MORE EXTRAORDINARY
USES
FOR ORDINARY THINGS

MORE EXTRAORDINARY
USES
FOR ORDINARY THINGS

1,700 WAYS TO SAVE TIME AND MONEY

Reader's
Digest

Published by Reader's Digest Association Ltd
London • New York • Sidney • Montreal

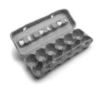

Welcome to a world of

brilliant ideas ...

where ordinary items from bicarbonate of soda to a pair of old tights can save you TIME and MONEY!

Step inside for hundreds of tips and hints

Clean your coffee grinder with rice

Don't bother with tools and brushes. Running a cup of uncooked rice through the grinder will give it an unbeatable scouring.

Spray away fresh carpet stains

A spray of non-gel shaving cream on a fresh carpet stain will make it a cinch to clean up.

Make your brass candlesticks gleam with ketchup

Put them in a pan, cover with ketchup, and bring to a boil for a spectacular shine.

Keep seedlings happy with aluminium foil

Place a sheet of aluminium foil underneath container seedlings to promote growth ... they love the warmth.

Cure your headache with coffee

Caffeine constricts blood vessels and alleviates the discomfort of a headache.

Banish weeds with salt and vinegar

Put an end to path and patio weeds with a salt and vinegar solution.
The weeds will shrivel and die from the roots.

Lighten a lipstick mark with bread

Blot a lipstick smear on fabric with the doughy centre of a white loaf,
kneaded into a small ball. It will lighten it ready for washing.

Unstick a stuck drawer

If wooden drawers get sticky, rub the runners
with a bar of soap, paraffin wax or lip balm.

Rub rust from metal tools with a raw potato

Dip a potato slice in salt, then rub away the rust spots
from knives, screwdrivers and other tools.

Loosen a stuck tap with a fizzy drink

Pour a few drops of a carbonated soft drink onto a tap
that won't budge to help loosen rust or corrosion.

De-bug your bumper with peanut butter

Insect casualties on the car are inevitable after a long journey.
Soften the remains with a smear of peanut butter then wash with soapy water.

Simple!

Clever!

Creative!

Fresh!

contents

Smart! Easy! Ingenious! Fast!

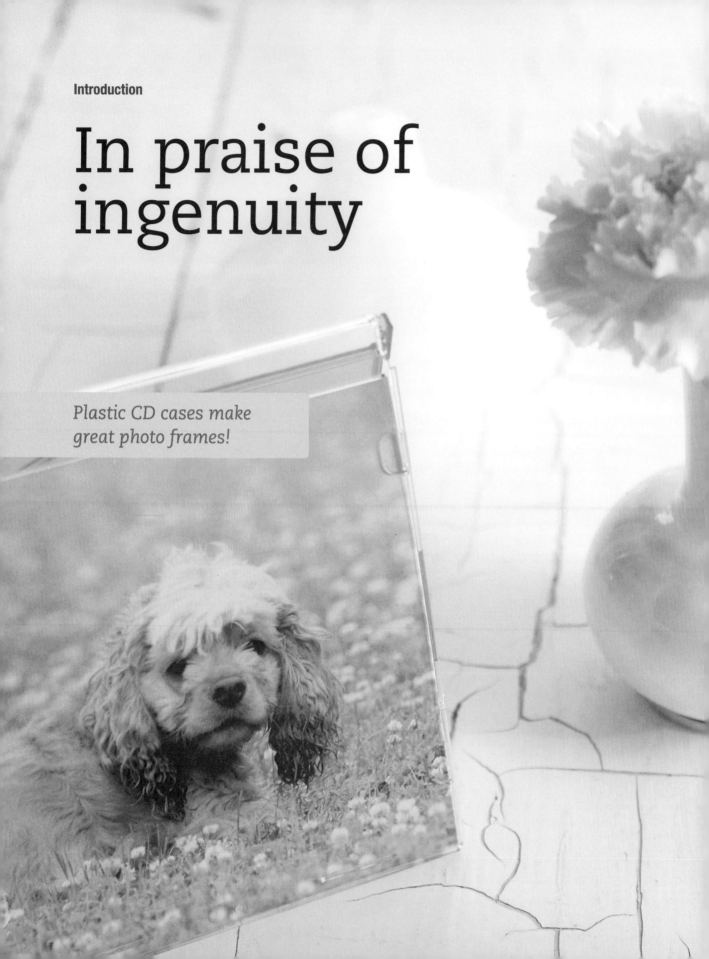

In praise of ingenuity

Plastic CD cases make great photo frames!

As they searched out clever ideas for better everyday living, the writers and researchers of *More Extraordinary Uses for Ordinary Things* often found out that necessity was the mother of invention. One expert made a serendipitous discovery. Trying to revive his dog's interest in dry food, this quick fix champion decided to mash a banana and stir a bit of it into his dog's bowl. The delighted dog ate everything and her finickiness is now a thing of the past.

The author of the cooking chapter struck gold when she asked family and friends about unusual ways of accomplishing common tasks. She quickly learned about buttering the lip of a pitcher to help stop dribbles, and using a garlic press to crush sugar cubes. One expert revealed that instead of buying an expensive electric sandwich maker, he uses a heavy cast-iron skillet. The results are even better – and the skillet is much easier to clean. This clever approach to everyday living is what 21st century folk wisdom is all about.

More Extraordinary Uses for Ordinary Things also provides a multitude of special features that inform, instruct, and entertain:

What's the story? brings you the surprising histories of household items, new and old.

Make your own... offers simple, natural recipes for everything from dog biscuits to nasal spray and natural insecticides for your plants.

Household superstar details some of the many uses for the most common and popular home ingredients, like sticky tape, petroleum jelly, plastic bags, salt, vinegar and WD-40.

Curiosity corner lets you dip into a veritable grab bag of curiosities, with some fascinating stories. Things like how many ingredients it took to build the world's largest sandwich; how

A NOTE OF CAUTION

Unlike many of their shop-bought equivalents, most of the cleaning substances and formulas found in this book are non toxic. Nevertheless, two of the harsher common household products must be used with caution. When working with either ammonia or bleach, throw open the windows for ventilation and wear gloves. In addition, never mix these two products when developing cleaning formulas of your own. Then there's the plethora of home remedies found in Chapter Six. The herbs used for infusions and teas are generally regarded as safe, but any plant with medicinal properties should always be used in moderation, and with your doctor's knowledge.

to estimate air temperature by the frequency of a cricket's chirp, and why red flannel was considered such a cure-all.

Plus there are the **Idea** features, highlighting particularly useful hints and tips for cleaning, curing, cooking and repairing that you can use as part of your regular household routine.

So whether you're excited by the possibility of experimenting with everyday things, or simply want ways to save a few pounds and do things better, this anti-gadget manual is for you. Dip into it and dip out, peruse the chapters closest to your heart, or read it from beginning to end ... no matter how you use it, this will become the busiest book in the house (and the garage, the garden shed, the utility room, the playroom, and pretty much everywhere else). And remember, the busier this book is, the more money and time you will save!

The Editors

Fruit,
bread and
vegetables make
terrific edible
bowls!

1 Cooking & serving shortcuts

Are a microwave and a freezer full of ready meals your ultimate kitchen allies? Or do you find yourself compelled to stand over a hot stove for several hours each night after a long day at work to make a meal for your family?

Whether you love cooking or find it a chore, there are lots of easier, faster and cleverer ways to happy home cooking that will not only save you time, but will make your meals even more delicious.

Not every hint in this magician's bag of cooking tricks will save you time. But money-saving, creative solutions to common kitchen problems are shortcuts to worry-free cooking and that's what this chapter is all about.

So, if your soup is too salty, add a bit of sugar. If a curry is too spicy, a spoonful of apple sauce will cool it down. If you run out of oil to grease a pan, use the cut side of a potato instead. The hints that follow will give you dozens of great ideas and in many cases may also get you out of an awkward spot. Turn the page to learn our secrets.

Fast food fixes

✱ Balance salt with sugar

If you've oversalted a stew or soup, save it with a teaspoon of granulated sugar. It will absorb excess salt and help to balance the taste. Or stir in a teaspoon of honey instead.

✱ De-grease gravy with bicarb

Sometimes the cooking juices used for gravy are so greasy that they look like an oil slick. Counteract the problem with a pinch or two of bicarbonate of soda, stirred into the juices just sufficient to absorb the grease. (Be careful, though, if you overdo it, you will taint the flavour and it will taste metallic.)

✱ Over-heated curry

Tone it down with apple sauce. Add 30ml of apple sauce for each 90ml curry sauce, then taste. If necessary, continue stirring in a little apple sauce until the curry is acceptable.

✱ Two extra for dinner

Perhaps you have cooked the perfect sized roast for a small dinner party – but – disaster. Meat shrinks when cooked, so it's a third smaller than you started out with and then the doorbell rings – with two extra guests to feed. Carve the entire roast into thin strips, toss a large salad, top with the beef and you should have substantially increased the size of your main course.

✱ Rescue a cracked egg

If you are boiling an egg and the shell cracks, simply add a teaspoon of vinegar to the cooking water. It will help to coagulate the egg white and stop it from seeping out.

✱ Salsa too hot?

Stir in a drop or two of vanilla extract and it should cool down. Whether it's the vanillin, sugars or amino acids in vanilla that takes the heat down a notch or two, vanilla extract is the coolest condiment for the job.

✱ Too much garlic in the soup

Pack a mesh pouch, gauze bag or metal tea ball with dried parsley flakes or fresh parsley sprigs and drop it into the pan. After 5 minutes or so, the flakes will absorb some of the taste of the offending ingredient. Once the garlic taste has been adequately toned down, simply remove the parsley and discard it.

tip ADD TASTE TO SUPERMARKET TOMATOES
The commercially grown red ping pong balls that often pass for tomatoes do have flavour hiding deep inside: just drizzle tomato slices with a little **rice vinegar** (available at most supermarkets). You'll be amazed at the difference it makes to the taste.

Fat catchers

Do you skim the fat off a simmering stew, soup or sauce with a teaspoon?
Here are three easy and effective alternative ways that you can
reduce the fat in the pot.

1

Float a large lettuce leaf
on the surface and it will
draw the fat in. Repeat
the process with fresh
leaves as necessary.

2

Float two or three ice cubes
on the surface and you will soon
see fat globules clinging to
them. Scoop the cubes
out (before they melt) and
continue cooking.

3

Slip an uncooked egg white
onto the simmering soup
or stew or sauce. Left alone
for a few minutes, it will
absorb the fat as it cooks;
simply scoop out the solidified
egg white with a slotted
spoon and discard it.

Perfect your poultry

✻ Simple skinning

Skin a piece of poultry or even a whole bird with ease. Put it in the freezer until it partially freezes (generally 1½–2 hours). You will be able to pull the skin off with no trouble.

✻ Chicken money-saver

Buy whole chickens and cut them up with poultry shears, rather than buying breasts or legs. Freeze in portion-size freezer bags. If chicken is a favourite dish, you will make up the cost of the shears (*c.* £10–15) in a few weeks.

✻ Butter(milk) up chicken pieces

To tenderise chicken pieces and pack them with flavour, rinse the meat, pat dry and marinate them in buttermilk (add a tablespoon of lemon or vinegar to create buttermilk) for 2–3 hours, in the fridge, before cooking.

✻ Stuffing stopper

When cooking a stuffed turkey, chicken or duck of any size, just place a raw potato in the body cavity and the stuffing will stay put.

✻ Tea-riffic flavour

To give chicken or turkey breasts or thighs a light, smokey flavour and help them to retain moisture as they cook, brew 2 strong cups of spice-flavoured tea. Once the tea cools, add seasonings such as black pepper, salt, paprika and garlic to taste, pour into a large self-sealing plastic bag and add the chicken or turkey pieces. Put in a shallow dish and marinate in the fridge for at least 2 hours before cooking.

✻ Carrot and celery rack

Don't use a roasting rack. Instead, crisscross whole carrots and celery stalks on the bottom of the roasting pan and top with your chicken or turkey. Once it's done, your bird will emerge from the pan without a hitch and the flavour of the gravy will be enhanced by the vegetables.

✻ Simple roux starters for gravy

Combine excess fat from a roasting pan with sufficient flour until you can roll it into small balls about half the size of a walnut and freeze on a baking sheet covered with a paper towel. When frozen, transfer the balls to a plastic bag and store in the freezer for future use. The next time you need to make gravy, take out a roux starter ball from the bag and melt in the saucepan before stirring in the other ingredients. If your cooked gravy is too thin, drop in a roux starter, whisk well, season to taste and serve.

tip GLAZE WITH VERMOUTH

About 15 minutes before you're ready to take a roast chicken or turkey out of the oven, brush the skin with a little **white vermouth.** The bird will take on a rich brown colour, thanks to the sugars in the fortified wine.

Double-duty kitchen tools

Some of the most ordinary kitchen gadgets and tools come in handy in ways that you may never have imagined, in some cases making them worth a lot more than you originally paid for them.

Vegetable peeler

Run a peeler along the corners of a block of cheese or chocolate to create thick, hearty ribbons that you can use as a garnish on salads or puddings.

Colander

Use as a steamer for vegetables. Fill a casserole dish with 5cm of water, bring to a boil, put a heatproof or metal vegetable-filled colander inside and cover.

Garlic press

Turn sugar cubes into granulated sugar by placing one cube at a time into a garlic press and squeezing it shut. One cube equals 1 teaspoon of sugar.

Melon baller

Use smaller ballers to core apples and pears and scoop biscuit dough onto a baking sheet. Use larger ones to scoop ice cream into a bowl.

Ice cream scoop

Lightly coat an ice cream scoop with cooking spray and use it to spoon even amounts of batter into cupcake or muffin tin liners. The sweeping release arm will help to clean all batter from the scoop and you won't waste a drop.

Pizza cutter

The sharp wheel on a pizza cutter makes cutting through all kinds of other foods a breeze. Use the cutter to separate waffle segments and to neatly slice a grilled cheese sandwich.

Tongs

Sturdy metal tongs measuring about 40cm long are like having an extra set of heatproof hands. Use them to turn meat on a ridged grill pan, to toss salads, to mix pasta with sauce and to rotate cake and pie tins in the oven.

Empty wine bottle

If you don't have a rolling pin or a meat pounder handy, use an empty wine bottle as a stand-in rolling pin (flour it first) or as a meat pounder to flatten chicken or veal cutlets for more even cooking.

Fish with finesse

✳ Keep fishy smells at bay

Before preparing fresh fish, halve a lemon and rub both hands with the cut ends to help to keep your hands from absorbing the fishy odour. (But if you didn't know you had a tiny scratch or cut on your hand, you will now.) If frying is your cooking method of choice, wash the pan you used and pour in 1cm white vinegar; the acetic acid should banish any lingering fish smell.

✳ Make scaling easier with vinegar

When scaling a fish, rub white vinegar onto the scales and let it sit for about 10 minutes. The scales will come off so easily that they may make more of a mess than usual, so put the fish in a plastic bag before you do this. Just scale the fish in the bag with one hand while holding it by the tail with your other hand.

✳ Keep poached fish firm

When poaching fish, squeeze fresh lemon juice into the poaching liquid to help the fish to cook evenly. For each 500g of fish, use the juice of half a lemon.

✳ Lock moisture in when baking

Low-fat fish like bass, halibut and red snapper can easily dry out as they bake. To seal in the moisture, simply wrap each fillet or whole fish in aluminium foil before putting it in the oven.

✳ Freezing fresh-caught fish

When you bring more fish home from a fishing trip than you can eat, here's the best way to freeze them. Take an empty milk carton large enough to hold each fish, place the fish inside and fill the carton with water. Seal the opening with tape and place the carton in the freezer. When you thaw the fish, you won't have to worry about scraping off ice crystals or pulling off some of the flesh with the wrapping.

✳ Cool down prawns

To ensure tender, well-textured meat, place prawns in the freezer for 10–15 minutes before you cook them. Just be sure not to overcook them because you think they need time to warm up in the boiling water. (They don't.)

✳ Make shucking oysters easier
Soaking oysters in soda water for 5–10 minutes will make it easier for you to open the shells.

✳ Stop lobster squirting
When cracking and twisting the legs and claws off a whole lobster or crab, guard against the occasional squirt by putting a napkin between the crustacean and your hand. Any squirts will hit the napkin, not your clothes.

✳ Improve the taste of canned seafood
If you detect a slight metallic flavour to canned seafood, soak it as directed below, drain and then pat the seafood dry with paper towels.
- **Water-packed tuna** Soak in a mixture of cold water and lemon juice for 15 minutes (2 parts water, 1 part juice).
- **Canned crab** Soak the crabmeat in ice water for 5–10 minutes.
- **Canned prawns** Soak the prawns in a mixture of 2 tablespoons vinegar and 1 teaspoon dry sherry for 15 minutes.

✳ Cut the salt in anchovies
If you like the taste of anchovies but wish they weren't quite so salty, soak them in iced water for 10–15 minutes and then drain them well before tossing them in a Caesar salad or arranging them on top of a pizza.

make your own...

SALT SUBSTITUTE
Here's a delicious, all-purpose, low-salt seasoning that will enhance fish, meat and poultry dishes. Make it in large batches so you always have some on hand.

Who-needs-salt mix
The citric acid, arrowroot and powdered orange peel in this recipe may sound unusual, but they can usually be found in supermarkets.

> 1 tablespoon celery seeds
> 1 tablespoon onion powder
> 1 tablespoon freshly ground black pepper
> 2 teaspoons cream of tartar
> 1 teaspoon garlic powder
> 1½ teaspoons sugar
> 1½ teaspoons arrowroot
> 1½ teaspoons powdered orange peel
> ¾ teaspoon citric acid powder
> ½ teaspoon white pepper
> ½ teaspoon dried dill
> ½ teaspoon dried thyme, crumbled
> ⅓ teaspoon powdered lemon peel
> ¼ teaspoon cayenne

1 Place all ingredients in a blender or food processor. Grind for 8–10 seconds or until the mixture is fine.

2 Use a funnel to fill a glass salt shaker with the mixture.

3 Put the rest of the mixture in an air-tight jar and store in a cool, dark place.

Red meat with relish

✱ Hamburgers with a difference

To add flavour and moisture to hamburger patties, add 30g finely minced onion and 2 tablespoons barbecue sauce. Blend the ingredients into the ground beef or turkey with your clean hands, taking care not to overwork the mixture.

Variations of the ingredients are endless – you can add everything from minced garlic or celery or other crisp vegetables paired with chilli sauce, ketchup or Worcestershire sauce. You could also mix a teaspoon of chilli powder or cumin (or ½ teaspoon of both) into the meat to give the patties a hint of Mexican flavour or even a drop of curry powder to add some Indian spice.

✱ Speed defrosting with salt

Defrost frozen meats quickly and safely by soaking them in cold salt water for several hours. Mix 50 to 100g sea salt or any other coarse-grained salt with 2 litres water, then submerge the meat and refrigerate it. Once the meat has thawed, just discard the salt water and cook as usual.

✱ Making better burgers

Although your usual hamburgers probably taste absolutely fine, you can notch up a burger's wow factor with a few easy tricks.

- **Keep them juicy** For a juicier grilled burger, add 100ml cold water to the minced meat and shape the patties as you normally would. Prepare the patties shortly before you grill them.
- **Flash freeze** Keep hamburger patties from breaking up during grilling by freezing them for 5 minutes just before they go on the grill.
- **Dented burgers** Use your forefinger to make two or three dents in the centre of a patty before placing it on the grill. This distributes heat more effectively so that the burger will cook faster.
- **Toast some herbs** You can easily flavour and scent grilled burgers on a barbecue by giving the hot coals an herbal treatment. Place fresh herbs like basil and rosemary directly on to the coals.

tip BASTE WITH A PAINTBRUSH

A clean paintbrush dipped in vegetable oil is perfect for making a grill pan nonstick before you place burgers or any other meat directly onto it. You can also season the steak, chicken or fish with the same brush, now dipped not in oil but a grilling sauce.

Bake your bacon for streaky strips that are crispier, meatier and less greasy.

✳ Bathe flank steak in ginger ale

Lend flank steak an Asian touch – and make it more tender – by marinating it in 150ml of ginger ale mixed with 3 minced garlic cloves, 150ml orange juice, 50ml soy sauce and ½ teaspoon sesame oil. Cover and keep in the fridge for 4–8 hours. This recipe makes enough marinade for 700g flank steak.

✳ Wake up a bit of brisket with coffee

This innovative method for cooking brisket of beef uses coffee and chilli sauce to give what can be a toughish meat a new twist. To enjoy this twice-cooked dish for yourself, combine 500ml brewed coffee with 320ml chilli sauce in a mixing bowl. Stir in a chopped onion, 2 tablespoons brown sugar and salt, and freshly ground black pepper to taste.

Place a 2.2kg brisket in a roasting pan, then pour the bowl of sauce over the meat. Cover tightly with a lid or foil and bake for 2 hours in a preheated 160°C/gas 3 oven. Remove the pan from the oven and transfer the meat to a platter

to cool. Now slice the meat, lay the slices in the sauce in the pan and cover again. Bake the joint at 160°C/gas 3 for another 2 hours or until the brisket is completely soft and tender when you insert a fork.

✳ Mix up in a bag

Put mince, breadcrumbs, chopped onions and seasonings for a meatloaf or hamburgers into a large self-sealing plastic bag and squish it about with both hands to evenly distribute the seasonings throughout the meat. Turn the bag inside out into a prepared loaf tin, gently press it into shape and bake. Your hands will be clean and there's no bowl to wash.

✳ Keep meatloaf moist

Spray the top of the loaf with water to keep it from cracking and drying out as it cooks. Open the oven door and brush tomato sauce or ketchup over the top of the loaf about 15 minutes before it has finished cooking

household superstar

10 KITCHEN USES FOR SALT

1 Sprinkle on a chicken 24 hours before cooking for the most flavourful and juicy roast bird you have ever eaten.

2 Release juices in meats by seasoning them with salt an hour before cooking.

3 Prevent pancakes from sticking to a griddle by wiping it between batches with coarse salt wrapped in cheesecloth. Caution: always wash cheesecloth before use.

4 Stop cheese from going mouldy by wrapping the cheese in a paper towel dampened with salt water.

5 Clean dirt and grit from leafy greens by soaking them in cold salt water for up to 15 minutes, then rinse in thoroughly under cold running water.

6 Keep apples, pears and potatoes from going brown as you slice them by placing into a bowl of lightly salted cold water.

7 Keep hard boiled eggs intact and make them easier to peel by adding a pinch of salt to the cooking water.

8 Make milk last almost twice as long in the fridge by adding a pinch of salt each time you open a new carton.

9 Neutralise bitter coffee that's sat too long by adding a dash of salt to your cup.

10 Enhance the flavour of cocoa drinks and desserts with a pinch of salt.

✱ Easy slices without tearing

To slice thin steaks or cubes from a roast prior to cooking, wrap the meat in heavy-duty cling film and freeze for 10 minutes. This method works for any cut of meat.

✱ Brilliant pork glaze

All you need is apricot jam, soy sauce and powdered ginger and you have the makings of a simple but delicious glaze. Just whisk together 3 tablespoons apricot jam, 2 tablespoons soy sauce and ¾ teaspoon ginger and brush it onto a pork loin or pork roast before cooking. If you are pan-frying pork chops on top of the hob, glaze the browned top of the chops after you've flipped them over once.

✱ A bit of a brew for lamb

To give lamb stew a beautiful dark colour and great flavour, add 1 cup black coffee to the stew pot about halfway through the cooking process.

Perfect pasta and just-right rice

✱ The ideal meal stretcher

An extra guest or two for dinner – even at a casual meal – can ruin the most carefully laid plans. Don't worry – make a beeline for the cupboard and get out the pasta – your best bet as a filling meal stretcher. You'll also need a can of chopped tomatoes. Boil the pasta while your friends mingle and eat nibbles, heating up the tomatoes at the same time. Drain the cooked pasta, put it into a large bowl and toss with the tomatoes and plenty of grated hard cheese, preferably Parmesan. (If you have no tomatoes, toss the pasta with a little olive oil and grated hard cheese – a surprisingly delicious combination.) Add the steaming bowl of pasta to the buffet table and your guests should be satisfied.

✱ Stop spaghetti showers

We've all probably done it – you're rummaging through a kitchen cabinet and accidentally knock over a half-used packet of spaghetti – and the dried strands cascade on the floor. How can you stop it from happening again? Save an empty Pringles box (tall and cylindrical and lidded) and recycle it as a dry pasta canister.

✱ Carrot ribbon pasta

Carrots add additional nutrients and some vibrant colour to a simple pasta dish. Clean and peel the carrots, then use the peeler to shave wide carrot ribbons. Sauté the ribbons in butter and seasonings, such as ginger, black pepper and salt, then add to cooked and drained pasta. You don't need a tomato-based sauce, simply toss with Parmesan cheese.

✱ Keep pasta from boiling over

Before adding water to a pasta pan, coat the interior lightly with nonstick cooking spray. The water won't boil over, even when you add the pasta. If you have no spray on hand, add a teaspoon of olive oil to the water as it cooks. This trick works for boiled rice as well.

✱ What to do with leftover pasta

Don't throw it out. Toss it in a nonstick, ovenproof pan with a teaspoon of olive oil, pour 2 beaten eggs over it, sprinkle with cheese and bake until golden brown. Slice the resulting frittata into wedges and have it for another dinner with a small green salad. It's money saving, simple and delicious.

✱ Jazz up rice

Instead of boiling rice in plain water, try using chicken or beef stock, tomato juice or even equal parts of orange juice and water. Or you could sprinkle dried oregano, cumin, turmeric and any other herb or spice into the water before adding the rice. You could also add finely chopped onion, garlic or plenty of lemon or orange zest to turn rice from a bland accompaniment into a brand new dish each time it appears on the table.

✳ Fluff it up!

It's easy to keep rice grains from sticking together as they cook. Try one of these methods to ensure you'll spoon out the fluffiest of servings.

- Soak the rice in a bowl of cold water for 30–60 minutes before cooking. Soaking will also make the rice cook faster. Drain and rinse before cooking.
- Put the rice into a colander and rinse it under cold running water several times to remove the surface starch that makes the grains stick together.

- Add the juice of half a lemon to the cooking water. Grating the lemon rind and adding the zest will give rice another taste note and some visual interest.

✳ Perfect rice noodles

Before being cooked, rice noodles need to soak in water at room temperature for several hours (for 1 hour at least). If you've soaked them but you can't cook the noodles immediately, keep them moist by sandwiching them between damp paper towels.

curiosity corner

THE GREAT SPAGHETTI TREE HOAX

Perhaps the world's greatest ever April Fools' joke was pulled on an unsuspecting British public on 1 April, 1957. The BBC news programme *Panorama* reported on a bumper spaghetti crop in southern Switzerland, the result, it was said, of an unusually mild winter.

'The spaghetti harvest here in Switzerland is not, of course, carried out on anything like the tremendous scale of the Italian industry,' reported the programme's presenter, Richard Dimbleby, as a family in rural Switzerland was shown harvesting spaghetti from tree limbs and tucking it into baskets. 'Many of you, I'm sure,' he continued, 'will have seen pictures of the vast spaghetti plantations in the Po Valley. For the Swiss, however, it tends to be more of a family affair.'

Dimbleby also explained the mystery of why tree-grown pasta came in uniform lengths, calling it 'the result of many years of patient endeavour by past [plant] breeders who succeeded in producing the perfect spaghetti.'

At the time, spaghetti was rarely eaten in the UK, where the food revolution of the 1960s and 70s was still years away. How many of the audience fell for the joke and how many knew at once that it was a brilliant hoax is unknown. What is known is that hundreds of viewers called the BBC to inquire about the story, many of them asking how they could grow and cultivate their own spaghetti trees. Staying in character (and impeccably so), BBC customer service representatives replied, 'Place a sprig of spaghetti in a tin of tomato sauce and hope for the best.'

Eggs and cheese

✳ Enrich omelettes and scrambled eggs

Give scrambled eggs and omelettes a silken texture and add a sinful dollop of richness by whisking in a tablespoon of good quality mayonnaise for each egg.

✳ No more cracks

Keep the shells of hard boiled eggs intact by rubbing them with the juice of a cut lemon before cooking. The shells won't crack and will be much easier to peel once they are cool. Achieve the same result by adding a teaspoon of lemon juice or a small wedge of lemon to the cooking water.

✳ Devilishly easy

When you are preparing devilled eggs, take two steps towards perfect alignment. Keep the yolks centred as the eggs boil by stirring the water non stop. Then cut a thin slice off opposite sides of the hard boiled eggs so that the halves sit up perfectly straight on the serving platter when they are stuffed with filling.

✳ Perfect slices

Ensure that slices of hard boiled egg are neat and clean by lightly wiping or spraying the knife blade with vegetable oil or cooking spray. If you don't have oil or spray on hand, run the knife under cold running water just before slicing.

✳ Spray before grating

A cheese grater can be a nightmare to get clean when the small holes are clogged with cheese, but you can make the job easier by taking action in advance. Just spray the grater with cooking spray or use a clean rag to rub it with vegetable oil.

what's the story?

THE REAL DEAL ON MOULDY CHEESE

Some cheeses, such as Roquefort, Danish Blue and Stilton, are designed to be mouldy. But the block of Cheddar at the back of the fridge has gone mouldy because it's been invaded by fungus spores. The good news is that it can be saved. Just cut away the mouldy area plus at least 2cm of mould-free cheese and discard it. If you spot mould on Brie, goat's cheese or another soft cheese, it can't be rescued – throw it out or you may risk getting violently ill.

You may have heard that you can 'treat' mould on cheese by rubbing a vinegar-soaked rag over the mould. It's not true. Nor is the advice to place mouldy cheese in a plastic bag with a few sugar cubes, mistakenly said to draw out mould. A food safety specialist advises that, 'By the time you see mould spots in cheese, the mould has already begun to put down its invisible 'roots'. That's why deep cuts are necessary to remove mould from hard cheese. Other advice is that you should not leave cheese out of the fridge for more than 2 hours and always keep your eye peeled for even the tiniest spot of mould.

Vegetables and fruit

✱ Rescue wilted veggies

You can revive wilted vegetables by soaking them for an hour in 500ml water mixed with a tablespoon apple cider vinegar. Pat dry and prepare as usual. Or plunge limp veggies into hot water, remove and then plunge them into a bowl of ice water mixed with a little cider vinegar.

✱ Easy-cheesy creamed spinach

If you like creamed spinach, try this yummy recipe. Sauté a clove of finely minced garlic in 1 tablespoons butter for 30–40 seconds. Add about 500g washed spinach leaves and toss until they are just wilted. Stir in 55g ricotta cheese and salt and freshly ground black pepper to taste.

✱ Liven up green beans

Add extra flavour to steamed green beans and give them a little kick as well by tossing them in this mixture: 2 tablespoons melted butter, ½ teaspoon chilli powder plus a dash or two of garlic powder.

✱ The benefits of a milk boost

Adding milk to cooking water can enhance the taste of certain vegetables. Two examples are:

- Keep cauliflower whiter by adding 80ml milk to the cooking water.
- Sweet corn-on-the-cob becomes even sweeter when milk is added to the water.

✱ 'Almost the real thing' vegetable lasagna

This recipe is suitable for strict vegetarians and may fool even the most die-hard carnivore. Replace the meat in a lasagna recipe with a mixture of diced courgettes, lentils and ground walnuts – a combination that closely resembles minced beef. Then just follow the recipe.

✱ Quick-bake potatoes

Cut potato baking times in half (without the help of a microwave) by choosing smaller potatoes and standing them up in the cups of a cake tin before putting them in the oven.

To reduce the baking time for a full-size spud by 15 minutes, try inserting a skewer into the flesh. This will help to distribute the heat throughout the potato more quickly.

✱ Keep baked peppers upright

Stuffed green peppers sometimes lean to one side while cooking. Give them firm footing by

tip USE A PLASTIC LID AS A FRUIT KEEPER
Instead of wasting cling film, try this method of storing a half grapefruit or small melon in the fridge. Simply set the fruit cut side down on a **clean plastic lid** from a large tin of coffee or a box of Pringles (for half lemons and oranges).

Store your lemons in water to make them jucier!

setting each pepper in the cup of a muffin or Yorkshire pudding tin sprayed with a little nonstick cooking spray to ensure easy removal.

✳ Cola-caramelised onions

For the best caramelised onions, you need only three ingredients: 2–3 sweet onions, brown sauce and cola. Slice the onions about 1.5cm thick and set in a microwaveable dish. Pour cola over the onions to cover. Stir in 2 teaspoons brown sauce and microwave at 50 per cent power for 30 minutes. No trouble, great taste!

✳ Save those veggie tops

Beetroot leaves? Fennel fronds? Carrot tops? Don't throw them out. Cut them away from their respective vegetables, wash and dry well, chop them and sauté them in a bit of olive oil with garlic to taste for a healthy side dish. Or mince them finely and mix together with scrambled eggs, salad leaves or leftover pasta.

✳ A toothbrush as a mushroom cleaner

Use a soft-bristled toothbrush to clean mushrooms and other soft-skinned vegetables before cooking. A medium or hard-bristled brush is more suitable for potatoes.

✳ Foolproof ways to slice dried fruit

Have you ever tried to cut dried fruit into small pieces only to have your knife stick on the fruit? Just squeeze a lemon quarter over the fruit you're about to cut or sprinkle the fruit with a few drops of pre-squeezed lemon juice. The knife will slice through with ease.

✳ More juice from your lemons

Store lemons in a sealed jar of water and when it's time to squeeze them, you will get twice as much juice. Another trick is to prick the lemon skin once or twice with a sharp knife and then microwave it on medium power for 15 seconds before slicing and squeezing.

Soups and salads

✳ A quick fix for bland soup

Boost the flavour of a so-so soup by dissolving a beef or chicken bouillon cube in a little hot water and whisking it into the soup.

✳ Soup stretchers

If you're heating up leftover soup for two or more people and it's looking skimpy, stir in cooked rice, pasta or pearl barley all of which are great soup stretchers.

✳ In the bag

As you prepare salad ingredients, put them into a small plastic bag. When you've finished, hold the bag closed with your hand and shake well. The ingredients will be thoroughly tossed and you will be able to refrigerate them in the bag until it's time to serve.

✳ Hold the tomatoes

Even when you need to make a mixed salad ahead of time, add sliced tomatoes only after the salad is on the plate. The greens in your salad bowl will stay crisper in the fridge without tomatoes, which will cause lettuce to wilt.

✳ 'Fast Italian' broccoli salad

For a classy, delicious salad, toss steamed broccoli florets cooled to room temperature in a dressing of 120ml plain tomato spaghetti sauce, 2 tablespoons olive oil, 1 tablespoon red wine vinegar, 1 tablespoon chopped Italian parsley and salt and black pepper to taste.

✳ Keep it fresh

Use this chef's trick to keep lettuce fresh for up to two weeks. Pull the leaves off the core, dry them well, fill a sink with cold water and submerge them for 20 minutes. Remove, dry thoroughly, wrap in paper towels and store in the crisper of your fridge.

---

idea

INSTANT THICKENERS FOR SOUP

To thicken a soup, add ...

Frozen spinach While the soup is cooking, put clumps of frozen spinach into the pan. If you prefer, defrost the spinach in the microwave and drain off excess liquid.

Sweet potato Prick a few holes in a small sweet potato and microwave it on high for a few minutes until it's partially cooked. Slice into quarters, mash with a fork and then add the lumpy pulp to the pot. As the soup cooks, use a fork to mash the pulp further, if necessary.

Bread As the soup cooks, remove the crust from a slice or two of bread and dice the bread into small cubes. A hearty multigrain will work like a charm and rich white bread will do the job, too.

Mashed potato or instant potato flakes If you don't want to change the flavour of your soup, add either mash or flakes.

Porridge oats Put a small amount of uncooked plain, quick-cooking oats or even leftover cooked porridge into the pot. Because they are bland, oats shouldn't affect the soup's flavour – but to counteract the blandness you may need to add more seasoning.

Clean hands and dry eyes

Any cook knows how hard it can be to get food stains and smells off hands and to chop onions without tears and pain. These hints will help on all fronts.

Stain-free hands

Rub with lemon juice. Berries and beetroots are notorious stainers. Remove stains by rubbing them with 1–2 teaspoons fresh lemon juice and then washing your hands with soap and water. Rub with a potato. Even chopped carrots, peppers and pumpkin can leave their marks. Rub a raw potato on your fingers to help to remove the stains.

Odour-free hands with onions, garlic, fish

Rub on a stainless steel surface. This strange-but-true chef's trick works: rub garlicky hands repeatedly on a flat stainless-steel surface and they will soon be fresh again.

Rub with rosemary. Rub your hands with sprigs of fresh rosemary to rid them of garlic and onion smells.

Rub with vinegar. Use a little white vinegar as a hand balm. To avoid oniony hands to begin with, rub vinegar over your hands before you start peeling onions.

Rub with salt. Sprinkle salt into your palm and rub your hands together to remove the smell of garlic and onions. Rinse and dry.

Scrub with sugar. Pour a tablespoon of sugar in your palm, wet it with a teaspoon of liquid soap and rub your hands and fingers together as when washing them. Rinse and dry.

Scrub with toothpaste. Handling fish can leave your hands with a lasting odour. Squeeze toothpaste on a facecloth dampened with cold water, then scrub to remove the smell.

Rub with lemon. Cut a lemon, squeeze a good bit of the juice over your hands and rub hands and fingers together as when washing. Rinse under running water.

Tips for tear-free eyes

'Bread' your knife. Cut a small piece of bread and insert your knife part of the way down to the hilt. As you slice the onions, the bread will absorb some of the fumes.

Toss onions in the freezer. Freeze onions for 10–15 minutes before slicing them. The cold helps to minimise the fumes that cause tears.

Chop near a stove burner. If you can safely position your chopping board on a gas hob, chop onions with one or two of the burners turned on low. The heat attracts the onion fumes and neutralises them.

Light a candle. Burn a candle near to your work area to burn off some of the fumes emanating from sliced onions.

Run the tap Bring your chopping board over to the sink and run the tap on cold while you slice your onion; the chemicals released are actually drawn to dampness (hence their ability to make your eyes tear), but will choose the running stream of water instead of your eyes.

Boosters for bakers

✳ Flour taste test

If you can't remember whether the flour in a storage jar is plain or self-raising, taste it. If it's salty, it's self-raising flour, so called because it contains baking powder and salt to make it rise.

✳ Is your baking powder fresh?

If you're not sure how long a pack of baking powder has been in the cupboard, you can easily tell whether it's still viable. Scoop ½ teaspoon of the powder into a teacup and pour in 60ml hot water. If it bubbles up, it's fine to use; if it fizzes only barely, it's time to buy a new pack.

✳ Make dough rise more quickly

Heat makes dough rise more quickly. But if it rises too quickly the flavour will suffer – something that cooks who have tried microwaving dough for a few minutes on low power could probably tell you. Instead, position the bowl or pan over the pilot light of a gas hob or on a medium hot heating pad.

✳ Keep hands clean when kneading

When working with dough, don't flour your hands to stop the mixture from sticking to your skin. Instead, pour a few drops of olive oil into your palm and work it into your hands as you would hand lotion.

✳ Easy greasing

Save the waxy wrappers of packs of butter and put their buttery residue to good use. Store them in a plastic bag in the fridge. When a recipe calls for a greased pan, bring one or two of the wrappers into service.

✳ Set cupcakes free

If cupcakes have stuck to the bottom of a metal tin, while the pan is still hot, set it on a wet towel. The condensation in the bottom of the tin will make the little cakes easier to remove.

✳ Steam for a better loaf

When you're baking bread, at the same time as you put the loaf tin in the oven, put a second tin containing 6–8 ice cubes on one of the oven racks. The steam that results will help the bread to bake more evenly and give it a crispier crust.

✳ Lighten up quick breads

If your banana and walnut bread, cinnamon coffee cake or carrot cake are tasty but heavy, substitute crème fraîche for the milk in the recipes; it should lighten the texture of any quick bread you bake. Experiment to find what gives you the best results: all crème fraîche, equal parts crème fraîche and milk and so on.

✳ Butter replacement

If a baking recipe calls for so much butter that you feel your arteries clogging just reading it, substitute a 50:50 mixture of unsweetened apple sauce and buttermilk. Best used in light-coloured or spiced cakes and breads, this substitute imparts a slightly chewier texture – so you may want to replace plain flour with a lighter special cake flour.

✳ A honey of a biscuit

Honey will help home-baked biscuits to stay softer and fresher for longer. Replace sugar with honey cup for cup, but decrease other liquids in the recipe by 50ml per 200ml honey.

Flowerpot cookery

Clay pot cookery is a kitchen tradition that goes back thousands of years. Wash an unglazed, unpainted, pot in hot soapy water and air-dry. Grease the pot's interior and lip with vegetable oil until the clay will absorb no more. Place the pot on a baking sheet covered with foil and place in a cold oven. Heat the oven to 200°C/gas 6 and then turn off immediately. Repeat the greasing and heating one more time and your pot will be ready to use.

Baking the bread:

1
Lightly grease the interior of a 15cm diameter flowerpot with vegetable oil or cooking spray.

2
Prepare your favourite bread recipe as usual and roll 250g of dough into a ball. Place in flowerpot and let rise according to the recipe.

3
Bake at 180°C/gas 4 for 25–30 minutes or until the top is golden brown. Let the bread cool on a wire rack and then gently tap the bottom of the pot to remove it.

The sweetest things

✱ Easy creaming

This important step in many a cake recipe – creaming the butter and sugar – can be a tedious and lengthy task. If the butter is cold, you can speed up the creaming process by warming the sugar a little on the hob or in the microwave. Or soften the butter by warming briefly in the microwave.

✱ One-egg replacement

If you are baking a cake that calls for one more egg than you have available, you can substitute 1 teaspoon of cornflour.

✱ Or go fruity

Replace one egg in a cake or sweet bread recipe with one small mashed banana or 120ml of apple sauce. For lovely moist chocolate cake, try substituting mashed prunes.

✱ Spaghetti cake tester

If you don't have a wire cake tester, use an uncooked strand of spaghetti instead. Gently push the spaghetti into the centre of the cake and pull it out. If your spaghetti comes out clean, the cake is done.

✱ Improvised cake decorator

Use a washed plastic mustard or ketchup squirt bottle as a cake decorating tool. Fill it with icing and then you will be able to pipe scallops, flowers and other designs onto cakes with ease. Or use it to make squiggles of pesto or cream on top of soups or chocolate on desserts.

✱ Pie bubbling over?

If a pie starts bubbling over as it is baking, cover the spills with salt. You'll prevent the spill

idea

YUMMY YOGHURTPOPS

Lollipops may be fat-free, but they are also mostly sugar. A custard-style frozen yoghurtpop, on the other hand, is full of healthy ingredients – and to most adult palates, is a lot tastier.

Making a yoghurtpop couldn't be simpler. Just spray flavourless cooking spray into a small paper cup, spoon in your favourite yogurt and freeze. After about half an hour, insert a sturdy plastic spoon into the middle of the cup.

Depending on the temperature of your freezer, the pops should be ready in about an hour. A great creamy variation is created by blending vanilla yoghurt with a little softened frozen orange juice concentrate. Then freeze as directed above.

from burning and avoid the terrible scorched smell. Best of all, the treated overflow will bake into a dry, light crust that you can wipe off easily when the oven has cooled.

✱ Make piecrust flakier

Flaky piecrusts are the talented baker's hallmark. You can improve the flakiness by replacing 1 tablespoon iced water in a crust recipe with 1 tablespoon chilled lemon juice or white vinegar.

✱ Fruit piecrusts too soggy?

To keep the juice in fruit from seeping into the crust of a baking pie, crumble up something to absorb it. A layer of plain, crisp flatbread will absorb the juice and introduce a savoury note to the pie, while biscotti or amaretti cookies will keep it tasting sweet.

✱ Slice meringue with ease
Your knife will glide through a meringue-topped pie if you butter it on both sides before slicing. It's a 10 second solution, if that.

✱ Thrifty chocolates
If you're a chocoholic, have extra freezer space and love saving money, buy chocolate Easter bunnies and Santas after the holidays when prices are slashed. Store them in the freezer and shave off chocolate curls to use in cooking. Or melt to create new chocolate shapes. Or, if you prefer, just thaw a Santa or bunny and gobble him up whenever you need a chocolate fix.

✱ Have coffee over ice
Pour cooled, freshly brewed coffee into several small containers such as clean yoghurt pots, to freeze. When frozen, remove the pots and then put the frozen coffee into a food processor. Process on the low setting until crystals form. Spoon the crystals into the cups and freeze for about a half hour before serving.

Options: Add milk and sugar to your coffee before freezing or just go with black coffee. Good toppings for granita include whipped cream and a sprinkling of cinnamon.

No cake tester? Use a strand of raw spaghetti instead!

Super-easy food improvements

✳ Marinate in plastic bags
Eliminate washing up bowls, spoons and even pots by marinating meat and poultry in large self-sealing plastic bags. Open the bag and pour in the liquids and seasonings – soy sauce, ketchup, ground ginger, black pepper, crushed garlic, herbs and so on. Zip the bag shut and shake it to blend. Now add the meat, zip the bag and shake. Refrigerate 6–8 hours or overnight. Occasionally take the bag out of the fridge and shake it to redistribute the marinade.

✳ Butter stops the dribbles
Dab a bit of butter onto the spout of your milk jug and you will put an end to the drips and dribbles.

✳ Oil your measuring cup
Sticky liquids like honey and syrup are difficult to measure and pour and a little always remains behind. Oiling the measuring cup will make it harder for viscous liquids to stick and will give you a more accurate serving.

✳ Keep salt on popcorn
If you want salt to stick to popcorn, give it something to cling to by lightly coating just-popped corn with a vegetable-based cooking spray. Avoid olive oil cooking spray because the flavour can overwhelm the taste of popcorn.

✳ Add tang to sauce with ginger ale
A little ginger ale will perk up tomato sauces, but be careful not to overdo it. A 80ml ginger ale added to a medium-size saucepan of tomato and garlic sauce or a tomato juice-based beef stew will help to subtly enhance the flavour.

✳ Brighten the taste of juice
For fresher tasting orange juice, add the juice of 1 lemon to each 4 litres. By the glass, squeeze in the juice of a quarter of a lemon, then place the peel on the rim for visual flair.

✳ Add flavour to plain crisps
It's so easy to make your own garlic-flavoured potato crisps. Just place a peeled garlic clove in a bag of plain crisps, fasten the bag shut with a clamp or clothespeg and let it sit for 6–8 hours, shaking the bag occasionally to even out the flavour. Open the bag, discard the garlic clove and crunch away.

✳ Dress up a syrup dressing
Adding chopped strawberries and a little lemon zest to the syrup you top pancakes with will make it a lot more interesting. Combine 120ml golden syrup, 100g strawberries and ½ teaspoon grated orange peel in a microwaveable bowl and heat on high power for 30–60 seconds. Top pancakes, waffles or French toast with the syrup and then tuck into what is now a much tastier and more healthy dish. (Strawberries are packed with vitamin C and the mineral, manganese.)

I'll be your substitute

✱ No lemon?

If a recipe calls for lemon juice, a lime is the best bet as a substitute. If not, you can use the same amount of white wine.

✱ Cut the salt – not the taste

A chef's trick for reducing the amount of salt in a recipe is to replace it with half as much lemon juice. If a recipe calls for ½ teaspoon of salt, substitute ¼ teaspoon lemon juice and there's no need to use the salt.

✱ Vanilla imitators

If you run out of vanilla just as a recipe for batter calls for it, you can substitute an equal amount of maple syrup or a sweet liqueur such as Bailey's Irish Cream.

✱ Powder for powder

Cake recipes often call for baking powder, but if you've run out, try this: For each teaspoon called for, substitute a mix of ½ teaspoon cream of tartar and ¼ teaspoon bicarbonate of soda. The mixture won't store well, so make it fresh should you ever need it again.

✱ Instead of breadcrumbs

If you are making meatballs or hamburgers, but you are running short of breadcrumbs, substitute oatmeal, crushed unsweetened cereal, crumbled crackers or instant mashed potato flakes instead.

✱ A surprising nonstick solution

You've chopped the vegetables, got the meat ready and you're about to fire up your grill when you find you're out of oil. Rub the grill with half of a potato and your food won't stick.

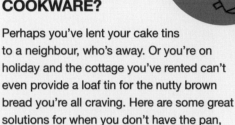

idea
CAUGHT WITHOUT COOKWARE?

Perhaps you've lent your cake tins to a neighbour, who's away. Or you're on holiday and the cottage you've rented can't even provide a loaf tin for the nutty brown bread you're all craving. Here are some great solutions for when you don't have the pan, cake tin or small appliance that you need:

Ceramic bowls Use an ovenproof ceramic bowl instead of a cake tin or try ovenproof cereal bowls for individual cakes. Just be sure to place them on a baking tray before putting them in the oven; bowls can be too hot to handle even with oven gloves or a tea towel.

Large can A quick bread will bake perfectly well in a large, wide-bottomed catering can. Be sure to coat the inside with grease or oil and dust it with flour.

Dutch oven if you don't have a slow cooker, a cast iron Dutch oven will do the job just as well. Combine the ingredients for your stew or casserole in the pan, cover and cook in a slow oven (140-180°C/gas 1-4) for 3–4 hours or until any meat in the dish is fork-tender.

✱ Soured cream stand-in

To make a substitute for soured cream, blend 225g cottage cheese, 40ml buttermilk and 1 tablespoon lemon juice until smooth. The lemon juice will sour its creamy partners.

Awesome advice

✸ Stop the drip
Wrap a towelling sweatband, headband or bandana around a bottle of olive oil to prevent drips. When the wrap becomes too oily, you can just throw it in the washing machine.

✸ An aid to elbow grease
If you struggle to twist the lid off a new jar of jam or marmalade, turn the jar upside down and give it a tap with the heel of your hand; you should hear a popping sound, signalling the release of air. Now turn the jar over and you may be able to twist off the lid with ease.

✸ Separate packaged bacon
Before opening a package of bacon, curl the package up with your hands a few times, turning it over each time. When you open the package, you should find it easier to peel away individual slices.

✸ Keep wooden tools in good shape
Sprinkle wooden salad bowls and chopping boards with salt and then rub them with a lemon to freshen them. The salt-and-lemon treatment will help your salad bowl to impart freshness, not smells, to the ingredients. And when you chop, slice and dice, your knife won't lift any dried wood bits from the board.

✸ 'Micropeel' garlic
Here's a tip to make working with garlic ultra easy. Microwave garlic cloves for 15 seconds and the skins will slip straight off, allowing you to slice, crush and chop without delay. Another hint: as you chop garlic, the juices released make tiny pieces stick to your knife. Sprinkling a little salt on both the chopping board and

idea

FLATTEN A COOKBOOK

Perhaps you're following a recipe in your favourite cookbook – a big book with lots of pages. But every time you turn your back to add a new ingredient or stir the batter, the pages turn over and you lose your place. It's enough to make your blood boil. To call a truce in the book battle, you could buy a clear plastic cookbook holder designed for the job. Alternatively, you could use something you already have: a clear glass baking dish. Just turn to the page where your recipe is printed and flatten the book with the dish. It will not only keep your cookbook open but will also give you a crystal-clear view of the type.

the garlic will go a long way towards solving the problem.

✸ Super lid opener
Too-tight lids on jars can make you feel like a weakling if they just won't budge. A simple way to get them open is to pull on a pair of rubber dishwashing gloves. With your grip secured, the lid will twist off with minimal effort.

✸ Don't forget the ice cube tray!
Whether you're preparing baby food, storing leftover sauces or making perfect-sized portions of no-cook fudge, a flexible plastic ice cube tray is your invaluable multitasker. It's a versatile kitchen aid you don't want to forget.

Who'd have thought it?

✳ Hair dryer as salad drier
If you have rinsed and spun your salad, but the leaves are still wet, set your hair dryer on cool setting and wave it gently over the leaves.

✳ A teaspoon as a ginger peeler
When you find it impossible to peel ginger without losing some of the flesh, try this. If you're right-handed, hold the ginger in your left hand and using a teaspoon, firmly scrape the edge of the spoon along the knob with your right. The papery skin will peel straight off.

✳ Dental floss as slicer
Held taut, fine floss can slice layer cakes, soft breads, soft cheeses, butter and plenty of other soft foods more effectively than a sharp knife.

✳ Plastic drink bottle as a funnel
Cut off the top third of the bottle and turn it upside down. Now you can easily funnel leftover sauces, gravies, kidney beans or even grease into containers for storage or disposal.

✳ A handsaw as a rib separator
A sharp (clean) handsaw works wonders when you're serving a juicy rack of ribs. Slip the blade between the bones, give it one or two saws and the ribs will separate cleanly and perfectly.

✳ A coffee filter as a gravy strainer
Beef and poultry drippings from a roast make the most delicious, flavourful base for gravy but are often packed with grease. Save the flavour and lose the fat by straining the cooking juices through a paper coffee filter.

✳ Scissors as herb chopper
Use clean household scissors to snip fresh herbs and spring onions into salads or mixing bowls. Scissors are also perfect for cutting steam vents in the crust of a pie before it goes in the oven.

✳ Flowerpots as kitchen tool caddy
Store serving spoons, whisks, tongs and other kitchen tools in flowerpots on a worktop. To make the pots more decorative, you could paint each one in a different pastel or bright colour.

✳ Wood rasp as lemon zester
A clean, fine metal rasp from a toolbox works perfectly as a zester for lemons, limes, oranges and other citrus fruit. Its tiny raised nubs scrape the fruit's skin to create perfect zest.

tip A SHOEHORN AS A CORN KERNEL REMOVER
A clean **shoehorn** has at least two uses in the kitchen. Scrape the wide end along a cob to remove the kernels and use the narrow end to gently release baked goods such as cupcakes, small pies or muffins from their tin.

Keeping fresh food fresh

✱ A surplus of spuds?

If you have peeled too many potatoes for a potato salad or casserole, don't get rid of the uncooked extras. Put them in a bowl, cover with cold water and add a few drops of vinegar. Now they will keep in the fridge for three to four days.

✱ Bag your lettuce

Lettuce will keep longer if transferred from a plastic bag to a larger paper bag before storing it in the fridge. Lettuce likes a little air, but you don't need to remove limp and discoloured outer leaves; although they are not pretty, these leaves help to keep the inner leaves crisper.

✱ A gentle touch in the crisper

Line the crisper drawer of your fridge with paper towels, which will absorb the excess moisture that does no favours for the veggies inside. Replace the towels as they become damp. Another way to dehumidify the drawer is to tuck two or three brand new clean kitchen sponges among the vegetables, squeezing moisture out over the sink as needed.

✱ Toast freshens lettuce

You can keep lettuce crisp in the fridge for longer if you store it in a sealed plastic bag with a slice of almost-burned toast. The ultra-dry toast will absorb some of the excess moisture that would otherwise cause the lettuce to wilt. As long as you replace the toast when it becomes soggy, the lettuce should stay crisp for up to two weeks.

what's the story?

DECIPHERING DATES ON FOOD PACKAGING

Most perishable foods are marked with a date indicating a time frame in which you may consume the product. This is how the three types of labelling work:

The sell-by date tells a shop how long to keep a product on the shelves. They are used by shops to help with stock control and are instructions for staff, not shoppers.

The best-before date is the last date that the product will be at its peak quality or flavour and has little to do with food safety except with regard to eggs which should not be eaten after the best-before date.

The use-by date gives the last day the manufacturer recommends that you should safely use the product, particularly with perishables such as fish, meat and prepared salads. Don't use food or drink after this date.

✱ Keep greens fork fresh

Keep kale, spinach and other greens fresh for longer by storing them in the fridge along with a stainless-steel fork or knife. Just open the storage bag, slip in the utensil and reclose.

✱ Special care for celery

It's crucial for celery to be crisp, so when it starts to go soft try this: put limp stalks in a

Keep your eggs fresh for weeks by coating them with oil.

bowl of cold water with a few slices of raw potato. After an hour or so in this starchy bath, the stalks may be restored to their crunchy best. To stop celery from going brown, soak them for 30 minutes in 1 litre cold water mixed with 1 teaspoon lemon juice before storing – a trick that will also crisp celery just before it's served.

✱ Get the most out of a lemon
When a recipe calls for just a few drops of lemon, simply puncture the rind with a toothpick and gently squeeze out the small amount of juice you need. Then cover the hole with a piece of tape and store the lemon in the fridge for later use. Waste not, want not.

✱ Oiled eggs
Prolong the life of fresh eggs by dipping a paper towel into vegetable oil and rubbing the shells before storing in the fridge. The oil will keep the eggs fresh for an extra three to four weeks.

✱ Vinegar and cheese
To keep cheese fresh, wrap it in a piece of soft clean cloth dampened with vinegar. It should come as no surprise that washed cheesecloth is ideal for the purpose.

✱ Store potatoes with ginger
Unused potatoes will last longer if you add a piece of fresh ginger root to the bin that you store them in. It's said that one root vegetable helps to keep another root vegetable fresh – and a potato tuber is a kind of root.

✱ Longer-lasting milk
If you buy more milk than you can use before the use by date date, extend its life with a couple of pinches of bicarbonate of soda. Bicarbonate of soda reduces the acidity of milk and will slow down the rate at which it goes off. But don't add too much or you'll notice the taste of the bicarb in your milk.

Storing bread and cakes

✳ Biscuits on tissue

Keep crisp biscuits crisp by crumpling plain tissue paper (the kind used as gift-wrap) and placing it in the bottom of the biscuit jar. It will help to absorb any moisture that may seep in.

✳ The birthday cake's in the bag

If you want to bake a sponge cake for a special occasion down the road – like your daughter's 21st birthday or your parents' golden wedding anniversary party – you can actually bake it several months ahead of time and freeze it. The trick is to triple-wrap the layers. Here's how:

1. After taking three layer cake tins out of the oven, let the layers cool completely.
2. Wrap each layer separately in cling film and then in aluminium foil, making each package as airtight as possible.
3. Place all three layers into a large freezer bag and seal it, squeezing out the air as you do.

When the day of the party arrives, defrost the layers before removing the cling film. Then assemble the cake and ice it, secure in the knowledge that your creation will taste as fresh as if it were baked yesterday.

✳ Instant cake dome

If you don't have a fancy cake plate with a glass dome, you can keep your cake fresh and the icing intact by covering it with a large bowl turned upside down.

✳ Well-bread cake

Once you cut into a scrumptious three-layer cake, the exposed part of what's left goes stale quickly. Here's a way to keep it moist for longer. Place a slice of bread over the cut surface of the cake and hold it in place with a couple of toothpicks. As the bread dries out, the cake will stay moist and taste better for longer.

✳ A trick for keeping pies fresh

Perhaps you've eaten two slices of a luscious peach pie and start to wrap the remainder with cling film. Stop. If you cover the pie first with an upside down paper plate or aluminium foil pie plate and then wrap it in plastic, you'll give the pie a little more breathing room and it will stay fresh for a week or more.

✳ Storing a meringue-topped pie

When storing the remains of a meringue pie in the fridge, how do you cover it without ruining the meringue? Rub a large piece of cling film with a little butter, making sure that it is greased completely. Fit it over the pie plate butter side down. The next time you want a slice of pie, the wrap will peel off without sticking.

✳ A crisp bread freshener

To keep sliced bread fresh for longer, just place a small, fresh stalk of celery in the bag with the bread. Celery has a high water content but stays dry on the outside, so what better moisturiser could you use?

✳ An apple every two days

The moisture from an apple will keep soft biscuits or cookies soft. Just place the biscuits in an airtight tin and put an apple slice (skin side down) on top before closing it. Replace the apple slice every two days to keep the treats inside at their very best.

Make freezing a breeze

The big icy compartment above (or below) your fridge can do far more than just act as a store for meat, ice cream and frozen vegetables. Here's how to use it to make everyday items (including ice cubes) go the distance:

'Instant' tea

When you brew a full pot of tea and have a lot left over, pour the tea into ice cube trays and freeze it. Later, you can use the tea cubes to chill a fresh batch of iced tea without diluting it or melt the cubes in the microwave instead of brewing a fresh pot. You can also freeze surplus coffee in the same way.

Freeze eggs?

Yes, but only raw yolks and whites. Break the eggs into an airtight plastic container and add 1 teaspoon of salt or honey for each five whole eggs. Cover the container and mark it with the additive you froze it with so that you'll know whether to use the thawed eggs in a sweet or savoury recipe.

Bag ice cubes

Keep ice cubes from sticking together by storing them in your freezer inside a paper bag. (It will also stop you from cursing and having to chip the cubes away from the shelves.)

Crystal-free ice cream

When you serve only part of a tub of ice cream and return the rest to the freezer, ice crystals tend to form on the surface. You can prevent crystals from forming by tucking a layer of cling film onto the surface of the ice cream before closing the carton and putting it back in the freezer.

Breathe life into leftovers

✳ Surplus grilled tuna or salmon

If you have leftover salmon or tuna from a dinner party, use it as the basis for a tasty salad. In a large bowl, combine 350g cooked tuna or salmon, a 420g can of white beans, 3 thinly sliced green onions, 2 tablespoons Italian parsley, 1 minced garlic clove and 60ml of an Italian dressing. Toss thoroughly and enjoy!

✳ A long life for extra veg

Save all leftover veggies for up to a week. Dice them; lightly sauté the mixture in olive oil with savoury seasonings such as oregano, basil and black pepper. Add some leftover rice or other grains. Use as filling for a quiche or to fortify mince-based dish.

✳ Get a head start on gravy

Did you know that you can whirl almost any kind of leftover soup that has no bones in a blender or food processor to make a quick sauce or gravy for vegetables or meat.

✳ Jazz up salsa

Add leftover corn kernels to a jar of spicy salsa or pickle. Stirring in corn will not only make it look more colourful but will also tone down an accompaniment that is too hot for your taste.

✳ Oatmeal muffins

Don't throw out unused porridge left in the pan when breakfast is finished. Instead, add it to batter when making muffins. Add the baking powder, eggs and other ingredients as the recipe directs and you may find you like the result.

idea

BE AWARE OF THE GREAT THAW

If there's a power cut while you're on holiday, you need to know about it before you go into the freezer. If the electricity was off for a long time and the food in the freezer has thawed and refrozen, the entire household could come down with food poisoning.

How will you be able to tell if the power has been off while you were away? Before you leave, place a plastic bag full of ice cubes in the freezer and check it when you return. If the cubes have become a solid block, a power cut of some duration has taken place. If the ice cubes are as you left them, all is well.

✳ Overripe fruit = great smoothies

Don't relegate overripe fruit to the compost or dustbin. Freeze it and use the frozen bananas, strawberries and peaches to make a delicious smoothie with yoghurt or your liquid of choice. Your smoothies may even taste better, thanks to the concentrated sugars in overripe fruit

✳ Leftover wine makes great salad dressings

Don't pour leftover red or white wine down the drain. Put it in an airtight jar and store it in the fridge. When it's time to make a vinaigrette, you can combine the wine in equal quantities with vinegar for a dressing with extra punch.

✱ Freeze leftover wine

If little bit of pinot grigio or zinfandel remains in the bottle at the end of a party or meal, don't let it go to waste. Pour it into an ice cube tray and the next time you're making a sauce, a casserole, soups or stews that call for a splash of white or red wine, you'll have it to hand. The cube will melt quickly, so no defrosting will be required.

✱ Use red wine to tenderise meat

If you have some leftover red wine, put it to work as a meat tenderiser and marinade. Simply put the meat in a self-sealing bag or lidded container and pour the leftover wine over it. Whether grilled or fried, the meat on the plate will have a juicy, tender texture.

✱ Remember the croquette

If you've just too much leftover chicken, ham or turkey, there's no need to let it go to waste. Make your own tasty croquettes. Mince the leftover meat or poultry very finely to make around 450g, add a tablespoon or two of prepared white sauce and a beaten egg, shape into tightly packed, small logs and refrigerate for an hour. Remove the croquettes from the fridge, roll them in fine breadcrumbs, heat up a few tablespoons of vegetable oil in a nonstick frying pan and lightly fry until golden brown. Perhaps the best bit comes last; if you don't finish these leftovers, they will freeze perfectly for up to six months.

✱ Leftover sauce from a stew?

Turn it into a homemade ragu so good that your family will think that a real chef is in the kitchen. Chop up the leftover meat into small pieces, return it to its sauce, add 480ml red wine and 2 cans of crushed tomatoes. Blend well, bring to a simmer, cover and continue to cook for 30 minutes.

household superstar

10 COOL USES FOR RESEALABLE KITCHEN STORAGE BAGS

1 Speed the ripening of fruit by sealing it in a bag.

2 Crush digestive biscuits for piecrust by putting them in a bag and running a rolling pin over it.

3 Crush nuts by placing them in a plastic bag and pounding them with a hammer.

4 Put the ingredients for hamburgers in a plastic bag, seal it and gently massage the bag.

5 Seal frozen poultry in a plastic bag and submerge it in cold water for several hours for the safest way to thaw chicken, turkey and game birds.

6 Marinate meat and poultry in a large plastic bag placed in a shallow bowl in the fridge.

7 Knead dough in a large plastic bag to keep your hands from getting sticky.

8 Turn a plastic bag into a pastry bag by snipping off a small corner.

9 Protect the recipe card you're using from splashes by enclosing it in a plastic bag.

10 Use a plastic bag as a glove when the phone rings and your hands are greasy or covered in flour.

A perfect table setting

✳ Mini bouquets

When your garden is in bloom, cut small bouquets and arrange them in empty jam jars, or glass water bottles. If you have a long table, line them up in the centre for a table decoration to delight your guests.

✳ Colour coordinate your vases

Add another dimension to floral arrangements with a dash of colour. A few drops of food colouring in the water of a clear glass vase will add extra interest to an arrangement.

✳ Can it

Many products these days come in beautifully decorated cans and containers. Once you've consumed the contents, use the cans to create a centrepiece. Set small leafy green plants of different heights in three cans and arrange the colourful planters in the centre of the table.

✳ The sit-down test

Before guests arrive, make sure that your centrepiece isn't so tall that it will block their line of vision: place your centrepiece in the middle of the table, pull out a chair and take a seat. If the tallest flowers or other decorative items are taller than face height, shorten them so that guests will be able to make eye contact.

✳ You've been framed!

Use small picture frames (matched or unmatched) as place card holders. If you're a skilled calligrapher, write each guest's name on a piece of good-quality paper cut to fit the frame or simply choose an attractive computer font and print out your guests' names. Slide each 'card' into its frame.

✳ Mix and (mis)match?

When good friends are coming over for a dinner party, make things more interesting and unexpected by varying the place settings – a brightly coloured plate here, a rose-patterned fine china plate there. The result is not only eclectic, but also a great conversation starter.

✳ Use grandma's silver

Gone are the days when silver was taken out only on special occasions; use it for everyday casual dinner parties as a reminder of that great woman. Don't worry if it's tarnished ... it will lend the table a bit of retro character!

Ready to serve

✳ No time to dust?

Let low mood lighting help out! Make a beeline for all the candles you can find and place them (carefully and not near curtains) around the living room and dining room – votive candles on windowsills, candelabras on the mantelpiece, pillar and jar candles here and there. If the lights in both rooms have dimmers, set the lights to low and bask in the complexion-enhancing, dirt-hiding glow.

✳ No-stick napkins

Keep napkins from sticking to the bottom of your drinking glasses by pressing the bottom of each glass in a plateful of salt, then shaking off the excess salt. However scant the coating, the salt should break the bond and keep napkin and glass separated.

✳ Chill wine in a hurry

Here's a foolproof way to chill champagne and other white wines quickly. Place the bottle in an ice bucket or other tall plastic container and add just enough ice cubes to make a 5cm layer on the bottom. Sprinkle the ice with a few tablespoons of salt and continue to layer ice and salt up to the neck of the bottle. Now add cold water until it reaches the top of the ice. After only 15 minutes (about half the time it would take in a freezer), you will be able to uncork the bottle and pour properly chilled bubbly for your guests.

✳ Wine bottle cork won't budge?

Run hot water over a towel and wrap the towel around the neck of a stubborn wine bottle. This easy treatment will help the glass neck of the bottle expand just enough to make the cork easier to pull out.

idea

SERVE FOOD IN FOOD

Fruits, breads and vegetables all make terrific edible receptacles.

Crusty rolls Slice the top off a crusty roll and remove the bread from the interior. Then fill with individual portions of tuna or chicken salad for each guest at your table.

Peppers Hollow out red, yellow or green peppers, slice a bit off the bottom so that they will stand straight and use as condiment 'dishes' on your buffet or picnic table.

Pineapple After you carve the fruit out of a pineapple, the shell makes a lovely serving platter – especially for a tropically themed party. Halve the rind lengthways and be sure to leave the leaves on.

Melons Hollow out a cantaloupe or honeydew melon half and serve honeydew chunks in the cantaloupe shell and vice versa.

✳ A stylish salad

Dress up simple salads by lining wide shallow glasses with lettuce leaves and adding a scoop of chicken, tuna or egg salad. Pierce an olive with a toothpick and set at an angle.

✳ Dine alfresco

Don't stay inside on a balmy evening. Cover a patio table with a cloth, bring chairs outside, light some candles and create a movable feast.

Wipe away
pencil marks
with rye bread!

2 Creative kitchen cleaning

The kitchen is the heart of everyone's home, but it can also be the messiest – and dirtiest – room in the house. With piles of unwashed dishes, over-full and disorganised cabinets and cupboards, a grease splattered hob and a filthy oven – if you have little time on your hands or a large and demanding family, you may think that a dirty kitchen is just a fact of life. But it doesn't have to be.

The good news is that you don't have to spend money on all kinds of miracle cleansers and other gimmicks that you see advertised on TV in order to keep a kitchen clean. For a tidy and efficient kitchen, you don't need a degree in organisational management, either. All it takes is a bit of resolve and a good browse through the following pages – all of them packed with time-saving, money-saving hints and tips on how to make your kitchen the clean, calm and hardworking centre of your home.

Wash up and wipe down

✳ Add vinegar to your bucket

Add a few drops of white vinegar to your mopping bucket to remove traces of soap. If the floor is linoleum or vinyl, add a little baby oil to the mop water to bring a soft gleam to the surface – but use a mere 1 or 2 capfuls at most or you'll turn the floor into a skating rink.

✳ Bleach painted walls

Mix a solution of 8 litres water and 120ml chlorine bleach to give your kitchen walls a brightening sponge-down after you've done a lot of cooking with a frying pan.

✳ Erase pencil marks with rye bread

Remove a young Picasso's pencil sketches from the kitchen wall with a slice of fresh rye bread (seeded or not). An artist's eraser can also get rid of the marks.

✳ Wash away wallpaper grime

If your kitchen walls are covered with waterproof wallpaper, remove excess dirt with a vacuum cleaner, then wash the walls with a solution of 120ml lemon juice, 120ml washing-up liquid and 1 litre water. Before starting, wash a tiny section in an inconspicuous place to make sure the paper will tolerate the mixture.

✳ Keep stainless steel stainless

Stainless-steel kitchen sinks aren't quite as immune to stains and marks as their name implies. Here are solutions to various problems:

- **Rust marks** Rub the area with a drop of lighter fluid and then clean it with non-abrasive scouring powder and water.
- **Water marks** Rub with a cloth dampened with surgical spirit.

- **Other marks** Rub marks with white vinegar or soda water, both of which are excellent polishers.

✳ Lemon stain lifter

Getting a tomato sauce stain off a worktop or cupboard door is easier than you think. Simply wet the stain with lemon juice, let sit for 30 minutes or so and then sprinkle bicarbonate of soda onto the abrasive side of a kitchen sponge and scrub the discoloured area. Most stains will vanish and your kitchen will smell fresher too.

✳ Sterilise your sink

Germs can lurk around in a sink on microscopic food particles. To kill them off, fill a spray bottle with full-strength surgical spirit. After you have finished washing dishes, spray the sink with the surgical spirit and then rub it down with a clean tea towel or paper towel.

✳ Tea thyme for porcelain

Attractive though they are, porcelain sinks can be hard to clean because abrasive cleaners dull (and often scratch) porcelain surfaces. Take the gentle route and clean your sink with fresh lemon thyme tea. Place 4–5 bunches of fresh lemon thyme in a large metal bucket and fill it with boiling water. Steep the thyme for 5–6 hours and then strain. Put the plug in the sink, pour in the tea and let it sit overnight. When you drain it the next morning, you will find a gleaming white sink with a delightfully fresh smell.

✳ Almost-free all-purpose cleaner

Why buy an antibacterial spray cleaner if you can make one in less than 5 minutes? Combine 240ml surgical spirit, 240ml water and 1 tablespoon white vinegar in a spray bottle. Spritz onto kitchen surfaces including tiles and chrome, then wipe off and watch how quickly the germ-killing polish evaporates.

✳ The dynamic grease-busting duo

The chemistry between bicarbonate of soda and vinegar is so powerful that the mix can flush grease out of kitchen drains. Pour 90g bicarbonate of soda into a blocked drain, followed by 120ml white vinegar. Cover the drain for a few minutes as the chemical reaction dissolves the grease – then flush the drain with warm water. Caution: You should never use this method after using a commercial drain cleaner which may react with the vinegar to create dangerous fumes.

✳ Ice-cold degreaser for waste disposer

Degrease a waste disposer unit by occasionally grinding five or six ice cubes along with 90g bicarbonate of soda. The ice quickly congeals the grease, priming it for attack by the fast-acting sodium bicarbonate and sending it down the drain. To flush out any residue, fill the plugged up sink with 5-8cm hot water and run the water through the unit.

household superstar

10 CLEANING USES FOR BICARBONATE OF SODA

1 Remove stains from plastic and rubber utensils with a bicarbonate of soda paste rubbed on with a scouring pad.

2 Protect stained enamel cookware, which can be scratched by abrasive cleaners, by coating the stain with a bicarbonate of soda paste – wipe it off after an hour.

3 To clean off grease add 2 tablespoons of bicarbonate of soda to washing-up liquid.

4 Deodorise a dishwasher by pouring in half a box of bicarbonate of soda and running the empty machine through the rinse cycle.

5 Dip a damp cloth in bicarbonate of soda and rub on china to blitz coffee stains.

6 Shine stainless steel by sprinkling it with bicarbonate of soda and rubbing with a damp cloth.

7 Moisten grease stains on your hob with water, cover them with bicarbonate of soda and wipe clean with a damp cloth.

8 Clean a coffee maker by brewing 1 litre of water with 45g bicarbonate of soda.

9 Loosen burned on food from a cast-iron grill pan by adding 2 tablespoons bicarbonate of soda to 1 litre water and boiling the solution for 5 minutes.

10 Remove residue from a Thermos by putting in 50g bicarbonate of soda and 1 litre water and letting it soak overnight.

Chase off kitchen odours

✳ Borax in the bin

Dustbins are great incubators for mould and bacteria that cause odours. To ward off accumulations of these microscopic marauders, sprinkle 90g borax in the bottom of your dusbin and renew it every time you empty the bin.

✳ Cabbage as culprit

Boiled cabbage is one of the healthiest foods around, but the smell it creates as it cooks is a major turn-off. To sweeten the air (and perk up the flavour of your cabbage at the same time), add half a lemon to the cooking water.

✳ Bake a batch of brownies

There's no better natural kitchen deodoriser than a batch of baking brownies. The gorgeous chocolate and vanilla smell will enhance any kitchen – and your family will thank you for it.

✳ Bake an air freshener

Don't buy an air freshener when you can get rid of kitchen smells at a fraction of the cost with baked lemon. Simply slice 2 lemons, put them on a foil-lined baking sheet and bake them in a low oven at 100°C/gas ½ for 60–90 minutes. To prolong the cleansing effect once the heat has been turned off, open the oven door and leave the lemons on the rack for a few hours.

✳ Odour-killing drain cleaner

Using salt and bicarbonate of soda to unblock a drain will put an end to awful drain smells at the same time. Pour 180g salt into the drain followed by 180g bicarbonate of soda. Pour a kettle full of boiling water down the drain and let the hard-working sodium freshen the drain.

✳ Disposer deodorisers

In places where scraps of food gather, bacteria follow, thriving in the cracks and crevices deep inside a waste disposal unit. To keep unpleasant smells from wafting out of your unit, try grinding any of these super fresheners:

● Citrus peel – lemon, lime, orange or grapefruit
● Two or three bunches of fresh mint.

tip SPICE IN THE AIR

When the air in a kitchen gets stale, liven it up by simmering a handful of whole cloves, 3–4 whole nutmegs, 4–5 **cinnamon sticks** and perhaps a few pieces of **orange** or lemon **peel** in a large pan of water for an hour. Then strain the cooled liquid into spray bottles and use it in the kitchen and elsewhere in your house whenever the air could use a little freshening.

Debugging the kitchen

✳ Store flour and rice with bay leaves

Tiny weevils and other small insects can enter paper or cardboard containers of flour, rice, porridge and breakfast cereal through the tiniest of cracks. Keep them at bay by putting a few dried bay leaves in the containers.

✳ Freeze them out

Some insects eggs may be in food containers before you bring your groceries home and have yet to hatch. Kill off any eggs by keeping new products in the freezer for the first day or two.

✳ Two other insect chasers

One or two whole nutmegs buried in a sack of flour or box of rice will help to keep weevils and other tiny invaders out. Some people claim to have successfully repelled insects by placing sticks of spearmint gum (unwrapped) at different points on the floor of the cupboard where susceptible foodstuffs are stored.

✳ Pop goes the weevil

If dried beans or peas are under attack by hungry weevils, add a bit of dried hot pepper to the storage container. You'll find that they hotfoot it out of the box or bag in a flash.

✳ Get ants on the run

Ants hate crawling over powdery or grainy substances. So if you see a line of ants on the march in your kitchen, spoon a long thin line of polenta, cornflour or another powdery foodstuff in their path and watch them beat a hasty retreat.

make your own...

FLYPAPER

Houseflies gravitate to the kitchen because they're drawn in by the food. Take a cue from housekeepers of old and trap flies with flypaper, which you can easily make all by yourself.

Super sticky flypaper

Hang these sticky strips beneath high cupboards, in doorways and from window frames. You don't need hooks – just secure the string hangers with a bit of tape.

1 brown paper bag
String
Tape
120g sugar
160ml golden syrup
160ml water

1 Cut the bag into strips 3cm wide and 30-90cm long. Cut 12cm-long pieces of string and secure them to the top of the strips with clear tape.

2 Combine sugar, syrup and water in a heavy 2 litre saucepan and bring the mixture to a boil over high heat.

3 Reduce the heat to medium and cook until the liquid thickens.

4 Use a pastry brush to coat the strips with the liquid and then hang them wherever flies congregate.

Keep insects out of your jars with bay leaves!

✳ Spicy ant repellents

If you want to stop ants from getting into the kitchen, sprinkle cayenne pepper or ground cinnamon outside the back door as an unmistakable 'not welcome' mat. Ants hate both the powdery texture and powerful smell of these spices.

✳ Fend off flies

There's no need to keep a fruit bowl empty just because these unwanted guests tend to help themselves to your apples and bananas. Send them packing with one of the following:

- **Mint or basil leaves** Scatter mint or basil sprigs near fresh fruit when you set it out; fruit flies hate the smell and will stay clear.
- **Surgical spirit** Rub a little surgical spirit on a worktop next to a bunch of bananas or a ripening melon, tomato or avocado.
- **Apple cider** Pour cider into a jar or bowl and fruit flies will be drawn to the sweet-smelling liquid.

✳ Non-toxic cockroach traps

Wrap the outside of an empty jam jar with masking tape and rub the inside of the jar with petroleum jelly. Pour in 2cm beer and top it with a few small pieces of ripe fruit and 4–5 drops of almond extract. Place the open jar under the sink or anywhere else cockroaches lurk. Cockroaches will be drawn to the appetising aroma, climb into the jar (the tape gives them traction) and drop inside to feast – but thanks to the slippery walls, they'll be unable to escape. To dispose of the tipsy cockroaches, fill the jar with hot water and flush the contents down the toilet.

✳ Borax on high shelves

Cockroaches like to roam any high spots they can reach, so fetch a stepladder and sprinkle borax on the top of your kitchen cabinets. Cockroaches poisoned by the borax will take it back to the nest, where their fellows will start dropping like flies.

Caring for your fridge

✽ Keep it clean

The surface of white fridges and freezers seem to positively attract dirt, especially around the handles. Even the hardware shows fingerprints and spotting. But you can make your fridge or freezer look bright and shiny by using one of these methods:

- Scrub it with a mixture of equal parts of ammonia and water.
- Rub it down with soda water, which cleans and polishes at the same time.
- For a glossier finish, wash and rinse the surface, then apply car wax and buff it to a shine with a clean soft cloth.
- Polish any chrome trim with a cloth dipped in surgical spirit.

✽ Keep a tight seal

The flexible rubber or plastic gasket framing the inside edge of your fridge door seals cold air in and warm air out. When cleaning the fridge, don't neglect it. Wipe grime – and often mould – off with a soft cloth dampened with surgical spirit and finish by rubbing the gasket with a little baby oil to prevent cracking.

✽ Scrub with salt

If you've crammed new groceries into the fridge, it's all to easy to displace a small bowl of leftover sauce in the back – that then gets wedged in at an angle and begins to leak. To get rid of the gummy mess that may result, sprinkle it with salt. Then dip a scrubbing pad or abrasive sponge in hot water and rub the stain vigorously. Repeat until it's gone, each time wiping the area with a wet paper towel.

✽ Litter box lesson

If cat litter can absorb the really pungent stinks that emanate from your cat's litter tray, it can certainly soak up the lesser odours that so easily arise in the fridge. Keeping a small, uncovered bowl of natural clay cat litter on a shelf of the fridge will help to block odours before they take hold.

✽ Deodorise with a spud

To diminish fridge smells, peel a raw potato, cut it in half and place each half on a small saucer. Now place the potato halves on different shelves in the fridge. When the cut surface turns

tip CHARCOAL BRIQUETTE ODOUR EATERS

Store three or four **charcoal briquettes** in the fridge to absorb smells. Simply put them in a small mesh bag (the kind that holds onions or fruit) and put them on a shelf. After a month, refresh the briquettes by putting them into a heavy stainless-steel pan and warming them; ventilate the kitchen well while doing this. Once the briquettes are cool, put them back in the bag and return them to the fridge.

black, trim the black part and return the potato to the fridge with its absorbent powers restored.

✳ A lemon-fresh fridge

Mould and mildew can take hold of your fridge and not let go – and banishing their odours takes drastic action. Squeeze a lemon into a cup of water and throw the peel in with the mixture. Unplug the fridge and empty it (we said it was drastic!), placing ice cream and other frozen items in a bath, sink or freezer bag filled with ice. Then, microwave the lemon water to almost boiling and place it inside the empty fridge.

Close the door and let the deodoriser sit for half an hour. The citrus fumes will freshen the smell and soften any accumulations of food. Remove the bowl, wash the interior of the fridge and restock it with your food and drinks.

✳ Two ways to speed up defrosting

If you have a freezer that doesn't defrost itself, you can speed up defrosting to keep frozen foods from spoiling or going soft. Hasten the process by aiming a stream of hot air at the ice with a hair dryer. Another trick is to boil water in a couple of saucepans, place them in the freezer (on trivets if the floor is plastic) and close the freezer door to trap the steam. In no time at all you should be able to pry off large slabs of ice with a knife.

✳ Use your oven when defrosting

If you have a self-cleaning oven, you can use it to store frozen foods as you defrost the freezer. These ovens are so well insulated that they should keep foods frozen for hours. Just remember not to turn it on.

curiosity corner

SALTY SUPERSTITIONS

In ancient times, salt was so highly coveted as a preservative and medicine and flavouring that it hastened the advance from nomadic to agricultural life, spurred the opening of new trade routes and influenced religious rites and rituals in almost every culture. In the Roman Empire, salt was considered so essential that Roman soldiers were given a regular *salarium* (salt allowance) as part of their pay.

(Salarium is the origin of the modern word salary.)

Not surprisingly, all kinds of superstitions grew up around this precious commodity. A vial of salt worn around the neck was thought to keep evil spirits away, though vampires could be repelled only by a direct assault with salt. According to Irish folklore, a bag of salt tied onto a child's nightgown would keep him or her from being stolen by fairies in their sleep.

The best known (and still current) salt superstition is found in many cultures around the world: 'Spilling salt brings bad luck.' And its second page: 'Toss a pinch of spilled salt over the left shoulder to keep the bad luck at bay.' Spirits who brought misfortune were thought to stand behind a person to their left and a spray of salt in the eyes would cause them to flee.

Hot tips for oven cleaning

✱ Keep the sides of your oven tidy

If crumbs, spills and stains stick to the sides of your oven, pick up some inexpensive plastic gaskets (usually used for electrical insulation) from a DIY store. Slipping them between a freestanding oven and the worktops will keep dirt and grease from sticking to the oven's sides. When the gaskets get soiled (and they will get filthy), simply remove them, wash them and reinstall them.

✱ Beat baked-on mess on a hob

If the pan supports on your hob are made of cast iron and a spilled substance has baked onto them, wipe them with non-toxic oven cleaner and place them in the oven the next time you self-clean it. Remove and wipe clean.

✱ Salt a grease spill while cooking

If grease spills over in your oven while you're roasting meat, sprinkle salt over the grease before it has a chance to bake on. Close the oven door and let the cooking continue. By the time you come to clean up, the spill will have transformed into an easily removed pile of ash.

✱ A poultice for grill pans

Grill pans with burned-on food are a major pain in the neck to clean. To make the job less of a chore, heat the pan and sprinkle washing powder over the affected area. Now cover the detergent with wet paper towels, wait 15 minutes, remove the towels and you'll find it much easier to scrape and scrub off the mess.

✱ In-the-bag oven rack cleaning

A typical way to wash a dirty oven rack is to submerge it in soapy water in the bath to loosen the grime – but who wants to clean a greasy bath afterward? Instead, put the rack into a large, heavy-duty plastic rubbish bag and add 160ml washing-up liquid, 240ml white vinegar and enough hot water to almost fill the bag. Seal the bag and place it in a bathtub full of warm water for an hour. Then remove the rack from the bag and scrub, rinse and air-dry.

tip CLEAN A GAS HOB WITH AN ICE SCRAPER

If you can't budge baked-on food on a gas hob, turn off all the burners and pilot lights, spray the area with WD-40, and let it sink in. After a few minutes, scrape the mess off the hob using a **plastic ice scraper.** Then wash the burners in hot soapy water and wipe dry with a tea towel.

* Ease a rack's slide

When you clean the shelves in your oven, don't forget to clean the ridges that they slide in and out on. Scrub with soap-filled steel wool pads, rinse off the soap and dry the ridges, then wipe them with a little vegetable oil to keep the racks gliding smoothly.

* A scrub for exhaust filters

Once a month, take the filter off the hood above your oven and spray it all over with WD-40. After an hour, scrub with a toothbrush and then put it in the dishwasher or rinse in hot water for a final cleaning.

* A shortcut to microwave cleaning

The quickest way to clean a microwave oven is to place a handful of wet paper towels inside and run it on High for 3 to 5 minutes. You don't need a science lesson to know that the steam from the towels will soften the grime. Once the towels cool down, use them to wipe the oven's interior.

* Carpet a dirty microwave floor with bicarbonate of soda

To remove cooked-on spills from the floor or turntable of a microwave, make a paste of 2 parts bicarbonate of soda to 1 part water and apply it to the hardened substance. After 5–6 minutes, wipe up the bicarbonate of soda with a wet sponge or cloth and remove any residue with a paper towel.

* Make a mini steam bath

The easiest way to melt the grease that accumulates on the walls of your microwave is to fill a heatproof glass bowl with water, run it on High for 2 minutes, don't open the door for another 2 minutes and then wipe with a soft rag. The steam will have softened the caked-on dirt and it will wipe away easily.

what's the story?

THE INVENTION OF THE MICROWAVE

Like a number of other machines, medicines and modern necessities, microwave ovens were invented by accident. In 1945, a self-educated engineer named Percy Spencer, who worked at the Raytheon company at Waltham, Massachussetts, USA, was visiting a lab where magnetrons were being tested. (Magnetrons are the power tubes of radar sets.) As he stood next to one of the machines, he suddenly felt the chocolate peanut bar in his pocket begin to melt.

His curiosity piqued, Spencer sent an assistant out for a bottle of popcorn kernels – and when he held the kernels near a magnetron, popcorn kernels exploded all over the lab. The next morning, Spencer brought in a kettle, cut a hole in the side and put in an uncooked egg. He then moved a magnetron next to the kettle and switched it on. A sceptical engineer looked into the hole just in time to get a face full of egg; the egg burst because the yolk cooked faster than the egg white.

Spencer had discovered that food can be cooked with high-frequency radio waves and in 1946 he patented the Radar Range, an oven the size of a refrigerator and costing $3,000 (almost £24,000 today). In the years that followed, the concept was refined and in the last 20 years, rare is the modern home, office or restaurant that isn't equipped with the machine that revolutionised the way we cook.

Delightful dishes

✳ Wash your dishwasher

After washing load after load of greasy dishes, your dishwasher gets dirty and its interior becomes coated with grease that will show up as film on plates and glasses. You can keep your dishes sparkling by taking the two simple steps below. (You may have to repeat the process once or twice to make sure the dishwasher's inner workings have been cleansed of grease.)

- Pour 240ml liquid bleach in a bowl and place on the bottom rack of the dishwasher. Then run the machine on the wash setting only.
- With the first washing complete, open the washer and pour 240ml vinegar into the same bowl and run the machine through a full cycle.

✳ Get ahead of dishwasher smells

A good way to keep odours out of your dishwasher in the first place is to simply add 120ml lemon juice to the detergent receptacle each time you use the machine.

✳ Give it the old-fashioned scrub

Save a few pounds on your electricity bill and get super-clean dishes in the process. Fill up the sink with warm water, add a few squirts of washing-up liquid, pull on a pair of rubber gloves and have a good scrub. If your dishes are a real mess, let them soak for 10 minutes in lemon juice-infused hot water; if they're still sticky, sprinkle them with coarse salt and a little more washing-up liquid, before rinsing them until they are squeaky clean.

Keep your dishwasher clean and it'll do a much better job on your dishes!

Washing dishes by hand

Washing dishes in the sink doesn't have to be drudgery. Only people who don't appreciate the simple satisfaction of doing things the old-fashioned way will really regard it as a chore. Some people find standing over the sink washing dishes gives them much-welcome 'quiet time', ideal for thinking or listening to music or the radio. And watching a beautiful china plate sparkle like new as you move it from the sink to the dish rack is very satisfying. There's surely no need to tell you how to wash dishes, but we're happy to offer three hints that may be new to you:

Clear up cloudy glass.
Ovenproof casserole dishes made of clear glass may be spoiled with large cloudy spots even though they are completely clean. Eggs, milk, cheese and other proteins are the culprits, but none can stand up to white vinegar. To remove them, just rub the spots with a vinegar-soaked sponge or cleaning cloth.

Banish germs with a short soak.
If you are one of those people who is so worried about germs that even an antibacterial washing-up liquid won't put your mind at ease, soak washed dishes in a sink in a solution of 1 tablespoon household bleach to 4 litres water. After 5 minutes, rinse well with fresh water and air-dry.

Keep rubber-gloved hands odour free.
Unlined rubber gloves may leave a smell reminiscent of car tyres on your hands. Prevent it by rubbing a little hand lotion on your hands before putting on the gloves. There will be no rubbery smell and you will get a great moisturising treatment as you wash.

Cleaning gadgets and appliances

* De-bitter your coffee grinder with rice

When you grind your own coffee beans, it's almost impossible to brush all of the residue out of the grinder when you have finished – and accumulated residue can make coffee taste bitter. To get rid of the residue, run a cup of raw white rice through the grinder once a month. The rice will clean the grinder and sharpen the blades at the same time.

* Hold the spices

If you sometimes use your coffee grinder to grind spices, be sure to clean all of the remnants out of the grinder before switching back to coffee beans or you'll affect the taste of the coffee. Clean it by grinding two or three slices of cut-up, plain white bread in the machine.

* Grind bread, clean meat grinder

Before cleaning a meat grinder, run a piece of bread through it to clean fatty meat particles out of the feed screw. Even regularly washing the parts won't get the feed screw truly clean.

* Purge coffee stains from a glass jug

Over time, caffeine will discolour the glass jug of your automatic coffeemaker, but you can easily make it look like new. Here's how:
1. Fill the carafe a quarter full of water.
2. Cut a lemon into 4 wedges, squeeze the juice of 2 of them into the water and drop all 4 lemon wedges into the carafe.
3. Add 2 tablespoons salt and swirl the carafe around for 2–3 minutes.
4. Empty the carafe and scrub the inside with soapy water. Rinse and dry and return the crystal-clear carafe to its base.

* Clean your toaster with a toothbrush

If your toaster is clogged with hard-to-reach crumbs, unplug it and loosen the crumbs with a small paintbrush or soft toothbrush. Avoid damaging the machine's heating elements by brushing very lightly. Once you've broken the stubborn crumbs apart, turn the toaster upside down, hold it over the kitchen sink and gently shake out the debris.

* Clean your oven window

If the window of your oven gets so caked with grime that you can barely see inside, try one of following fixes:
- Open the oven door and the spray the glass with a solution of 2 parts hydrogen peroxide, 2 parts white vinegar and 1 part dishwashing liquid. Let stand for half an hour.
- Wipe the window with household ammonia and let stand for 20–30 minutes.

Wipe off either substance with paper towels. If any residue remains, scrape it off with a plastic (not metal) windscreen scraper. Finally, clean the oven window with a spray of vinegar or commercial glass cleaner.

* Melted plastic on your toaster?

If you accidentally leave a plastic bag or plastic wrapping so close to a toaster that it touches the metal surface, the plastic will melt onto it when you toast bread – and won't come off with normal washing. To get rid of it, let the

Give uncooked rice a whirl in your coffee grinder to clean it!

toaster cool down thoroughly and try one of the following methods.

- Rub the melted plastic vigorously with a damp sponge coated with bicarbonate of soda.
- Coat the plastic with petroleum jelly and then toast a slice of bread. The heated jelly will soften the plastic and make it easier to wipe off with a soft cloth. When the toaster cools, scrub the residue with bicarbonate of soda and a damp sponge.
- Spray the plastic with WD-40 and let it soak in for a few minutes. Then wipe off with a damp cloth.

✱ Easy blender cleaning

Although you probably flush out your blender jar under the kitchen tap and sometimes even give it a proper wash, that isn't enough to keep it really clean and hygienic. Pour 240ml water and 60ml vinegar into the jar and add a squirt of washing-up liquid. Put on the jar top and blend the mixture for 1 minute. Now rinse the jar and wipe it dry and your blender will be ready to whir and free of germs.

✱ Hose out stuck food

If a bit of food has become lodged in a food processor or blender and trying to remove it is driving you mad, take the machine's bowl or jar outside to direct a strong stream of water from the garden hose on to the clogged-up works. Take a newspaper with you and place the machine on it so that it doesn't get soiled.

✱ Keep appliances dust-free

Sometimes it seems that dust gathers more quickly on worktop appliances than anywhere else. If this happens to you, cover the appliances with tea towels or – if you're always looking for

still one more way to use a pair of tights –
a stocking leg cut to size.

✳ Brush away espresso

If you're a fan of espresso, you'll also be
familiar with how finely ground Italy's favourite
coffee is. To keep it from clogging up the filter
screen on an espresso maker, scrub the screen
gently after each use with a soft toothbrush. If
any bits remain, remove them with a pin.

✳ Rack it up to prevent sandwich toaster fires

One of the leading causes of sandwich toaster
fires comes from a greasy, grimy rack: from
burned cheese or baked on sugar with both
leading to the possibility of a spark on the
heating element. The next time you clean your
real oven – if it is a self-cleaning one – remove
the sandwich toaster rack and wipe it down
with non-toxic oven cleaner. Then simply place
them inside your oven to be cleaned.

✳ De-pulp a juicer

It's easy to forget that electric juicers are traps
for all manner of fruit (and therefore, food)
particles. Keep it spotlessly clean to prevent
bacteria buildup by cleaning it thoroughly:
dismantle it, wipe out the pulp and discard and
fill the kitchen sink with hot, soapy water. Soak
everything but the motor casing for 10 minutes,
remove the pieces from the sink and scrub with
a soft toothbrush. Dry well and reassemble.

household superstar

9 PRACTICAL USES FOR VINEGAR

1 To clean your fridge, wipe it inside and out with a 50/50 mixture of white vinegar and water (don't forget the door gasket).

2 Prevent mildew in the fridge's vegetable bins by washing them out with full-strength vinegar.

3 Steam clean your microwave oven's interior by putting a bowl with 60ml vinegar and 240ml water inside and microwaving it on High for 5 minutes.

4 Disinfect a wooden chopping board by wiping it with full-strength white vinegar after each use.

5 Deep clean and deodorise a waste disposal unit by grinding ice cubes made with half vinegar, half water.

6 To make glasses gleam, add 2 tablespoons vinegar to the dishwasher as the rinse cycle begins.

7 Remove coffee stains from china cups by scrubbing them with equal parts vinegar and salt.

8 Clean a coffeemaker by running 500ml vinegar and 250ml water through a brewing cycle.

9 Eliminate mineral deposits in a kettle by boiling 750ml full-strength white vinegar in it for 5 minutes, then letting the vinegar sit in the kettle overnight.

Pristine pots and pans

✳ Choice cast-iron cleaners

Both coarse salt and borax (sodium borate) are better for cast iron than washing-up and dishwasher detergents, so use either to get burned food off a treasured pan. Sprinkle the crystals into the pan and scrub with a wet sponge or paper towel. Then rinse with fresh cold water and dry immediately as cast iron rusts easily.

✳ Oil your grill pan

Rub vegetable oil on the inside of a cast-iron ridged grill pan to keep it seasoned – do it after each wash and any time you feel it is necessary.

✳ Don't soak a cast-iron grill pan

Soaking a cast-iron grill pan in soapy water can deplete the fat that seeps into the porous surface and seasons the pan – and an unseasoned grill pan is a recipe for frustration. Food will stick and burn and become almost impossible to clean off.

✳ Scrub away scorched milk

If you've let a milk pan boil over, it's probably burned milk onto the hob and filled the air with a scorching smell. Get rid of it by wetting the bottom of the pan – and the hob – and sprinkling it with salt. Let the salt sit for about 10 minutes and then wash the pan as you usually do. The pan and hob will be clean and the odour will vanish.

✳ Boil away burned-on food

If burned food won't come off a pan, fill it with water and add a squirt of washing-up liquid and 1 tablespoon salt. Bring the water to the boil and then turn off the heat. After about 15 minutes, discard the mixture and use a scourer or scrubbing brush to remove the loosened material.

✳ Two aluminium restorers

When aluminium pots and pans become discoloured after extended use, you can revive the lustre with either cream of tartar or vinegar and then wash and dry as usual.

- **Cream of tartar** Fill the pan with hot water and add cream of tartar (2 tablespoons powder to 1 litre water). Bring to a boil, then reduce heat and let the mixture simmer for 10 minutes.
- **Vinegar** Combine equal parts white vinegar and water in the pan and simmer for 10–12 minutes.

Note: Avoid using alkaline cleaners like bicarbonate of soda and bleach on aluminium, which may discolour it further.

✳ Rub out rust with a potato

With regular use, metal pie tins can rust. To get rid of rust, cut a potato in half, dip the exposed flesh into scouring powder and rub the rust with your spud 'sponge'.

✳ Toothpaste for stainless steel cookware

If there are fingerprints all over your nice, sparkling new stainless steel cookware, dampen it with lukewarm water, apply 2cm low-abrasion toothpaste and brush away the unsightly marks. Rinse, dry and you can enjoy your new shiny cookware again.

Four ways to clean copper pans

Copper pans are beautiful – and great for cooking. To keep them looking their absolute best, try these out-of-the-ordinary cleansers.

1
Salt and vinegar
Fill a spray bottle with vinegar and 3 tablespoons salt, shake until the salt dissolves and give the copper a good spray. Let the pans sit for 10–12 minutes and then scrub them clean.

2
Lemon juice and cream of tartar
Mix these into a paste that's thin enough to spread but thick enough to cling. Apply to copperware with a clean cloth and let it stand for 5 minutes before washing with warm water.

3
Worcestershire sauce
Soak a sponge with a little Worcestershire sauce and rub it over the surface of copper pots and pans. Let it sit 1–2 minutes and then wipe clean. Rinse well and dry.

4
Half a lemon and salt
If you find stubborn stains on your copperware, dip lemon halves in salt and rub the stains away.

Cleaning china, glassware and utensils

✱ Spot-free glassware

To prevent spotting on glass jugs, candlesticks, drinking glasses and any other glassware, soak each piece for 3–4 minutes in a bath of 8 litres water and 120ml white vinegar. Shake off any remaining water droplets and then dry and polish the piece with a clean soft cloth.

✱ Protect a teapot

When you store a treasured china teapot at the back of a cabinet for a long time, chances are it will be banged by the dishes up front at some point. To protect the spout from damage, slip a toilet paper tube over it and secure the tube with masking tape. Or sheathe the spout with the thumb from an old leather glove or thick mitten. It's also worth using one of these protective sheathes when you're packing the teapot for a move.

✱ Remove invisible film

Though drinking glasses, mugs and everyday plates and bowls might look clean after they have been washed, they may still be covered with a thin film of grease that is invisible to the naked eye. See for yourself by making a thin paste of bicarbonate of soda and water, dipping a sponge into it and rubbing the glass or china surface well. Rinse, dry with a soft cloth and your dishes may sparkle as never before and even feel different to the touch.

✱ Tea for crystal

If residue dries inside a crystal jug or vase that won't bear hard scrubbing without becoming scratched, fill it with a mixture of 2 parts strong black tea and 1 part white vinegar. Leave overnight, discard the solution and wash the item with a soft cloth dipped in soapy water.

✱ Cleaning etched crystal

If you have some pieces of deeply etched crystal, use an old-fashioned shaving brush or large make-up brush to work soapy water into the ridges and crevices when you are cleaning them. These brushes are rigid enough to root out dirt without scratching the crystal. To rinse, hold each piece under running water.

✱ Smooth out nicks and scratches

If you notice a small nick on the edge of a drinking glass, use an emery board to smooth it out. To eliminate a scratch on a glass, rub it out with non-gel white toothpaste on a soft cloth, then rinse. The mildly abrasive toothpaste will smooth the glass just enough to make the scratch invisible.

✳ No spots on your stainless steel

If you think that vinegar and a paper towel are all you need to rub spots off stainless-steel knives, forks and spoons, you're missing a trick. The spots will come clean only if you dip the vinegar-soaked paper towel into a saucer of bicarbonate soda. After rubbing off the spots, wash the utensils as you usually do and dry them thoroughly right away.

✳ Whiten bone handles

In time, bone-handled knives begin to yellow. Unless you love the antiqued look, wrap a yellowed handle in a piece of flannel moistened with hydrogen peroxide. Let it sit for a day or so, then unwrap. Rinse and dry a knife and the handle will be good as new.

✳ Easy waxing for wood

To keep wooden spoons and salad servers looking like new, wash and dry, and then rub down with wax paper. The thin coating of wax will help to keep wood from drying out.

✳ Scrub a chopping board

Keep your chopping board clean by scrubbing it well with a lightly abrasive cleansing powder and a scrubbing pad or brush and wiping down with hot, soapy water. Rinse, dry and you can be assured that the board is free from bacteria.

idea
KEEPING CHINA PERFECT

If you have a set of fine bone china you may avoid using it in case you damage a precious piece. Follow our guide to ensure that your precious service stays intact and you can enjoy using it more often.

- Rinse dishes quickly after use so that food does not have time to stick and stain.
- Line the bottom and sides of the sink with a soft towel or rubber mat.
- Wash one piece at a time and use mild detergents with a sponge or soft dish cloth.
- Use only warm water and slide china into the water to allow time for the temperature to distribute evenly.
- Never use hot water on china with a metal trim. The hot water will cause the metal to flake away. Never rub any detergent on the metal trim, which can also cause it to flake.

✳ Wrap silver in plastic

When putting away silverware, wrap each utensil in two layers of cling film to shut out air. Exposure to air causes the oxidation that tarnishes silver.

tip NO CIGARETTE STAINS ALLOWED

When you throw a party and you're tolerant enough to let smoking guests puff away on the patio, you may find cigarette stains on a piece of china as you collect all of the post-party dishes. To make short work of the stains, dip the **cork from a wine bottle** into some salt and use it to scour away the tobacco tar.

Bits and pieces

✳ Shake it freely

Salt and pepper shakers tend to clog up in humid weather. To keep the moisture out of salt, add a few grains of raw rice or some crumbled salty crackers to the shaker. To keep ground black pepper from clogging, add a few black or white peppercorns.

✳ Keep brown sugar from hardening

Prevent brown sugar from turning into a brick by putting either a few dried prunes or a 2 x 6cm strip of orange peel in the box. Then tape the box closed and store it in a sealed plastic bag – preferably in the freezer.

✳ Keep olive oil fresh

Unless you use olive oil in large quantities, try this trick to make your supply last: add a drop of sugar to the bottle and it will stay fresher longer. And keep it away from your cooker, where the heat will turn it rancid.

✳ Storing things within things

If you don't have much kitchen storage space, store other items in containers that you rarely use. One neglected container is a coolbag that is only likely to be used in the summer months. Likewise, a little-used casserole dish in the back of a cupboard could hold napkins and other items bought in bulk.

✳ Number your containers

If you have lots of plastic containers, you know how frustrating it can be to match them to their lids. A simple solution is to label both container and lid with a number. It's much easier to match a 2 with a 2 or a 5 with a 5 than repeatedly trying lids on for size.

Tame stray paper bags with a trouser hanger!

✳ Hang paper bags

If you're a natural-born hoarder but have no place to store paper bags you have collected while shopping, clamp them together with an old trouser hanger and hang them from a hook on the pantry or utility room door.

✳ Clean that can opener

To loosen the grime on an electric or manual can opener, spray the blade and gears with WD-40 and let it sit for 6–8 minutes. Then brush away the grime with an old hard-bristle toothbrush. You could also tackle the blade and gears with a toothbrush dipped in hot soapy water – ideally an antibacterial washing-up liquid.

✳ Storing a Thermos

Empty Thermos flasks tucked away in cupboards can take on a sour smell, but you can guard against odours after washing and drying a just-used Thermos:

- Drop a few denture cleaning tablets into the Thermos and fill it with water. Let it sit for an hour or so, then wash, rinse and dry.
- Put a teaspoon of sugar in the Thermos and screw the lid on tightly. The sugar will absorb unwanted odours.

✳ Keep your board from sliding

To keep a chopping board from slip-sliding away while you're trying to chop on it, try this simple trick: dampen a small piece of paper towel and place it between the bottom of the board and the worktop. Press down and your board won't budge.

✳ Cleaning chopping boards

Freshen both the look and smell or a stained or greasy chopping board by sprinkling it with salt and rubbing the board with the cut side of half a lemon. If a much-used wooden chopping board really won't come clean, try sanding the

idea

KEEPING SPONGES FRESH AND FRAGRANT

When a sponge starts to smell like a dead animal, it's time to throw it away. What's not so obvious is that even slightly smelly sponges should be disposed of. These innocent-looking objects are hotbeds of germs that can quickly become one of the filthiest things in your kitchen – the reason you should clean seemingly fresh sponges every three or four days at the very least. Two sponge-cleaning tricks:

- Soak a sponge overnight in a mixture of 240ml hot water, 120ml white vinegar and 3 tablespoons salt. The next day, rinse and squeeze the sponge several times to rid it of all of the cleaning liquid.

- Put a wet sponge (emphasis on wet) in the microwave and heat it on High for 2 minutes. Stay there until the microwave beeps because there's a chance (though an extremely slight one) that the sponge could burst into flames.

entire surface with very fine-grit sandpaper, pressing lightly. When it is smooth, coat with olive oil to keep the wood from drying out and give it an attractive sheen.

✳ Keep garlic fresh for longer

When the papery peel from garlic is left with the bulb, it releases enzymes that help to keep garlic fresh. So when you peel a clove, put the skin back in the container with the rest of the bulb.

Polish silver with a banana skin!

3 Housekeeping secrets

The many miraculous cleaning products that you can buy today – everything from labour-saving devices like self-propelling 'robot' vacuum cleaners to multi-programmed washing machines – are astonishing in their scope. But do they really make our lives easier?

Or are they just more stuff that needs looking after. Could a more old-fashioned approach be more effective? In fact, some of our favourite 21st-century housecleaning methods and items have been used for many hundreds of years: salt, tea, vinegar, lemon and any number of other all-natural items cut through grime just as well now as they did in days long past.

Lifting grease off wallpaper with a slice of bread, polishing bronze with a wedge of lemon, scattering tea leaves on the floor before sweeping – such simple techniques are timeless. This isn't to say, of course, that modern science hasn't advanced housekeeping in ways that make it infinitely easier. But supplementing commercial products with the no-nonsense cleaning and laundering methods found in the coming pages is more than worthwhile. As you try them, you'll discover the pleasures of self-sufficiency and save pounds in the process.

Cleaning floors and walls

✱ Wipe scuffs off wooden floors

Go into the bathroom to arm yourself with the tools to remove scuff marks. First, try squeezing a little toothpaste (the non-gel, non-whitening kind) onto an old toothbrush, scrub the marks gently and wipe up the paste with a damp cloth. If that doesn't work, dab a little baby oil or petroleum jelly onto a dry cloth and rub the mark, then remove any residue with a cotton rag or paper towel.

✱ Protect floors when rearranging furniture

If you have to move heavy furniture out of the way to clean or are rearranging the living room for a big party, protect wooden floors – and save yourself the trouble of dealing with scratches later – by pulling heavy socks over furniture legs and securing them with masking tape. This trick will also make it easier to push heavy furniture around. For everyday floor protection, consider putting adhesive plasters or soft patches on the bottom of furniture legs. If you have a rocking chair, fix a long strip of masking tape to the bottom of each rocker to help to keep wooden floors unspoiled.

✱ Get rit of waxy build-up

If you wax a vinyl or linoleum floor, you will know how wax builds up over time. Here are two easy ways to remove it:

- **Soda water for vinyl** Working in sections, pour a small amount of soda water onto the vinyl floor and scrub it with the abrasive side of a kitchen sponge. Let the soda water sit on the floor for 5 minutes, then wipe up the loosened wax with a wad of cheesecloth or a pair of tights.

- **Surgical spirit for linoleum** Mop a linoleum floor with a solution of 750ml water to 250ml surgical spirit. Use a sponge mop to scrub it in well, then rinse it thoroughly.

idea

DEALING WITH UNSEALED CONCRETE FLOORS

They're often the least considered floors in your home, but garage floors take a lot of hard knocks, on a daily basis. If you store a lawnmower, leaf blower or strimmer in this space, you are likely to experience all kinds of oil and grease spills. And if the floor is made from porous, unsealed cement – and it probably is – the surface will absorb smells like a sponge. The simplest way to remove odours is to go to the nearest pet shop and pick up a large bag of non-clumping cat litter.

1. Blot any oil or grease from the surface with newspaper; the floor should be fairly dry.

2. Spread a healthy amount of cat litter on the stain and using a broom, sweep it over the area until it is covered.

3. Let it stand for 24 hours and then sweep or vacuum up the litter.

✳ Liquidate heel marks on vinyl

Vinyl floors are highly susceptible to heel marks, especially from rubber heels. An easy way to wipe the marks off is to spray them with WD-40, let it sit for 5–6 minutes and then rub the marks with a soft cloth.

✳ Vinegar for tiles and linoleum

These materials are practical choices for flooring in kitchens, bathrooms and utility rooms – all of which receive some of the most punishing wear in the house. Keep cleaning these areas simple by mopping with a solution of 120ml white vinegar to 4 litres warm water.

✳ A clean sweep with tea

Rural Japanese housekeepers traditionally strewed still-damp tea leaves over the floor before sweeping – and some no doubt still do. Dust and dirt cling to leaves and are easier to push into a dust pan. You can then throw the contents into a garden bed or compost heap. (Talk about an eco-friendly cleanser!) Just don't use tea leaves on unbleached wood or carpet, as the tea may stain.

tip MORE VINEGAR FOR STONE AND BRICK

These tough flooring materials can put up with a larger dose of **vinegar**, so scrub stone or brick floors with a solution of 240ml vinegar in 4 litres water. The operative word is 'scrub', as the most effective way to clean is to get down on your hands and knees with a stiff scrubbing brush.

✳ Erasing crayon marks from walls

Your child may be a budding Rembrandt, but even so, you probably don't want him defacing your walls with crayons. Try these techniques to clean up surprise murals.

● Lightly rub the area with a clean, dry fabric softener sheet.

● Rub vigorously with a clean artist's eraser – or ask your young artist do it.

● Squirt shaving cream onto the markings and scrub gently with a toothbrush or a scrubbing brush.

● Soften the markings with a hair dryer and wipe them off with a cloth moistened with a little baby oil.

✳ Cleaning wood-panelled walls

Most wood panelling needs only a good dusting every once in a while, but you can give it a more thorough cleaning with a simple homemade solution – one best applied with a pair of tights, whose texture is perfect for abrasive yet gentle scrubbing. Combine 500ml water, 250ml white vinegar and 60ml lemon juice in a bucket and mix well. Dip a handful of wadded-up tights into the solution and wipe the panelling, working from the bottom of the wall upwards so you won't have to deal with drips.

✳ How to wash up wallpaper

How can you restore the lustre to dingy washable wallpaper? First fill a bucket with 1 litre water and mix in ½ teaspoon washing-up liquid. Then dip a soft cloth in the liquid and wring it out until no excess water remains. Gently rub the wallpaper with the cloth and blot it dry with a lint-free towel.

If the wallpaper has become soiled with a greasy stain, try one of these remedies:

● Brush talcum powder onto the stain, let it sit for at least half an hour and then brush it off; repeat as necessary.

make your own...

FLOOR CLEANER

Clean a wooden floor with herbal tea? You can, as long as it's combined with a few other ingredients. The tannic acid in some herbs – in this case, peppermint – attacks dirt without damaging the finish of the floor. Wring the mop several times as you clean; letting the floor get too wet could warp the floorboards.

Pep-it-up floor wash

To make the peppermint tea good and strong, use 6 tea bags to 1 litre water and let the tea steep for at least 2–3 hours.

1 litre water
6 peppermint tea bags
1 litre white vinegar
2 tablespoons baby oil
1 teaspoon washing-up liquid

1 In a large saucepan, boil 1 litre water, remove from heat and add 6 peppermint tea bags. Let steep for 2 hours.

2 Pour the tea into a mop bucket and add vinegar, baby oil and washing-up liquid. Stir with a large spoon to mix.

3 Dip a clean mop into the solution, wring or squeeze it out and mop away.

● Fold a brown paper bag and hold it over the stain. Press a warm iron to the spot so that the grease is drawn into the paper. Repeat as necessary until the spot is gone, repositioning the bag each time.

Caring for carpets

✱ Baby your carpet

Cooking fumes, cigarette smoke and other smells cling to carpets and make a whole house smell musty. To freshen up, spread a liberal coat of baby powder over the carpet using a flour sifter. Leave the powder in place for a few hours or overnight, then vacuum it up. Bicarbonate of soda will do the same job; with a darker carpet you may want to throw in a bit of ground cinnamon or nutmeg to sweeten the smell.

✱ Steam away furniture footprints

When you move a piece of furniture in a carpeted room, its footprints remain. You can spruce up the crushed fibres using your iron and a fork. Put the iron onto the steam setting and hold it about 0.5cm above the carpet, then fluff out the steamed fibres with the tines of the fork.

idea

CHOOSE YOUR RUG WISELY

It happens all the time: a stunning rug catches your eye and you pay hard earned cash for it, imagining how its delightful pale colours will lighten up your living room. You bring it home, put it down and it looks superb. Unfortunately, the dog and cat are just as drawn to it as you are and like a big vomit magnet, it seems to attract your furry friends at the precise moment that they need to get rid of a hairball or throw up a biscuit. (Sound familiar? It's remarkable!) Remember this the next time you go rug or carpet shopping and plan accordingly. You will still have to clean it, but your stain woes will be much less serious if you don't buy a light-coloured rug.

A sprinkling of bicarbonate of soda will freshen a carpet!

PEANUT BUTTER TO THE RESCUE

Peanut butter as a carpet cleaner? It's a nutty idea, but nutty in a good way. Peanut butter helps remove chewing gum from a carpet. First, heat the area with a hair dryer to loosen the gum. Press the area gently with a plastic bag, which should lift at least some of the gum; you could also try scraping it up with a plastic spatula. Some gum will remain in the carpet, which is where the peanut butter comes in: the natural oils help the carpet fibres to detach from the gum.

Rub a small blob of peanut butter into the spot, let it sit for 5 minutes and then wipe it up with a damp cloth. To finish off, dab the spot with warm water mixed with 1 teaspoon washing-up liquid.

✳ Inexpensive homemade carpet cleaner

Mix 1 part white vinegar to 10 parts hot water or if you choose, 120ml household ammonia in 480ml hot water. Use it either in a carpet-cleaning machine or apply with a scrubbing brush and elbow grease. Rinse the cleaned carpet with a damp cloth. To help to dissipate any lingering odours, open the windows and, if necessary, place an oscillating fan in the room.

✳ Clean up paint spills with vinegar

Don't waste time crying over spilt paint on your carpet. Instead, spring into action before it sets: mix 1½ teaspoons vinegar and 1½ teaspoons laundry detergent into 500ml warm water. Now sponge away the paint (a task that takes time and a lot of elbow grease) and rinse with cold water. If you're lucky, what might have been an unwelcome (and permanent) decorating touch will be gone.

✳ Beat a rug

Dust and pet dander collect daily on (and in) the fibres of rugs, so shake them out the old-fashioned way to get rid of it: hang the rug over a rail or taut clothes line and beat it with a tennis racquet or a cricket bat.

✳ Flip an expensive rug

Has your beloved but incontinent dog relieved himself on the priceless Peshawar rug that you inherited from Aunt Mabel? There's no need to cry or rehome the dog. Scoop up the mess, turn the rug over, place a bucket under the offending spot and pour water – repeatedly – through the underside of the stain and into the bucket until the spot is gone. This will clean the delicate fibres without the need for scrubbing.

✳ The brilliance of baby wipes

Yet another great use for mild baby wipes is as a simple carpet stain cleaner. Blot up a spill with a damp (but not soaking wet) baby wipe. This will lift out the stain before it sets.

✳ Shaving cream to the rescue

To clean a stain that hasn't yet set, squirt non-gel shaving cream directly onto the stain and wipe clean with a damp rag or sponge.

✳ Soda water with a twist

Every waitress and barman knows how reliable a stain remover soda water can be. To use it on a stained carpet, pour it onto the stain, leave it for 3 minutes and then dab it up with a paper towel or sponge.

Common carpet stains

Below are treatments for five common carpet stains – and they're treatments that work on upholstery as well. After removing as much of the stain as you can, rinse the wet spot with warm water, then lay a heavy cloth towel or several layers of paper towels on top. Weigh it down with heavy books or pots and pans and leave it in place until the treated spot dries.

Red wine

Liberally pour salt onto the stain and dab with a cloth dipped in soda water. Or blot the spill with a paper towel, pour a little white wine onto the stain and scrub with a damp cloth. If neither method works, mix 1 teaspoon washing-up liquid with 240ml warm water and pour a little onto the stain; then blot the stain with a paper towel and repeat with a solution of 80ml white vinegar and 160ml water.

Fruit and fruit juice

Pick up any solid pieces of fruit, then stir 1 tablespoon liquid laundry detergent and 1½ tablespoons white vinegar into 500ml water. Work the solution into the stain and blot.

Grease or oil

If you've accidentally dropped fried chicken or another greasy food onto a carpet, sprinkle the grease spots liberally with some cornflour, let it sit for several hours and vacuum it up. Or work shaving cream into the stains, let it dry and rub it off with a damp soft cloth.

Coffee and tea

Choose one of these three methods and act fast. Pour soda water liberally onto the stain and blot, repeating as necessary. Or blot with a solution of equal parts white vinegar and water. Or beat an egg yolk, rub it into the stain and blot it.

Ketchup

Jump right on this one because once a ketchup stain sets, it won't come out (ever). Grab a salt cellar and sprinkle it over the spill, let it sit for a few minutes and vacuum. Sponge up any residue and continue salting and vacuuming until the stain has completely disappeared.

Fixing up furniture

✳ Double-duty dusting formula

Here's a dusting formula that will also moisturise dry wood. In a teacup, mix 60ml linseed oil with 1 teaspoon lemon balm tea. Dip your dusting cloth into the mixture (soaking up only a small amount at a time) and rub it vigorously into the wooden surface to be cleaned. Use a soft clean cloth to wipe away any residue.

✳ Removing stuck-on candle wax

If a candlelight dinner party has ended with hot wax dripped onto your treasured dining table, here's how to remove it without scratching the wood. Put a few ice cubes in a plastic bag and rest the bag on the wax until it becomes brittle. Then gently lift the wax with the edge of a spatula or credit card. Gently rub a soft cloth dampened with a solution of 1 part apple cider vinegar to 10 parts warm water to take care of any residue.

✳ Three fixes for wood finishes

You don't have to look any farther than the kitchen or bathroom when you need to take care of these three problems.

- **Stuck-on paper** To remove paper that's stuck to a wooden surface, pour a few drops of olive oil over the paper, wait about 20 minutes as the oil softens it and then use a clean dry cloth to remove the paper and oil. (Not only is olive oil harmless to wood, but it may do it some good.)
- **Burn mark** If a wood surface suffers a slight burn from a mislaid cigarette or a lit match, rub a little mayonnaise into the burn, let it sit for a few minutes and wipe it off with a clean damp cloth. Mayonnaise will also remove crayon marks from wood.

idea

A BLAST FROM THE PAST

Stripped pine furniture may be regarded by interior decorators as 'so seventies', these days but what's wrong with lending a touch of hippie chic to a room? A stripped table or armoire can look like a million dollars in the right sort of setting.

Stripped wood furniture may be fashionably retro, but it's also quick to dry out. Besides regular dusting and the occasional wipe-down with soapy water, it needs a little oil – and here's how to make a moisturiser and apply it:

Stir ½ teaspoon lemon oil into 240ml mineral oil (not to be confused with mineral spirits, a paint thinner). Put only a drop or two of the mixture on a soft cloth and rub it onto a small area of the wood with a circular motion, repeating until all surfaces are oiled.

Now step back and admire your spruced-up sideboard – now looking so good that you may decide it's just the place to display your mood ring and Led Zeppelin LPs.

- **Tape** If adhesive tape has stuck to a wooden floor or piece of furniture, don't yank it off or you may remove some of the finish. Apply a little surgical spirit to the tape, then rub the area with a cloth dipped in a solution of 1 teaspoon washing-up liquid and 500ml warm water.

✳ Get rid of water rings and spots

If a party guest doesn't use a coaster and their

glass leaves a white ring or spots on a wooden table, the unsightly marks will disappear like magic if you dampen a cloth, apply a dab of toothpaste and rub the area gently. For a stubborn spot, add a little bicarbonate of soda to the toothpaste. Dry the area and then polish the surface as usual; if you're lucky, all traces of the damage will vanish.

✳ Homemade furniture polish

A simple polish made from two kitchen staples will leave wooden furniture with a lovely shine and pleasant smell. Combine 600ml vegetable oil with 360ml lemon juice, mix well and pour the solution into a spray bottle. Spray onto finished wooden surfaces and polish well with a soft cloth. As the polish contains lemon juice, you'll have to store it in the fridge, where it will keep for up to six months. The oil won't congeal, so the polish won't need 'thawing'.

✳ Caring for vinyl upholstery

Though vinyl upholstery is durable, it has a weakness – oil from skin and hair can cause it to harden and even crack. To keep vinyl-covered furniture in good shape, clean it regularly, especially when it gets a lot of use. Dampen a cloth in water, dip it in white vinegar and gently wipe the vinyl surfaces to cut through oils. Then add a few drops of mild washing-up liquid to a bucket of water, stir well and wash the vinyl with a soft cloth dipped into the soapy water. Rinse with a damp cloth and dry.

✳ Foam away dirt

For spot cleaning dirty the corners of dirty sofa cushions, upholstered chair arms and similar, whip up some foam. First, make sure the fabric can be safely cleaned with water-based agents (check the cleaning instructions tag). If it can, vacuum the soiled fabric thoroughly to remove loose dirt. Mix 1 part mild liquid laundry

Give melted-on candlewax the freeze!

curiosity corner

THE UGLY FURNITURE CONTEST

Few pieces of furniture vary so much in style as the large multi-seater item of furniture that dominates our living rooms. Do you call yours a sofa, a settee, a couch or do you have a louche chaise longue? In the US, they have a contest that seeks to find the most hideous sofa in the country! The Ugly Couch Contest was started in 1995 by a slipcover manufacturer as a way to promote the company's product. Little did they expect the flood of photos that poured in: couches held together with duct tape and bits of wire, sofas with patterns so awful one had to shield one's eyes, settees so creatively shaped that they elicited peals of laughter.

Not only did the contest continue and grow but it inspired dozens of other ugly couch contests. An Internet browse of this curious battle of the couch potatoes reveals a worldwide Ugly Couch Contest – proof that the French expression *chaque à son goût* ('each to his own taste') applies throughout the world.

detergent with 4 parts distilled water in a bowl. (Distilled water doesn't leave watermarks on fabric.) Using a hand mixer, beat the solution until a you build a good head of foam. Carefully apply to the upholstery, working in small sections and using a clean sponge or cloth. Let dry, then wipe it off with a cloth dampened with white vinegar diluted with distilled water (1 part vinegar to 6 parts water).

✱ Removing stains from vinyl furniture

To remove stubborn marks from vinyl furniture, try rubbing the stain with a cloth dipped in milk. (Whether the milk is skimmed, semi-skimmed or whole doesn't matter.) Then wash with soapy water as directed above and dry.

✱ Scorch mark on upholstery

Whether someone has been smoking on the sly or accidentally dropped a match on your best armchair is irrelevant: you now have an expensive repair to deal with. It may not be the disaster it seems. You may be able to blot out the mark with paper towels. Wet a paper towel with distilled water and dab it onto the mark (but don't rub). Now blot it with a dry paper towel. If that doesn't work, put a drop of mild liquid laundry detergent onto a wet paper towel and treat the spot. After a minute or two, blot up the detergent with a wet paper towel and then blot the area one last time with a dry one.

✱ Touching up leather

Though leather is hard to stain, it can easily sustain watermarks. Just wipe these away with white vinegar – but only after testing on an inconspicuous area of the upholstery. To get rid of scuff marks, rub them with a pencil eraser.

✱ Take a leather lesson from the stables

If you're lucky enough to own a sofa or club chair made of heavier, saddle leather, take care of it not with expensive, specialised leather cleaners, but with old fashioned saddle soap. Treat once or twice a year, depending on how dry or humid your home is.

Get glass and metal gleaming

✱ Keep glass tabletops sparkling

If you have a glass table, you'll be used to cleaning it frequently to remove smudge marks. To add a shine every time, squeeze the juice of a halved lemon onto the surface and rub it with a clean cloth. Remove any excess juice, then buff the tabletop with a wad of newspaper.

✱ Cut down on mess when cleaning a chandelier

To clean all the pendants and bangles and bits on a crystal chandelier, do you have to go to the trouble of taking it apart? Not if you use this easy method and don't mind standing on a ladder. First, make sure the ladder is secure and that your shoes have soles with a good grip. Then push out the tray at the top of the ladder and set a small bowl of diluted surgical spirit on top (1 part alcohol to 3 parts water). Slip an old cotton glove over your hand, dip your fingers into the alcohol and wipe the glass clean with your forefinger and thumb. Then soak a second cotton glove in fresh water and go over the same areas again. Then dry all of the parts of the chandelier with a clean, soft cotton cloth and it should sparkle again.

✱ Cleanups for drippy candlesticks

You might have more than romantic memories to remind you of your candlelight dinner: a table full of wax-encrusted candlesticks. Gather up the candlesticks and go into the kitchen, where you have several cleaning options.

- Hold the candlesticks under running hot water and rub the wax off with a soft cloth Wash them in hot soapy water until any wax residue is gone.
- If the candlesticks are glass, lay them in the microwave on a paper towel and run the oven at its lowest setting for 3 minutes. When you open the door, you'll find the wax on the towel, not the candlesticks.
- Pop candlesticks of any material into the freezer for a couple of hours. When you take them out you will probably be able to lift the wax off completely.

tip PEWTER TO BE PROUD OF

Pewter bowls and candlesticks are not only attractive but also easy to clean – you can usually restore the gentle sheen by simply wiping pewter pieces with a damp cloth. If smudges and smears remain, go to the fridge or fireplace. A rubdown with **cabbage leaves** or moistened ashes from a wood fire will make pewter look like new.

household superstar

10 WAYS TO CLEAN WITH LEMONS

1 Shine chrome with the inside of a lemon peel.

2 Remove drink stains from marble by rubbing it with lemon juice.

3 Remove water spots from the metal parts of shower doors with juice.

4 Mix lemon juice with borax to clean a toilet bowl.

5 Deodorise a musty humidifier by pouring 3–4 teaspoons of lemon juice into the water.

6 Sweeten the smells coming from the fireplace by throwing a few bits of lemon peel onto the burning logs.

7 To keep ants, fleas and other insects away, add the juice of 1 lemon to 4 litres of mop water when washing the floor.

8 Rub petroleum jelly on the insides of your nostrils to moisten the mucous membranes and make nosebleeds less likely.

9 Protect the recipe card you're using from splashes by enclosing it in a plastic bag.

10 Soak delicate fabrics in lemon juice instead of bleach.

✱ Clean stove doors

When the doors of a woodburning stove are covered with soot it can spoil the cosy effect of a fire. It's not hard to clean the glass. If the dirty side of the glass is easy to reach, leave the doors attached when cleaning. If you need to remove the doors, lay them on a soft towel to clean. (Most doors have spring-loaded clips at the top for easy removal.) Start by scraping away any built-up deposits with a razor blade. Then fill a bucket with water, add 240ml white vinegar and ½ teaspoon washing-up liquid and scrub with newspaper crumpled into a ball. Rinse well with a clean sponge or towel, dry the doors and stand back and admire the view.

✱ Mirror, mirror …

Your mirrors will be streak-free if you wash them with equal parts water and white vinegar. But it's your technique that matters: spray-cleaning a mirror can result in moisture seeping behind the glass and turning the silvering black. Instead, dip a clean sponge or wadded-up newspaper (without coloured ink) into the solution and clean the mirror. Wipe dry with a soft cloth, a paper towel or more newspaper.

✱ Cleaning monitors and TV screens

Less is more when cleaning a computer monitor or TV screen. Turn off the monitor and then simply dust with a clean cloth, preferably an antistatic wipe. Wipe the screen with a clean cloth barely dampened with water, from top to bottom; if fingerprints and other marks remain, add a small amount of white vinegar to the cloth and wipe again. Liquid crystal display (LCD) laptop screens should be wiped very lightly and only with a clean cloth (paper towels can scratch the sensitive surface). Never clean an LCD screen with commercial glass cleaners, which contain ammonia, acetone, ethyl alcohol or other substances that can do serious damage.

✳ Reduce tarnish with charcoal or rice

Although sooner or later you'll need to polish silver cutlery or other items, you can make the task easier by keeping tarnish to a minimum. Protect your silver from moisture that can cause tarnishing by placing a few charcoal briquettes or a small bowl of rice in the cabinet where you keep the silver; both are highly absorbent. Place a briquette inside a silver teapot or coffee pot to prevent moisture from building up.

✳ Shine silver with banana peels

Is your grandmother's cherished silver tea set tarnished? Polish it up with a banana skin or toothpaste. Whichever you use, rinse the pieces well after wiping them clean and then buff them dry with a soft cloth.

● **Banana peel** Remove the banana (and eat it – it's packed with potassium that's good for the heart) and gripping it, massage your silver with the inside of the peel. For tougher tarnish, purée the peel in a blender and massage in the paste. Remove with a soft cloth.

● **Toothpaste** Rub non-gel white toothpaste onto the tarnished pieces and work it in with a damp soft cloth.

✳ Keep brass looking golden

For a tarnish-free shine, clean any brass item in one of these two ways: sprinkle a slice of lemon with bicarbonate of soda and rub it onto the brass. Or sprinkle salt onto a soft cloth dipped in white vinegar and rub the surface. Rinse the brass with a cloth dipped in warm water and then buff it dry. For some extra shine, rub just-cleaned brass with a little olive oil.

✳ Ketchup makes brass shine

A good way to clean knickknacks, drawer handles and other pieces made of brass is to boil them in ketchup or a hot sauce like Tabasco. Just put the items in a saucepan, cover with ketchup (more practical and economical than using Tabasco), and place the pan over a high heat. Bring to a boil, then lower the heat and simmer until the brass shines like new. Rinse with warm water and dry with a soft cloth.

Tips for tiresome chores

✱ Use a ruler to clean your louvres

The slats in louvred doors and shutters attract dust in a flash, but cleaning them can be a real chore. Speed the task with fabric softener and a ruler. Wrap a fabric softener sheet (or a cloth sprayed with fabric softener) around a ruler and clean the louvres by running the makeshift tool over each slat. A bonus with this method is that fabric softening agents repel dust, so you won't need to dust quite so often.

✱ Freshen artificial flowers

Fake flowers do attract lots of dust. You can't use water on silk or crepe, so give the flowers a bath in bicarbonate of soda instead. Put at least 180g bicarbonate of soda in a large plastic bag, insert the flower heads and close the top of the bag around the stems. Grasp the top of the bag tightly and shake it hard so that the soda can absorb all the dust and grime. Remove flowers, shake off soda and dust residue off the petals with a soft toothbrush or artist's paintbrush.

✱ Stained marble tabletop?

Marble makes a beautiful worktop or tabletop, but this porous stone is a real stain magnet. To remove a drink stain, rub a paste of bicarbonate of soda and equal parts water and lemon juice into the area, rinse with water and wipe dry.

To remove other kinds of marble stains (including scuff marks on a marble floor), shake a good amount of salt over the area. Wet the salt with soured milk for as long as two days, checking periodically to see whether the salt–sour milk mixture has done its job. When it has, mop up the salty puddle with a sponge.

✱ Scrub away soot

It's hard to keep a fireplace spotless, but these easy tricks will help it to look miles better.

- Clean the tiles or bricks with a scrubbing brush moistened with white vinegar.
- Rub soot marks off the hearth and tiles or bricks with an artist's eraser.
- After removing ashes from the fireplace, set a plate of bicarbonate of soda inside for a day to get rid of the sooty odour.

✱ Vinegar for vases

It's hard to clean dirty, long-necked vases and bottles. Make the task easier by filling the vessel with warm water and an equal amount of

tip FRESHENING A MATTRESS

To rid a mattress of urine smells or any other unpleasant odours, sprinkle it liberally with **bicarbonate of soda,** let sit for a day or two and then vacuum well.

Buff up your books

Almost everyone has their own library. It doesn't have to be a wood-panelled room lined with oak shelves; a library is simply a collection of books. And whether books are shelved in a special room or stacked haphazardly in a single bookcase, they must be cleaned. Keep your tomes in best-selling shape and you'll have them forever.

To dry a damp book, fan out the pages and sprinkle on cornflour or talcum powder to soak up the moisture. Let it sit for 5–6 hours and then brush off the remaining white stuff.

To get rid of insects that reside in books, place an infested book in a plastic bag and pop it into the freezer for a day or two to kill off the insects and their larvae.

To freshen up a musty volume, pour some clean cat litter into a paper bag and keep the book in the bag for a week or so. Then remove the book and brush off any litter.

If pages are mildewed, wipe away the mould with a cloth that's been barely moistened with a solution of 1 part white vinegar to 8 parts water. To dry, open the book to the affected pages and place it in the sun; let it sunbathe for no more than half an hour or the paper will fade and yellow.

Use a clean, soft paintbrush to dust one book at a time, brushing the covers and the outer edges of the pages. Do not dust a shelf of books with a feather duster, which will only redistribute most of the dust on to the other books.

household superstar

13 REASONS TO TAKE SALT SERIOUSLY

1 Extend the life of a straw broom by soaking the bristles in hot salt water.

2 Throw salt onto a log fire to prevent soot from building up in the chimney.

3 Keep windows frost-free by wiping with a sponge dipped in salt water.

4 Remove watermarks from wooden tables with a paste of salt and water.

5 Spruce up wicker furniture by scrubbing with a stiff brush dipped in salt water.

6 Clean copper, bronze, brass and pewter with a paste of salt and white vinegar.

7 Scrub away rust stains with salt mixed with turpentine.

8 Brighten chopping boards by rubbing with a damp cloth dipped in salt.

9 Refresh kitchen sponges by soaking them in salt water.

10 Pour salt into a washing machine overflowing with suds.

11 Add salt to a washing machine's rinse cycle to sharpen colours.

12 Make wooden clothespegs last longer by boiling them in salted water.

13 Sprinkle salt on to an ironing board to clean an iron.

vinegar. Add up to 140g uncooked rice and shake vigorously. (If cleaning a vase or a bottle without a lid, put a sheet of aluminium foil on the top, mold it to the sides and grip the top tightly as you shake.) The rice acts as an abrasive that scrapes the glass clean.

✳ **Whiten piano keys**

If you wonder how your piano keys became so yellow, don't despair: you can restore their whiteness in a few simple ways. Use a soft cloth to rub the keys with lemon juice and salt or with a 50:50 mix of surgical spirit and water; or apply mayonnaise and gently scrub with a soft cloth or soft toothbrush.

Whichever method you choose, prevent seepage by holding a piece of cardboard between the keys as you work your way down the keyboard. Wipe off each key with a slightly damp cloth before moving on to the next one. Let the keys air-dry and the piano will soon be fit to be played again.

✳ **Dusting a ceiling fan**

All you need to clean a ceiling fan without getting covered in dust is a ladder, an old cotton sock and a bucket of soapy water. Stir 1 teaspoon washing-up liquid into 4 litres water. Dip the sock into the water and wring it out. Slip the sock over your hand, climb the ladder and rub your stockinged hand over each blade. Take care to clean the blades on both sides – the heaviest dust layer is on the top. The dust will be transferred directly to the damp sock, not into the air.

Buff up your bathroom

✱ Keep showerheads unclogged

If you live in an area with very hard water, you'll have noticed how mineral deposits can block showerheads. Don't need to buy a new one – use denture tablets or vinegar to unclog it.

- If you can remove the showerhead, dissolve 4–5 denture tablets in a bowl of water and put the head in to soak. Or let it soak overnight in white vinegar. (For extra cleaning action, heat the vinegar in the microwave first.)
- If the showerhead isn't removable, pour the denture tablet solution or vinegar into a plastic bag, tape or tie the bag to the fixture so the showerhead is completely immersed and leave the bag in place for 1–2 hours.

To make sure the showerhead is completely unblocked, clean out the holes with a needle, piece of wire or toothpick. Then wipe the head with a cloth dipped in vinegar.

✱ Good-bye to grime and soap scum

Forget about purchased 'miracle' products. Instead, stir 3 tablespoons bicarbonate of soda and 120ml household ammonia into 480ml warm water. Once you've wiped the solution on

idea

SEPTIC SYSTEMS AND BLEACH

While bleach is a must-have cleaner that can do everything from whiten laundry to kill off mould spores, it has to be used carefully in homes with septic systems. To make sure that no bleach gets into your groundwater or septic tank when you're scrubbing your tile or sink, use a toothbrush and be sure to wipe any excess off the surface material with a water-dampened cloth.

and rinsed it off with a sponge or rag, bathroom surfaces will gleam.

✱ Make glass shower doors sparkle

Glass shower doors are a convenient addition to any bathroom but can quickly cloud up with soap scum. For some heavy-duty cleaning, try:

tip KEEP CHROME SHINY

Chrome taps and other bathroom fixtures get spotted in seconds, but you can shine them just as fast with **fabric softener sheets.** Keep some on hand in the bathroom and wipe off fixtures as needed. Surgical spirit, white vinegar and the inside of a lemon peel will do a good job, too.

- **Shaving cream** Squirt on the foam and wipe clean with a dry rag; the foam will leave a film that keeps the door from fogging and makes it harder for scum to stick.
- **White vinegar** Keep a spray bottle filled with vinegar and a sponge by (or in) the shower so you can make washing down the surfaces part of your post-shower routine.
- **Bicarbonate of soda-plus** Make a solution of 60ml washing-up liquid, 60ml hydrogen peroxide and 45g bicarbonate of soda. Then scrub it on the doors with a sponge.
- **Vegetable oil** Simply pour a little vegetable oil onto a sponge or paper towel and scrub the doors, adding more oil as you need it.
- **Furniture polish** Use a cloth to rub polish directly on doors, then wipe it off with a clean cloth. The polish will not only clean but will protect against the future build-up of soap scum.

✳ Mildew-free shower curtains

The moist environment of a bathroom is just made for mildew, so don't be surprised when it appears on your shower curtain. You can keep it at bay for a while, at least, by soaking curtains and liners in salt water before hanging them. Once they're up and any mildew appears:

- Add 90g borax and 120ml vinegar to 480ml water, pour onto the affected areas and let sit for 8–10 minutes. Then scrub with a sponge or cloth.
- Mix 2 tablespoons washing-up liquid with 500ml household bleach and spray the solution on the curtain.
- Make a paste of vinegar and salt, and spread it onto the mildewed area. Let it dry for 1–2 hours and then clean it off with a damp cloth.

✳ Lemony toilet cleaner

Make a paste of 2–3 parts borax and 1 part lemon juice (stir the juice in gradually until you have the right consistency) and apply it to a stained toilet bowl, rim included. Let it sit for 1½–2 hours and then scrub it off with a toilet brush. This treatment is especially effective for getting rid of the ring that often appears at water level on the toilet bowl.

✳ Clean that ceiling

You're probably so busy cleaning the fixtures and tiles in your bathroom that you don't even think about the ceiling. Look up, but prepare yourself what you might see – mildew, spots, built-up grime. To clean it easily, fill a mop bucket with equal parts water and white vinegar. Then put on goggles or other protective eyewear. Dip a long-handled sponge mop into the solution, squeeze it out and reach up to clean one section of the ceiling at a time.

✳ Good riddance to grout grime

The grouting between bathroom tiles is a magnet for dirt and germs and it's easy to miss these hard-to-reach crevices during regular cleaning. It also looks awful so every so often:

- Make a paste of 1 part borax, 2 parts bicarbonate of soda and 1–2 parts water and scrub it onto the grout with a toothbrush.
- Rub away grime with a new pencil eraser, that's well suited to reaching these narrow spaces.
- Scrub with a mouthwash containing a tooth-whitening agent.
- Soak a cotton wool ball in household bleach and set it on a spot of badly stained worktop grout for a few hours; for walls, attach the cotton ball with gaffer tape.

✳ Solutions for stubborn scum and water spots

Many surfaces in the bathroom – including ceramic tiles around sinks and tubs, and glass fibre and acrylic shower units – can become dulled by water spots and built-up scum just as easily as tubs and sinks. Tackle these heavily soiled surfaces with vigour and ...

- 360g salt dissolved in 4 litres hot water.
- 120ml vinegar, 120ml ammonia and 45g bicarbonate of soda in 4 litres warm water.

idea

TOILET CLEANING MADE EASY

Cleaning a toilet is no-one's favourite job – no matter how keen a housekeeper, but it's one you have no choice but to tackle regularly. Here are a few ways to make the job easier and cut the cost of specialist cleansers.

Chalky tablets Drop 2 antacid tablets or 1 denture tablet containing sodium bicarbonate into the bowl, let them dissolve for about 20 minutes, then scrub the bowl with a toilet brush. A vitamin C tablet will do the trick as well.

Mouthwash Take a bottle of mouthwash from the medicine cabinet and pour 60ml into the toilet bowl. After about half an hour, scrub the bowl with a toilet brush and flush.

Cola Empty a can of cola into the toilet bowl and let sit for 30–60 minutes before scrubbing and flushing.

Apply one of the solutions, let sit for about 15 minutes, then scrub off and rinse.

✳ Brush away rust stains

To get rid of hard-water rust stains on toilets, baths and sinks, just squeeze a little toothpaste onto an old toothbrush and scrub away. Or scrub at the stain with a paste of borax and lemon juice or a solution of equal parts turpentine and salt. Whichever method you choose, attack the rust stains right away. The sooner you deal with them, the easier they will be to remove.

Window treatments

✳ Gelatine for window curtains

Machine washable cotton curtains may emerge from the washer fresh as a daisy, but more often than not, they come out so creased that you're in for a tough time at the ironing board. How to keep creasing to a minimum when washing cotton curtains? Dissolve 1 tablespoon plain gelatine in 240ml boiling water and add to the final rinse cycle. The same trick will restore shine to glazed cotton curtains.

✳ Use a blackboard eraser

You've washed your windows and when you step back to admire your handiwork you spot the dreaded streaks. What's worse, you can't tell whether they're on the inside or the outside of the pane. You'll have to clean the panes on both sides again, but with what? One of the best tools is a clean blackboard eraser, rubbed in a circular motion. To keep from guessing about which side of a window is streaked, try this trick next time: use an up-and-down motion when cleaning and drying one side of the window and a back-and-forth motion on the other side. You'll now know which side to 'erase'.

✳ Two old window-washing standbys

People have probably argued about the best ways to clean windows since glass was invented. Two formulations that never disappoint are 1) 120ml ammonia in 8 litres warm water or 2) 240ml white vinegar in 1 litre water. To remove isolated smudges and sort other spots swiftly, wipe windowpanes with a soft cloth dipped in white vinegar.

tip STREAKING: READ ALL ABOUT IT!

One of the biggest window-washing challenges is to prevent streaking. To begin with, wash your windows on a cloudy day, when they'll dry more slowly and leave fewer streaks. Use the right equipment, which needn't be costly or even commercial. Crumpled up, **newspaper** without coloured ink is ideal for streak-free cleaning and drying. So is the packing paper used by professional movers – simply newsprint without ink.

✱ Effervescent washer

One of the simplest and most effective glass window cleaners around is soda water, which dries without streaking. Just pour it into a spray bottle and spritz the windows, then dry with a cloth.

✱ Solve the dirty windowsill problem

If you like fresh air and keep your windows open, it can be hard to keep out all the dust and soot that soils indoor sills, especially if you live in an area with heavy traffic. Outdoor sills fare even worse, of course, since their surfaces tend to trap dirt in pits and cracks. To make cleaning windowsills a breeze, wash them thoroughly, let dry and spray the sills lightly with a little clear floor wax.

✱ Awesome awnings

A good spray with the garden hose every once in a while will help to keep awnings clean and free of debris, but they also need a thorough clean every few months. Scrub awnings that are made of canvas and most other materials with a brush dipped in warm water and a mild detergent. If you're faced with stubborn stains or mildew, sprinkle bicarbonate of soda onto a stain and let it sit for about 5 minutes before rinsing it off with a garden hose. Treat mildew with a solution of 1 part colourfast bleach and 3 parts water; just let it soak into the material for 3–4 minutes and then rinse.

✱ Don't wash windows on a hot day!

It might be tempting to do your window washing on a warm day, but you'll find you're in a worse situation than you were when you started. Why? Your window washing solution will dry on contact, leaving the windows streaky.

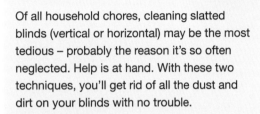

idea
CLEAN YOUR BLINDS

Of all household chores, cleaning slatted blinds (vertical or horizontal) may be the most tedious – probably the reason it's so often neglected. Help is at hand. With these two techniques, you'll get rid of all the dust and dirt on your blinds with no trouble.

Clean with a glove All you need to wash blinds is a clean thick cotton glove (a gardening glove is ideal) and a small bowl of fabric softener. Pull on the glove, dip your fingers into the bowl and simply slide your forefinger and middle finger along both sides of each slat. Fabric softener not only cleans hard surfaces but also slows the build-up of dust.

Clean with a kitchen spatula Wrap a cotton cloth around a spatula and secure it with a rubber band. Dip the spatula in either a 50:50 vinegar-water solution or surgical spirit and run your makeshift cleaning tool along the slats. You could also apply vinegar water or alcohol to the blinds using the gloved-hand technique above.

✱ Super-green curtain poles

For smaller windows, try a natural alternative to a traditional curtain rod. Find an appropriate length and width of fallen tree branch – say 1.5m long and 7cm in circumference for a 1.2m wide window – and run it through the tops of curtains or through the curtain rings.

Get rid of pests

✳ Lure ants with sugar

Give ants what they want: sugar. Make a trap by adding 2–3 teaspoons sugar to 240ml water, moisten a few paper towels or old kitchen sponges in the solution and set them in spots where you have seen ants. Leave the traps overnight and check them in the morning. If they're crawling with ants (almost a certainty), sweep the traps into an empty dustpan and pour a kettle of hot water over them. Repeat the process until there are no ants left to lure.

✳ Repel ants with vinegar

If ants love sugar, it only makes sense that they hate vinegar. To get rid of these unwelcome visitors, mix equal parts white vinegar and water in a spray bottle and squirt it on worktops, windowsills, kickboards and anywhere else ants are to be found wandering.

✳ Spiced-out silverfish

These wingless insects enjoy munching on, among other things, paper, glue and starch. But they don't like herbs. Leave sachets or tea bags of dried lavender, mint, sage or bay leaves in bathroom and kitchen cabinets, where silverfish typically congregate. Wiping down surfaces with lavender oil or a similarly potent herbal solution should also encourage silverfish to go somewhere else.

✳ A lethal treat for cockroaches

Ingesting bicarbonate of soda will kill cockroaches, but you will need to make it palatable. Bait them by mixing bicarbonate of soda with equal parts of icing sugar and sprinkling the mixture inside cabinets and other potential cockroach hidey-holes.

✳ Minty mouse repellent

Whip up a litre of peppermint tea – not for your morning pleasure but to repel the mice you've heard scurrying about at night. Boil 500ml water, turn off the heat and add 4–6 peppermint tea bags and let the tea steep for 6–8 hours. Now stir in 2 teaspoons washing-up liquid to make the super-strong solution stick to surfaces for longer. Fill a spray bottle with the tea and coat kickboards and any areas where you suspect mice may be getting into the house.

✳ Ground flying insects

As much as you may enjoy the aromas of basil, oranges and cloves, flies and other flying insects are repelled by them – one whiff and they'll wing their way elsewhere. So chase them off while treating yourself to some delightful scents.

- Put dried basil in organza and muslin sachets (sold at craft and kitchenware stores). Hang the bags in the kitchen and anywhere else flies and other winged pests like to buzz around and they'll quickly stop dropping by.
- Make a pomander – a whole orange stuck with cloves. Hang it from a light fixture or hook and you'll enjoy pest-free air and a fruity scent as well.

Everyday laundry tips

✳ Outfox the sock bandit

The invisible sock bandit who hangs around washing machines and snatches one sock from a pair will probably never be apprehended, but here's a way to thwart him. Give each family member a mesh bag for their dirty socks. Then, on washday, close the bags and throw them into the washing machine. The sneaky thief will leave empty-handed and you should only have to replace socks when they wear out.

✳ Freshen a laundry basket

Hampers are handy for keeping dirty laundry in one place, but they can get a little ripe when packed with soiled clothes. Here are two ways to prevent stale clothes smells:

- Cut the foot off a pair of old tights, fill it with bicarbonate of soda, knot it and throw the makeshift odour eater into the basket. Replace the bicarbonate of soda every month or so.
- Keep a box of bicarbonate of soda next to the basket and sprinkle some on to the soiled clothes as you put them into the washing machine, where the soda will freshen and soften the load.

✳ Whiter whites

Do your white T-shirts tend to go grey? White socks look dirty no matter how many times they're washed? Try one of these tried and trusted methods for making whites stay white.

- Soak in a solution of 4 litres water and 180g bicarbonate of soda.
- Soak in hot water in which you've dissolved 5 aspirin tablets (325mg each).
- Add 240ml white vinegar to the washing machine's rinse cycle.

make your own...

FABRIC SOFTENER

There's no need to spend money buying fabric softeners when you probably have all the ingredients you need to make your own. See for yourself with this simple recipe.

Super fabric softener

You can also use this solution to make a fabric softener sheet to toss in a tumble drier. Just dilute with water, dip in a washcloth and wring it out and add the washcloth to your load of wet clothes.

480ml white vinegar
360g bicarbonate of soda
1 litre water

1 Combine ingredients in a large bucket or pan and stir to dissolve the bicarbonate of soda.

2 Pour the solution into a plastic bottle with a lid. (An old liquid detergent bottle is ideal.)

3 To use, add 60ml softener to the washing machine's final rinse cycle.

✳ Blacker blacks, darker darks

While faded and distressed-looking garments are sometimes the height of fashion, you may prefer not to look as if the last time you went clothes-shopping was 1998. Here are some tips

Add coffee to your rinse cycles to keep dark clothes dark!

for keeping black and dark-coloured clothes looking like new.

- For black clothes, add 2 cups brewed coffee or tea to the rinse cycle.
- For dark colours like navy blue or plum, add 180g table salt to the rinse cycle.
- To keep denim from fading quickly, soak jeans in salt water or a 50:50 solution of water and white vinegar before the first wash. Turn the jeans inside out before putting them in the machine and turn the temperature setting to cold.

✳ Two starch substitutes

There's no need to run out and buy starch to stiffen shirt collars or restore body to shapeless clothing. Make your own by pouring 500ml water into a jar and adding 2 tablespoons cornflour. Screw the jar lid on tightly and shake well. Now pour the solution into a spray bottle for use when ironing.

If some garmets are looking a bit shapeless, don't use starch when ironing. Instead, add a cup of powdered milk to the final rinse cycle of the wash to give the fabric back its body.

✳ Boil yellowed cottons

With time, white cotton and linen tend to turn yellow – hardly the fresh, crisp look for which cotton is famous. Mix 45g salt and 45g bicarbonate of soda with 4 litres water in a large pan. Add the yellowed items and boil them for 1 hour to get rid of the yellow.

✳ Brightening rugs and curtains

If cotton rugs or cotton curtains have faded, simply add 60g salt to your laundry detergent to brighten the colours. If a rug is too large for machine washing, scrub it well with a clean rag dipped in salt water.

✳ Banish odours

Get rid of dye or chemical smells in new sheets or shirts and the rank odour of sweaty gym clothes left to fester for weeks. Here are two old but effective deodorising standbys. First, add 90g bicarbonate of soda to 4 litres water and presoak any smelly washable items for about 2 hours. Then, as you machine-wash them, add 120ml white vinegar to the rinse cycle.

✳ Dry sweaters with a pair of tights

Don't peg sweaters directly onto the line; run an old pair of tights through one sleeve, the neck and out the other sleeve and peg on to the line.

✳ Clean your drier vent from the outside

Stuffed-up drier vents can, in worst case scenarios, cause fires, but most of us never think of examining the vent from the outside, on a regular basis. To do so, carefully lift up the vent flap and clean it out.

✳ An improvised drying rack

To save money, air-dry any items you can. But you don't need a sunny day. Suspend an old fridge shelf or oven rack from a beam in your utility room and hang wet clothes on coat hangers onto the rack.

idea

A SUPER-CLEAN IRON

You're pressing your best blouse or shirt in preparation for dinner with your boss when the iron leaves a black streak on the collar. You won't have to worry about ruined garments if you clean your iron regularly. Try one of these methods to rid the soleplate of burned starch and other debris:

- Lay several sheets of wax paper on the ironing board, turn the iron on low and the steam off and run the iron back and forth over the wax paper several times.

- Fill the iron with white vinegar, turn the heat on high, switch on the steam and let it puff steam for about 5 minutes. Empty the iron and refill it with cool water. Shake gently, drain it and wipe the soleplate with a clean cloth.

- Unblock steam vents by poking them with a cotton swab dipped in a solution of equal parts water and white vinegar. A toothpick will unblock smaller vents.

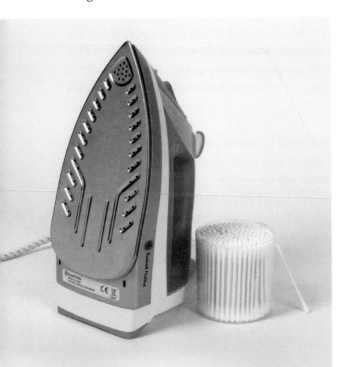

The science of stain removal

With the right formula you can remove almost any kind of stain from clothing and there's no reason not to experiment with ingredients that 'do no harm': bicarbonate of soda, cornflour, flour, lemon juice, liquid detergent, a raw potato, shampoo and white vinegar. Follow stain treatments with a regular wash. (To treat garments without machine washing, see 'Saving stained clothing', on pages 197-98.)

Blood	As quickly as possible, soak a bloodstained item of clothing in a pan of cold salted water. After 3–4 hours, rub the stain with liquid detergent and launder.
Coffee	Presoak the stain in a solution of 1 litre water, 1 tablespoon white vinegar and 1 teaspoon laundry detergent.
Grass	Either soak grass stains in full-strength white vinegar or brush non-gel, non-whitening toothpaste directly onto the stain.
Gravy	Cover the stain with bicarbonate of soda, cornflour, flour or salt, all of which soak up grease. After brushing off the substance, pour liquid laundry detergent and hot water directly onto the stain.
Ink	Pour salt onto an ink stain that's still wet, gently dab with a wet paper towel and then brush off the salt; repeat as necessary.
Mud	Rub the stain with a peeled slice of raw potato and then soak the garment in cold water for at least 15 minutes.
Mustard	Stir 1 tablespoon white vinegar and ½ teaspoon liquid laundry detergent into 1 litre warm water. Sponge the solution on the stain and let it air-dry. Before washing the garment, apply liquid detergent directly to the spot.
Ring	Rub shampoo directly onto the stain with your finger or around a toothbrush. Let it sit for 25–30 minutes before washing the collar of the shirt. (Make sure the shampoo you use contains ammonium lauryl sulphate, an ingredient that cuts through oil.)

Special care for special items

✳ Fluff fluffy stuff with a trainer

When drying a feather-filled item – whether a pillow, duvet or parka – toss a clean old trainer into the tumble drier (the less smelly, the better). The soft-soled shoe will make a bit of noise, but will fluff up the item nicely as it bounces around.

✳ Speed-dry a wet blanket

Make a soggy blanket fresh from the washing machine look warm and welcoming again in no time. First, put two large towels in the tumble drier and let them heat for 20 minutes. Now throw in the blanket and let the towels soak up the moisture. Take the blanket out when it's still damp and drape it over the backs of two chairs (ideally, garden chairs out in the sun) or two parallel clothes lines to air-dry.

✳ Prevent runs in tights

Runs in a pair of tights can ruin the look of the sharpest outfit, so take preventative action before you wear them. Wash new tights, let them dry and then soak for 3 hours in a solution of 4 litres water and 360g salt.

✳ Salt your new jeans

Nothing's more comfortable than a pair of jeans, but it can take a little time before the stiffness wears off. Hasten the process by throwing a new pair of jeans into the washing machine with 90g salt. They'll feel softer the first time you pull them on.

✳ New life for soiled whites

It's a sad day when a favourite white shirt or blouse just can't be seen in public anymore – yellow stains, a dreary cast and seemingly permanent ring around the collar. But all is not lost. Perk up the garment (and yourself) by working a paste of vinegar and bicarbonate of soda directly onto stained and soiled areas, then hang the garment outside in the sun for a couple of hours. If the collar remains soiled, pour a capful of 3 per cent hydrogen peroxide along the ring. Now wash in hot water as you normally would and welcome your favourite back into the cupboard.

✳ Kettle-clean a felt hat

To deep clean a wool felt hat, fill a kettle with water and bring to the boil. Carefully hold the hat above the steam, rotating it as necessary. Brush with a dry toothbrush and let it dry.

✳ Wash silk in hair shampoo

Use a protein-based hair shampoo and cool water to hand-wash silk garments; the protein will feed the protein in the silk, giving the garment body and making it last longer.

Corral outdoor shoes in a laundry basket!

4 Winning the war on clutter

Some people keep their living quarters so orderly that it's almost scary. Others seem entirely incapable of controlling mountains of clutter and their houses always look as if they've just had a burglary or been turned over in a police raid.

From all appearances, a talent for organising is like music or athletics or maths: you either have it or you don't and if you're reading this, you probably know who you are.

Many of the simple solutions in this chapter may work so well that keeping your house tidy will not only be easy, but fun, as well. Clutter-controlling hints also give you creative ways to use things you already have, such as cardboard boxes, shoe boxes and plastic containers. Other hints call for common items that aren't normally used for storage, but which work perfectly, like a suitcase, a casserole and even a pair of tights. It's a well-known fact that organised surroundings have a positive psychological effect on the psyche. So applying the advice found in this chapter might not only help you to emerge from under the mess, but boost your spirits, too!

Smart storage strategies

* How to clean out a drawer

To organise a drawer in the most efficient manner, you need to have a plastic bin bag and three shoe boxes or similarly sized containers by your side. Dump the contents of the drawer onto the bed or floor or a table and start sorting the bits and pieces, distributing them like this:

- Put anything you want to throw away in the bin bag.
- Place anything you want to store elsewhere in the first box.
- Put anything worth giving to charity in the second box.
- Save any candidates for a car boot or jumble sale in the third box.

Now put everything that's left over back in the drawer. Then take the bag and the boxes and plan your trip to the dump, the storage facility, your favourite charity and an upcoming car boot or jumble sale.

* No cheese, please

The next time you order a takeaway pizza in person, chat up the cashier and ask if you can have an extra box. Pizza boxes make excellent containers for everything from road maps to souvenir newspapers to children's artwork.

* CD storage

When you have completely filled up your CD rack and you've taken to stacking new CDs beside it on the floor, it's time to put an empty shoe box to good use. Sort your CDs and put the ones you rarely listen to in the box; label each box according to genre of music and return it to its former place (probably on a cupboard shelf). Stack other shoe boxes on top as your CD collection grows.

* Special storage for special stuff

Turn shoe or hat boxes into a treasure box for each member of the family. Covering the boxes in differently coloured contact paper will distinguish them from one another and make them more durable as well. You could also let a child use tempera paint to paint his or her box. The boxes will ensure that all medals, ribbons, special greetings cards and any other bits and pieces worth keeping don't get submerged amid everyday clutter.

tip THE HOME ORGANISER'S DREAM BOX

Wine and spirits boxes usually have 6-12 compartments, each about 30cm high and just made to hold rolled-up posters, Christmas decorations and other kinds of flotsam and jetsam that you want to keep in order. The boxes are always easy to come by, since wine merchants are more than happy for you to take a few off their hands.

Marvellous mini containers

Some common items found in the average home have achieved such status among organised housekeepers that we've inducted them into the Mini Container Hall of Fame. Buy an indelible marker and a roll of tape that you can write on and label all your items. When the contents change, peel off the old labels and make a new one.

Cigar box
These are hard to find, but when you do, they're worth their weight in gold. Look for them at car boot sales.

Fruit basket
This small, ventilated plastic basket from the supermarket is good for storing anything that needs a little air, such as kitchen sponges.

Coffee can
It's roomy and has a lid. Who could ask for more? Just keep the contents dry.

Film canister
Soon to be extinct, but not yet. Hoard film canisters and use them to hold rings and earrings, small change for tolls, fishing flies and garden seeds.

Hanging shoe bag
One of the best all-purpose holders ever created. Hang it on a wardrobe door, in a bathroom, in a home office or in a child's room and use the roomy pockets for just about everything.

Baby wipes container
Sturdy and stackable, this rectangular plastic receptacle is ideal for small office supplies, sewing paraphernalia, small tools and biscuit cutters.

Ice cube tray
The plastic ice cube tray has more compartments than an egg carton but no lid – which makes it the perfect drawer divider for tiny odds and ends. Fill it with small office necessities or rings and earrings.

Egg carton
Six to 12 (or even 15 or 18) small compartments and an attached lid make this lightweight container a great choice for buttons, washers, tacks, paperclips and drawing pins.

make your own...

NEWSPAPER CLIPPING PRESERVATIVE

The acidic nature of newsprint means that newspaper clippings will not only yellow but will also eventually disintegrate. To save articles of personal significance or historical importance, give the clippings a bath in Milk of Magnesia. Though 'milk of magnesia' is a common term for magnesium hydroxide, $Mg(OH)_2$, it is trademarked as an over-the-counter antacid and laxative medicine.

$Mg(OH)_2$ clipping saver

Before soaking a clipping, make sure that the ink doesn't run by adding a drop to a tiny area of print, preferably outside the margins of the article you want to preserve.

1 Milk of Magnesia tablet
1 litre soda water
1 large bowl (not aluminium)
Shallow glass dish

1 Combine the tablet and soda water in a bowl and let it sit overnight.

2 Pour a 0.5cm layer of the soda mix into the dish and submerge the clipping for 60–90 seconds.

3 Lay the clipping on a double layer of paper towels and then cover with another double layer and press gently to absorb the water.

4 Remove towels and air-dry the clippings on a wire rack or screen.

✴ Storing gift-wrapping paper

Save long cardboard tubes and use them to store leftover wrapping paper. The tubes can be stored in the corner of a large wardrobe or understairs cupboard. You could also attach a plastic bag filled with gift cards and spools of ribbon to a tube with a metal binder clamp or a clothespeg. Tape the tubes together with masking tape and group by occasion.

✴ Jot it down

Perhaps you reorganised your drawers and cupboards a while ago and now can't remember where you put the measuring tape or box of recordable CDs. Don't waste time hunting things down. Instead, record their new locations in a notebook labelled 'Where it is'. Better still, use your computer and save the list on your hard drive so that you won't have to hunt for your notebook.

✴ Curtail junk mail

A combination of three things will slow the seemingly never-ending flow of junk mail that adds to clutter: 1) a pen or computer; 2) paper; and 3) a stamp. Write and ask the Mailing Preference Service to remove your name from the list. You can contact them at Mailing Preference Service (MPS), DMA House, 70 Margaret Street, London, W1W 8SS, telephone 0845 703 4599 or go online at www.mpsonline.org.uk to register with them. It should remove your name from up to 95 per cent of direct mail lists. But don't expect a quick fix; it takes a few months for the MPS to stop the flood of mail. You should expect to continue to receive mailings from companies with whom you have dealt in the past as well as small, local firms. If you want to stop these mailings as well you will have to contact the firms individually.

Streamlined halls and living spaces

✳ Here's your hat (and your keys)

A hat rack in the hall is the handiest place to put jackets, scarves, dog leads, keys and hats. If you're a skilled woodworker with an artistic bent, you could turn the right fallen tree limb into a sculptural rack that works equally well as a functional item and decorative feature.

✳ A hanger rack from scratch

Turn a straightened coat hanger and some clothespegs into a hanger rack on the back of a cupboard door in your hall. Do the same on the back of a kitchen cupboard door to hold extra tea towels.

1. Measure the door and cut a piece of wire that will leave 5–8cm of space at each end.
2. Mount a screw eye in the centre, then another at each end. Run the hanger wire through the screw eyes and bend both ends around the outer eyes with pliers.
3. Now clip some clothespegs to the wire and use them to hold mittens, caps and other small items of clothing.

✳ Wet shoe catcher

Devote a plastic laundry basket not to your wash, but to wet shoes. Place it just inside the hall or utility room door as a catch all for trainers, wellies and anything else muddy. (A large, shallow basket is more attractive, but plastic is much easier to clean.) To speed the drying of wet shoes, use two items that normally belong in the kitchen: a baking sheet and a wire cooler rack. Place the baking sheet

Use a wire cake rack to dry off soggy shoes!

household superstar

27 THINGS TO STORE IN A PAIR OF TIGHTS

Among the multitude of items that you can stash in a stocking leg or foot are these:

1 Apples	**2** Badminton shuttlecocks	**3** Coloured pencils
4 Curling irons	**5** Dog toys	**6** Easter egg moulds
7 Flower seed packets	**8** Golf balls	**9** GPS trackers
10 Hair clips	**11** Instant porridge	**12** Jelly beans
13 Kazoos	**14** Lightbulbs	**15** Mothballs
16 Narcissus bulbs	**17** Onions	**18** Ping-pong balls
19 Q-tips	**20** Ribbons	**21** Takeaway menus
22 Underwear	**23** Vampire teeth	**24** Walkie-talkies
25 X-ray specs	**26** Yo-yos	**27** Zips

near the door, set the rack on top to make a wet shoe catcher that allows for better air circulation – and quicker drying.

✶ Clear the way

If access to your garage is through the laundry room, you don't want to have to dodge clutter each time you pass through, especially if space is tight. One way to keep the coast clear is to mount two plastic milk crates side-by-side on the wall above the washing machine. Use them to hold your detergent and other laundry supplies and they'll not only stay out of the way but will be at hand when you need them.

✶ Impromptu umbrella holder

If you have a tall cylindrical rubbish bin that's seen its day, think twice about retiring it. A coat of paint or a layer of contact paper will turn it into an umbrella stand for your hall. The real article can often be quite expensive, but you'll find that your recycled stand will work just as well. Note: If the bin is metal, coat the interior with clear varnish to prevent rust.

✶ Try a little feng shui

According to the principles of the ancient Chinese art of feng shui (pronounced fung schway), placing furniture and objects so that they align with magnetic north will optimise the energy flow or chi and make the home environment more harmonious. If you want to give feng shui a whirl, rearrange your furniture accordingly to see if it makes a difference in your sense of orderliness and well-being. Lots of people swear by it.

✶ The magazine mountain

It just keeps mounting – and can take up precious space. To reduce clutter without giving up the articles, use a craft knife to slice out the pages you want and then save them in a 'To

Store guestroom blankets or pillows in an antique suitcase!

Read' file. A craft knife will not only give you a cleaner cut but will also do the job three times faster than a pair of scissors.

✳ Mount a CD cabinet in a hallway

Get rid of a picture you don't much like and replace it with this organising marvel. Essentially a bookcase divided into individual squares meant to hold ten or so compact discs each, it's also a perfect way for family members to keep their keys and mobile phones instantly 'grab-able' first thing in the morning.

✳ Take care with collectibles

The best storage compartments for delicate antiques are polyethylene plastic containers, acid-free cardboard boxes and enamelled metal storage cabinets. But if a lack of space demands that store collectibles in a wooden cabinet or drawers, take these measures to keep stamps, dolls, textiles and metals (including coins) from being damaged by the acidic vapours that may be given off by unfinished and painted wood.

- Keep items out of contact with the wood by wrapping them in acid-free tissue paper or pre-washed, unbleached cotton muslin.
- Seal interiors of wooden boxes with at least two coasts of polyurethane varnish.
- Whether you collect comics or stamps, give them the right conditions: no excessive light, heat, moisture or dust.

✳ Double-duty furniture

Your great-great-grandfather's old chest in the attic can do more than just gather dust. Topped with a runner, it makes a coffee table that's stylish and interesting as well as a useful storage unit. Pack it with extra blankets or sheets or use it for board games, playing cards and any sports equipment small enough to fit in.

The sorted bedroom

✱ Between the sheets

If there's no room for the set of new bedlinen you were given for your birthday, where can you keep it? Hide the two halves of the set side by side between the mattress and the box springs at the foot of the bed.

✱ A square metre of extra space

It doesn't sound like much, but it's enough to hold the towels or shoes that won't fit into your bulging linen cupboard or even the stack of weekly magazines you insist you'll get around to reading one day. What is it? A suitcase. If you're going away, just dump the contents in a cardboard box you store in a corner of the bedroom with a sheet thrown over it. Whether you're home or away, your stuff is still all in one place and out of sight. But don't store things in a suitcase that smells of mould or mildew, which will do whatever you've put in it no favours. And be sure to wrap any glass or ceramic objects in bubble wrap to protect them when the suitcase is moved.

✱ Two-level clothes rail

If the clothes rail in your bedroom wardrobe is high up, suspend a second rail below it. Cut a second rail to the desired length and then do the same with two vertical lengths of light but sturdy chain. Attach steel rings to both ends of the chains and hang the lower rail from the original.

✱ Under-the-bed dresser drawer

If you have an old dresser in the attic, you probably use it to store things that you don't need all the time. But you can also bring one of the drawers into your bedroom and keep it out of sight. Just attach casters to the bottom four corners for a rolling chest that you can keep under the bed.

✱ Homemade sock organiser

You may not be able to keep a sock from losing its mate, but you *can* bring order to the pairs you keep in a dresser drawer. To avoid rummaging through a big pile of socks to find what you want, cut shoe boxes in half and then position them so the open ends fit snugly against the front of the drawer. (Or, if you're handy with a saw, cut two or three hardboard dividers to the depth of the drawer.) Sort smart socks, casual socks and sports socks into the appropriate compartments and you'll be able to home in on what you're looking for at once.

✱ Make door stops into hangers

When screwed into the back of a wardrobe door, door stops with rubber tips make excellent hangers for shoes. Group the stops in pairs, setting them a few inches apart. Hang the shoes and clear some valuable floor space.

✱ Swinging from the ceiling

A length of brightly coloured plastic chain will keep the stuffed animals in a child's bedroom off the floor and out of the way. Hang the chain in a corner at the appropriate height, fixing the ends to both walls. To make it possible for your child to hang up the toys, stitch a loop of cotton tape to each one and use S-hooks to suspend the stuffed animals from the chain.

Storing your jewels

Keeping jewellery neat and accessible can be a challenge for even the most organised person. For every perfectly arranged jewellery box, there are at least ten with a jumbled mess of necklaces, bracelets, rings, brooches and mismatched earrings. To sort your precious gems, try these no-extra-cost storage ideas.

Silverware box

If your grandmother's wooden cutlery box is sitting empty in the attic, odds are that the velvet-lined interior is in good enough shape to hold your jewellery. The velvet will slow silver jewellery from tarnishing, while the compartments will keep it in order, particularly necklaces, which can be held in place by the utensil dividers. Polish the exterior wood to a sheen and keep it on your chest of drawers as a showpiece.

Needlepoint canvas

Tiny squares of leftover needlepoint canvas are perfect for storing pierced earrings. Make them more secure by slipping the mesh into a plastic bag before storing them in your jewellery drawer.

Plastic pill bottles

Don't throw these out when they are empty; the tinted brown plastic is just transparent enough to show the jewellery.

Egg cartons and ice cube trays

The compartments of egg cartons and ice cube trays are just the right size for keeping jewellery separated, organised and visible. They are especially good for keeping pairs of earrings together. Line up side by side in a drawer.

Pierced earring holder

Clip a skirt hanger onto the waistband of an old pair of tights to make an instant pierced earring holder. Just push the studs through the nylon and attach the backs. Hang from a wardrobe rail. You'll be able to see your collection all at once, keep pairs of earrings together and have immediate access.

Herb or spice jars

Re-use clean plastic or glass spice jars as jewellery holders. They are small, see-through and perfect for keeping pairs of earrings together and storing rings, brooches and chain-link bracelets. Keep in a jewellery drawer or in a suitcase when travelling.

✳ Storing loose change

Instead of keeping loose change in a dish on your dresser, let resealable plastic kitchen bags be your cash organisers. Sort the change into small separate plastic bags. Then stack the bags in the corner of a drawer until you're ready to cash in the coins for notes.

✳ A pared-down 'wallet'

When leaving for your morning walk or run, you may take a few £5 notes along in case you decide to stop for a sports drink or newspaper on the way home. The easiest and most lightweight alternative to a wallet is a metal binder clip, which will firmly secure the bills (and your ID, if you like) to the waistband of your running shorts or tights.

✳ Jewellery within reach

Draping necklaces and bracelets from the hooks on a coat rack mounted on the wall next to your dressing table is a smart idea. For one thing, your baubles are right at hand. For another, they add a nice decorative touch to an expanse of bare wall.

✳ A jewellery hanger

Use a padded coat hanger to store a variety of different kinds of jewellery. Put necklaces and bracelets round the neck of the hanger, then use the padding to hold pierced earrings and pin on brooches. You could colour code hangers to hold jewellery to go with a range of outfits.

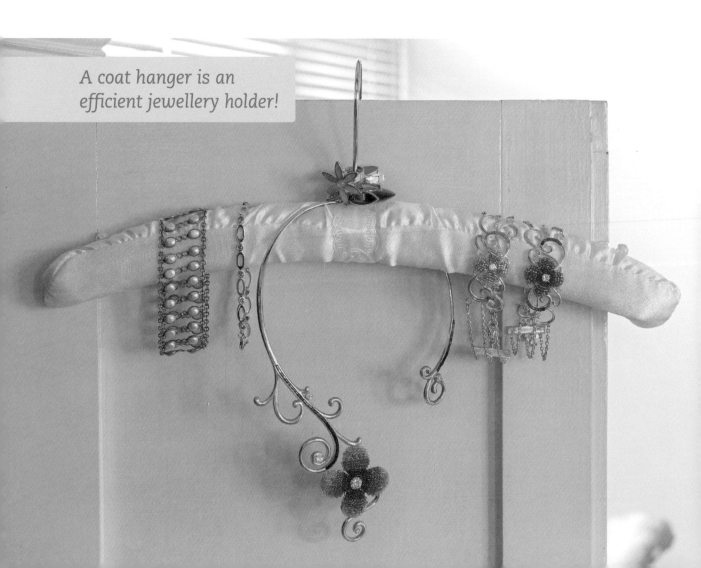

A coat hanger is an efficient jewellery holder!

The organised kitchen

✳ Compartmentalise your cabinets

To keep your kitchen cupboards from becoming a jumble of boxes and bags and cans, gather some flat-bottomed rectangular baskets or small wooden or cardboard boxes – shoe boxes are usually ideal. Line up the containers on the shelves and reserve each for a different kind of food – one for sugar, syrups and other sweet things, one for baking-related items like flour and bicarbonate of soda and so on. If you use boxes, you can paint them to blend with your kitchen's colour scheme. Whether you decorate them or not, label the containers with their contents so you don't confuse sugar with salt.

✳ Organise spices by style of cuisine

Is your spice rack a mess? Can't find the cumin when you need it? Arrange spice bottles in a low-sided, unlidded box (old cigar boxes work brilliantly) by type of cuisine. So whenever you're cooking Italian food (or Chinese, French, Thai, Indian, Middle Eastern or simply the best of British), the appropriate spices will be together in one place. Cumin, tamarind, coriander and chillies? Probably Indian or Thai. Tarragon, parsley, sorrel and bay? French. Label each box according to its nationality and hopefully, whenever you're in the mood for that style of cuisine, your search for the right spices will be kept to a minimum.

✳ A new rack means less racket

If you are fed up with having to take the pots and pans out of a cabinet to get to the baking sheets on the bottom, transfer a metal desk file organiser to the kitchen. This compartmentalised metal rack will allow you to store baking sheets, swiss roll tins and thin

idea

THE LOWDOWN ON LABELLING

Some people get so excited about labelling devices that they go on a binge – labelling every shelf in the larder and linen cupboard and even toying with the idea of labelling pets and children.

But used sensibly, compact label printers can be a real godsend for anyone whose constant refrain is, 'If I could only remember which box I put that in ...' It's amazing how many boxes are left unlabelled when people move house. They then have to sift through a stack of boxes to find the can opener or a vegetable peeler – or go and buy a new one.

And it's not just boxes you should label, moving or not. Marking home videos, CDs, file folders and any other objects that don't immediately reveal their contents will make your life much easier and also remind other family members where to put things.

Although you can use your computer to print out sheets with labels and tape them on to boxes, it's faster to key in the letters on a specialised labeller and then print out the self-sticking tag. You can use different colours and styles of print for different rooms and to code different kinds of objects.

wooden or acrylic cutting boards vertically. As a result, you will be able to pluck flat items out of a crowded cupboard with ease.

Protect knives with a paper towel tube!

✱ Newspaper buffers for nonstick cookware

When you nest nonstick saucepans one inside one another, you're almost sure to scratch the delicate coating. To keep nonstick cookware scratch-free, simply tuck a newspaper sheet into each pot and nest them without worrying.

✱ Rack 'em up

Rummaging through a cluttered cupboard full of pots and pans in order to find a matching lid can be an exercise in extreme frustration. A solution to the problem is in your toolbox. Just mount an ordinary towel rack or two on the back of the cupboard door and slide in the lids between rack and door. The knobs on the lids will stop them from falling through the rack.

✱ Keep your storage lids on

If you've ever found the perfect storage container for a batch of tomato sauce or soup, but the container lid has made its way somewhere else entirely, you can stop it from happening again. Keep all the lids together – by storing them inside a large storage bin.

✱ Storing fine china safely

When stacking fine china in the cupboard, keep dinner plates scratch free by alternating them with paper plates. For salad plates and saucers, use coffee filters. China teacups are best stored right-side up. If the cupboard won't take all the cups, create an extra tier of shelf space by setting a coated wire rack inside. But why not hang the cups from hooks attached to the bottom of the shelf above? Hooks are fine for everyday china, but hanging antique teacups means that they will be bearing their own weight – a bad idea if you want to give these heirlooms the tender loving care they deserve.

✱ Let it slide

In some wooden kitchen cupboards, drawers sit on wooden slides on the bottom rather than lubricated metal slides at the sides. Dirt can accumulate on the slides and opening and closing drawers may be difficult. Clean the wooden slides with soap and water. Then, when the slides are dry, rub candle wax on all wood-to-wood contact points. Friction-worn wooden slides can also be easily fixed with the insertion of one or two smooth-headed upholstery tacks.

✱ Multi-purpose furniture

If you have an old china cabinet lurking in the attic, put it to use in the kitchen. Turn it into storage for spices, measuring cups and baking equipment or anything you don't use all the time that clutters your cupboards.

✱ Hats off to plates

Whether you keep inheriting piles of plates from relatives or you can't resist them at car-boot sales and antique fairs, don't let them overrun your cupboards. Use old hatboxes, to store plates on top of each other, separated by pieces of soft cardboard or paper plates. Label and store in the attic or a garage shelf.

✱ Sheathe your kitchen knives

The sharp knives you use for cooking can be dangerous, so never keep them loose in a drawer. If you don't have worktop space for a knife holder, create protective sheaths for knives from empty paper towel tubes. Just flatten a tube, fold over one end and staple or tape it closed, then slide a knife in the other end. For smaller knives, use toilet paper tubes.

what's the story?

THE ARRIVAL OF PLASTIC

When did man-made plastic first appear? It made its debut at the 1862 Great International Exhibition in London, the work of British chemist Alexander Parkes, who named his cellulose-derived creation Parkesine – the first organic material able to retain its shape after being heated and moulded. Six years later, an enterprising printer from Albany, New York, named John Wesley Hyatt discovered that the solvent action of camphor on cellulose nitrate under heat and pressure created a clear and durable material – celluloid, which transformed photography and, in the early 20th century, movie film.

The first mass-marketed plastic, Bakelite, was introduced in 1907. The phenol-formaldehyde resin – perfected in Yonkers, New York, by Belgian-born Leo Hendrik Baekeland – was used to manufacture everything from telephone handsets to kitchenware to engine parts. Teflon made its first appearance in 1937 and nylon one year later. The arrival of polyester in 1942 would transform the manufacture of clothing, as anyone who donned a leisure suit or pink polyester trousersuit in the 1970s could attest.

Today's liquid crystal polymers and other new plastics in no way resemble Mr Parkes's rudimentary invention. Little could he have dreamed that a century and a half later, flying machines would be as ubiquitous as horse-drawn carriages and that one of those machine's bodies would be plastic: the Boeing 787 Dreamliner, made from the same reinforced plastic used for golf club shafts.

✳ Keep small appliances in clear plastic containers

If your kitchen worktops are in such a mess that you can't find the coffee grinder behind the electric pepper mill, large, clear plastic storage containers are a great way to keep small tools that are used infrequently out of the way, but still in sight.

✳ Repackage dried food to save space

If kitchen cupboard space is cramped, repackage the dried food products that you buy. Gain precious room by transferring most of your dry food into see-through plastic containers (and then label and date them). Flat rectangular containers work best, as they're stackable and ideal for storing tea bags, dried beans, rice, pasta and cereal.

✳ Ready-made picnic carriers

A six-pack cardboard container (the kind used for cans or bottles of beer) is ideal for carrying picnic supplies from the kitchen to the car or a picnic site. Bind plastic utensils with a rubber band and put them in one compartment, then fill the other compartments with picnic paraphernalia such as rolled up napkins, salt and pepper shakers, squeeze bottles of ketchup or mustard or mayonnaise and an insect repellant.

✳ Smart idea for storing leftovers

If you have a label-making machine, this is an idea that may not have occurred to you. Store all of your leftovers on the same rack and label the shelf so no one forgets where to put them. If you don't have a machine, cut a piece of paper to size, write 'Leftovers' in indelible ink and tape the label onto the rim of the rack with clear tape. Designating a leftovers shelf and labelling it will make it much less likely that the remains of the steamed broccoli you enjoyed in April won't be covered in mould in June.

✳ A movable sweet bin

When organising kitchen cupboards with the aid of baskets or boxes, keep a special one for sweets. Either place the treats bin on a low shelf that the children can reach or on a high shelf where it's out of reach.

✳ Three-ring recipes

A box will keep your recipe cards all in one place, but a three-ring binder will go one better. Slip the cards into the pocketed plastic photo holders made for ring binders. Arrange recipes by type and then tape a coloured plastic file tab onto the first page of each category: soups, chicken dishes and so on. Using a binder will make it easier to browse through your cards and choose the perfect recipe for the occasion.

tip DECANT BIG BAGS OF FLOUR

If large bags of flour, sugar, cereal or pasta are on sale, and you use enough regularly to justify the purchase, empty the bags into individual, supersize clear plastic **storage containers,** label them and stack them on an out-of-the-way shelf in a pantry or utility area until needed instead of taking up valuable space in the kitchen.

The clutter-free bathroom

✳ Downsize your essentials

If there are only three people in your household, do you really need 18 bath towels, 12 hand towels and 10 facecloths? And how many bottles and tubes of cosmetics and ointments and painkillers crowd the shelves of medicine cabinets and bathroom unit drawers? The first task for the clutter fighter is to get rid of what you don't need; the second is to look for ways to save space – and here are ways to do both.

● To free up shelf space, attach three or four towel rails on the back of the door and hang a week's supply of towels from the rails.

● Make up two bathroom toolkits and store one in a clear zipped plastic bag for packing. Include tweezers, nail clippers, scissors, cotton buds and cotton wool balls.

✳ Search out shelf space

Use space above a window or door to put up brackets and a simple shelf to hold towels and other bathroom supplies. A 60cm expanse of wall is enough for two or three-tiered shelving, good for holding supplies of any kind. Get more mileage out of it by attaching a board to the bottom with hooks for hanging wet towels.

✳ Racks to the rescue

If you wish you had more towel racks in your bathroom, forgo time-consuming installation and simply stand a coat rack in the corner – ideal for hanging towels and bathrobes.

When it comes to storing towels, a wine rack meant for worktops fits the bill. You should put the rack, which will accommodate from five to

idea
FROM LUNCH BOX TO FIRST-AID KIT

Although your son outgrew his superhero lunch box a long time ago and it's been consigned to the attic, there's still life in the colourful carrying case. It's just the right size to hold bandages, gauze, scissors and tape on one side and an antiseptic spray, cream or ointment – plus the cottonwool balls used to apply it – on the other.

Keep the kit in a bathroom cabinet and you'll be able to grab everything at once whenever you have to go into the garden to treat your family's cuts and scrapes.

ten rolled-up towels, depending on the design – wherever it seems most practical – the floor, perhaps or on top of a cabinet. Besides saving space, the rack will bring an attractive architectural feature to the bathroom.

✳ Hang tiered baskets

The tiered wire baskets made for decluttering the kitchen will come in handy in the bathroom as well – and the less room you have, the more you need to make use of the bathroom's 'air space'. Hang a set of tiered baskets from the ceiling and then place rolled hand towels in the largest basket and toiletries and other small items in the smaller ones.

An unused lunch box makes a perfect first-aid kit!

✱ Toiletries on the move

Here's a clever space-saving idea for large families with limited bathroom space. Turn small wicker baskets into toiletry holders and keep one in each family member's bedroom. Everyone can then carry his or her toiletries to the bathroom as needed.

Paint each basket a different colour and fill it with customised supplies – for Dad, his preferred toothpaste, shaving cream and razor and other grooming supplies; for Mum, cosmetics, hair-care products and similar. Whatever you load into the baskets will help to keep bathroom worktops clutter-free.

✱ Move medicines out

Removing your prescription and over-the-counter medicines from a bathroom cabinet to the kitchen or bedroom will do more than save space in one of the home's smallest rooms. The warmth and humidity in bathrooms can degrade the stability and potency of some drugs.

Instead, put them in a lidded plastic container or shoebox and store them in a cool, dry place. Make sure that the medicines are stored well out of the reach of children.

✱ Mount a magnet

A magnetic knife holder mounted on the bathroom wall makes an ideal holder for small metal necessities like nail clippers, tweezers and toenail scissors. You won't have to search around for small items in a messy drawer.

✱ A hair accessories box

Present a little girl with a compact box with a clasp and lots of compartments (a flat fishing tackle box is ideal) and ask her to sort her hair accessories into the compartments by type. If she is very young, ask her to bring it to you whenever she likes. As she watches you taking items from the box and returning them to their proper places, she will learn to keep her hair accessories and other belongings in order.

Whip your workshop and garage into shape

✳ The magic of magnets

Given a magnet's powerful hold over metal, it's no wonder that so many DIY fans feel such a strong attraction to magnets. They come in handy for a multitude of tasks around the workshop – everything from organising a workbench to cleaning up spills. Here are a half-dozen fantastic ways that you can put them to work for you.

- Fix a large round magnet to the wall next to your workspace (or suspend it from the ceiling, if necessary) to keep small metal parts and tools from getting lost in the middle of repair work.
- Before using steel wool, wrap a small bar magnet inside the pad to catch any loose steel strands or particles and keep them from messing up your work area.

idea

TIDY WAYS TO STORE TIMBER

Keeping loose timber around your workshop can be dangerous for you and damaging to the wood. But an old wooden ladder can straighten things out. Secure the ladder rail to a wall with wooden brackets and then use the spaces between the rungs to sort different lengths of timber. You could also stand several pieces of timber in an old golf bag or keep them bound together inside a trouser leg cut from an old pair of jeans.

Make the most of magnets in your workshop!

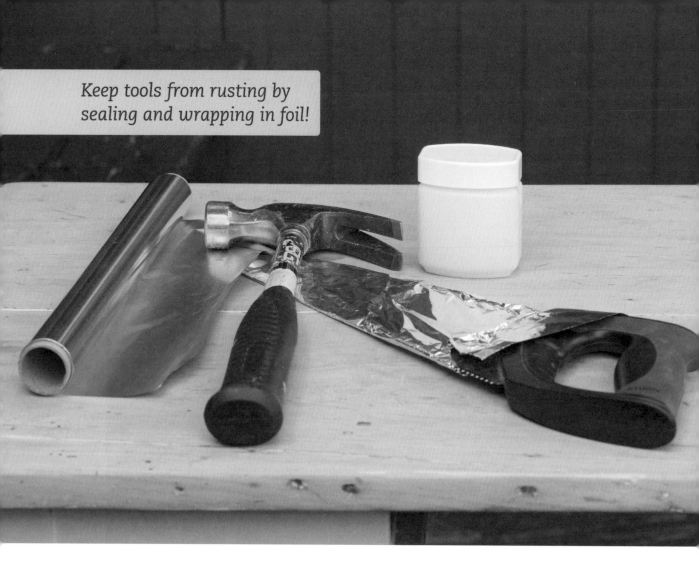

Keep tools from rusting by sealing and wrapping in foil!

- Place small round magnets inside jars or boxes of screws and brads to prevent or contain spillage if they are accidentally knocked over.
- Put a bar magnet inside a plastic sandwich bag to pick up spilled nails, nuts or washers – or even to clean up metal filings. The objects will stick to the outside of the bag, which you can then turn inside out to contain them.
- Magnetise the head of a screwdriver by rubbing it several times with a small horseshoe magnet. You won't lose nearly so many screws in future.

- Hot-glue several magnetic strips inside your toolbox or workbench drawer to keep most-used flat tools at the ready.

✳ Cords for clamps

Don't throw away old bungee cords; when wrapped around furniture, appliances and other household items, they make excellent band clamps when you are tackling a range of repairs. Although the cords aren't adjustable, they can be combined to create almost any length desired or, in the case of long cords, easily shortened by multiple wrappings.

✳ Keep supplies in the gutter

Who says gutters have to be outside? Not the clever DIY-er. Mount a couple of pieces of plastic guttering around your work area for an inexpensive yet sturdy way to store lengths of moulding, timber, pipes and dowels. Simply screw the mounting brackets into the wall studs and snap in the gutters. You could also use the bare gutter brackets to hold wire coils, extension cords and hoses.

✳ Make the cut

Here's a sharp idea: remove the serrated cutting strip from a box of aluminium foil or plastic wrap, cut it in half with a metal cutter or shears and tack or nail one of the sections to the least-used side of your workbench – well away from where you put your hands. Make sure the teeth are positioned slightly above the top of the surface and you should never have to search again for a knife or scissors to cut a piece of tape, rope or sandpaper.

✳ A place for parts

Make your own parts bins out of recycled plastic milk cartons. Leave the caps on the cartons (seal them with a bit of glue, if needed), and cut off about a third of the side panel with a utility knife or scissors. Fill the cartons with nails, screws, nuts and other small items, then place them on a small bookshelf or cabinet. You can also stand the cartons upright, of course and the handles make for easy transport.

✳ Prevent rust on tools

If your garage tends to be damp and you store tools there, prevent rusting by lightly coating them with petroleum jelly or car wax. If you are storing tools that you don't often use, spray them with a silicone lubricant and wrap them in aluminium foil. The next time you use the tools, just wipe them with a soft cloth.

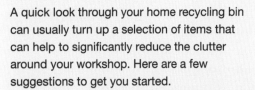

THE REWARDS OF REPURPOSING

A quick look through your home recycling bin can usually turn up a selection of items that can help to significantly reduce the clutter around your workshop. Here are a few suggestions to get you started.

- Use empty prescription pill bottles, film canisters, glass jars, used cans and the see-through plastic tops from CD spindles to hold nails, screws and other fasteners.

- Turn an old ice cube tray or a muffin tin into an organiser for washers, tacks, nuts and bolts.

- Number the compartments in an egg carton and use each cup to hold disassembled parts in the order that they're removed.

- Use cardboard tubes from paper towels, gift-wrapping paper and toilet paper rolls to neatly hold extension cords, ropes and pieces of dowelling.

- Mount a large block of recycled polystyrene near your workbench to use as a 'pincushion' for drill bits, screwdrivers, pens, punches, wrenches and other tools.

- Glue a piece of cardboard onto the bottom of a building brick (the type with holes in it) and use the brick to hold files, drill bits, brushes and craft knives.

The orderly home office

✴ The No. 1 home office storage space

Forget about fancy desk dividers or expensive built-in shelves; the most important home office storage space under your roof is the hard drive of your computer. Your address book, diary, desk calendar and business card holder (not to mention pictures of your children) that seem to move around all over your desk will be immediately available in the most uncluttered way possible, if you spend time digitising them.

✴ Turn a filing cabinet into conference table base

Perhaps not the usual long table but a round conference table that can seat two or three people and provide useful extra workspace. The space between the tabletop and the floor won't go to waste if you use a metal filing cabinet or an old bedside chest as a support. Use 9mm plywood for the top and bolt it to the top of the cabinet. Then cover with a tablecloth that almost reaches the floor. Store rarely used files in the cabinets below and you should only have to crawl under the table on rare occasions.

✴ A secret filing cabinet

There's no intrigue here – just a filing cabinet that looks like anything but what it is. What is it? A straw rectangular basket with a lid, something more often found in a living area than a home office. A basket with dimensions of roughly 45 x 45 x 22cm should accommodate around 30 files of average size or up to a dozen well-stuffed file folders. Placed under or beside your worktable, the basket is decorative as well as functional.

✴ Invest in a small safe

Store deeds, birth certificates, insurance information and passports in a fireproof safe that can be stowed on the top shelf of a wardrobe. It may be out of sight, but it won't be out of mind.

✴ Door-top bookshelf

When you run out of space for books, put a shelf in the space above the door and below the ceiling. If you have a piece of timber in the garage or storeroom, you can make a shelf whose only cost is the support brackets purchased at a DIY store. A coat of paint on a sawn-to-size board will keep it from looking like a makeshift shelf in a college dormitory.

✴ Keep paper-shredder blades sharp

Cutting aluminium foil will sharpen your scissors with ease and the shiny stuff will also do the same for the blades in your paper shredder. Lay a sheet of A4 paper on two sheets of heavy-duty aluminium foil as a cutting guide. Feed the sheets of foil through the shredder one at a time and the blades will get sharpened with minimal fuss.

✴ A good-looking bulletin board

A jungle of Post-it notes and envelopes and papers stuck to a bulletin board isn't the prettiest sight to behold. So make your easy-to-reach 'filing system' more attractive by covering the board with felt and attaching ribbons to hold your stuff. Start by choosing felt in the colour of your choice. Then cut it 10cm larger than the board on all four sides, pull it taut over the board and staple the extra to the back. Use upholstery tacks to secure ribbons to the board, pulling them as taut as possible so that paper

Tips for packing and posting

Some of the things you're trying to keep in order are sent to you and others are things you want to send – say a package to your son or daughter on a gap year in Africa. Here are a few tips for making things run smoothly when you prepare a letter or parcel for posting.

Rustle up free packing material

Wadded-up newspaper is probably the first thing you reach for when packing something in a box, but you can also use several other items you most likely have on hand – like these:

• Plastic grocery bags
• Paper grocery bags
• Dry cleaning bags
• Paper strips from a shredder
• T-shirts bound for the dustbin

Store such stuff in paper bags in the or garage so they won't take up unnecessary space in your cupboards.

Pop some popcorn

Unbuttered air-popped popcorn makes excellent packing material because it's soft and light as a feather. It's also green – because it is completely biodegradable.

Towel fragile items

If you've collected together a whole lot of items to send to a child at college or a relative abroad, use bath and tea towels to protect any breakable objects. Wrapped several times around fragile items, towels provide protection and make a nice gift.

No-stick hands

Polystyrene packing peanuts cling to your hands when you unpack a mail-order package. To keep the peanuts from sticking, simply rub your hands with a fabric softener sheet.

slipped behind the ribbons won't fall through. You could crisscross the ribbons to create a diamond pattern over the whole board or position them to look like latticework – as long as it works, the design is up to you.

✱ A real vertical file
A vertical file is US business slang for a wastepaper basket. But there is another kind of vertical file that you can borrow from your child's toy box which will keep post, tickets and papers of similar size from cluttering up your workspace. What is it? A Slinky. Set it on your worktable and slide stray papers in between the wires.

✱ A business card album
A small photo album is ideal for keeping business cards in order. Simply slip a card or two in the protective plastic sleeves made for ring binders. With a ring binder to leaf through, your days of shuffling through a stack of cards for the one you need are over.

✱ An office in a cupboard
If you're short of space but desperately need a home office, turn a spare understairs cupboard into your workspace at home. Remove the doors, attach a thick plank of plywood from one inside wall to the other; use the upper shelves to store less frequently used items such as a dictionary, extra stationery and your computer. Slip a low filing cabinet under the 'desk', add a lamp and you'll have a useful space to work in.

✱ Keep documents in a scrapbook
Scrapbooks equipped with plastic sleeves or pockets are ideal for keeping business contracts and other documents in order.

tip MISPLACED YOUR PENCIL SHARPENER?
At a pinch, you can sharpen a pencil with a **vegetable peeler.** This kitchen staple is better than a penknife when you can't find your usual sharpener.

Dealing with decorations

✱ Tangle-free twinklers

What are the parties and celebrations without strings of lights, whether they illuminate trees, mantels or garden displays? And what are fresh-out-of-storage strings of lights if not tangled? All you need to keep them orderly is an empty coffee or cocoa can and its lid.

First, slice the plastic lid of the can with a sharp knife and insert one end of the light cord. Then wrap the cord of lights around the can, taping the end to the can to keep everything in place. Before putting on the lid, fill the can with extra bulbs and an extension cord.

✱ Give fragile items top billing

Christmas tree ornaments range from wooden toy drummers to delicate winged doves made of crystal – the latter and their ilk needing special care. If you pack fragile items with other ornaments, first wrap them in tissue and put them in a self-sealing plastic bag. When putting them in the storage box, be sure to place them on top of the other ornaments so they won't be damaged as you search in the box next year.

✱ Storing big stuff

If you're one of those people who likes to make a big display on the lawn or roof at Christmas, you probably have a problem with storage the rest of the year. The components of your tableau are probably made of moulded plastic that can't be squashed flat – and unless you have room to spare, they create a storage problem bigger than Santa's toy bag. Your first step toward clever storage is to save zipped garment bags, which should be large enough to hold one or two or the pieces – or more, depending on their size. Then hang the bags from rafters in the attic or a shed. You could also consider hanging a hammock between two rafters and putting the bagged pieces into it.

✱ Make bows easy to spot

Do you have a spare glass canister that you don't really have a use for?

If it's tall and has a lid, store self-sticking bows in the canister so that, come gift-wrapping time, you can see at a glance what your choices are.

✳ How to store candles

If stored in a hot place, candles tend to warp and curve – and a curving candle is good only for the person who enjoys candle making and melts down candles. Prevent the problem by choosing a storage spot that stays below 20°C all year, even if that means the cellar or a closet. Wrap individual candles in tissue paper and lay them flat in a plastic container or a cardboard box – or, in the spirit of repurposing, paper-towel tubes or cylindrical potato crisp cans.

✳ New life for wrapping paper

Don't throw away wrapping paper and tissue that piles up as your family opens gifts. Instead, use it to keep the holiday ornaments you'll soon be storing from getting scratched or chipped or donate it to a local vet. Choose one or all of these three options:

- Wrap each ornament in leftover paper when placing in the storage box. If desired, store ornaments by type and Christmas tree balls by colour. However you choose to store, label each box with the contents.
- Feed the wrapping paper into a shredder. Then use the paper ribbons as packing material to keep your ornaments well protected.

- Donate shredded wrapping paper to a veterinary clinic. Many vets use shredded paper as bedding for the animals in their care. Just call first to make sure the paper is wanted and needed.

✳ Holiday spirit in a black plastic bag

Look at old clothing, furniture, books, toys and odds and ends of any sort not as 'just something to get rid of' but as items that would be welcomed by the less fortunate. Organisations or charitable groups will accept virtually anything that is still in good condition – check that they can accept electrical goods – many can't. Clean clothing in good condition can be donated to a number of different charities.

A cardboard box filled with gently worn shoes or a black plastic bin bag filled with towels and sheets that no longer match your colour scheme becomes a vessel of hope, not of refuse bound for the dump. Deliver your goods to the charity in person or place them in one of the genuine charity bags that are regularly posted through the door. You'll create more space and someone in need will benefit from a 'new' shirt, pair of shoes, sofa or even the key connection to the world at large, a computer.

tip GREETINGS CARD ART

If you enjoy doing craft projects with your children or on your own, look at the **Christmas or birthday cards** you receive as a wealth of raw material. Snipping images from the cards and using them to create collages or abstract compositions gives you artworks suitable for framing. And it consolidates the good wishes of friends and family into a memento that's attractive and meaningful.

Easy ways to store a garland

The beautiful garlands you draped along the staircase drew a host of compliments from friends and family last Christmas, but this year you're not sure how they were put together. How do you eliminate the guesswork when you want to recreate a previous success? Take these three simple steps before putting the garlands away for storage.

1
Tag the lengths with their location, numbering them in order from the top railing to the newel post at the bottom.

2
Use twist-ties to mark the spots where the lengths were tied to the banister to make swags.

3
Label the storage box clearly ('Staircase Garland') so it won't be confused with any other garlands you might have used.

Everyday organisers

✻ Elevated cellar storage

Storing furniture and other large items in a basement or cellar can be risky because of the potentially damp conditions. If you have no choice but to keep precious old inherited furniture there for a while, safeguard it or any other vulnerable item from moisture by placing it on a wooden pallet and covering it with a large tarpaulin.

If you're wondering where to find a free pallet, check with a local DIY store or timber merchant. An alternative platform is a thick slab of plywood that is supported by bricks or breeze blocks.

✻ Attic air-freshener

Your attic probably contains everything from hanging bags of clothes to old hats and gloves and scarves. But how can you stop it from smelling like a dusty old store room? Banish mustiness with the lava rocks used for barbecues. Just scoop rocks into four or five mesh bags and hang the bags from the attic's beams. Every few months, refresh the rocks by setting them outside in the sun for 4–6 hours. Lava rocks left out in the sun should absorb musty odours for years on end.

✻ The wandering shower caddy

You don't need to confine that most useful of small storage systems, the shower caddy to the bathroom. You can use it anywhere inside the house to stock items of all sorts – utility and laundry room supplies, gardening products and small tools and so on. Just hang the caddy from a doorknob or from a sturdy hook or nail on the wall of the garage, basement, workshop or garden shed.

✻ Looking after anything framed

You should not only store framed photographs and artworks properly to extend their life but also label them as clearly as possible – the latter accomplished by taping a photograph of the framed item to its wrapper (use a Polaroid or the printout of a digital shot). Wrapping paintings, framed prints, lithographs and photographs takes some time, but pays off in the end. Wrap each piece in acid-free tissue paper and sandwich it between two layers of 0.5cm foam board cut a little larger than the frame. Tape the corners and middle of the board, then wrap the package in brown paper. After taping the paper at every seam, attach the photograph of the piece within.

Extra hint 1: Never wrap artwork of any kind in plastic, which can trap moisture and cause warping or the growth of mould.

Extra hint 2: Wear cotton gloves when handling an oil painting. Touching the surface (back or front) will leave oils and salts from your hands – substances that can eventually crack or otherwise damage dried oil paint.

✻ Two ways to hang string

Say that you need to keep three balls of string fairly handy – jute twine for tying together newspapers and flattened cardboard for recycling; nylon garden twine for tying plants to stakes; and coloured string for gift-wrapping. How would you go about saving yourself from fishing around for them in a drawer or tool box? Try these two tricks:

● Install three hooks on a wall or on the back of a door, spacing them 13-18cm apart. Now slide a cord or ribbon (or a length of string from the ball itself, for that matter) through each spool and knot it. Hang a ball of string from each hook and your string is easily accessible.

- Use funnels instead of hooks. Choose funnels large enough to hold a ball of string and nail the top rim of each to the wall. Put a ball of string in each funnel and run the ends out of the spouts – and you have made a string dispenser that works like a charm.

✽ Bank on this one

Bank statements seem to accumulate faster than you can say 'special interest rate', especially when you're so busy you can't find the time to check them. Try this quick organisational fix. Each time a statement arrives in the post, scan it and save it as a file in your computer. The result? All the information you need and no paper to take up space or waste time searching through.

✽ Free labels for your stuff

Some charities that send out promotional mailings include a small batch of personalised address labels in the packet. If they have your name and address right, you can use the unsolicited gift to label personal items as well as envelopes. Paste the labels inside books, on the underside of staplers and other small pieces of office equipment and on the back of your mobile phone. Using a bit of tape, you could even fix one of the labels to your umbrella or the inner cuffs of mittens or gloves.

what's the story?

THE SCIENTIFIC TAKE ON TANGLING

When you put away last year's Christmas tree lights, you probably looped the strings carefully so that they wouldn't get tangled. And when you got them out again they were a mess of knots. Why does it happen?

Apparently it's physics, not you, that is to blame. In October 2007, experiments conducted at the University of California, San Diego, showed that strings basically tie themselves when agitated. Professor Douglas Smith and his research assistant Dorian Raymer wrote in the Proceedings of the National Academy of Sciences that they had developed a mathematical formula that explained why strings and cords knot so easily. Their method involved shaking strings placed in boxes and they discovered that roughly half of the shaken strings came out of the box knotted.

Professor Keith Devlin of Stanford University explained why it happened: '[Smith and Raymer's] programme gave them tremendous insight into how Christmas tree lights or iPod earphone cords ... get tangled up. What we know now is that roughly half of the times a knot forms, it begins to form within the first two or three seconds of shaking. So even if you've only taken a Christmas tree box up the stairs into the attic, the chances are high that you're going to tangle it.'

So the tangling of strings of lights isn't always caused by our haphazard storage habits but rather by forces way beyond your control.

Turn your living space into a photo gallery with a clothes line!

5 Making your space into a perfect home

If you are looking at a major revamp of your home or simply want to freshen it up, our list of helpful household items and intuitive but surprising tips includes almost everything in the house. You'll feel as if you could easily teach a top interior designer a thing or two.

This chapter is about using what you already have to make the place you call home look, feel and function to meet your needs, your style and your budget. You will find loads of practical ways that you can create fresh looks by reusing, refurbishing and repurposing.

Have you ever thought of whitewashing or glazing wallpaper to give it a brighter feel or using a beaten-up old ladder as a design feature? Have you ever thrown away a piece of fabric or an old glass bottle simply because you're not sure what to do with it? You're about to discover how easy it is to update all sorts of furnishings and accessories by using what you have on hand. So get inspired, get to work and get ready to delight in being your own interior decorator.

Making changes around the house

✴ Looking for free design inspiration

It's easy – strip the room back to basics. This two-step trick will turn you into an interior decorator without costing a penny.

1. 'Edit' a room by putting everything that *isn't* furniture out of sight. Remove personal items, linens (leave the curtains if it's a pain to take them down), cushions, rugs, lamps, artwork, electronics, books and magazines.

2. Look at what's left. By getting down to the bones of a room, you will gain a better perspective on what you have and whether it works for you.

You will probably decide to reposition or eliminate some furniture. Perhaps a fresh coat of paint or adapting your existing window treatments is all you need. Or it may have been all the 'stuff' that was making an attractive room look dowdy or overcrowded. With the room stripped down to basics, you can envisage the space and its contents anew, see fresh possibilities and improve the room – and at no cost whatsoever.

✴ A laundry basket as a cushion holder

What can you do when all your lovely cushions get in the way? Convert an old wicker laundry basket into a cushion holder. If you have a plastic laundry basket, cover it with a sheet by setting the basket on it and folding the sides and corners into the basket itself (as if you were wrapping a gift). Fill with cushions and you'll have a chic container for almost no cost.

✴ New furniture from spare chairs

Nobody ever seems to have enough small tables, but many of us have too many chairs. If so, think about converting those extra chairs into something more useful. In most cases, straight-backed armless chairs with hard, flat seats are the easiest to work with.

● Paint two chairs of different designs in the same colour to make an attractive pair of bedside 'tables'.

● Refinish or paint a straight-backed chair that has arms and put it in the hall as a catch all for hats, bags and umbrellas.

tip PUT TOGETHER A NO-FRILLS DESIGN KIT

Use a design-planning method that's easy, cheap, fun and entirely free of any sales pressure – a do-it-yourself design kit put together from a **ruler,** a **pencil,** a few sheets of graph paper and a tape measure.

An old woven basket will make a great place to store cushions!

● Make a coffee table substitute with two or three wooden chairs; they don't need to match as long as the seats are approximately the same height. Saw off the back of each one at seat level and sand well; you may also need to trim off any corner protuberances that rise a bit above seat level. To guard against stains, paint the chairs with water-resistant gloss. When the paint dries, line up the little tables as a unique and practical coffee table.

✱ Don't destroy, redeploy
When you are renovating a kitchen, resist the urge to throw away or break up the old units before considering how you might reuse them in another part of the house. You could ...
● Hang wall cabinets in a workroom, removing the doors for open shelving.

● Put two single or one double wall cabinet (standard depth approximately 30cm) in a child's room to hold toys and clothes or use as a hall cupboard for storing seasonal items.
● Add casters to a base cabinet to make a rolling laundry bin.
● Make a study desk or work table with a couple of base cabinets topped with a plain, smooth-surfaced old door.
● Stack two single or double top cabinets to make a useful storage unit for sewing and craft supplies.

✱ Create a strong focal point in any room
The focal point of a room is the first visual element to which the eye is immediately drawn. Rooms without an obvious focal point can look bland, disorganised or incomplete, regardless of

the style or quality of the furnishings. To add flair to an unfocused room, a quick and inexpensive fix is to use items you already have. Decide on the logical focus of attention and then go through your storage cupboards and loft for things you may have tucked away or forgotten.

- Bright throw cushions or a quilt will add impact to a dull bed.
- Frame a beautiful silk scarf or lace shawl that you haven't worn in years and hang it on the wall behind the bed.
- If your fireplace and mantelpiece don't grab the eye, use leftover paint to set them off with a floor-to-ceiling background panel of a different colour. Hang a large mirror or a display of eye-catching plates above the mantelpiece.
- Get rid of clutter to draw the eye to a focal point: remember that less is more, so rotate collectibles instead of displaying all of your treasures all the time.

✳ Shelving from odds and ends

Instead of spending lots of money on shelving, look around you. Perhaps you have some wooden trays you never use? A shallow drawer from an old dresser or desk? Or the sturdy in-out boxes someone at work was about to throw away? Maybe the decorated drawer fronts from a baby's old chest would make fun shelves for a growing youngster. The size and weight of a makeshift shelf will determine the kind of brackets and hardware you need when attaching it to a wall, so take your 'shelf' to a good hardware or DIY store and ask for advice. If you plan to load heavy items like books onto the shelf, make sure it's on a load-bearing wall.

idea
A TINY TOUCH OF ORIGINALITY

Can you remember what fridges used to look like? Today they're likely to be covered with more magnets than a millipede has legs. While the fridge makes a great magnetic bulletin board filled with Post-it notes, photos, takeaway menus and other reminders, it will benefit greatly from the occasional decluttering. And why not make your own unique fridge magnets? You can simply hot glue small magnets, sold at craft stores, to tiny souvenirs and found objects like small seashells; clip-on earrings (with the clips removed); lapel pins from museums or other visits that you've enjoyed; smooth, flat rocks; or unusual buttons.

✳ New ways with louvres

Don't get rid of old louvred doors until you've considered their possibilities. Hinge three or more together so they will fold accordion-style, to create practical screens for indoors and out. Long narrow doors make an attractive screen to separate sleeping and dressing areas in a bedroom or to shade a sunny area on a porch or patio. Secure a panel of hinged louvres to the wall behind a plain bed for an unusual headboard. If you have a corner space calling out for something to fill it, stand up a tall louvred screen to soften the angle.

Colour your world

✱ Save leftover paint

Whenever you get the urge to redecorate, you'll be very glad that you didn't throw away all your half-empty paint cans. Keep them so you can create small 'patch' tests when you are redecorating. Better still, use them for:

- Patching nicks and scratches in existing painted walls
- As a primer for new paint
- Redoing or touching up old furniture and accessories
- Painting a cupboard or pantry
- Painting the inside of a small cupboard
- Tinting other paints to create customised colour washes
- Creating multicolour faux finishes
- For decorative stencilling
- Painting trim and beading on everything from furniture to picture frames

Transfer small amounts of leftover paint to wide-mouthed plastic storage containers, such as clean mayonnaise or marmalade jars. Label by colour, type of paint and manufacturer. Air and moisture are the enemies of stored paint, so be sure that the tops and lids seal tightly. Oil-based paints will form their own protective skins in the containers. For emulsion (water-based) paint, lay a layer of cling film on top of the paint before putting the lid on. And always store leftover paint in a cool, dry place, away from direct sunlight.

✱ Create depth with colour

One of the simplest ways to add depth to a room is to paint or wallpaper the inside backs of built-in bookcases and display shelving – a great way to use leftover decorating materials. If you paint, keep in mind that darker colours appear to recede, fooling the eye into seeing a deeper recess – and a larger room. A solid or discreetly patterned wallpaper will achieve the same effect.

what's the story?

THE NOVELIST WHO 'INVENTED' INTERIOR DESIGN

Much of modern interior design owes its origins to a great American novelist. Edith Wharton (1862–1937) was born Edith Newbold Jones to a socially prominent New York family. She went on to skewer her own class in *The House of Mirth,* her Pulitzer Prize-winning *The Age of Innocence* and other widely read novels and story collections. But it was her first book, *The Decoration of Houses* (1897) that punctured the pretensions of upper-class Victorian decorating and set out many principles that still guide interior design today.

In collaboration with architect Ogden Codman Jr., the well-travelled Mrs. Wharton brought her knowledge of French and Italian decorating styles into the mix, comparing European lightness, elegance and comfort to the 'exquisite discomfort' of the dreary, cold, overstuffed drawing rooms of New York's upper crust. Her book is credited with elevating interior decoration from a lady's hobby to profession. Although not the bestseller she hoped for, *The Decoration of Houses* did earn her first royalty cheque, sold steadily for many years and is studied today.

How to age furniture with candles

Do you like the worn, 'shabby chic' look that's all the rage but don't want to spend the substantial amounts of money that the 'distressed' look can cost? Use a household candle to reproduce the look on any wooden piece of furniture – new or old – that you plan to paint.

1

First, prime the piece with an under-colour primer (as though the furniture had been painted this colour previously) and allow the primed coat to dry thoroughly.

2

Rub a white candle along edges and corners, around knobs and handles, randomly over chair arms – wherever the furniture finish would be worn away by frequent use. Be generous with the wax but brush away any flaky bits.

3

Now paint the piece with a coat of the main colour, which won't adhere to the wax. If you need another coat of the top colour – a possibility if you're painting a light colour over a darker one – rub a little more wax over the exposed places.

4

When the item is completely dry, just rub away the wax with a soft cotton cloth dipped in warm water.

✷ Spruce up mouldings and woodwork with colour

Before starting a large-scale redecoration, look at the woodwork and mouldings and check your supply of leftover paints. In general, a single colour is used throughout the home to unify the spaces from room to room. But you could add colour to a child's room or playroom by painting the woodwork in an accent colour. (To maintain the visual flow with the rest of the house, keep doors and window frames the same colour as elsewhere.)

✷ Don't strip old wallpaper; glaze it!

If your wallpaper has fallen out of style but you dread the tedious job of stripping it, applying a glaze will soften colours and tone down patterns. It will create less mess, take less time – and with luck, you already have the key ingredients: white emulsion interior paint, acrylic glazing liquid, water and a small amount of coloured emulsion for tinting the wash. This is a great two-person project – the application requires coordination but goes very quickly.

1. Mix 1 part white emulsion to 1 part glaze. Add water to thin. As you add the water, test the mix on a paper remnant or a small, out-of-the-way patch of wall. If the wash is too strong, add more water and test again. (Water can account for up to half of the finished product.)
2. Once you're happy with the look, wash the mix over the paper with a lint-free cloth, using a swirling motion as if you were cleaning the wall. Work in sections and work fast, because glaze dries rapidly.
3. Use a brush to apply the glaze wash at corners and edges, tamping with a cloth to remove brush strokes.

✷ Take an old ladder and ...

Give it a new lease of life. It may be too wobbly to stand on safely any more, but an aged wooden ladder – with its many nicks, paint splatters and worn-down rungs – has lots of *character* and plenty of potential uses.

- Prop it against an outside wall and use the rungs to display plants.
- Add some heavy-duty hooks and hang the ladder horizontally on a utility room or hall wall to make a handy place to put coats, hats, gloves, wet swimsuits and towels, and whatever other items family members tend to dump on the floor.
- Suspend an old but still-sturdy ladder from the kitchen ceiling and equip it with metal S-hooks for a unique, cost-free pan rack. So the old ladder may not be ready for retirement yet – just a change of career.

✷ Add a rainbow of colour to dreary outdoor furniture

Outside, you have five garden chairs that have undoubtedly seen better days. Inside, you have five tins of leftover paint. Here's your chance to make good use of the paints you have been saving and to go a little crazy with colour to boot. There's no rule that all outdoor furniture has to look the same, so be adventurous and go for the bold approach. As long as you prepare surfaces well by sanding and cleaning and follow manufacturers' instructions, you can use leftover interior paint on outdoor pieces and protect them with a coat of polyurethane varnish. Rusty metal furniture should be scraped as needed and primed with a rust-resistant undercoat. Thanks to modern technology, you can also spray paint faded plastic garden furniture.

Bright ideas for lamps and lighting

✳ Use a light-diffusing slipcover for a shade

Lamplight often owes its beauty more to the lampshade than the bulb. To soften harsh light from a fabric or paper shade, try a gathered slipcover – it is especially easy for a round shade. Check flame-retardent remnants and the linen cupboard for a lightweight fabric in a pale-to-medium colour or pattern and a piece of narrow ribbon to gather up the fabric.

1. Cut the material about twice as wide as the smaller circumference of the shade (longer for a shade with one very wide end) and about 5cm longer than the top-to-bottom measurement. Piece together the fabric if necessary, perhaps alternating solid and patterned panels.

2. Sew the short sides of the fabric together. Fold over and stitch the top and bottom edges to make 1cm pockets, leaving a small opening in each. Now take the ribbon and cut lengths twice as long as the shade's top and bottom circumferences and wrap one end of each length tightly with adhesive tape, so it looks like the tip of a shoelace.

3. Thread the ribbon through the pockets, playing with the fabric so the gathers are evenly distributed. Tie off any excess ribbon as little bows. To secure the cover, tack down the top and bottom edges with thread or double-sided fabric tape. The finished lampshade will look as soft and pretty as the lamplight.

Caution: Halogen lights get very hot, so stick with heat-appropriate shades for those lamps.

✳ Perk up your lampshades

Did you know that you can spray paint a fabric shade to give it a new look? And you won't have to buy paint if you have some craft paint or leftover emulsion on hand.

● Using a ratio of 1 part paint to 10 parts water, mix enough to fill a 500ml plastic spray bottle. Ensure that the lampshade is clean and free of dust. Protect the inside of the shade with paper secured by masking tape. Begin by spraying a light, even coat; let it dry. Spray on more paint, drying between coats, until you have achieved the intensity of colour that you want.

● Add a design by using masking tape to make vertical or diagonal stripes. Or cut shapes from a coated paper, attaching them to the unpainted shade with spray adhesive (follow instructions for a temporary bond). After spray painting, remove the cutouts once the paint is dry. For a soft, mottled effect, use the same paint formula and dab paint, a little at a time, directly onto the shade with a natural sponge. The fabric will diffuse the colour, creating a light and airy look.

✳ Silhouettes on the shade

Add extra interest to a plain paper or fabric lampshade with dark or black construction paper cutouts – also a fun way to decorate for special occasions. (You could try leaf patterns for an autumn celebration, snowflake silhouettes for a winter one, hearts for Valentine's, pumpkin lanterns for Halloween, footballs for an FA Cup party.) A medium-weight card works, too. Translucent white, cream, gold, beige and pastel shades give the best effect. When cutting out the shapes, size them to the shade – not too large and not too small. Fix the shapes to the inside of the shade with double-sided tape, taking special care that the paper doesn't touch or lie too close to, the lightbulb. Now turn on the lamp and see how the silhouettes appear almost 'embedded' in the light. Paper cutouts will begin to curl over time, but they're easy to remove and replace.

✳ Almost anything can be a lamp base

Picture a beautiful ceramic flowerpot illuminating your living room. It's relatively simple to convert just about any non-fragile container, large or small, into a one-of-a-kind lamp base. Most containers need a hole drilled into the bottom or side for the cord. You can cannibalise an old lamp for no-cost parts, but if you lack experience with electrical wiring you should take your object of choice to an electrican for help. You might have to spend some money (shop-bought lamp kits have almost everything you need) – but compared to a new, unique lamp, you may be surprised by how much you can save when you create your own design. Wonderful lamp bases can be repurposed from old:

- Inexpensive vases
- Car boot sale jugs
- Large coffee mugs
- Overturned ceramic mixing bowls

Decorate a drab lampshade with a paper silhouette.

- Loving cup-style trophies
- Books that have been placed on top of each other and glued together
- Antique wooden boxes
- Flower pots

✳ Paint an old lamp base

Spark up an old or inexpensive wooden, metal, plastic or even glass lamp base with a coat of paint. Use paint you already have, but check the information on the can to be sure the paint is suitable for the lamp base material. If you need to buy paint, one spray can or one small can of enamel should be plenty for a pair of medium-sized lamps. (Glass requires special paint, available from craft suppliers, to achieve a permanent finish.) The colour and design are up to you. Anything goes, from an antique finish to a thoroughly modern industrial look.

Before painting, use masking tape to protect the fittings and any areas that you want to keep paint-free, such as a metal base or trim. Also tape over the top of the socket to avoid getting paint on the contact points.

✳ Bedazzle an ordinary chandelier

A plain chandelier can become a dazzler when hung with artful strands of crystals and beads. Go through what you have already – leftover glass beads and faux pearls from other craft and sewing projects, crystal baubles from an unused chandelier, beads from broken or no-longer fashionable costume jewellery. Look for beads with sparkle. Though stringing with pliable wire will allow you to form shapes, dental floss and beading thread are just as strong as wire. String baubles and beads in interesting combinations and then loop and swag them on your light fixture (turned off at the switch) until you have a look you like. Then turn on the light to appraise the dazzling results.

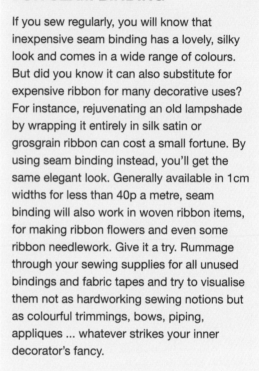

idea

STUNNING USES FOR SEAM BINDING

If you sew regularly, you will know that inexpensive seam binding has a lovely, silky look and comes in a wide range of colours. But did you know it can also substitute for expensive ribbon for many decorative uses? For instance, rejuvenating an old lampshade by wrapping it entirely in silk satin or grosgrain ribbon can cost a small fortune. By using seam binding instead, you'll get the same elegant look. Generally available in 1cm widths for less than 40p a metre, seam binding will also work in woven ribbon items, for making ribbon flowers and even some ribbon needlework. Give it a try. Rummage through your sewing supplies for all unused bindings and fabric tapes and try to visualise them not as hardworking sewing notions but as colourful trimmings, bows, piping, appliques ... whatever strikes your inner decorator's fancy.

✳ Paint a simple ceiling medallion

Plain, flush ceiling light fixtures are the Cinderellas of room lighting; they work so very hard, yet no one pays them any attention. But with a little leftover emulsion paint, some string and a ladder, you can dress up a dull ceiling light. The idea is to mimic a circular plaster medallion. On paper, work out an attractive design, such as concentric circles in different colours and shades. Remember that you'll be painting upside down, so keep the design simple.

Tie a pencil to one end of the string, tape the other end to the centre of the fixture and mark off your outside circle. Use the string compass to mark other circles and semi-circles and a straight edge for lines. Evaluate your design from ground level before painting. If you're not confident of your painting abilities, use flexible tape to outline sections of your medallion as you proceed. Wipe away any mistakes with a wet cloth. With some advance practice, you might add shading and highlighting to give your faux medallion a 3-D look.

✳ Make dinner more intimate

Soft lamplight adds intimacy in restaurants and clubs. You can duplicate this kind of romantic lighting in your dining room, using a lamp and a table runner you already own, plus some masking tape. Lay the runner on your dining table and position the lamp. If the runner has a cutwork pattern, you may be able to slip the lamp flex through. Otherwise, cut a slit in the runner, just wide enough for the plug, at the point where the flex exits the lamp base. (You can also do this with a tablecloth you don't mind cutting.) Run the flex under the fabric and tape it to the table. Now tape the flex to the inside of a table leg and run it to the nearest electrical outlet. To keep anyone from tripping,

tape loose flex unobtrusively to the floor. Dim the room lights to get the full effect.

✳ Beautiful botanical candles

Turn plain candles into really special botanical beauties, using the bounty of your garden and nonflammable household glue. Choose small, flat-faced flowers like violets, pansies or nasturtiums and press them for a few hours in a telephone book. Flatten ordinary grass (unmowed), fern stems, plant leaves and flower petals in the same way. Glue the natural material to the lower half of candles. Tip: If you're not going to use the candles immediately, dip them in paraffin melted in a double boiler. A thin coat of paraffin will protect the botanical items and preserve their colours.

✳ Tea lights in a sandy bed

Here is an economical way to transform any fairly large, shallow, flameproof container into an unexpected light show. From a treasured silver or wooden tray to a serving platter with gently sloping sides to a simple baking sheet – you're sure to have a suitable container around the house. Even the lid from a large tin of sweets or biscuits will do. Line the container

tip ADD THE BEAUTY OF BEESWAX

Beeswax candles can be expensive. If you've got a few ordinary candles you haven't yet used, you can get the unique appearance of beeswax by wrapping them in **a sheet of beeswax.** A number of craft suppliers sell affordable sheets of beeswax (around 30cm wide and 12-25cm deep) in plain or honeycombed textures. With a sharp craft knife, cut a rectangle equal to the circumference and height of your candle. Use a hair dryer to soften the beeswax just enough to make it pliable. Wrap the candle and press the edges together to close the seam.

Ordinary items worth hanging on to

You can't hang on to everything, no matter how devoted a problem solver you are. But there are some basic decorating tools and materials that are worth saving for new uses. Here are some more prosaic leftovers that won't need to be bought again. Plus, they all have everyday household uses, so saving them means that you can find them when you need them.

Special purpose **glues** and adhesive tapes

Paint **solvents**

Metal hooks and **brackets** of any size

Picture **hangers**

Hole punching tools

Metal **hinges**

Speciality **cutting tools** and scrapers

Cleaned **paint brushes,** rollers and wooden stirrers

Dust **cloths**

Regular and heavy-duty metal **staples**

Upholstery **tacks**

Curtain **rails,** hooks and rings

Metal hooks and **brackets** of any size

Sandpaper and steel wool

Measuring cups and spoons no longer used for cooking

bottom with aluminium foil and add a smooth layer of clean sand. If you don't have any sand, try table or sea salt or small dried pulses such as green lentils and yellow split peas or black beans. Embed the tea lights to the top of their sides. Use a small paint or make-up brush to sweep away any material on the candle itself.

✳ Sparkling candle holders

A little glitter and clear-drying household glue will turn a humble candle holder into the shimmering, sparkling star of any candle display. Check first that both glitter and glue are not flammable. Brush the candle holder with glue and roll it in glitter. A really thorough coat of glue will produce a nearly opaque glitter covering; less glue, applied randomly, will give the look of a dusting of glitter. If you don't have any glitter, lightly brush on glue and roll the holder in granulated sugar, table salt or sea salt. You won't be able to wash these candle holders, but when stored in cling film they will keep their sparkle for quite some time.

✳ Glassware candleholders

If you have masses of candles but not enough candle holders to display them in, look through your good, better and best glassware as well as more mundane items such as jam jars, canning jars, tumblers and printed drinking glasses.

A mix of pretty glasses with candles – different sizes, shapes and colours – will make an intriguing arrangement on a table and mantelpiece. Two or three stemmed crystal wine or water goblets can be sublimely elegant candleholders on a formal dining table. Float tea candles in cocktail glasses, filled about two-thirds with water. Pillar candles will rest easily inside flat-bottomed water glasses.

For glassware that has a concave or convex base, stick pillar candles or tapers to the inside of the base with removable putty and then pour

idea
MANTELPIECE LIGHTS

During religious holidays, illuminated nativity scenes and menorahs, and all kinds of other religious or merely decorative lights take pride of place on mantelpieces the world over. But why not light up a mantel at other times as well? Don't pack away your string of lights this year and hang onto the extra bulbs. Here are five ideas to get your imagination going – but first, some cautions: be very careful that lights are never near water or flammable materials and unplug lights whenever there's no responsible adult in the room, when you leave the house or when you turn in for the evening. Use lights that don't heat up and always check wiring for breaks and wear before using.

- Hide lights in an arrangement of silk flowers or a leafy artificial topiary.

- Feed a strand of lights loosely into a large coloured glass bottle or jar.

- Arrange lights in polished silver or brass bowls and cups lined up across the mantel.

- Encircle the frame of a mantelpiece mirror with lights taped behind the frame edge.

- Fill a long, narrow metal tray with marbles or flat, Asian-style river rocks and embed twinkle lights among them.

in enough salt to support the candle. (The salt will catch any wax drips and can be easily disposed of later.)

To get a really spectacular look, use a dripless candle and substitute metallic glitter or glass seed beads for the salt.

Decorating for a party

✴ Garden-fresh flower arrangements

Instead of spending money at the florist for a flower arrangement, pick flowers and greenery from your own garden. If you don't have a garden, explore the floral section of your local supermarket for bargains on bunches of flowers that are several days old but still fresh. A well-stocked farmers' market may also have a selection of cut-price blooms. Another idea is to fill in fresh floral arrangements with the odd quality artificial flower. Amid the tangle of blossoms and leaves, it's hard the see the difference between real and faux.

✴ A pumpkin vase for autumn flowers

Remove the top of a medium-sized pumpkin and scrape out the seeds and pulp, as you would for a Halloween lantern. In the bottom, cut a hole slightly larger than an ordinary glass kitchen or canning jar that will fit comfortably inside the pumpkin. Fill the jar with water and add your flowers. You can cut the pumpkin a day or two in advance if you have a cool, shaded place to store it (outside, if the weather is cooperative). Wrap the pumpkin inside and out with several layers of wet paper towels, re-wetting them as needed to keep it looking fresh.

✴ Protect your decorations from the pets and children

Are you worried about pulling out Grandma's priceless collection of special porcelain decorations from the attic, only to have your new puppy, kitten or grandchild knock them over? Worry no more. Attach a drop of blu-tak to the bottom surface of your treasures, display them as planned and they'll stay put until the celebration is over.

✴ Don't hide the silver

Silver used to be pulled out only for special occasions, but there is no better way to add a splash of sparkle to any room than to stand up silver utensils in tall, clear glassware; for a rustic look, place silverware in coloured antique bottling jars and arrange together on the mantlepiece or wherever a bright light might shine down to illuminate the collection.

tip DRESS A TABLE WITH NATURE'S BOUNTY

An autumn centrepiece of **leaves** at the height of their colour is cost-free and beautiful. Add some of nature's dried bounty, like thistles and wild grasses and light the table with earth-toned candles. You can also use leaves as place cards; write names in metallic permanent marker. If you have clear glass serving plates, slip a large perfect autumn leaf under each server when you set the table.

✱ An autumn arrangement from the wild

To make a gorgeous dried arrangement for an autumn mantlepiece, coffee table or sideboard, fill a plain, tall glass vase or deep glass bowl with brown rice, dried beans or bird seed – simple staples that will help to support your arrangement and look make it look surprisingly elegant. Or go on a hike and collect dried grasses, thistles, milkweed and other long-stemmed flora.

✱ Create a cost-free lightscape with glasses

Forget expensive flowers and instead gather an interesting selection of drinking glasses, glass bottles and decorative glass vases and bowls. Include cut-glass pieces if you have any. Arrange glass items almost randomly on your dining table or buffet and add ordinary white candles to some of the containers. Clear glass and crystal will create a wintry look; a mix of clear and coloured glass will yield a jewel-like effect.

✱ A hearts-and-flowers centrepiece

How can you create a romantic dining table without a lot of cost or effort? You'll need a handful of common household items, one of the little plastic sharpeners children keep in their pencil boxes and thin bamboo skewers.

1. Cut two lengths of waxed paper 45 x 60cm long. Place a larger piece of newspaper on your ironing board and then lay one sheet of waxed paper on top.
2. With a pencil sharpener, shave pink and red crayons and then scatter the shavings randomly over the surface of the waxed paper, making sure that there aren't any clumps or hard pieces.
3. Lay the second sheet of waxed paper over the shavings-covered sheet, then place another piece of newspaper on top. Run an iron on a low-medium setting (don't use steam) over the newspaper until the crayon shavings are melted and the waxed paper sheets stick together completely.
4. After the paper has cooled, use a template to trace hearts in several sizes. Cut them out and attach a bamboo skewer to each heart with a couple of drops of glue.

Add the hearts to your floral arrangement so that they appear to be sprouting upward. The hearts will be gracefully translucent in the candlelight and should help to create a romantic atmosphere for a special dinner.

✱ A creepy Halloween door wreath

Add some ghoulish fun to your home to show that you're in the mood when trick-or-treaters come to the door at Halloween. Some of the essentials, including a magazine and weary flowers, are probably right at hand in the house or garden.

1. Tear pages from a magazine and crumple the paper to make something resembling a chrysanthemum bloom. The resemblance doesn't have to be close; you're going for an effect, not realism.
2. Glue the 'flowers' to cover a wreath form, then spray the wreath and flowers with black paint. So that you don't saturate the paper, apply the paint in several layers, letting it dry between coats.
3. If you have some dead and dry garden leftovers, such as purple echinaceas, zinnias or magnolia leaves, glue them into the wreath. To finish, tie 1m or more of wide red ribbon diagonally around the wreath and let the ends trail. Or tie a bow if you have enough extra ribbon.
4. Hang the wreath on your front door and wait for the arrival of small goblins, witches and ghosts armed with capes, vampire teeth and paper bags.

Create a table centrepiece
with seasonal objects

You can create stunning centrepieces for tables and sideboards from the most mundane objects. Here, you'll need a mirror, a few wide-bottom candles, putty and some pieces of extra greenery from the garden.

An inexpensive, bevelled mirror, 60cm to 1m long and 30cm wide

Platter 'feet' or low wedding cake separators

2–3 wide-bottom candles, depending on the length of the mirror

Plumber's putty

Greenery and flowers

If your dining table is long enough, use a mirror that's 1m long and 30cm wide; the narrow size will enable guests to see each other and to chat over dinner. Plumber's putty and feet can be purchased inexpensively at any hardware or DIY store.

1. Turn the mirror over and glue the small, round platter feet at each corner. This will prevent your centrepiece from sitting flush to the table.

2. Turn the mirror back over and stand each candle on its surface, at equal distances from each other. If you are using a 1m long mirror, attach three candles, equidistant, starting with the middle candle.

3. Apply plumber's putty to the bottom of each candle and secure it to the mirror by pressing firmly but carefully. Repeat with each candle.

4. Cover the mirror with seasonal decorations such as pine trimmings, rope, Christmas decorations and poinsettias. For Easter, nestle coloured eggs among the trimmings.

5. At the end of the celebration, dispose of any fresh trimmings, carefully remove the candles, wipe the mirror with a solution of 50 per cent water and 50 per cent white vinegar, dry and store safely until the next celebration.

Clever cover-ups

✳ Slipcover a headboard

Do you remember how your grandmother would fold her best quilt or bedspread over the foot of the bed so it didn't get crumpled during the day? That's the inspiration for quick, cost-free and very modern loosecovers that you can make to go on your bed – one at each end. Use fabric or a bed sheet you already have; only a few yards will bring a whole new look to a plain bed. Take the vertical and horizontal (between the end posts) measurements for the head and footboards, then double the vertical measurement of each board. (If the horizontal measurement is wider than your fabric, you will have to sew two lengths together.) If you use a sheet, cut it down to size. Hem the edges and add fabric ties to both sides. This look can be as nostalgic as grandma's bed or as sleek as a city studio. Loosecovering is also a smart way to protect the finish on an antique or much-treasured bed and continue to use it as intended.

✳ Window drapery to doorway curtain

Curtaining doorways is a traditional but effective way to keep heat in or out of interior spaces (think tent flaps or alternatively the thick, interlined velvet curtains you sometimes see on doors in old houses). So if you have a set of long curtains that you don't use much, you have a set of ready-made door curtains. For a standard door, mount a curtain rod at or slightly above the door frame. Extend the rod 12cm or more beyond the frame, creating room to slide the curtain to one side so that you can easily open and close the door. Then hang one curtain panel that's long enough to reach to the floor. (Standard door frames are approximately 2m tall, but measure yours just in case.) Metal or plastic curtain rings or clips will make it easier to move the curtain along the rod. To prevent the curtain from billowing on windy days you can sew weights such as metal washers inside the hems.

household superstar

10 TAPE FIXES FOR STICKY SITUATIONS

Solve your decorating dilemmas with a bit of tape

1 Fabric tape to mend split seams in loose covers.

2 Masking tape to make even stripes while painting, without measuring.

3 Masking tape to mask edges of baseboards and door and window frames when painting.

4 Brightly coloured, waterproof electrician's tape to decorate and identify children's plastic toys and adult tools.

5 Double-sided tape to secure rugs to the floor and seat cushions to chairs.

6 Clear parcel tape and a permanent marker to label paint and solvent cans.

7 Masking tape to wrap the metal portion of paint brush handles to catch drips.

8 Non-slip tape to mend worn spots on the underside of rubber-backed bath mats.

9 Double-sided acid-free mounting tape to mount and frame precious artworks on paper.

10 Adhesive-backed Velcro tape as a temporary closure on a cabinet door with a broken latch.

✳ Tile an old tabletop

A battered and bruised wooden coffee table or small side table can become a canvas for tiles, even for beginners. You could use tiles left over from a kitchen or bathroom, specially collected decorated tiles or new ones purchased in a sale. Measure the tabletop to determine how many you will need. If you are careful with your measurements and buy tiles of the correct size, you can probably cover the entire top without making any cuts in the tiles. Bear in mind that you should leave approximately 2–4mm of space between the tiles for grouting.

● Sand the tabletop and clean off the dust. (If you want to refinish or paint your table, do so before sanding.) Then lay out the tiles on the tabletop in your pattern of choice and make any changes and adjustments. Fix the tiles with tiling adhesive or white glue. (If using glue, be sure it's dry before grouting.)

● Grout the tiles with commercial grout, which is available in many colours. As you work, wipe off excess grout with a damp sponge. To remove any remaining grout film, wash again with water after the grout has dried. And there you have it – a brand new look for a tired old table.

✳ A quick change for dining chairs

If the upholstered seats of your dining room chairs are removable – some lift out and others are attached only by screws underneath – you are in luck. You can make a quick, temporary change with some fabric and a bit of strong masking tape. Use what you have on hand: fabric remnants, a tablecloth or bed cover, large scarves, sheets or pillowcases. Mix and match colours and patterns if you like. Choose a medium-weight material, as heavy or highly textured fabrics won't always give a smooth, finished appearance. Remove the chair seat and use it as a template to cut a piece of material extending 7–10cm beyond the edges. Then centre the seat, top down, onto the wrong side of the fabric. Drape the fabric over one side of the bottom of the chair and secure it with a piece of tape. Do the same on the other side, pulling the fabric taut. Repeat on the other two sides and then tape all four folds all the way to the corners. Fold the fabric over each corner for a neat finish. Secure the cover with an extra layer of tape, replace the seat and you've transformed a chair.

✳ Rug on rug

Wall-to-wall carpet often gets flattened, matted and stained in a heavily trafficked area but elsewhere is in good condition. The solution is to search your home for the perfect rug to cover the trouble spot – a rug that might be in the next room or stored away in the attic. If you have a carpet remnant that would look good but is too large, you could ask a local carpet dealer to cut it to size and bind the edges.

✳ Covering the nicks

Has an elderly relative accidentally barged into your treasured coffee table with her walker? Or perhaps your grandson motored his tricycle through the house and into the legs of a treasured antique rolltop desk? Don't weep and don't call in a professional to fix the damage. If the nick is shallow, you can colour it with a similar-hued indelible marker. If the nick is deep (but still superficial), soften a small amount of white candle wax and, using a small butter knife, massage it into the gash. Wait for it to harden and then colour it with the correct colour marker. If the damage is any deeper than that, you will need a professional to fix it.

✳ Wallpapered storage boxes

Cardboard boxes – free from the supermarket or wine merchant or purchased from a storage

idea
LEAF IT TO YOU

Leaves make beautiful printing stamps for decorating fabric – and hey – they fall free from the trees! Even if you live in the most urban of cities, you can find leaves in parks, public gardens and on your own potted plants sitting on your windowsill. Look for fresh, well-shaped leaves with prominent spines and veins.

- Flatten the leaves by pressing them for a day or two in a phone book weighted with something heavy, like more books.

- To use a leaf to stamp fabric, brush fabric paint evenly on its top side. Test the leaf stamp first on a fabric scrap, laying the leaf on the material and pushing – not rubbing – it down with your fingers.

Practice until you get the look you like and then stamp fabric for a tea towel, a cushion cover or whatever else you want to make. Leaf stamps won't last very long, but you can always gather more as they fall.

specialist are probably the world's favourite storage units. They're also ugly and not always easy to put out of sight. So make them look better with leftover wallpaper, preferably vinyl coated. Prepasted wallpaper can be cut to size, dampened and pasted on relatively quickly. Unpasted paper can be stuck down with wallpaper paste, craft glue or rubber adhesive. Arranged on open shelves or neatly stacked under a desk or along a wall, revamped boxes look attractive and their wallpaper covers are durable enough to take a good deal of wear.

Add flair with fabric

✳ Embellishment for cushions

To jazz up throw cushions and cushion covers, look through your sewing box for interesting and unusual embellishments. Ribbons, lace, braid, buttons, beads, tassels, bits of fabric for appliqué, wool, netting, old handkerchiefs and antimacassars, stencils and decorative stamps for fabric painting – practically anything that won't break and will wash can perk up a plain cushion cover. Here are four simple, quick and virtually cost-free ideas:

● Tie on a satin or grosgrain ribbon. Two metres or less will wrap around a 30 x 30cm cushion and let you tie a pretty bow. Tack under the bow and on the back of the cushion.

● Sew a band of lace or decorative trim around the hem of an open-ended cushion cover. Seam the trim to cover the seam line at the opening.

● Sew a row of mismatched buttons in any direction – vertical, horizontal or diagonal – on one side of a tailored cushion for a fun, trendy look.

● Sew pretty tassels to the corners of a cushion or sew or glue tasselled fabric trim around the cushion edges.

✳ Make a duvet cover with sheets

Sleeping under a down-filled duvet is blissful, but washing or dry cleaning it frequently can be expensive. Make a protective cover out of cheap white cotton or a couple of flat bed sheets that fully cover your duvet. Pin the sheets together, right sides facing and sew bottoms and sides together with a straight seam. Turn the cover right side out and slip it over your duvet. The simplest closures are sewn-on ribbon or fabric tape ties, Velcro or snaps.

Now you have a low-cost duvet protector that can be washed as often as you like; under normal conditions, your duvet will need washing or cleaning just once or twice a year.

✳ Save a too-short curtain

If you've just moved house, don't throw away the old curtains if they are too short for your new windows; just add a bottom panel. If you have a collection of fabric remnants, search through them and be ingenious. If not, look out some toning fabrics at a furnishing fabric shop. For one panel, measure the width of your curtain and add seam allowances. Now work out how much you need for the length you want; include seam and hem allowances. Remove stitching from the curtain hems and trim. Cut the extra fabric to fit your measurements. Seam, hem and then hang up your 'new' old curtain.

✳ A plush bath towel shower curtain

If you enjoy the feeling of thick towelling bath sheets, use them to make a luxurious shower curtain. You'll need to use a waterproof liner with it. Two towelling bath sheets are a similar size to a standard shower curtain. Use bath sheets that you already have: white bath sheets create a spa feeling; bright colours can add punch to a plain bathroom. Don't seam the towels; simply overlap the edges and sew together, stitching down the selvage. Add eyelets near the top (eyelet kits are available from most fabric shops). The standard number of holes is 12. To determine the spacing, measure the full width of the sewn curtain and subtract 10cm so that you leave 5cm free at each side. Divide the remainder by 12.

A home gallery

✷ Cheap artworks

When looking for ways to decorate your walls, think outside the box for items that are not an automatic choice for framing. You could, for example, frame an interesting magazine cover, a child's painting, a piece of needlework, a collection of men's silk ties, coins, exotic stamps, a photo collage or a map or postcards from your favourite holiday spot. As an example, save the seed packets that are left after you have planted in the spring; open the packets at the back to preserve the graphic fronts. You may already have some small picture frames that you can use; if not, you can buy inexpensive photo frames. Cover the cardboard backing that comes with the frames in leftover wrapping paper or fabric, then attach the seed packets with double-sided tape. Now just find the right place to hang your new 'botanical prints', which are quick, easy, cost-free and a pleasing memento of your summer garden.

✷ Old frames in new colours

Use leftover paints to refurbish old picture frames for a cost-free way to highlight artwork and add splashes of colour to your home.

Remove everything from the frame and clean it well; if the frame is ornate, use damp cotton buds to get into the nooks and crannies. Dry thoroughly, sand lightly if the frame is wood and simply brush or spray with your colour choice. You can give your frame an antique

tip SHOE POLISH FOR AN ANTIQUE FINISH

Sand a new wooden picture frame and then rub on and buff off a thin coating of brown or reddish-brown **shoe polish** to give the frame an antique finish.

If you're a keen gardener, frame vintage seed packets for a decorative touch.

finish by sanding the dry paint back to the original finish and rubbing the whole frame with brown shoe polish, buffing well. Create a contemporary frame by painting it with high-gloss car paint.

✳ Making unique picture mats

Apart from paintings on canvas, most graphic art is framed under a mat – a cardboard border with a quality paper veneer – that prevents the image from touching (and sticking to) the glass. Cutting mats the meticulous professional way isn't easy, but even an amateur can make attractive mats with glue and materials found around the house. Start with the cardboard mat that came with the frame; if the border is just paper, use it as a template to cut a piece of cardboard. Choose something attractive to cover the cardboard. Consider the frame and the photo or artwork and pick something that will complement both. It won't take much of any of the following to create an individualised mat:

- A remnant of wallpaper
- Curtain or upholstery fabric
- Any leftover medium-weight fabric
- Fake leather, suede or fur
- Wrapping paper or foil
- Parchment paper
- Card stock
- Origami paper
- Shelf or drawer lining paper
- Wide ribbon or lace
- Magazine or old book pages

Cut a piece of material that is slightly larger than the dimensions of the mat. Thinly coat the cardboard with glue and then fix the material, smoothing it carefully to eliminate air pockets and creases. When the glue has dried, cut away the material from the outside edges. Now turn the mat face down and cut excess material diagonally from each top corner to opposite bottom corner, taking care not to cut into the cardboard. Fold the flaps over, trim away all but about 1cm and glue the edges.

✳ Whitewashing a gilt frame

When a new gold gilt or painted frame looks *too* new, you can tone it down with a wash of white. Dilute a small amount of leftover white emulsion paint with water or eggshell with turpentine – to make a thin wash. Ensure that the frame is clean of dust and grease. Use a clean cotton cloth to apply the wash, wiping away excess paint as you go. Let it dry. One or two coats should be enough – you want to calm down the flashiness of new gilt, not cover it up.

✳ A CD case photo gallery

This is a great decorating project for teenagers, who tend to take lots of photos and have plenty of empty CD cases. Twelve or more clear transparent CD cases, stuck to the wall with Blu-tak or low-tack, double-sided tape, make a brilliant, ever-changing gallery. Standard cases measure 12.5cm square – just right for many photo prints and other lightweight items. The pictures can be changed instantly, whenever the mood strikes, just by opening the case.

✳ 'Clothes line' photo displays

Create a modern photo display by using these everyday office supplies. Search in your stationery supplies and desk drawers for clear document sleeves and some small metal binder clips. Mount your photos or other items in the sleeves and nail both ends of a length of wire or rope to the wall, like a washing line, leaving a little slack. (If you have some thin computer cable that you are not using, use it to give the display a high tech look.) Now clip the photo sleeves to the hanging line. Because it is so easy to change photos whenever you want, you will never get fed up with your display.

make your own...

AIR FRESHENER

You'll never buy a commercial air freshener again when you've made your own! Many people swear by homemade fresheners made with bicarbonate of soda or vinegar, which act as deodorisers as well as adding a gentle scent.

Double treat room spray

Both lemon and bicarbinate of soda are traditional odour eaters and this recipe couldn't be simpler.

1 teaspoon bicarbonatet of soda
1 tablespoon lemon juice
480ml water

1 Combine the ingredients in a bowl and let the mixture fizz.

2 When fizzing subsides, stir well.

3 Pour the mixture into a spray bottle that produces a fine mist. Spray rooms that need freshening two or three times a day.

The glue gun:
every decorator's best friend

Whether you are a new convert to re-making and finding new uses for old items or you are a seasoned pro who sews your own curtains, you should always have a glue gun in your home toolkit. Costing around £20, a basic model of this most versatile item will enable you to add your own personal touches to virtually every room in your house, from the bedroom to the bathroom and beyond.

If you have some beautiful linens or textiles that you don't want to get rid of, use them, along with your glue gun, to add appliqué decorations to curtains, wallpaper, shower curtains, bed coverings, headboards and other furnishings. Be creative: appliqués can mean far more than just cut pieces of cloth or textile. Look in your sewing kit for some older-looking buttons to create a unique design statement.

Are there too many Christmas ornaments on your tree? Make a reusable holiday wreath by glue-gunning extra ornaments onto a twig wreath form (available at craft shops); you'll be able to use it again next year.

Create one-of-a-kind gift boxes with everything from plain cardboard posting boxes to dilapidated shoeboxes: cover with fabric, glue-gun in place and dress up with buttons, bows and trim. What does it cost? Virtually nothing.

A bargain lamp with a boring shade can be transformed with a little inexpensive fringe or seam edging, glue gunned to the edging of the shade.

Decorate to celebrate

✳ Spotlight the tree

Forget tangled ropes of tree lights and use a spotlight instead. If you have track lighting, position your tree so the track fixtures can bathe it in light. Or use the portable indoor uplight that's currently highlighting a big houseplant. A swivel desk lamp will also work; locate it so the light strikes the tree but not people's eyes. Essentially any light you can direct will bring out the beauty of your Christmas tree, without all the fuss and bother.

✳ Fragrant holiday window box

Use your winter garden as the palette from which to fill a detachable window box with aromatic pine and pinecones; spruce and cedar clippings; sprigs of boxwood, holly or mistletoe; and clusters of red or white berries. Place it on an inside window ledge, mantle or fireplace shelf or even your holiday table – a picturesque way to bring the colours and fragrances of winter indoors for Christmas.

First, remove any soil and wash the box with bicarbonate of soda or vinegar and water. Most fresh-cut winter greenery will last for a week or more if you mist it daily. If you plan to add water to the box, plug the drainage holes with clay or putty. Protect paint finishes and furniture from drips and condensation by cutting a disposable nappy to the size of the bottom of the box and laying it, plastic side down, under the box. (Check and change this makeshift 'soak pad' as often as necessary.)

✳ Offbeat homemade gift-wrapping

Instead of buying expensive wrapping paper, look around the house for creative and eco-smart substitutes. Newspaper, paper bags, crepe paper, parchment paper, paper place mats, fabric napkins you don't use, comic book pages, children's graph and drawing paper, bubble wrap – the possibilities are endless. Use stamps, stencils and stickers to embellish your wrappings and substitute brightly coloured wools, workshop twines and flexes, fabric trims and bindings, torn strips of fabric or an old fabric measuring tape, for purchased bows.

✳ Dried citrus ornaments

Extra oranges and lemons in the fridge that may be past their prime can be transformed into warmly translucent tree ornaments. Cut fruit into 0.5cm slices, lay the slices flat on a nonstick baking sheet and place in the oven on the lowest setting for several hours. Test for dryness by lightly touching the pulp; if it feels sticky, leave the slices in the oven for a little longer; it's important to remove the fruit before it begins to brown. Cool on a wire rack. Thread the dried fruit slices with ribbon or wool and hang them where they will catch the tree lights. Preserve your dried fruit slices by spraying or painting them with a clear acrylic finish.

Dyeing Easter eggs
(with help from nature)

In this chart, quantities are based on 1 litre of liquid. Amounts of dyeing ingredients are approximate; more dyestuff and longer dye baths produce the deepest colours. All boiled eggs should be stored in the fridge and any that have soaked in hot or warm water for several hours should not be eaten.

Dye source	Quantity	Colour
Beet juice	half strength or more of the vinegar water	deep pink
Cranberry juice	full-strength	light pink
Paprika	3 tablespoons or more	brick red
Yellow onion skins	250g	sienna
Turmeric	3 or more tablespoons	yellow-green
Brewed coffee	1 litre strong coffee plus water to cover	brown
Blueberries	up to 400g	lavender
Purple grape juice	half or more of the liquid	blue-grey
Red cabbage	400g (boil and then soak overnight)	robin's egg blue
Spinach or grass	450g	green
Red wine	full strength or diluted with water only	deep purple

✳ Easter eggs, naturally

Budding young chemists and curious children will really enjoy helping to make naturally coloured Easter eggs with ingredients that come straight from the cupboard and fridge. This family project costs nothing, but the delight in learning is priceless.

1. Gently wash eggs with soapy water and dry.

2. Place a single layer of eggs in a non-metal pot with the dye source (see chart at left).

3. Add 2 tablespoons vinegar to 1 litre water. Bring to a boil, reduce to a simmer for 15–20 minutes and remove pan from the heat. If you like the colour as it is, dab off excess dye with a paper towel and set the eggs on a rack to dry. To deepen the colour, leave eggs in the pot until cool. To get even richer shades, put cool eggs in a bowl, strain the dye water and pour it over the eggs. Store the submerged eggs in the fridge for a few hours or overnight.

✳ Snow globes from empty jars

Make your own old-fashioned snow globe at home with clean, plain, glass kitchen jars and whatever small Christmas items you have available – such as little plastic Santas and reindeer and ceramic elves and angels. Don't use wood or metal items. Any size glass jar will work, as long as the objects will fit inside and the lid fits tightly. Small and medium olive and baby food jars are ideal for small globes. You may have to buy several items – waterproof epoxy glue, distilled water, white glitter and glycerine (available from pharmacies and online suppliers) – but you will only need small amounts.

1. Roughen the inside surface of the jar lid with sandpaper or steel wool and then glue on your object or objects with epoxy; let it

idea

SUPERLATIVE STRING

Beautiful filigree balls can be made for almost no cost. All you need is a spool of household string, white PVA glue, water and a balloon.

- For each ball, soak several metres of string in a mixture of 1 part white glue to 1 part water. Blow up and tie a small round balloon.

- Wrap the balloon with the saturated string, wrapping randomly. When you like the look of it, clip the string and set the balloon on top of a drinking glass. Allow the string to dry for at least a day or until the balloon begins to deflate.

- Pop the balloon and remove it. Then spray the ball with gold, silver or copper metallic paint. Dust with glitter for a more glamorous look, if you like. Pile the finished balls in a shallow bowl for a stunning, low-cost centrepiece.

dry. Fill the jar almost to the top with distilled water and add a drop of glycerine.

2. Glycerine thickens the water so glitter will swirl; for larger jars, add a couple of drops. Now add a pinch or two of glitter.

3. Screw the jar lid on tightly, being careful not to dislodge the glued-on object. Finally, turn the jar over and enjoy the snowstorm.

If you have arthritis – reach for the turmeric!

6 Nature's home remedies

We're all obsessed with our health, using both established pharmaceutical remedies for what ails us (such as aspirin and Alka-Seltzer) or the kinds of time-honoured folk cures that your grandmother swore by: witch hazel and Epsom salts, camomile tea and castor oil, hydrogen peroxide and mustard plasters.

And while many of these remedies are valid and useful, there is also wisdom in the proverb, 'Moderation in all things'.

That said, it really does pay to stock your medicine cabinet with home remedies. Homemade witch hazel is more effective than its commercial equivalent because it isn't distilled. The herb feverfew will stave off migraines more effectively when you chew the fresh leaves instead of swallowing a capsule. A hair dryer may help to stave off a cold better than a pill. And our distant forebears found a multitude of uses for salt and stinging nettles, cloves and castor oil. Leafing through the pages that follow may encourage you to emulate those hardy souls. (But remember to consult your doctor before using all but the most benign remedies.)

Fighting colds and flu

✳ Kick chicken soup up a notch

When science proved that grandma's chicken soup really does help to fight colds, the legendary broth secured its place in the pantheon of healing foods. Chicken soup works not only because steam rising from the bowl helps to clear congestion, but also because anti-inflammatory compounds in the broth slow the movement of neutrophils, white blood cells that spur the formation of mucus in the lungs and nose. To notch up the cold-fighting abilities of chicken soup even further, add two peeled and crushed garlic cloves to a simmering pan. Garlic contains antiviral sulphur compounds and it is also said to boost the immune system.

✳ Fire up the hair dryer

When you feel a cold coming on, inhaling heated air can stunt its severity. Studies show that warm air kills rhinoviruses that are working their way up the nose. In one British test, subjects who breathed warm air had half the symptoms of those who inhaled air at room temperature. Set your hair dryer to warm (not

idea

BEATING 'RUDOLPH SYNDROME'

You might think that the reddening (and soreness) of the nostril rims that results from constant nose blowing would have a name. Up until now, it hasn't, so let's call it Rudolph Syndrome (RS), after Santa's favourite reindeer. Stop the unsightly, uncomfortable redness by rubbing petroleum jelly or lip balm on the rim of the nostrils.

hot), hold it at least 45cm from your face and inhale the warm air for as long as you can – preferably 20 minutes or so but 2 or 3 minutes at the very least.

✳ Sip (and gargle) echinacea tea

Echinacea purpurea or purple coneflower, can indeed help to prevent colds and relieve the symptoms of colds and influenza alike. It works partly by boosting levels of the chemical properdin, which strengthens the body's defence mechanisms against infections. Drinking 3 cups of echinacea tea (left) a day will guard against colds, but it's best not to take it all the time. Limit consumption to three weeks in every four to avoid nausea, fevers and other side effects. You can also gargle echinacea tea up to three times a

Increase the cold-fighting properties of chicken soup with a touch of garlic!

day to soothe a sore throat. Because it stimulates the immune system, echinacea should not be taken by people with autoimmune conditions such as lupus or multiple sclerosis, or by anyone with AIDS. It may also interact with some drugs, so do tell your doctor if you plan to take echinacea and are on any other medications.

✳ Cool a fever
In the first stages of a cold, you can help your body to bring down a fever by giving yourself a sponge bath every hour or so. Dip a sponge in tepid (not cold) water, lightly wring it out and use it to bathe your face, shoulders, chest and extremities. If the fever persists, drink 1–2 cups of ginger tea every few hours; the ginger will promote sweating, which is the body's way of cooling itself.

✳ Fight coughs with thyme
Thyme is a natural expectorant, so brew a pot of thyme tea to fight a nagging cough. Just steep 2 tablespoons dried thyme leaves in 6 cups hot water for 10 minutes. Strain the liquid into a teacup, sweeten with honey if desired and sip a cupful two or three times a day.

✳ Three simple sore throat gargles
Invade the kitchen cabinet rather than the medicine cabinet to cure your sore throat.
- **Honey** Honey coats the throat and has mild antibacterial properties. Stir 1–3 teaspoons into 240ml warm water and gargle two or three times a day.
- **Salt** Salt water has been used as a gargle for centuries because it works so well. It draws moisture from the mucous membranes (and

helps to dilute the mucus) and helps to cleanse the throat of phlegm. Dissolve ½ teaspoon salt in 240ml warm water and gargle the mixture three or four times daily.

- **Peppermint** The menthol in peppermint helps open the nasal passages, especially when you gargle strong peppermint tea. Pour 240ml boiling water over 3 peppermint tea bags and let steep for 4–5 minutes. Gargle with the cooled solution two or three times a day.

✱ A fiery gulp

For a practical way to get rid of a congested throat, use kitchen staples honey and Tabasco (right). Whisk 1 teaspoon honey into 240ml warm water. Now whisk in ½ teaspoon Tabasco or hot red pepper sauce. (If this is too spicy for you, experiment by adding a few drops at a time.) Drink the concoction slowly; follow it with a small glass of ginger ale, which will cool the burning feeling.

✱ Swat a flu bug with elderberry

If you feel that you've been bitten by the flu bug, drink 3–4 cups of elderberry tea daily or take 20–30 drops of elderberry tincture in a glass of water. In Europe, elderberry (*Sambucus nigra*) has a long history as an antiviral herb and research bears it out. In one study, nine out of ten test group subjects who had consumed elderberry saw their flu symptoms subside in two days, while symptoms in the group that consumed no elderberry continued for six days.

curiosity corner

THE POWER OF RED

Over a century ago, one of the most common cold cures was bought by the yard: red flannel, which was associated with warmth and healing. Why red? Because of the superstition that the colour red kept evil spirits at bay. Less metaphysically, flannel was said to 'draw out' a cold when worn next to the skin.

Flannel came on the scene in the late 19th century, when a napped cotton called flannelette became widely available. While considered inferior to wool, this new fabric didn't feel itchy on the skin as wool did. Mothers tied red flannel scarves around their children's necks to relieve sore throats (in addition to keeping away the evil eye). Many men wore red flannel underwear under their clothing to protect themselves not only from colds and the flu but to prevent attacks of gout and rheumatism. For back pain, flannelette bands were worn around the waist. In time, the fabric that sealed in heat without itching came to be known simply as flannel and widely used for the tartan shirts beloved of lumberjacks and the checks, stripes and paisleys used in several generations worth of flannel pyjamas.

Easing asthma, bronchitis and allergies

✳ Inhale eucalyptus vapours

If you're lucky enough to have access to dried *Eucalyptus globulus*, just boil the crumbled leaves and let them steep for 4–5 hours and strain out the bits of leaf before heating the liquid for inhalation. (Alternatively, add 5–10 drops commercial eucalyptus oil to the steaming water.) Place the bowl at the edge of a table, sit down, bend your head over the bowl and put the towel over your head to form a tent. Breathe the vapours for about 10 minutes, taking care not to get too close to the steam. Your lungs will clear and you'll get a facial as a bonus.

✳ Bronchitis double dose

The head-clearing pungency of freshly grated horseradish paired with the acidic aroma of lemon helps to dissolve mucus in the sinuses and bronchial tubes. To make a cough medicine, grate a peeled horseradish root into a bowl (or cheat and use prepared horseradish) and transfer 50g grated horseradish to a small bowl. Add 80ml lemon juice and stir well. Dose yourself with ½ teaspoon of the mixture at a time, taking it two or three times a day. The expectorant action should set up a cough after each dose, helping to rid your lungs of mucus.

✳ Loosen mucus with mullein

Mullein (*Verbascum thapsus*), a longtime folk remedy for respiratory ailments, contains saponins that loosen phlegm and promote expectoration. It also contains gelatinous mucilage that soothes the mucous membranes. To make mullein tea, steep 2 teaspoons dried mullein leaves in just-boiled water for 10 minutes. Herbalists advise drinking the tea up to three times a day to ease bronchial distress.

✳ Elecampane the expectorant

Buy elecampane tea or liquid extract, sweeten the tea with honey and drink 1–2 cups a day to stimulate the lungs' natural 'housecleaning' mechanism. The active principle in elecampane (*Inula helenium*) is alantolactone, a proven expectorant. Use of elecampane dates back to

tip FIGHT ASTHMA WITH FISH

Omega 3, the fatty acids found in **sardines,** tuna, salmon, mackerel and other oily fish, works in much the same way as a class of drugs called leukotriene inhibitors, which disable bodily compounds that contribute to inflammation of the airways.

some of the earliest European settlers in the Americas, who used it to treat the symptoms of asthma, whooping cough, pneumonia and tuberculosis.

✱ Camomile's two faces

For an allergy-fighting tea, pour 240ml boiling water over 2–3 teaspoons crushed flower heads of German camomile, steep for 10 minutes, strain and drink three to four times daily. Caution: while camomile is a traditional hay fever fighter, it can aggravate symptoms in anyone who is allergic to ragweed, a camomile cousin. For everyone else, the azulene content in camomile has anti-inflammatory properties that have led doctors worldwide to prescribe camomile preparations for respiratory tract infections and allergies.

✱ Use bleach to quell sniffles

If you have a sudden case of the sniffles that won't go away and you don't have allergies (or a cold), you may unknowingly be living with mould. Check for spots in the bathroom or beneath windows subject to condensation and kill mould instantly with a 50:50 mixture of bleach and water. Spray it directly onto the offensive spots and let it sit. The mould should be stopped in its tracks within minutes, along with (hopefully) your runny nose.

✱ Nettle and hay fever

If you have access to fresh stinging nettles (it's a common garden weed), wear gloves when harvesting and washing the leaves (the plant's not called stinging nettle for nothing). Add 120g of the leaf to 6 cups of boiling water. Lower the heat and simmer until the water turns green, then strain through a fine sieve into a large teapot. During the hay fever season, drink a cup of nettle tea in the morning and one in the evening, sweetening it with honey if you like.

make your own...

NASAL SPRAY

This is a homemade spray that will help to flush allergens out of your nasal passages. The isosmotic solution parallels the concentration of salt found in the body, making the spray mild but effective.

Salt water sniffle-stopper

This spray works best at room temperature. Discard any unused solution after two days or it may become contaminated.

1 litre water
1 tablespoon camomile tea
2 teaspoons salt

1 Place water in a medium saucepan, add tea and salt, and bring to a low simmer.

2 Stir until salt is dissolved, then let it cool to room temperature.

3 Pour solution into an empty nose spray bottle. Spray twice in each nostril as needed, holding the other nostril closed each time.

Studies have yet to definitively confirm the efficacy of stinging nettle (*Urtica dioica*) for treating hay fever, but legions of people swear by nettle's powers to ease runny noses and watery eyes.

What does that term mean?

You probably already know the meaning of many of the words in this list, not all of which apply only to herbal remedies. But when it comes to self-treatment, having a fuller grasp of the terminology becomes all the more important.

Active principle The ingredient of a plant remedy that is responsible for its medical effect.

Antiseptic A substance that prevents or stops the growth of microorganisms that cause infection.

Astringent A substance that draws together the soft tissues, such as skin or mucous membranes.

Decoction A drink or liquid extract made by boiling plant bark, roots, berries or seeds in water.

Diuretic A substance that increases the flow of urine.

Emollient A substance that softens and soothes the skin and mucous membranes.

Essential oil A plant oil that readily vaporises and is often obtained by steam distillation.

Expectorant A substance that loosens and helps to expel phlegm.

Infusion A preparation in which flowers, leaves or stems are steeped in water that is not boiling.

Liquid extract Concentrated infusion made by soaking a herb in distilled water, grain alcohol or glycerine for a long period.

Mucous membrane Lining of a body passage, such as the throat, that protects itself with secretions of mucus.

Photosensitivity Sensitivity to sunlight, causing rash or burning sensation on exposure. May be brought on by ingestion or application of certain substances.

Plaster Gauze or cloth impregnated with chemicals or wrapping medicines applied to the skin.

Poultice A soft, moist mass, often containing herbs, that is usually applied directly to an affected area to relieve pain or swelling.

Purgative A very strong laxative.

Tannins Astringent and bitter compounds found in plants, especially grape seeds and skins, which slow oxidation and ageing.

Tincture An herbal liquid extract that generally involves macerating the herb in alcohol.

Volatile oil A plant oil that readily vapourises and is often obtained by steam distillation; used interchangeably with essential oil.

Wash A liquid herbal medicine preparation for external use.

No-drugs headache relief

THE FUSS OVER FEWERFEW

Feverfew *(Tanacetum parthenium)*, has been used to treat everything from joint pain to melancholy and fever. In the 1970s, clinical trials in London showed that the herb was an effective treatment for migraines.

The active principles in feverfew leaves and flowers, called parthenolides, inhibit the body's release of serotonin, prostaglandins and histamines into the bloodstream, all of which can inflame tissue and trigger (and worsen) migraine headaches. The herb, which modern herbalists also recommend for colds, indigestion and diarrhoea, is sold in capsules and as liquid extract. Feverfew is also the perfect candidate for a physic garden (page 167), because freshly plucked leaves are said to be more effective than processed feverfew. To help to prevent migraines, chew two or three freshly picked feverfew leaves after breakfast and dinner each day, swallowing only the juice. (Caution: Some people develop sores and other mouth irritations after chewing feverfew – so stop chewing the fresh leaves at the first sign of any oral irritation.) Another unprocessed option is an infusion made from feverfew flowers and leaves.

✳ Running hot and cold

To cure a tension headache (caused by contractions in the head and neck muscles and brought on by – among other things – stress, anxiety and lack of sleep) without painkilling drugs, dip a facecloth in hot water, wring it out and fold it into a compress. Now place it on your forehead or the back of your neck to relax tight muscles. To ease a vascular headache (including migraine and cluster headaches and stemming from the contraction and expansion of blood vessels in a particular area of the head), follow the same procedure, but use cold water, which constricts the blood vessels and reduces blood flow, taking the pressure off a painful head.

✳ A cup of tea makes a headache flee

A clinical trial in Illinois, USA found that caffeine, which reduces the swelling of blood vessels, can reduce both the intensity and frequency of headaches. Subjects in one group were given caffeine alone; 58 per cent reported complete relief. Subjects in the other group were given caffeine in combination with ibuprofen and 71 per cent saw their symptoms disappear.

✳ Sinus headache self-massage

Use your middle fingers to massage the points of the face just opposite your nostrils – that is, at the level of the tip of your nose. Massage in clockwise circles for 2 or 3 minutes.

To sooth a throbbing headache, soak your feet – in hot water and mustard!

✱ Head-to-toe headache remedy

Blood drawn to the lower body will reduce pressure in the blood vessels of the head. What could be lower than your feet? To help to soothe a throbbing vascular headache, soak your feet in a small tub filled with hot water mixed with mustard powder. After a half hour or so, remove your feet from the water, dry your feet and you should feel better.

✱ Sip ginger tea

When it comes to treating headaches, ginger works especially well for migraines and can help to alleviate the nausea as well as the pain. You can make a tea by pouring 3 cups water over 2 tablespoons freshly grated ginger. Let steep 4–5 minutes, then strain through a small sieve into a teacup. Ginger tea bags are also available, but the tea lacks the punch of fresh ginger root tea.

tip WEAR A HEADBAND

Tie a **scarf, tie or bandana** tightly around your forehead to reduce the flow of blood to your scalp and in turn, to throbbing, swollen blood vessels.

Eyes, ears and mouth

✳ Eye can see clearly now

Carrots, celery, kale and parsley can all contribute to the trouble-free operation of the optic system. Either juice the vegetables to make an eye-boosting drink or purée to make a cold soup. The ideal proportions are 2 parts carrots, 2 parts kale, 1 part celery and 1 part parsley. For the best results, consume 2 cups of juice or soup a day. Vary the mix by incorporating spinach, tomatoes and melons.

✳ Tea for two

We're talking about puffy eyes. Take two cool, wet tea bags, place them on tired or swollen eyes and lie down for 15–20 minutes as the tea soothes and refreshes. Green tea is ideal for these mini-compresses, but black tea and herbal teas work well. Some herbalists also claim that tea-bag compresses speed the healing of a black eye.

✳ Let's 'ear it for mullein and garlic!

Paired with garlic, mullein (*Verbascum thapsus*) makes soothing drops for an earache that you can keep on hand in the fridge. In a sterilised jar, combine 1 crushed clove garlic with 2 tablespoons dried or fresh mullein flower (crushed if fresh) and 120ml olive oil. Screw the lid on tightly and shake to blend. Store in a cool, dark place, shaking the jar daily. After two weeks, strain the oil into another jar and store it in the fridge. To treat an earache, bring the oil to room temperature or hold the jar under warm running water. With a sterile eyedropper, add 2–3 drops to the ear, then gently massage the ear to help the oil to move through the ear canal. Do not use eardrops if you think you could have a perforated eardrum.

Help lower blood pressure with a banana at breakfast!

✳ Bubble away ear trouble

Dropping 3 per cent hydrogen peroxide into the ear makes earwax easier to extract. Fill a sterile eyedropper with peroxide, lie on your side and squeeze the liquid into the affected ear until it feels full. Let the peroxide bubble away for 3–5 minutes, then press a facecloth or folded paper towel against the ear and turn over to let it drain. Rinse the ear by repeating the process with water then allow to dry. Never use hydrogen peroxide in your ear if you suspect that you have a perforated eardrum.

✳ Homemade breath freshener

To make a mouthwash, pour 240ml water into a saucepan and add 1 tablespoon cardamom seeds and 1 tablespoon whole cloves. If you like, add a few mint leaves and a little sugar to improve the taste. Bring to the boil, remove from heat and let steep for 3–4 hours. Strain the solution into a bottle and gargle as needed.

✳ Brown stains on teeth?

If your teeth advertise your fondness for coffee, tea or cigarettes, supplement a whitening toothpaste with a dash of bicarbonate of soda.

✳ Saltwater rinse for toothaches

Swishing warm salt water in the mouth can relieve the pain of toothache in the short term. Use 2 to 3 teaspoons salt in 240ml warm water.

✳ Lips chapped?

Soothe cracked, dry lips with a drop of olive, corn or sunflower oil. Margarine and petroleum jelly also work well.

✳ Don't dry your eyes

Dry eyes are so common that over-the-counter remedies for this ailment abound. What are the causes? Everything from pollution and smoke to age. A good cure is to leave packaged remedies

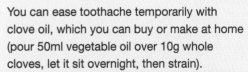

CLOVE OIL TO THE RESCUE

You can ease toothache temporarily with clove oil, which you can buy or make at home (pour 50ml vegetable oil over 10g whole cloves, let it sit overnight, then strain).

Put a few drops of clove oil onto a cotton wool ball, place the ball on your sore tooth and bite down. Keep your jaw shut tight for 3–4 minutes as the oil numbs the pain and kills bacteria. Now remove the cottonwool ball and make a mouthwash from 180ml water, ¼ teaspoon salt and 6–8 drops clove oil. Swish the solution around in your mouth for about 30 seconds to kill still more bacteria and rinse.

Caution: undiluted clove oil inside the mouth can cause burning, tissue or nerve damage and pain. In large doses, clove oil taken orally can cause vomiting, sore throat, seizure, difficulty breathing, kidney failure or liver damage. Clove oil shouldn't be applied to broken skin. Children, pregnant or nursing women and people with diabetes, kidney or liver disease or bleeding disorders should avoid taking clove oil.

at the chemist's and eat a banana instead. Bananas are rich in potassium, which helps to control the balance of sodium and the release of fluid in your cells.

✳ Help lower blood pressure with bananas

Slice a banana into your breakfast cereal in the morning to get the benefit of Nature's potassium-laden gift to those with high blood pressure. Check with your doctor first.

Soothing back, joint and muscular pain

✳ Tin can massage

A cold, unopened 330ml drink can makes a great back massager, whether it's filled with cola, lemonade or beer. To loosen muscle tissue and spur blood flow to the area, stand against the wall with the can on its side wedged between your back and the wall. Then move from side to side to make the can roll. This impromptu massager does an especially good job of relaxing the muscles next to the shoulder blades and lower down the back.

✳ A back support for drivers

To make a lower back support to use in the car when you are driving, fold a medium-size bath towel lengthways, then roll it up; the roll should be about 30cm long. Cut the leg of an old pair of tights to size and slip the towel inside. In the car, tuck the makeshift cushion between the small of your back and the car seat and you should be able to ride in comfort and with a back-friendly posture.

✳ A plaster from the past

To give this favourite old pain remedy a go, combine powdered mustard seed and plain flour in a bowl (1 part mustard seed to 2 parts flour) and slowly stir in water to make a paste. Spread the mixture on one side of a 30cm square of cheesecloth and fold. Now place the plaster on the ache, securing it with a bandage or slipping it under a tight T-shirt. Leave the plaster in place for no more than 20–30 minutes at a time. If any skin irritation occurs, remove the plaster immediately.

✳ More curry = less arthritis pain

Turmeric, one of the principal spices in curry powder, is as medicinal as it is culinary. The compound in turmeric called curcumin has been shown in clinical trials to reduce swelling associated with arthritis. If you find curries too spicy, use powdered turmeric as a seasoning, sprinkling it over meat, eggs and dark green leafy vegetables such as spinach.

✳ Eat and drink ginger

Incorporating ginger into your diet may bring some relief from rheumatoid arthritis and osteoarthritis pains. For best results, take ½ teaspoon of powdered ginger or 6 teaspoons of fresh ginger once a day, whether in food or tea.

✳ Painful leg cramp relievers

Standing barefoot on a cold floor decreases blood flow and could help to relax tightened leg muscles, so if you're hit with painful leg cramps in the middle of the night, get out of bed and stand on a cold floor.

✳ Quinine for cramping

To prevent cramps, make tonic water part of the 240ml of water we're told to drink eight times a day. Quinine, from the bark of the South American cinchona tree, is the only drug that has actually proven to be effective for leg cramps, but its serious side effects, including irregular heartbeat, put neat quinine on the prescription only list. What you can buy anywhere is tonic water – so-called because it is flavoured with small doses of quinine.

Calming gastrointestinal distress

✳ Stomach soothers

Certain herb leaves, flowers and seeds have traditionally been used to remedy such gastrointestinal problems such as indigestion, nausea and tummy ache. Among them are angelica, anise, caraway seed, camomile, cinnamon, fennel seed, ginger, marjoram, oregano and peppermint. And all can be used to make a herbal infusion or herbal tea.

✳ Tummy taming turmeric

To alleviate stomach cramps, add a teaspoon of this very mild-flavoured, bright red powdered herb to 240ml glass of water or simply sprinkle it over whatever you are eating. Turmeric is an ancient Indian and Middle Eastern remedy for treating babies with colic and is a recognised antispasmodic.

✳ Sort out problems with wind

To help to keep flatulence under control, try one of these herbal teas or infusions.

- **Caraway seed** (right) Pour 240ml boiling water over 1–2 teaspoons freshly crushed caraway seeds. Steep 10–15 minutes, then strain. Drink a cupful two to four times a day between meals.
- **Fennel seed** Follow the directions given for caraway seed tea, substituting fennel, then drink before or after meals.

- **Dried peppermint leaf** Pour 240ml just-boiled water over 1 tablespoon dried peppermint, infuse for 10–15 minutes and strain. Drink a warm cup of tea three or four times a day.
- **Dill seed** For a mild dill seed infusion, pour 240ml just-boiled water over 1 teaspoon ground dill seeds and let it sit for 10–15 minutes. Strain, then drink before or after meals.
- **Anise seed** Follow the directions for infusing dill seed, substituting anise for dill seed. (Caution: Some people may be allergic to anise.)

✱ Go for the ginger

Sip a cup of virtually miraculous ginger tea after meals to help to keep your digestive system in good working order. Ginger root, which could be called the queen of digestive herbs, has been used for thousands of years to treat indigestion and diarrhoea. Research over the past 25 years has shown that two compounds in ginger – gingerols and shogaols – also work on the inner ear and central nervous system as well as the gastrointestinal tract, helping to reduce nausea and dizziness.

✱ Sip cider vinegar

Stir 2 teaspoons cider vinegar into 240ml water and enjoy a 'vinegar cocktail' up to three times a day to improve digestion and to fend off an impending stomach ache. Apple cider vinegar, unlike white vinegar, contains malic acid, and can help to balance the stomach's pH (the balance of alkalinity and acidity).

✱ Treat diarrhoea with berries

Simmer 1–2 tablespoons astringent bilberries, blackberries or blueberries or their dried leaves in 360ml water for 10 minutes, then strain, for the relief of diarrhoea. Drink 1 cup of this diarrhoea-fighting tonic several times a day, preparing it freshly each time. Some herbalists recommend that you should drink 2 tablespoons every 4 hours.

✱ Old-time constipation cure

Your grandmother was devoted to it for a reason: one of the primary uses for castor oil is as a laxative; taking 1–2 teaspoons on an empty stomach will give results in about 8 hours. Castor oil works because a component in the oil breaks down into a substance that stimulates the large and small intestines. Caution: This remedy is not recommended for repeated use, as it impairs the absorption of nutrients.

✱ Ease constipation with blackstrap molasses

This byproduct of sugar refining contains lots of calcium, magnesium, potassium and iron, in addition to easing constipation and is available from online suppliers. As it is essentially concentrated cane sugar you must brush your teeth after swallowing to protect your teeth. Take 1 tablespoon before going to bed.

---

what's the story?

CASTOR OIL: OUR ANCESTORS' CURE-ALL

Well into the 20th century, a bottle of castor oil could be found in virtually every doctor's office, hospital and home. It was used primarily as a laxative and stomach ache cure but also to treat colds and skin problems.

Children in particular were subjected to the foul-tasting oil, which was given at the first hint of a sniffle, cough or cramp. Many adults took it once a week as a purgative believed to 'clean out the system'. The oil was also used to induce labour and to help a mother recover after childbirth.

Castor oil is extracted from the seeds of the castor bean plant (*Ricinus communis*) – the source of ricin, a deadly poison. But the oil is denatured and made safe to use when it is extracted through cold compression and undergoes steam treatment. The venerable product is still on the market, so why not hold your nose and give it a try?

How to grow a physic garden

Physic gardens were collections of healing plants grown by physicians and monks in ancient times. Plant your own using some of the herbs shown here. By investing a little time and the cost of seeds, you'll have the makings of infusions, teas and balms. Choose a sunny spot with rich soil for your garden. Perennials will grow from season to season, while annuals must be reseeded or transplanted.

Basil
Annual. Harvest the young leaves of 'the king of herbs' as needed. Uses: flatulence, lack of appetite, cuts and scrapes.

Camomile
Annual. Use the flower heads for infusions and salves. Uses: indigestion, anxiety, skin inflammations.

Feverfew
Perennial. Use leaves and flowers for teas; chew leaves to ease headache pain. Uses: headaches (including migraines), arthritis, skin conditions.

Lemon balm
Perennial. A relative of mint, lemon balm is a versatile medicinal herb. Uses: anxiety, insomnia, wounds, herpes, insect bites, flatulence, upset stomach.

Parsley
Biennial. Like its curly cousin *P. crispum*, this herb is loaded with nutrients. Uses: flatulence, bad breath.

Sage
Perennial. Sage's genus name, Salvia, means 'to heal', reflecting its early use as a medicinal, not culinary, herb. Uses: mouth and throat inflammations.

St John's wort
Perennial. The glossy leaves and yellow flowers are this herb's active parts. Uses: mild to moderate depression. (Talk to your doctor first.)

Thyme
Perennial. The active principle in thyme, thymol, is a strong antiseptic. Uses: coughs, congestion, indigestion, gas.

Problems with 'plumbing'

✱ The little red infection fighter

To prevent urinary tract infections (UTIs), drink 360ml to 1 litre of unsweetened cranberry juice each day. Capsules of dried cranberry powder are also available – but in some brands, six capsules are the equivalent of only 80ml juice. Medical researchers learned as early as the 1840s that the hippuric acid in cranberries inhibits the growth of E. coli bacteria, the most common cause of UTI. The acid also keeps *E. coli* from adhering to the urinary tract walls and from spreading from the bladder to the kidneys. Caution: cranberry juice can interfere with the action of anticoagulant drugs such as warfarin, so consult your doctor before using.

✱ Eat your parsley to ease your pain

Crush parsley leaves, add 1 teaspoon to 240ml boiling water and let it steep for 3–5 minutes. Strain, then drink up to 3 cups of tea a day. Because a volatile oil contained in the leaves and roots of parsley has diuretic properties, parsley tea is useful for treating mild bladder problems, reducing urinary tract inflammation and even helping the passage of small kidney stones. Caution: Anyone with chronic kidney disease should consult a doctor before using parsley and excessive ingestion of the herb can cause the skin to be photosensitive.

✱ Cornsilk – a natural diuretic

Place washed cornsilk, the stigmas from the female flowers of maize, in a teapot and add boiling water (9–12g washed corn silk to each 240ml water) for a natural diuretic. Let it steep

what's the story?

IS 'NATURAL' SAFE?

Not always. Even plain water can be lethal if you drink too much of it. (A water overdose actually dilutes the salt in the body and can lead to a condition called hyponatremia.)

- Always ask a doctor or medical herbalist about any possible interactions with prescription medications and only use natural or herbal remedies under the advice and supervision of a doctor or herbalist.

- Never use herbal remedies when pregnant or nursing except under the direction of a doctor or medical herbalist.

- If you don't grow your own herbs, buy only from reputable sources, preferably at a shop with reliable sales staff.

- Never exceed the recommended dosage.

- Discontinue use if you notice any negative side effects.

- Store products in a cool, dry place out of the reach of children.

- Do not use commercial products after one year from the date of purchase.

for 5–6 minutes, then strain into a teacup and drink up to 3 cups a day. This natural remedy has been shown in tests to have anti-inflammatory properties that fight UTIs; it is also a traditional remedy for cystitis and inflammation of the urethra and prostate.

✳ We love lovage
To ease the discomfort associated with a mild inflammation of the urinary tract, make lovage tea by pouring 240ml boiling water over 1 teaspoon crushed dried lovage root, which is a member of the carrot family but tastes more like celery. Steep for 10 minutes, then strain and drink. Caution: Do not use if you have a history of chronic kidney problems.

✳ Drink to the health of your kidneys
Making sure you drink one or two 240ml glasses of fruit juice (especially cranberry juice, fresh lemonade or orange juice) a day will help the overall health of your kidneys. The ascorbic and citric acids in the fruit juices acidify the urine and have an antiseptic effect on the kidneys. Don't drink too much – a good rule to follow in any case, but especially when ingesting anything acidic. Do not drink cranberry juice if you are taking warfarin or other anticoagulants.

✳ Praise the weed and pass the teapot!
The dandelion isn't just any old weed: it has at least two benefits for the kidneys. First, dandelion increases urine flow and reduces fluid retention resulting from kidney disorders. Second, dandelion may be able to speed the passing of a small kidney stone. If you feel the pain that signals movement of a stone, drink as much dandelion tea as you can. A strong diuretic, dandelion stimulates blood circulation through the kidneys, increasing urine output and helping to flush out the stone. Dandelion tea bags are available, but you can also make your own. Wash dandelion leaves and roots thoroughly and then chop finely. Add 3 tablespoons to 480ml water, boil for 3 minutes and let it sit for 10–12 minutes before straining.

Dandelion tea may hasten the passing of kidney stones!

Caring for your feet

❋ Beat athlete's foot

To put athlete's foot on the run, make a footbath with 1 tablespoon salt dissolved in 6 litres warm water. Soak the affected foot for 10 minutes to help to kill the fungus. To make the solution even more strongly antifungal, add 1–2 tablespoons tea tree oil.

❋ Fight toenail fungus

If you think you can't control a fungus without prescription drugs, think again – in the short term, at least. Mix equal parts warm water, vinegar (white or cider) and mouthwash, with a tablespoon of powdered cinnamon. Soak, dry feet and then sprinkle with cornflour. There's no guarantee that the fungus won't return, but you can keep it in check without expensive drugs.

❋ Beat stinky feet with tea

Strong black tea will not only kill the bacteria that cause odours but will close pores and help to keep your feet less sweaty. Simmer 3 black tea bags in 240ml water for 15 minutes, then dilute the tea with 2 litres water. Once it has cooled, pour the tea into a plastic tub and soak your ripe lower limbs for around 30 minutes. It should put an end to smelly feet.

❋ A salty cure for sore feet

While Epsom salt – named for the Surrey town where its efficacious waters were found – has long been used to soothe dry, sore feet, ordinary table salt will also do. Pour 8 litres warm water into a plastic tub, add 200g table salt and stir with your hand to dissolve. Soak your feet in the solution for at least 20 minutes, then rub them vigorously with a towel to slough off any dead skin cells.

idea

AN ODOUR EATER FROM THE KITCHEN CUPBOARD

Take shoes (warm and airless), sweat (secreted by the glands on the soles of your feet), and poor hygiene (neglecting to scrub your feet when you shower) and you have a recipe for smelly feet. Whether your stockinged feet are only mildly odoriferous or bad enough to fell a crowd at 40 paces, turn to the kitchen cupboard to help to control the odour.

Use bicarbonate of soda and cornflour. Mix the powders 50:50 and sprinkle the mixture on your feet before you put on your socks. Bicarbonate of soda helps to neutralise the skin acids that harbour bacteria that cause odours, while cornflour absorbs sweat. Sprinkling some of the powder into your shoes will also help to neutralise smells.

❋ A trick for tired feet

If your feet are tired and aching, scatter a few pencils onto the floor and then pick them up ... with your toes. This little workout will rejuvenate and invigorate your feet as much as a quick foot massage.

❋ Cool hot feet with peppermint

Chill down hot feet by soaking them in iced peppermint tea for 10 minutes. Once they are pepped up, they should be ready to take you on a 3 mile jog or an hour long power walk.

Healing cuts, bruises and other skin problems

✽ Treat a cut with garlic

To treat a cut or abrasion, gently wash the wound with soapy, warm water and pat it dry with a clean, soft cloth. Then bruise a peeled clove of garlic and press it against the cut for 5–10 minutes, securing it with a bandage if you like. Garlic contains allicin, which has been shown to inhibit the growth of several kinds of bacteria and protect against infection. (Caution: Fresh garlic is an irritant, so never leave garlic in any form – infused, minced or whole – on the skin for more than 20 minutes at a time. Remove it immediately if it irritates the skin.)

✽ Black pepper stops bleeding

Shaking a good amount of black pepper onto a bleeding cut will stop the blood flow swiftly. It works because the pepper constricts the blood vessels. Many people who have tried this remedy also claim that a wound treated with black pepper heals with less scarring.

✽ Reduce bruising with an onion

If you have just bumped your arm, leg or knee (or other body part) and you're worried about bruising, immediately press the cut end of a raw onion onto the bruised area and keep it in place for 15 minutes. The allicin in onions (the compound that makes your eyes water) helps to stimulate the lymphatic flow in the body, helping to flush away excess blood in the just-injured tissue that creates the discoloration we call a bruise. Caution: only use onion on intact skin, not if the skin is broken.

idea

GET ALOE STRAIGHT FROM THE LEAF

Commercial aloe vera lotions and creams are widely available, but an aloe treatment is yours for free if you have access to an aloe vera plant. Better still, fresh gel is generally more effective than shop-bought lotions, which often contain more non-aloe emollients than aloe.

To get the real stuff, go straight to the leaf itself. Aloe vera plants will keep well indoors, in a cool, sunny spot.

1. Cut off a 7cm section of fleshy aloe leaf, slice open the inner portion and scrape out the mucilaginous gel with a spoon, stopping short of the rind.

2. Apply the gel to the skin two or three times a day, washing the skin between applications to make it more receptive to glucomannan and aloe's other anti-inflammatory substances.

Be careful not to get aloe gel on your clothes, as it can leave a yellow stain.

Kill bacteria on a cut finger with garlic!

✳ Soothe sunburn with green tea

Just add 3 green tea bags to 1 litre just-boiled water, remove the pan from the heat and let it steep for 2–3 hours. Use a cotton wool ball or a very soft cloth to dab the sunburned area with the cooled tea and allow the cooling tannins to do their work.

✳ Conquer lice with alder bark

To get rid of lice, simmer 2 tablespoons chipped alder bark in 2 litres white vinegar, then let it cool before straining into a container with a lid. Using a cotton wool ball, apply to the scalp or other affected areas four times daily. Caution: Do not ingest the mixture and be aware that alder bark may temporarily colour the skin.

✳ Camomile salve

Melt 120ml petroleum jelly in a double boiler and stir in 1 tablespoon camomile flowers. Heat for 2 hours or until the flowers are crisp. Tightly fit a jam strainer on top of a glass jar and squeeze the hot mixture through. Once the salve cools, apply to a mild skin rash up to four times a day. For best results, choose the more efficacious German camomile (*Matricaria recutita*) over Roman or English, camomile (*Chamaemelum nobile*).

✳ Double-duty paste for bee stings

A bicarbonate of soda–vinegar paste applied to a bee sting immediately after you remove the sting will get both alkaline and acidic action going (use 2 parts bicarbonate of soda to 1 part vinegar) and reduce the pain. When the paste dries, wipe off with a clean, damp cloth.

✱ Oatmeal and tights to cure a case of hives

Cut the leg of a pair of tights off at the knee and put these four ingredients into the foot: 50g rolled oats; 60g dry powdered milk and 12g each dried camomile flowers and lavender. Knot the nylon bag closed and hold it under warm (not hot) running water as you fill your bath. Submerge the bag and let the water cool. (Hot water makes hives worse, not better). Soak for half an hour and every 5 minutes or so, hold the bag over the rash and squeeze to release the soothing stuff inside.

✱ Witch hazel for skin rashes

The bark and leaves of the witch hazel plant contain high proportions of naturally astringent tannins and an aromatic oil – the perfect recipe for soothing itchy skin rashes.

✱ Spot buster pastes

Applied to spots and pimples, these quick and easy homemade pastes will make blemishes disappear quickly. Try these three.

- **Bicarbonate of soda** Moisten ¼ teaspoon bicarbonate of soda with a few drops water and dab it onto spots. Leave for 5 minutes, then wipe off with a facecloth dipped in cool water.
- **Oatmeal** Use some of your morning porridge as a scourge for spots. Dab the cooked, cooled porridge onto blemished skin, cover with a warm-water facecloth compress and let it sit for 15 minutes. Repeat daily until the spots are gone.
- **Cornflour and lemon juice** Make a paste with 1 teaspoon cornflour and 1 teaspoon lemon juice. Apply to spots and let it sit for 4–5 minutes before gently washing your face with cool water.

idea
WITCH HAZEL FROM YOUR GARDEN

If you have a witch hazel bush *(Hamamelis virginiana)* in your garden and it is at least 1m tall, you can prepare your own witch hazel astringent for treating skin irritations, cuts and scrapes. Going the homemade route has two advantages: it allows you to be more self sufficient and, more importantly, your homemade astringent will be more effective than witch hazel products that have undergone steam distillation and lost most of their tannins.

Because the leaves have to dry, it takes about a week to make witch hazel. Snip leaves at the stem base and rinse them well. To harvest bark, lop off a branch and scrape off the bark. Place the leaves and bark on paper towel–lined trays and store them in a dark place at 21–36°C for seven days.

While witch hazel can be prepared in a number of ways, the easiest is to use a blender. Blend the dried plant matter for 1–2 minutes, then combine it with water (1 tablespoon plant matter to 240ml water). Pour into a saucepan, bring to a boil and simmer for 20 minutes. Remove from heat and let steep for 2 hours. Strain through cheesecloth or a fine sieve into sterilised jars and use as needed.

✱ Sunscreen and spot buster

The white zinc oxide cream that cricketers spread over their noses as a sunscreen is also an effective acne fighter. Dab on a little zinc oxide cream before bed and it will not only help to dry up pimples but is also said to prevent scarring.

✱ Wards off vampires, too!

Rubbing a freshly cut clove of raw garlic on to a pimple will help to dry it up and make it disappear. Just treat pimples straight before bed, as garlic doesn't have to be on your breath to make those around you wrinkle their noses.

✱ A kitchen-cupboard eczema salve

A white creamy substance good for soothing eczema comes not from the medicine cabinet but the fridge: vegetable margarine. Coat the affected area with margarine, cover with cling film and secure the film with surgical tape. Leave it on for 2–4 hours at a time, if possible, repeating daily until the rash calms down.

✱ Two ways to stop shingles from itching

Shingles or herpes zoster, is caused by the varicella-zoster virus – the same virus that causes chicken pox. (It isn't as contagious as chicken pox but can be passed on to anyone who's susceptible.) The rash consists of small, crusting blisters that itch terribly and both of these home remedies can bring relief:

- **Aloe gel** Apply gel to affected area to calm the itch.
- **Nail polish remover and aspirin** Pour 3 tablespoons nail polish remover into a small cup, add two crushed aspirin and stir until the aspirin dissolves. Use a cotton wool ball to apply the solution to shingles blisters and let it air-dry to give hours of relief.

✱ Cure warts with a 'garlic press'

Slice a freshly peeled garlic clove, place it on the wart and bind it with a gauze bandage. Leave the garlic in place as long you're able to and repeat the process morning and night. Because of its general antiviral activity, it has been claimed that garlic can cure warts even when other methods have failed.

✱ Rosewater for chapped skin

To make a lotion for chapped skin (and a fragrant one, at that) mix 120ml rosewater with 60ml glycerine and rub it into the skin as needed. This essential cupboard companion is as popular as ever in Asia and the Middle East, where it is used both to flavour food and in rituals. Find it in pharmacies and health-food stores.

tip ALOE FOR BLISTERS

Get a blister to heal more quickly by rubbing it with gel from an **aloe vera** leaf. Slice open a leaf and use a spoon to scrape out the gel (see 'Aloe Straight from the Leaf', page 171). Dab it on the blister, cover with a bandage, then reapply and re-bandage once a day.

✱ T(r)opical wart remover

Make several shallow cuts in an unripe green papaya and collect the sap that it releases. When it congeals, mix it with water to make a thin paste. Before applying the paste, protect the skin surrounding the wart by swabbing on a thin layer of petroleum jelly (papain, the enzyme in papaya, is an irritant so powerful that it's an ingredient in meat tenderisers). Using a cotton bud, carefully apply the paste to a wart morning and night until it breaks down and disappears. Papain breaks down proteins in dead tissue, making it a wart remover of long standing.

✱ Turmeric for treating ringworm

If you have a bottle of the Indian spice turmeric in your kitchen cabinet, you have an antiviral powder that has been used in Asia as a ringworm remedy for centuries. In a small bowl, mix enough of the powdered root to make a paste. Apply the paste to the affected area with a cotton bud, cover it with a bandage and leave it on for 20–60 minutes. Repeat three or four times a day. Caution: Turmeric may irritate sensitive skin, so test it first on clear skin; if redness develops, try another treatment.

✱ Seal in moisture with margarine

Dry skin and rashes will both benefit from a soak with a wet facecloth for several minutes, then a gentle rubdown with a bit of margarine. Cover the affected area and leave it on for 1–2 hours. Wipe the margarine off with a clean soft cloth and repeat the treatment as needed.

idea

1,001 WAYS TO REMOVE WARTS

We're not promising to run down all of the folk remedies tried over the ages to remove warts, since that would be one of those lists that stretches all the way around the equator. Untold numbers of methods have been recorded. People washed warts in rainwater pooled in tree stumps. They pressed raw potatoes, banana peel and any number of saps and oils on warts. They also believed in the Theory of Transference – the notion that an ailment could be transferred from the patient to a tree, animal or object. Blood was drawn from a wart, placed on a grain of corn and fed to a chicken. Warts could also be 'sold' to a folk healer called a wart charmer.

Surprising as it is, many of the most far-fetched wart remedies have been documented as being successful. Some medical researchers now believe that the body may be able to rid itself of warts through the power of hypnotic suggestion. One doctor who had had no success in treating a man with a case of multiple warts put the patient in an X-ray room and told him he was going to zap him with radiation. In fact, the doctor ran the X-ray machine without delivering any rays – but the man's warts fell off the next day.

Aiding sleeplessness and anxiety

✳ A tryptophan snack before bed

Serotonin is a brain chemical that helps you sleep and tryptophan is an amino acid the body uses to make serotonin. Two tryptophan-rich foods are turkey and bananas, and eating a little of either of these before bed could help you to have sweeter dreams.

✳ Drink passionflower tea

Despite its name, passionflower won't make your honeymoon memorable. In fact, it will put you to sleep. Infuse 3 passionflower tea bags in 720ml just-boiled water for 30–60 minutes and sip a cup half an hour before going to bed. (The 'passion' in the name of the flower refers to the Crucifixion of Christ, not lust.) Alkaloids in the flower can help to allay both insomnia and anxiety, conditions that often go hand in hand. Caution: talk to your doctor before using passionflower as it may interact with certain drugs, especially anticoagulants.

✳ Calming Epsom salts bath

To calm yourself, pour 450g Epsom salts into a warm bath and soak to your heart's content. Epsom salts (magnesium sulphate) cleans and tones skin but also may lower blood pressure.

✳ Make a hops pillow

Take a cushion cover with a zip and stuff it full of dried hops (available at herbal stores, online and perhaps at the local brewery). If you like, throw in a handful of dried lavender, also a sedative herb, to sweeten the smell. When you retire for the night, put the pillow near enough to you head that you will be able to breathe in the aroma. To keep the hops active, you will need to dampen them with grain alcohol every three or four weeks.

✳ Try St John's wort as a mood booster

A cup of St John's wort tea can safely be drunk up to three times a day to allay mild depression, nervousness and insomnia; capsules and liquid extracts are also available. The herb is Germany's leading antidepressant, outselling even Prozac. Studies show that hypericin and other compounds in St John's wort act together to prevent the enzyme monoamine oxidase (MAO) from breaking down serotonin, dopamine and other amines that elevate mood and emotions. St John's wort interacts with various drugs, so always check with your doctor before use. Caution: certain people who have used the herb have experienced delayed photosensitivity – an abnormal reaction to sunlight that usually results in a skin rash.

✳ Stop snoring with a can

If your bed mate's snoring is cutting into your sleeping time, put a small can of tomato paste in the pocket of a cotton T-shirt and secure it closed with a safety pin. Get the snorer to put the shirt on backward before going to sleep and it should stop him (or her) from rolling over into the prime snoring position – on the back.

✳ Give yourself a soak

There's a good reason why some parents give their babies warm baths before bedtime or a nap: warm water is a natural relaxant. So fill the bath, turn the lights down low, soak for a few minutes and crawl into a freshly made bed for some superlative sleep.

✳ Pre-sleep sip

Camomile, which is known to have sedating qualities, is an ideal sleep inducer. If you can get good-quality tea bags, they will work perfectly; if you can grow fresh camomile in a small pot on a windowsill, all the better. Snip them about 2cm below the flower, tie a few of them together with kitchen string and steep them in a mug of hot water for a delicious calming drink.

✳ White noise as sleep therapy

A number of studies have shown that white noise – defined as noise that combines sounds of all different frequencies so that they virtually cancel each other out – is an effective, completely non-narcotic, safe and peaceful sleep aid. Where can you get it? You can buy white noise machines or even less expensively, CDs and tapes. Load them into a CD player in the bedroom, turn the lights down, climb into bed and remember to set the alarm.

✳ Keep your cool!

The term 'warm and cosy' doesn't always translate to the right conditions for falling asleep; so resist the urge to keep the heat up and instead, lower your bedroom thermostat to around 18°C and if possible, open the window a little for good ventilation. Most sleep experts maintain that bedroom temperatures that are slightly cooler than living areas result in a sounder, better snooze.

household superstar

8 SOOTHING WAYS WITH PETROLEUM JELLY

While petroleum jelly is usually thought of as a moisturiser, it was originally developed as a salve to heal and protect cuts and abrasions.

1 Prevent chafing of skin subjected to a backpack's straps and upper thighs clothed in denim by rubbing petroleum jelly onto the vulnerable areas.

2 Rub petroleum jelly onto dry, scaly patches of psoriasis to lubricate them and reduce itching.

3 To keep a crusted cold sore from bleeding, coat it with petroleum jelly applied with a cotton bud, not your fingers.

4 Spread a thick layer of petroleum jelly onto an infested scalp and when you wipe it off, the lice should go with it.

5 Dab a haemorrhoid with petroleum jelly, which is contained in many over-the-counter haemorrhoid treatments.

6 A layer of petroleum jelly dabbed on a small wound will keep moisture in and bacteria out.

7 Dab petroleum jelly under your nose to trap pollen spores that may be making their way towards your nostrils.

8 Rub petroleum jelly on the insides of your nostrils to moisten the mucous membranes and make nosebleeds less likely.

Caring for your baby

✳ Nappy rash soothers

Prolonged contact of a baby's skin with urine and faeces causes nappy rash, especially when nappy changes are delayed – so the best treatment for nappy rash is to leave the nappy off for as long as possible. Soap can irritate the skin even more and so can wipes that contain alcohol – though most commercial baby wipes are alcohol-free. Here are three cost-free nappy rash soothers you're likely to have at home:

● **'Toasted' cornflour** Although moisture-absorbing cornflour can be used straight from the box, it works better when dried in the oven. Just spread it on a baking sheet and dry it in a very low oven for 10 minutes. Let cool before using.

● **Honey** The sugar in honey absorbs water, denying the bacteria that cause infection the moisture they need to survive. Ask your doctor before using honey on children under 12 months of age; don't give it to your child to eat – if ingested, honey can cause botulism.

● **Petroleum jelly** Wiping petroleum jelly on the rash gives your baby's skin a protective coating so that the rash can heal.

✳ A spicy baby powder substitute

The spice fenugreek has been shown to soothe nappy rash. Apply directly to the skin, like baby powder or mix it with a little water to form a paste to apply sparingly to irritated areas.

✳ Prevent nappy rash with salt and zinc

Stir 1 tablespoon salt into 1 litre boiling water and let the solution cool to room temperature. Wipe it onto your baby's bottom, then gently dab it dry. Then apply a zinc oxide lotion to create a barrier against further wetness.

✳ The easiest rash preventive of all

The less time a baby's bottom is covered by a nappy, the less she risks suffering nappy rash. At nap time, just place an unfastened nappy under your child or put the baby on towels placed over a waterproof sheet.

✳ A rash remedy from the garden

Calendula, a cousin of marigolds, has long been used to treat skin rashes, so keep a homemade wash in the nursery to soothe your baby's skin. Cut the flower heads from a calendula plant and let them dry. Pick the petals off over a bowl and put 1 heaping tablespoon petals into a bowl. Pour 720ml just-boiled water over the petals, let steep for 1 hour, then strain into a bottle. Apply to the baby's bottom or other red or itchy areas up to four times a day.

✱ Camomile for congestion?

If your baby is 6 months or older, try easing her congestion with weak camomile tea – weak meaning 1 chamomile tea bag steeped in 480ml hot water for no more than 3 minutes. Put the lukewarm tea in her baby bottle and let her sip on it two or three times a day. Check with your doctor first; camomile can trigger allergic reactions in some people.

✱ Soothe heat rash with a bicarbonate of soda bath

Heat rash can make babies miserable. Here's a way to help to 'take the red out': add bicarbonate of soda to your baby's lukewarm bathwater – 2 teaspoons to each 8 litres water. Then let your baby air-dry instead of wiping him with a towel. Or gently press the rash with a cool, wet facecloth several times a day.

✱ Soothing a sore throat

If your baby is old enough to be eating solids, warm drinks like tea or broth can be soothing to a sore throat. But don't add honey to the tea as honey may contain spores that could grow in the baby's immature digestive tract. Cool apple juice is another effective sore throat soother for a baby or small child.

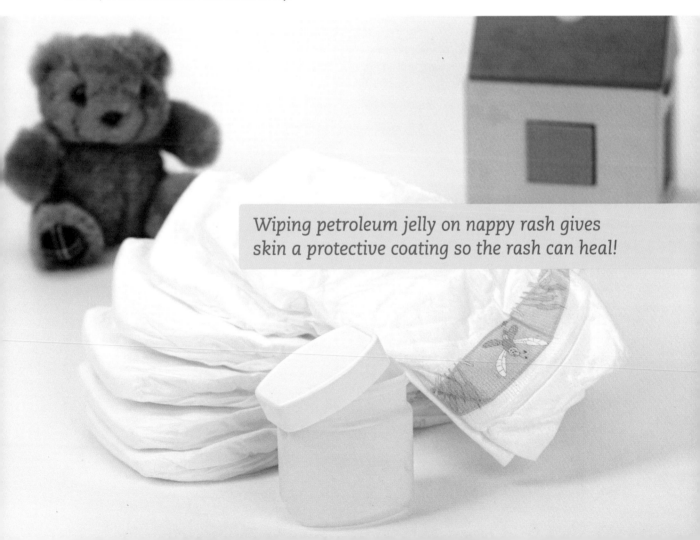

Wiping petroleum jelly on nappy rash gives skin a protective coating so the rash can heal!

Remedies from the folk doctor's medicine bag

✱ Homemade hydration aid

Sports drinks are full of electrolytes – the salts that need replenishing after the body sweats – and are very helpful for keeping athletes and runners hydrated. You can make your own for next to nothing. Dissolve 1 teaspoon salt and 4 teaspoons sugar in 1 litre water to make a drink that isn't coloured or adorned with a fancy label but that will nonetheless maintain your electrolyte balance and keep you hydrated.

✱ Milk thistle for liver health

Our forebears used the weed milk thistle to 'clean the liver' and they were on to something. Silymarin, contained in the seeds, prevents toxins from penetrating the liver and stimulates the regeneration of liver cells – the reason milk thistle has been used in the treatment of hepatitis, cirrhosis and jaundice.

If you think you can just harvest milk thistle weed and use the seeds to make a therapeutic tea, it's not the case. Teas are ineffective because the active principles in milk thistle seeds aren't water-soluble. Instead, try milk thistle capsules and liquid extracts, making sure they contain 200–400mg silymarin.

✱ Peanut butter for hiccups

Believe it or not, peanut butter may be able to sort an annoying case of hiccups. It's not the peanut butter per se that works but what it takes to swallow it. Eat 1 heaped teaspoon of peanut butter (plain or crunchy) and take some time to swallow it. As you chew and use your tongue to clean it off the roof of your mouth and your teeth, your breathing patterns will be interrupted and may stop hiccups.

curiosity corner

'LIKE THINGS FOR LIKE THINGS'

Since the Middle Ages, one of the 'laws' of folk medicine was based on the principle *similia similibus* – 'like things for like things'. When it came to medicinal plants, those whose characteristics match the body's organs were believed to have a curative effect, a belief that in time came to be called the Doctrine of Signatures and that eventually was proved utterly false.

As late as the nineteenth century, liverwort (*Hepatica* ssp.) – so named because its leaves are the shape of the liver – was used to treat liver ailments. Plants with red sap were applied to bleeding wounds and the fuzzy burrs of the burdock plant were said to cure baldness. The Doctrine of Signatures was rooted in the belief of an inherent affinity or sympathy, between living things and the forces of the universe – and for this reason it was often referred to as 'sympathetic magic'.

✱ Oil and vinegar remedies

Take some oil and vinegar from the kitchen cabinet when you need a quick remedy. You can do a lot more than dress a salad with these staples.

- Vinegar takes the pain out of a bee or jellyfish sting. Scrape the stinger off with a credit card and then pour undiluted vinegar directly on the sting.
- White vinegar dries up a cold sore when rubbed on the sore three to four times a day.
- White and cider vinegar take the burn out of sunburn. They also take the itch out of poison ivy rashes and insect bites.
- Olive oil can stand-in for shaving cream.
- Soaking in a bath to which you've added 120ml olive oil and 360g bicarbonate of soda will stop skin from itching and will soften it as well.
- Add 2–3 drops warm (not hot) olive oil to the ear to soften earwax. Drain your ear after 5 minutes. Caution: Never do this if you may have a perforated eardrum.

✱ Fight herpes with lemon balm tea

The volatile oil in lemon balm contains two substances that fight herpes simplex type 1 virus (HSV1), which usually affects the lips, mouth and face and HSV2 or genital herpes – the reason that the herb is widely used in European over-the-counter herpes products. To make an infusion, pour 240ml just-boiled water over 2–3 teaspoons finely chopped lemon balm and let it steep for 10–12 minutes before straining into a jar. Soak a cotton wool ball in the solution and apply it to herpes blisters several times a day.

✱ Remove splinters with an onion

Here's a pain-free (if rather smelly) way to get a splinter out of a finger or foot. Place a 0.5cm slice of onion over the splinter and wrap a bandage around the affected area to keep the onion in place. Leave the onion poultice on overnight and by morning the skin should have shrunk and allowed the splinter to work itself out.

✱ Cider vinegar tea for fatigue

Vinegar perks up a recipe and it may perk you up, too. Every morning before breakfast, whisk together 240ml warm water, 2 tablespoons apple cider vinegar and 1 teaspoon honey. Sip the tea slowly until you've downed the last drop and within a week you may find yourself feeling more energised.

✱ Treat thrush with goldenseal

Thrush or candidiasis – an infection of the mucous membranes of the mouth, vagina or digestive tract – shows up in a whitish, 'furry' tongue or a white discharge. The dried root of goldenseal (*Hydrastis canadensis*) has a long history as a thrush treatment and clinical trials have confirmed its efficacy. To treat thrush, make goldenseal tea by pouring 240ml boiling water over 2 teaspoons powdered root; steep for 5–10 minutes. Let it cool before using as a gargle or douche or drink as a hot tea. Caution: do not take goldenseal internally if you are a pregnant woman or have high blood pressure.

Keep a straw
hat looking
sharp with
hairspray!

7 Looking your best

Fashion and grooming slip ups affect all women – and usually at the worst possible time: a snagged, laddered pair of tights, a broken heel, smudged make-up. For men it might be a tomato sauce stain on a shirt front, no shaving foam and a grey ring around the collar. And both sexes can be affected by bad hair days, broken zips and clothes as creased as the face of Methuselah (who supposedly died at the age of 969). What should you do?

Just flip through the next 23 pages where you will find more than a hundred creative solutions to the often infuriating grooming and clothing problems that plague us all, using items you probably already have. Here, you'll learn how to recycle old garments and make them look brand new; make very cool jewellery from old-fashioned typewriter keys; whip up homemade skin treatments that will leave you glowing; revitalise your hair with beer and avocados; and even remove lipstick smears with a piece of bread. What's more, making your own grooming products is simple, environmentally friendly and inexpensive. If our ancestors did it, there's no reason why we can't.

Home help for your skin

✳ Tape out a furrowed brow

Is a furrow in your brow starting to become your own small Grand Canyon? Smooth it out by putting a piece of tape on your brow overnight, every night for a month. Before going to sleep, rub moisturiser on the crease and wipe off any excess. Now smooth the furrow with your fingers, hold it taut and secure a piece of tape across the spot. Some people recommend surgical tape, while others make do with any sticky tape. (Just make sure it extends beyond the moisturised area or it may not stay on through the night.) Taping works by retraining the face muscles to relax – and, unlike Botox or plastic surgery, costs only pennies.

✳ Look younger (and sweeter!)

Discourage wrinkles by applying a facial mask made of honey once a week, like Cleopatra did. Honey has properties that soften and hydrate skin and help it to retain moisture, as well as antioxidants and various compounds that can soothe irritations and inflammations. To make a honey mask, warm the honey. While it's heating, press a warm facecloth to your face to open the pores. Carefully spread the honey around the face, keeping it away from your eyes. Relax for 15 minutes and then rinse the mask off, using cold water in the final rinse to close the pores. Although your skin may not look like a baby's, it should feel almost as soft.

✳ Soak in a hot tea bath

If a cup of tea in the afternoon is a calming break, a hot green tea bath in the evening after a tough day can be a little touch of heaven. Place 2 tablespoons dried green tea leaves in the toe of an old nylon stocking, then bunch it up and close with a twist tie. Put the bundle into a hot bath or tie it with string over the tap opening so that the water will run through. While you're enjoying the hot soak, the antioxidants in the tea will go to work, smoothing, soothing and calming you both outside and in.

✳ Chocolate body wrap

Do you love chocolate so much that you could bathe in it? Here's your chance. Just warm 120ml honey in a microwave or the top of a double boiler. Then stir in 150g unsweetened cocoa until it dissolves. If the mixture cools, reheat it, but don't let it get hot. Now spread

tip TURN A SOCK INTO A WASHCLOTH

If you have lots of **lonely sports socks,** you're not the only one. At bath time, simply turn a single sock inside out (terry cloth on the outside), fit it over your hand like a mitten and use it as an exfoliating scrubber.

curiosity corner

SKIN-SATIONAL FACTS

The skin is the body's largest organ. It grows faster than any other organ and continually replenishes itself. It's waterproof, flexible, generates all the hairs on the body and can repair itself. And if you think that's amazing, read on.

- The average-size person's skin weighs about 4kg or about 16 per cent of total body weight.

- An average-size person's skin would cover an area of about 1.6 to 2m² if laid out.

- Your skin has approximately 72km of nerves and more nerve endings than any other part of the body.

- The entire top layer of dead skin cells sloughs off and is replaced every month, yet we barely notice it.

- In an average lifetime, about 18kg of dead skin cells are shed and replaced.

- In 6cm² of skin there are 65 hairs, 100 oil glands, 650 sweat glands, 1,500 nerve receptors and countless blood vessels.

- There are 5 million hairs on the body, with only 100,000 growing on the scalp.

the mudlike paste evenly over your body. Now comes the good bit: wrap your legs, arms and torso in cling film to seal in the paste and sit tight (or lie down) for 20 minutes. When you have finished, peel off the wrap and wash away the paste in a warm shower or bath. Your skin should feel silky smooth, thanks to the hydrating and revitalising antioxidants in cocoa and honey. And all without a single calorie!

✱ Indigestion tablet facial

It's strange but true: many indigestion medicines that contain salicylic acid, such as Pepto-Bismol, are beneficial to the skin. It's because salicylic acid helps to slough off the top layer of dead skin cells and bring new healthy skin cells to the surface. Squash a few cotton wool balls together in your fingers, pour on some of the medicine and apply it to your face, taking care to avoid the eyes. Let it dry for about 15 minutes, then rinse and pat dry. Your skin will not only stomach this facial but will thank you for it.

✱ Condition your legs

For a smooth leg shave without shaving cream or gel, substitute hair conditioner or an all-in-one shampoo-conditioner, both of which contain ingredients that soften, smooth and moisturise hair. They will do the same for hair and skin on your legs, underarms and, for men, the face.

✱ A summertime citrus body splash

Squeeze the juice from a lime, filter out the pulp and pour the juice into a spray bottle. Add 120ml surgical spirit and 3 teaspoons lemon or orange extract. Screw the lid on the bottle and shake well. Spritz it on for a great way to cool down in summer. Caution: store the spray in the refrigerator with an identification label so no one will think it's safe to drink.

✱ Prolong the scent

Make perfume last for hours by first dabbing a tiny bit of petroleum jelly on your wrists, neck, ear lobes and anywhere else that you usually apply a drop of the fragrance.

Delicious natural skin scrubs

Facials, masks, scrubs and other methods speed the process of shedding dead skin cells, known as exfoliation. Sloughing off dead cells exposes cleaner, smoother cells that lie just beneath the skin's surface. Exfoliating also stimulates circulation, bringing a healthy glow to skin. There are lots of products available that exfoliate and stimulate skin renewal while salons and spas charge a good bit of money for one session. Save money by sloughing off skin using items from your cupboards and fridge. Gently massage the exfoliants shown here into the skin, using circular motions. (When applying an exfoliating facial or mask, avoid the area around the eyes.) After rinsing and patting skin dry, apply some moisturiser and you'll feel renewed.

1
Strawberry scrub
Mash 5 or 6 strawberries, then mix in 1 tablespoon ground almonds and enough yoghurt (about 2 tablespoons) for the mixture to be thick enough to apply.

2
Oatmeal ouster
Blend together 2 heaped teaspoons finely ground uncooked porridge oats with 1 teaspoon bicarbonate of soda. Stir in water slowly until you have made a spreadable paste.

3
Ginger snapper
Blend together equal amounts of freshly crushed ginger and brown sugar, then add vanilla extract or sweet almond oil to make an energising body scrub. Ginger contains valuable antioxidants and is known to stimulate circulation.

Keeping eyes bright

✶ Tighten up tired eyes

Many models and performers have long held the secret to reducing puffiness and wrinkles no matter how late they were up the night before and it's not an expensive eye cream. It is in fact haemorrhoid cream, which tightens puffy areas and wrinkles. If the smell of the cream is too strong, mix a little moisturiser into it before applying. And be careful not to get any of the cream into your eyes; after all, it's designed to be used elsewhere.

✶ A spoonful of energy

The next time your eyes need a pep-up, take two metal teaspoons from the kitchen drawer and hold them under very cold running water for a few minutes. Then lie down and place the bowls of the spoons over your eyelids for 30–60 seconds. The sharp cold of the metal will revive tired eyes and may boost your energy level at the same time.

✶ Teething ring eye booster

If the baby has been crying all night, leaving you with tired eyes, don't worry. While he has a nap, put two of his teething rings into the freezer until they're ice cold, stretch out on the sofa and place the rings on your closed eyelids for about 10 minutes. The cold will not only reduce puffiness but you'll feel invigorated as well.

✶ Lighten dark circles

For many people, tiredness causes dark circles under the eyes – 'panda eyes' that can add years to the appearance of men and women alike. If you can't catch up on your rest, place slices of ripe avocado under each eye or apply a paste of

ground almonds and milk to help to lighten the dark shadows.

✶ Cool as a cucumber

When your eyes are all red and puffy from late nights or overwork, cut a couple of slices of cold cucumber, lie down and put a slice over each eye for 30 minutes. When you get up, your eyes will be brighter and your body refreshed.

✶ De-puff with tea

Tea – which contains natural tannins – is a mild diuretic and has long been used by grandmothers and catwalk models alike to reduce eye puffiness. Soak two tea bags in warm water and then chill the bags for a few minutes in the fridge. Place one tea bag on each eye and leave it for 5 minutes. When you remove the bag, your eyes will feel as fresh as a daisy.

Make-up miracles

✻ Firming up melted lipstick

If your bag has been sitting in the sun for too long and you find that the heat has softened up your lipstick, simply pop it into the fridge for a fast 5 minute fix.

✻ Emergency lip colour

Perhaps you can't decide whether a new dress you're trying on flatters your face but without extra colour on your lips it's even harder to tell. So you look in your handbag only to discover that you've left both your lipstick and lip pencil at home. If you have a brown eyeliner pencil, use it on your lips instead. You may find that it looks fantastic.

✻ A cheesy solution

Have you run out of cottonwool balls and make up remover pads and don't like to use tissues because of the residue they leave on your skin? Cut a few squares of washed cheesecloth for wiping off make-up. It's soft, porous and absorbent. Use a bigger swatch as a covering for sloppy facials so that they don't drip onto the floor or yourself; pat the cloth very gently over the mixture, just until it adheres.

idea

SORT SCENT OVERLOAD

Have you ever accidentally doused yourself with just a little too much cologne?

If soap and water won't correct the problem, go to the cupboard and take out a bottle of vodka. Dab a little onto the places where you applied the cologne or perfume and the nearly odourless spirit should quickly knock out the excess scent.

✻ No eye shadow applicator?

Use a cotton bud instead: it's softer, the tip can be used to smudge and soften eye liner and you can throw it away when you have finished.

✻ Make-up mistakes

If you go overboard with the mascara or sustain a smudge elsewhere during your make-up application, just wipe off the slip-up with a cotton bud dipped in petroleum jelly. Then start over again but using a lighter hand.

tip HOMEMADE LIP GLOSS

To make your own lip gloss, scoop the last bit of lipstick from the tube and blend it with a little **petroleum jelly.** Put the mix into an empty lip gloss pot and it's ready to use. For a firmer gloss, refrigerate the mixture for an hour.

Hair care solutions

✱ Instant dry shampoo

If you've no time to wash your hair or are caring for someone who can't get into a shower or bath, a dry shampoo will do the job. Take 1 tablespoon of cornflour and sprinkle the powder into the hair; massage it in section by section and comb out any tangles. Brush well to remove all the powder, stopping often to shake out the brush. The powder absorbs dirt and excess oil, leaving hair looking clean and shiny.

✱ Two-ingredient revitalising conditioner

Give drab hair new life with this luscious conditioner – made with only two ingredients. Take half of a ripe avocado, scoop out the fruit and mash until smooth. Slowly stir in 60ml coconut milk; the mixture should look like a thick gel, so add more milk as needed. Work all of the mixture into your hair, then comb smooth. Wait 10–15 minutes before rinsing thoroughly. Your hair should feel thicker and look richer. (For an extra treat, use the other half of the avocado to whip up a little guacamole.)

✱ Gloss up with vinegar

Your hair has lost its lustre, so you've switched shampoos which helped for a while, but now your hair looks dull again. It's due to a build-up of the residue left by shampoo and other products. Vinegar will safely remove the residue and restore your hair's natural acidic pH balance, leaving it shinier, smoother and easier to manage. Just mix 2–3 tablespoons apple cider vinegar with 1–2 cups of water in a jar. Then shampoo your hair as usual and rinse. Shake the vinegar solution and use it as a final rinse. Any vinegar smell will disappear as soon as your hair dries.

✱ A hair mousse alternative

You've shaken the can of mousse and turned it upside down, but not a drop comes out. Don't panic. Try a little shaving cream mixed with a drop of surgical spirit to keep your hair in place and moisturise it at the same time.

tip SUPER (BOWL) HAIR

If you have some **beer** left over from a weekend party, use a little to make a hops shampoo that will give your hair body, shine and volume. In an enamel-lined saucepan set over medium heat, bring 180ml beer to a boil, then simmer briskly until it reduces to 60ml. Cool, then mix with 240ml of your ordinary shampoo. Transfer it to a jar with a lid and shake before using.

make your own...

HAIR RINSE

Herbal formulations have been used on hair for thousands of years. The bergamot in this herbal rinse helps to control itching and dandruff, while the rosemary (which is often used as a fragrance in soaps and perfumes) provides the lovely fresh scent.

Herbal rise and shine

If the lid of the jar you use to steep the herbs is metal, place cling film or wax paper between the lid and the jar to prevent the vinegar from corroding it.

12g dried rosemary leaves
12g dried bergamot
480ml cider vinegar
500-750ml warm water

1 Place the herbs in a heatproof, thick glass jar, such as the kind that are used for jams and preserves.

2 Heat the vinegar until very hot but not boiling, then pour it over the herbs. Cool, then cover tightly.

3 Keep the jar in a warm spot for a week, shaking it once a day.

4 Line a funnel with washed cheesecloth and place the funnel over a jar. Strain the rinse into the jar and screw on the lid.

5 When ready to use, mix 80ml of the rinse with up to 750ml warm water. Then pour over hair once or twice as a rinse.

✱ Hair mousse but no gel?

Raid the pantry! Mix up some flavourless gelatine and you may never go back to the salon variety: dissolve from ½ to 1 teaspoon unflavoured gelatine in 240ml warm water and refrigerate. It won't last as long as ordinary hair gel – up to a week in the fridge – but gives a super firm hold.

✱ No hair spray?

Chop up 1 lemon and add it to a pan filled with 480ml water. Boil until the water has reduced by half. Cool, strain and pour into a spray bottle; add 30ml surgical spirit. Stored in the fridge, the spray should keep for three to four weeks; unrefrigerated, it will last for two weeks.

✱ Tame hairline frizz

The hardest place to control frizz is in the area around your hairline. To deal with irritating stray frizz and wisps, saturate an old toothbrush with hairspray and brush them back where they belong. Hold in place with your fingers until the hairspray dries.

✱ Make your own scrunchies

If you have long hair and can't find something to tie it back with, get out a pair of 'emergency' tights – the ones with runs that you only wear under trousers. Just cut the length you need and you will be ready to run for miles. Black and coloured tights will look the most fashionable, but flesh tones will do if you are stuck. Tights have the added advantage of not bruising or breaking your hair, as elastic sometimes does.

✳ Eyeball those roots

If you're of a certain age, you may colour your hair and white roots seem to appear faster than a racing car on the Silverstone track. Here's a quick fix if you don't have time to apply full colour. Apply your mascara to the roots with an old toothbrush, blending it in as you go. This trick works best with dark hair. What should you do if you have blonde hair? Try beige or taupe eye shadow as temporary camouflage.

✳ A sage decision for brunettes

Applied to brown or black hair, sage will darken grey hairs. Put 12g dried sage into a bowl and pour 480ml boiling water over it. Let the mixture steep for 3 hours or overnight before straining it into a bottle or jar. Shampoo your hair as usual, rinse and then apply the sage tea to grey hairs one area at a time, dabbing it on with a cottonwool ball or a wad of cheesecloth. Air-dry or use a hair dryer, but *do not* rinse. You will probably need to repeat the process once a week until you get the colour you want.

✳ Spike it with petroleum jelly

If you want a new way to style a short hairstyle, use a drop or two of petroleum jelly to spike your locks into place. As a bonus, when you wash the petroleum jelly out, your hair will be softer and shinier.

✳ Shelve the dye for darker locks

Leave chemical dyes on the shelf and colour your dark hair the way the ancients did: with rosemary. Pour 500ml boiling water over 50g fresh chopped rosemary leaves, allow it to stand until cold, then bottle it and rinse hair after washing. It's a natural solution for greys.

household superstar

6 QUICK BEAUTY FIXES WITH A LEMON

Considering its size, the vitamin C powerhouse we know as the lemon provides an astonishing number of beauty benefits, six of which are listed below. (One word of caution: lemons can cause skin to be extra-sensitive to sunlight, so don't expose yourself to the sun for too long after a skin treatment.

1 Exfoliate dead skin and bring new skin to the surface by washing skin with lemon juice mixed with a little sugar.

2 Smooth wrinkles by boiling 240ml milk, 2 teaspoons lemon juice and 1 tablespoon brandy. Cool the mixture to room temperature, apply and let dry before wiping it off.

3 Lighten age spots by dabbing them with lemon juice and rinsing off after 15 minutes. Repeat once later in the day.

4 Mix the juice from 1 lemon with 60ml olive oil or sweet almond oil for a facial that both exfoliates and moisturises.

5 Fight dandruff with a daily scalp massage with 2 tablespoons lemon. Rinse with water and follow with a rinse of 240ml water mixed with 1 teaspoon lemon juice.

6 Whiten and clean fingernails by soaking them in 240ml lukewarm water and the juice of ½ lemon for 5 minutes, then rub the inside of the lemon peel against the nails.

The home nail salon

Why spend money at a nail salon when you can achieve the same look in the privacy of your own home? Here's how.

Cleaning nails

Soak dirty nails for 5 minutes in a bowl of water into which two denture tablets have been dissolved. While this method may seem odd, it works because teeth and nails are made of the same substance – keratin.

Caring for cuticles

Don't waste money buying specialised cuticle cream. Use olive oil, sweet almond oil, baby oil, margarine or even lip balm instead. Taking good care of cuticles will also discourage hangnails – a sign that both your nails and cuticles are too dry. As you massage oil into your cuticles, oil the whole nail. There should be no splits, no breaks and less chance of an annoying and painful hangnail.

Instant polish touch-up

If you have a chip in a polished toenail and not somewhere that you can repair it properly, look in your make-up bag and use a lip pencil or lipstick to add colour to the chipped spot. It won't hold for long, but it ought to get you through lunch or dinner or a film. And you can always reapply your temporary fix in the ladies' room.

Freeze-dry your wet nails

If you're late for a special appointment but your nails are still too wet with polish to risk opening the car door, open the freezer and stick your hands in. Your nails will be dry in a jiffy and you can get on your way without ruining your manicure.

Keeping clothes in shape

✱ Put a stop to static cling

Lack of humidity in the air is the main cause of static electricity in your clothes. Men have to worry only about trouser legs clinging to the skin, while women wearing nylon tights experience the problem much more often. Try one of these methods to keep clothes static-free.

- **Spritz with hairspray** Spray a little hairspray along the underside of trousers or skirts. Or spray a paper towel and wipe the hairspray on the inside of the fabric.
- **Dampen with water** Wet a paper towel or your hand with water and run it along the exterior of tights and the interior of a skirt or pair of trousers. Or you could use a spray bottle to mist the inside of the clothing.
- **Separate with a coat hanger** Move a hanger up and down between the inside of clothes and tights or a slip.

✱ The incredible shrinking waistband

It's not that unusual to find that an elastic waistband has shrunk or expanded when you're putting on trousers, shorts or a skirt that you haven't worn for months. For a quick fix: open the waistband on the inside of the garment. Cut the elastic inside the band and insert a piece of taut elastic from the waist of an old pair of tights or a section of a stretchy headband. Attach the insert to one side of the cut elastic with a safety pin. Stretch the insert to the fit you want and safety-pin it to the other side of the original elastic. Cut off any excess for a flatter appearance and then smooth down the waistband with your fingers. Cover any telltale bulge with a sweater, T-shirt, blouse or jacket.

✱ A little glue to keep buttons on

Buttons on new clothes will stay put longer if you dab the threads above the buttons with white, clear-drying glue. Use a cotton bud to apply it neatly.

tip BLOWIN' IN THE WIND

Prevent skirts from flare-ups on windy days by sewing two or three small **keys or coins** into the hem as weights. Wedding dress seamstresses use this trick to keep the hems of bridal veils hanging properly, choosing weights that can't easily be seen through gossamer fabrics – among them, the flat glass beads used in flower arrangements and fish bowls.

✳ An iron-free crease solution

Lay the creased garment on a flat surface (a worktop or dresser top will do). Hold a hair dryer a few inches above the shirt and aim the hot air at the crease while smoothing it out with your other hand. After a few minutes the crease should either be less noticeable or gone.

✳ Banish mustiness with vodka

What can you do when you pull out an outfit you haven't worn for a while and it smells rather musty? Pour a little unflavoured vodka into a spray bottle and lightly mist the outfit. The alcohol kills the bacteria that create odours without adding an unwanted smell of its own.

✳ Let appliqués save the day

When a favourite garment – particularly a summer skirt or dress – seem beyond repair because of holes or stains, don't automatically get rid of it. Consider hiding the damage with a series of carefully chosen appliqués. They not only hide problem areas but also provide a new decorative look. Many appliqués are iron-on these days, so you may not need to sew.

✳ Rid sweaters of pills

Pilling can ruin an otherwise perfect sweater. Use a razor or an electric shaver to cut the fuzzy pills off, taking care not to make a hole in the weave. Other handy tools for de-pilling are an emery board, a pumice stone and the rough side of a piece of Velcro. With any of these, take care to rub very lightly in just one direction until the pills disengage.

✳ Keep a zip moving

If a zip has become stuck, take a closer look at the teeth. If there is any lint or dirt between them, brush the teeth with dry toothbrush bristles, then rub them lightly with the stub of a beeswax candle. The zip should now glide

what's the story?

CINCHED IN TOO TIGHT

During the 19th century women were famous for their hourglass figures and for fainting – and one wonders whether they were aware that the two were related. Ladies owed their curvaceous figures to tight-fitting corsets that cinched in the waist and enhanced the bosom. The corsets were heavy and stiff, reinforced with wood, whalebone or steel ribs.

Once a woman was laced in, her posture was admirably erect. And no wonder: she couldn't bend. Worse, women often had trouble breathing. Corsets restricted the normal movement of the diaphragm, the muscle below the lungs. When the diaphragm moves down, it allows the lungs to expand and take in fresh oxygen; when it moves up, the lungs contract and exhale carbon dioxide. In other words, the breath was actually being squeezed out of these wasp-waisted, corseted ladies. Not surprisingly, as corsets fell out of favour, so did the smelling salts that were used to revive a person who fainted.

smoothly on its waxed track. If a zip has *too* much zip and comes undone on its own (usually at the most embarrassing moments), use a cotton bud to coat the teeth with hairspray after you've put on the garment and zipped it up. Hairspray will hold both sides of the zip together just enough to keep them from coming apart.

Storing clothes in style

✳ Perfume your lingerie

When you have just dabbed the last drop of your favourite perfume on your wrist, you can still enjoy its fragrance if you put the empty bottle in your lingerie drawer. The scent will waft up each time you open the drawer and will perfume your underwear as well.

✳ Eliminate unwanted trouser creases with bubble wrap

How many times have you pulled on a pair of trousers only to take them off because coat hanger creases have made them unwearable? Wrap the hanger bar in a layer of bubble wrap with the smooth side facing out (secure the wrap with gaffer tape). Other coverings that work just as well are strips of quilt batting or soft foam sheets used as filler in packing boxes.

✳ Hang spaghetti straps securely

If tops and dresses with spaghetti straps are forever slipping off their hangers, the easiest way to secure them is simply to clip both straps to the hanger with clothespegs. Or sew a button to a padded hanger to provide a stop for the strap.

✳ Stay-put scarves

A neat way to store scarves so that each is within easy reach is to attach a few shower curtain rings to the bottom bar of a coat hanger, thread a scarf though each one and then hang them on the wardrobe rail. Arrange them by colour and you'll find that it's much easier than rummaging through a pile of scarves in your drawer to find the one you want.

✳ Cedar scent

Cedar blocks have long been used as an alternative to strong-smelling camphor to keep moths from eating holes in your clothes. If your cedar has lost its woodland fragrance, don't spend money to replace the blocks. Just use sandpaper or an emery board to rough up the wood and release the scent.

Moths also shy away from a host of other strong natural fragrances including the scent of dried bay leaves, dried lavender, dried orange peel, cloves and whole peppercorns. Place some of these in the feet of a pair of old tights to make cheap and inconspicuous sachets for your wardrobe or drawer.

tip DOUBLE YOUR HANGING SPACE

You don't have to redesign your wardrobe to increase your hanging space. Just slip a sturdy **shower curtain ring** over the necks of your hangers and hook a second hanger onto them to create a hanger that takes twice as many clothes.

Help for holey hosiery

What? In a book like this we're actually talking about wearing a pair of tights instead of using it as an emergency fan belt or dog lead? We are. And these four hints about the hosiery itself are all to do with keeping it in good condition.

1
Prevent runs

You'll get a lot more wear from a pair of tights if you first soak them for 30 minutes in a solution of 90g salt dissolved in 1 litre of water. Rinse and drip dry. When you don't have time for pretreating, soak the tights in salt water after use and then wash. Whatever you do, the salt strengthens the nylon fibres, making them less likely to tear.

2
Lengthen the life

Dampen a pair of tights and place them in a sealable plastic bag in the freezer. Remove the frozen tights, then defrost (not in the microwave) and drip dry. Freezing the fibres hardens them and your tights will last through many more wearings.

3
Soften to avoid runs

Rinsing a pair of tights with a drop or two of fabric softener in the water is a good anti-run tactic. The fabric softener makes the nylon mesh more stretchable and less prone to runs caused by tautness. To dry, roll the tights in a towel instead of wringing them out and hanging them.

4
Nip runs in the bud

If you don't have any clear nail polish to stop a run in its tracks, rub a small amount of liquid soap along the run's top, bottom and sides. The soap hardens into a barrier as it dries, preventing the run from continuing on its path. Rubbing a bar of wet soap over the run will also work.

Super saves for stained clothing

✳ Wash out make-up spills with bicarbonate of soda

If you've spilled liquid foundation onto a blouse, go to the kitchen and get some bicarbonate of soda. Sprinkle the powder onto the stain until it's completely covered and press it gently into the fabric. Wet a nailbrush or a toothbrush and lightly brush the spot. If any make-up remains, repeat the process until all traces have disappeared.

✳ Lipstick smear remover 1: petroleum jelly

Dabbing petroleum jelly onto lipstick marks before washing a garment is a removal method used by stain specialists. If it's good enough for pros, it should be good enough for you.

✳ Lipstick smear remover 2: bread

Tear out the doughy centre of the bread and knead it into a ball, then blot the smear repeatedly with the dough until the stain lifts from the fabric. Now wash the garment. The dough ball is also safe to use on lipstick marks on dry-clean only woollen clothing.

✳ Soak out tomato sauce stains

It's a brave person who's prepared to eat spaghetti while wearing a white shirt without a large napkin tucked into the collar. If you do spill, for an effective tomato sauce spot eradicator, combine 120ml 3 per cent hydrogen peroxide and 720ml water in a bowl or clean sink. Soak the stain in the solution for 30 minutes before washing the shirt.

✳ Shaving cream tomato sauce remover

Take a can of non-gel shaving cream and spray it onto the stain, rub it in gently and let it dry before washing.

✳ Foundation shaker

Blot up foundation marks on washable fabrics with a piece of fresh white bread kneaded into a ball. The bread treatment should also erase pencil marks on woollen and washable clothing. Resist the temptation to use the pencil's eraser to rub out the marks; in most cases it will only make them look worse.

✳ Milk an ink stain

To get rid of a nasty ink blot on a shirt, put 2–3 tablespoons cornflour into a bowl and then stir into whole milk until you have made a thick paste. Cover the stain with the paste and let it sit for 3–4 hours. Then brush off the paste and wash the shirt. Another paste to try is 2 tablespoons cream of tartar mixed with 2 tablespoons lemon juice.

✳ Remove red wine stains

Although the wine tasted terrific, the drops left on your trousers don't look all that great this morning. Soda water is a common antidote for red wine stains, but if that doesn't work, try one of these treatments:

● **Borax** Dissolve 1 tablespoon borax in 480ml warm water. Submerge the stained part of the garment in the solution and soak for 1 minute, then put the item in the washing machine.

- **Washing-up liquid and vinegar** Dilute washing-up liquid and gently scrub it into the stain; rinse gently with water, then apply a drop of white vinegar. Pat dry and rinse again with water.
- **Salt and boiling water** Pour a generous amount of salt onto a still-wet stain and see if the salt turns pink as it soaks up the wine. If it doesn't, pour boiling water over the salt. In either case, wash the stained garment as soon as possible.
- **Bicarbonate of soda** Heap bicarbonate of soda on the stain and let it sit for an hour or more to absorb the stain. Then shake off the bicarbonate of soda and wash the garment.

✱ Prevent perspiration stains

Spread baby powder or talcum powder along the collar and underarms of soiled clothing and press gently with a warm iron. The powder should absorb the sweat and make it easier for the rest to come out in the wash.

✱ Pop out bloodstains

Perhaps you're nearing the end of a charity bike ride when your front wheel hits a pothole, sending you and your bike clattering to the ground. Fortunately, all that's hurt is your pride and your bleeding elbow which goes messily all over your clothes. You remember that a friend who knows about such things told you to soak bloodstains overnight in cola. You try it and find out that she was, in fact, right – not insane.

✱ A toast to soda water

The most successful way to get rid of stains is to treat them before they dry and become set in the fabric. If you spill food onto your clothes at a dinner party or in a restaurant, ask for a glass of soda water and a lint-free kitchen towel.

make your own...

STAIN REMOVER

Vinegar, bicarbonate of soda and ammonia are a mighty trio beefed up even more by the addition of liquid castile soap. Even Lady Macbeth would have killed for this homemade cleanser, that's specially for stains that have already dried.

Out-darned-spot spray

Treat grease, coffee, fruit juice and other common stains with this spray, shaking it well before using. Liquid castile soap is sold in natural products stores, online and at some supermarkets.

120ml white vinegar
80ml clear household ammonia
45g bicarbonate of soda
2 tablespoons liquid castile soap
1.5 litres water

1 Combine all ingredients into a 4 litre container and stir well. Pour into a suitably sized spray bottle.

2 Spray the solution onto a stain and let it set for 3–5 minutes.

3 Rub the stain gently with a soft cloth and then wash the garment as soon as possible.

Retire to the bathroom with the soda and apply as much as you can. Wait 1 minute, then blot the stain gently with the towel.

Quick fixes and mends

✳ Salvage discoloured whites

Don't get rid of drab and dingy whites just yet: dissolve 1 teaspoon cream of tartar in cold water in a clean plastic washing-up bowl or sink and soak the garment for a few hours before washing. (This is also a great way to restore old handkerchiefs.) To whiten yellowed clothes, soak the items overnight in a solution of 120ml white vinegar and 1.5 litres warm water before washing.

✳ Restore crispness to lace

If you have a lace scarf or shawl that's gone limp, wash it as you normally would and then dip it in a solution of 9 litres warm water and 180g Epsom salts. The salts will cling to the fibres and add body.

✳ No-snag, soapy thread

When you're sewing on a button and the thread tangles or knots it can be hugely frustrating. To stop it happening, run the thread lightly over a bar of soap before you begin sewing. The waxy coating will make thread easier to untangle and unknot.

✳ Rethread a drawstring

If a drawstring has come out of a hood or pyjama trousers, attach a safety pin to one end of the string and use the closed pin to push the string back into place.

✳ Use marbles to help to mend gloves

Drop a marble into the fingertip of a glove that needs mending so that you'll have a stretched, smooth surface on which to sew. Mend the toes and heels of socks in the same way, using a tennis ball or billiard ball.

idea

FIX A SCORCH MARK

Perhaps you've pressed some unfamiliar garments – but have heated up the iron much too high – leading to some serious scorching. Luckily scorch marks don't have to be permanent. Here are four techniques to try:

- **For white cottons** Take a cotton cloth dampened with 3 per cent hydrogen peroxide and dab at the scorch until it has completely disappeared.

- **For coloured cottons** Wet a lint-free cloth with 3 per cent hydrogen peroxide or white vinegar and lay it over the scorch. Press with the iron on low.

- **For all washable cottons** Cut an onion in half, rub it on the scorch, soak overnight in cold water and then wash to get rid of the smell.

- **For woollens** Dampen the scorch with water and dab cornflour onto it. Let it sit for 20–30 minutes and brush off.

✳ A sewing kit in a film canister

If a button falls off your blouse while you're en route to an appointment, you can make sure you're prepared. You can store everything you need in a plastic film canister in your handbag – a few shirt buttons, a set of sewing needles still stuck in their cardboard holder, thread and a variety of different-sized safety pins.

Just for men

✳ Hardworking hand lotion

Even if you're someone who takes really good care of your fingernails, hands that have rough, dry skin can take you down a notch on the 'good grooming' scale. To take care of the problem as you sleep, whip up a thin paste by mixing together 2 tablespoons avocado oil, 1 tablespoon honey and 2 teaspoons glycerine. Now stir in 150g finely ground rolled oats or almonds until you have the right consistency. 'Wash' your hands and fingers in the paste, then slip on a pair of rubber or cotton gloves before going to bed.

✳ Skin rejuvenator

Diluted vinegar will not only tone your skin but also help to protect it from infections – and it's easy to make a vinegar-peppermint concentrate you can keep with your toiletries. Place 1 teaspoon dried peppermint (or 1 tablespoon fresh) in a sterilised bottle with a cap, then pour in 80ml apple cider vinegar. Screw the cap on tight and set aside for ten days.

Strain the mint-scented vinegar into a second sterilised bottle. To use, dilute 1 tablespoon of the scented vinegar with 120ml boiled or distilled water and splash it all over your face to pep up the skin.

✳ Homemade aloe face mask

Men are no longer strangers to facials (some of them at any rate), but you don't need to go to a salon to get one. Prepare a skin-friendly, moisturising mask at home with an aloe vera leaf, an egg yolk, honey and powdered milk. Start by slicing the aloe leaf open lengthways and scraping 1 teaspoon aloe gel into a small bowl. Beat in 1 egg yolk and 1 teaspoon warm

(not hot) honey with a spoon, then stir in enough powdered milk to make a thin but spreadable paste.

Use your fingers to spread the paste from hairline to chin, steering clear of the area around your eyes. Leave the mask on for 20–30 minutes, then remove it with your fingers and a wet facecloth. Follow your facial with a splash or two of skin toner.

✳ Experiment with aftershave

For an antiseptic aftershave that smells really good, play around with some apple cider vinegar and the likes of orange flower water, witch hazel and essential oils such as bergamot and neroli. Experiment with different proportions until you find the formulation you like best, then store it in a sterilised bottle with a lid.

✳ Double-duty scent for drawers

Keeping a bundle of cedar shavings or pine needles in a drawer full of T-shirts, sweaters or any other garments will not only give a fresh, woodland scent to your clothes but will also keep moths and other insect pests at bay. (You will find that dried bay leaves are an excellent choice, too.) Just place a handful of the shavings, needles or herbs into the centre of a handkerchief, bunch the four corners together and knot the bundle loosely before tucking it into a drawer.

Keeping shoes shipshape

✳ Bubble wrap keeps shoes in shape

You don't need expensive shoe trees to keep your shoes in good shape: use bubble wrap. Cut two pieces small enough to roll up and fit into your shoes and boots. When packing a suitcase, remove the bubble wrap and stuff tights or socks inside the shoes to retain their shape and free up space in the suitcase. Finally wrap the bubble wrap around the shoes so that they won't dirty your clean clothes.

✳ Serving spoon shoehorn

Cinderella's stepsisters struggled to fit their feet into the glass slipper, but you don't have to struggle if you find yourself without a shoehorn. Take a narrow serving spoon with a blunt end and place your heel into the bowl of the spoon as you work your foot into the shoe.

✳ Instant shoeshine

You don't need to buy special shoe polish to get the shine you want on leather shoes. Just put a few drops of baby oil, olive oil (below) or even castor oil onto dull-looking leather and buff with a soft cloth. You'll not only have shiny shoes again, but softer ones, too. These oils lubricate the leather, softening stiff spots and creases. They also work on patent leather and leather jackets, handbags, belts and briefcases.

✳ Smooth out heel creases

The smart high-heel shoes that you spent your bonus on still look as good as new – except for a bit of creased leather on the heel where they got caught in a grating. Fix them yourself with a hair dryer and leather glue. Put your hair dryer on the warm setting and direct air to the heel. The warmth will soften both the remaining original glue and the leather, allowing you to smooth the leather out from top to bottom. Glue down any loose edges and you'll be ready to step out in style again.

✳ Cover up spots with a marker

When your dark shoes are scuffed and you don't have time to polish them, you can quickly cover up the scuffs using a permanent marker pen in a matching colour.

✳ From plain Janes to fancy Janes

If you have a pair of plain patent strap shoes, slip-on ballet shoes or plain heels and want them to look a bit more special, dress them up with a pair of big sparkly clip-on earrings that you don't wear any more. The extra colour or glitter may be just the touch of glamour that you want for a party.

Hats and handbags

✳ Polish leather with a potato

Rub a cut potato across the surface of your dull leather handbag, give it a buff with a clean, soft cloth and it'll look good as new.

✳ Steam your suede

To clean stains and spots on a suede handbag, first lightly rub the spots with fine-grained sandpaper or an emery board. Then hold the bag 15cm away from a kettle or pan with steaming water until the stain gets a little warm, making sure the steam doesn't saturate the bag. Brush with a suede brush or toothbrush, repeating the brushing once the suede is dry.

✳ A space-saving handbag rack

If you have recently replaced a tall wooden stepladder, use the old one to store handbags – an especially helpful trick if you are short of shelf space. To make the ladder prettier, paint it in a toning shade to go with the rest of the furniture or cover the steps with adhesive shelf paper or glue on decorative fabric swatches.

✳ Re-size a special hat

If you've found a perfect hat at a car boot sale charity or vintage shop, the type that's worn with the brim low on the forehead, but it's just a little too big for you, buy it, then wear a sweatband under the hat to fill in the extra space. If the sweatband is too thick and makes the hat too tight, try using a more stretchy, thinner headband – one of them should work. Just remember to take the band and the hat off at the same time or you'll reveal your little secret. For a more permanent fix, lightly tack the band that fits inside the hat, using long tacking stitches.

idea

DON'T LOSE YOUR KEYS

Who doesn't lose keys in a handbag – especially a big one – now and then? A simple solution is to attach a key line. Measure your handbag from the bottom to the base of one of the handles and then add 10-15cm. Cut a piece of dental floss, fishing line or a thin corded ribbon to that length. Thread your keys onto the line and knot the end. Place this end into your handbag and wrap the other end around the base of the handle, knotting it tightly. Now, whenever you need your keys, just pull out the line. You shouldn't have to fish for them anymore.

✳ Restore shine to straw hats

Over time, many straw hats lose their crisp, shiny look. You can spruce up yours in time for the its summer outing by spraying it with a light coating of hairspray and letting it dry thoroughly before wearing the hat again. Always be sure to spray in a well-ventilated area or outside.

✳ Stuff hats to save their shape

Have you noticed that the brims of hats in hat shops don't ever touch the shelves? Milliners know that brims that rest on shelves will flatten out, so they overstuff the crowns with tissue paper to let hats rest on the paper instead. If you don't have any leftover tissue paper, use bubble wrap, dry-cleaning plastic, plastic shopping bags, old socks or tights or a discarded sweater as stuffing.

Jewellery

✳ Buttons for your wrist

If you like to make your own bracelets and necklaces, alternating beads with some spare buttons that you've collected will make an unusual accessory. String buttons and beads of different colours and sizes onto two strands of dental floss, fishing line or heavy-duty thread. Then experiment with a variety of combinations until you've fashioned a piece of jewellery worthy of a chic boutique.

✳ Magnetic brooch holder

When it comes to silk blouses, dresses or jackets, the last thing you want is to poke tiny holes in the smooth, expensive fabric with a pin. Instead, use magnets to attach the brooch. Remove the shaft of the brooch and attach one magnet to the back with superglue. Make sure that the glue dries completely before wearing the brooch. Place it in the desired location on the garment, holding it with one hand. With your other hand, place the opposing magnet behind both fabric and brooch. The magnets will securely lock the brooch in place.

✳ Buttons for your toes

Don't think that adding a bit of glam to plain pumps isn't jewellery ... it is. Rummage through a button collection for two oversized and interesting ones; then glue gun them to the vamp of your shoes and give them a new life.

✳ Wristwatch earring holder

If you've ever left your pierced earrings in a hotel room or had one mysteriously disappear from a dressing table never to be seen again, keep them safe and secure with another accessory: your wristwatch. After taking off

what's the story?

JEWELLERY FOR MEN

Some style gurus believe that a man should never wear more than a wedding ring and a watch, but these days most people would disagree. But understatement did have its day, which ran from the late 18th century until the 1970s – when open shirts and a chestful of medallions were all the rage. The style victims of the 70s were bringing things full circle: until Louis XVI lost his head in 1793 and male adornment went out of style, men of a certain rank were loaded with jewellery.

Prehistoric humans of both sexes decorated their bodies with beads and feathers. Centuries later, Tutankhamun's mummy was covered with amulets, pendants, bracelets, earrings and other pieces of jewellery. In ancient Rome, jewellery was widely worn and the gold ring – once reserved for dignitaries – appeared on the fingers of lower ranks and soldiers. In Renaissance Europe, men's jewellery flourished among the aristocracy and portraits of Henry VIII show his garments and hat brim studded with jewels.

By the early 20th century, men's jewellery was no longer associated with rank. Still, the common man's adornment was generally limited to a pocket watch and a ring. Only later did the love beads of the hippie era, the medallions of the disco days and the bling of the hip-hop age bring flash to a man's wardrobe that rivalled (or outshone) that of earlier kings.

Organise your everyday jewellery by tacking it to a bulletin board!

your earrings, insert them into the holes of a leather or plastic watchstrap or between the links of an expandable metal band. You can now rest assured that they will still be there in the morning. If you don't have a watch, use the holes of a belt as a temporary earring holder.

✻ Unstick a stuck ring

Your one and only has just proposed marriage and you want to slip on the engagement ring. But at this moment of a lifetime, you just can't get the old ring off your finger. What should you do? Get some mayonnaise and rub it on your finger. It's not romantic but it will help the proposal to go more smoothly. Make a fist to help the mayonnaise to seep under the band of gold or silver. The ring should now slide off easily. Wash your hands and then mentally rehearse a funny family story you'll be able to share with your grandchildren.

✻ Bulletin board jewellery 'box'

If you're tired of having to empty out all your precious jewels to find the one necklace you really want to wear today, buy an inexpensive bulletin board and some colourful drawing pins. Then paint the board in your favourite colour and hang each necklace and each ring on the board to keep them from getting scratched and to keep them organised.

✻ Fix necklace knots with powder

It takes a lot of patience to untangle a knot in a necklace chain. How can you complete the task in less time? Sprinkle the knot with talcum or baby powder, cornflour or vegetable oil and use a straight pin or two to prise the knot apart. The powder and oil lubricate the links, helping them to slide and separate more easily. Afterwards, wash the untangled chain with a mild detergent, rinse and pat dry.

Specs savers

✳ Protect glasses from hair dye

Whether you are highlighting your hair at home or having it coloured at a beauty salon, it's possible that a little dye may drip onto the sidepieces of your glasses. To protect the arms, simply wrap them with cling film until the new colour is finished.

✳ A screw loose?

The tiny screws holding your glasses frames together never seem to stay tight for long, especially when the specs are reading glasses. One way to keep things tight is to dab the threads with a little clear nail polish when replacing a screw, then coat the screw heads again once they are in place.

✳ Seeing is believing

Glasses cleaner is expensive these days, but some people are aware that two common household products will clean and polish lenses just as well – try soda water or surgical spirit, the latter used either full strength or diluted with equal parts water. Keep your cleanser in a handy spray bottle and use a soft lint-free cloth to dry the lenses.

✳ Clearing up foggy specs

Having your glasses fog up is no fun. It happens in cold weather when you go from outside to inside, when steam billows up from a pan of boiling water or even when you're eating very spicy food. As a preventative measure, clean your specs with foamy white shaving cream, which will leave an invisible coating on the lenses that keeps water drops from sticking.

Shaving cream is also a fantastic cleaner for glasses. If you've accidentally got hairspray on your glasses and can't get it off, a dab of shaving cream on each lens will clean it up.

A dab of nail varnish can save your specs!

Store tiny
toys in an empty
milk container!

8 Great ideas for parents and children

In an age of constant media bombardment and pester power, it may seem like a novel idea, but you can entertain children without buying them the latest computer game or the newest toy to hit the market. And you don't have to break the bank to keep children happy, healthy and clean.

This chapter is bursting with great ways to provide for your children's needs, teach them interesting and important things in fun ways and keep them engaged and entertained ... all without having to take out a loan. Where do we even begin when it comes to the fun of sculpting with salt dough that you make from scratch (instead of its commercial counterpart)? Best of all, you will find simple suggestions for keeping children safe, secure and happy and keeping all their bits and pieces organised at little or no cost.

Bath time brilliance

✴ A laundry basket 'bathtub'

When your baby can sit by herself but is still too wobbly to go in an ordinary bath, a plastic laundry basket – the kind with perforations in the sides – is a great solution. Set the laundry basket in the bath, add a few inches of water and put your baby in this 'bathtub playpen'. Be sure that the holes in the laundry basket are large enough not to catch your baby's fingers or toes and that all plastic edges are smooth and safe. And follow the number one safety rule: Never leave a baby or small child unattended when she is in or near water.

✴ Infant seat in the bath

If you need an extra pair of hands when bathing a baby, a plastic infant seat will make bath time safer and less stressful for everyone concerned. Remove the seat pad, buckle and straps, and then line the seat with a soft towel folded to fit. To prevent slipping and sliding, lay another towel on the bottom of the bath and set the seat on the towel. Then put your baby in his place and run just enough water into the tub for the bath. The infant seat supports your baby and lets you use both hands to bathe him easily.

✴ Petroleum jelly = no tears

Babies can't stand getting anything in their eyes at bath time, be it shampoo or water. Whether you have no-tears shampoo on hand or have to make do with a bar of mild soap, dab a tiny drop of petroleum jelly across your child's eyebrows, gently wiping off any residue with a soft cloth or tissue. The jelly will deflect water and shampoo from the eyes and keep your baby happy and comfortable.

make your own...

BUBBLE BATH

Few can resist the appeal of a warm, frothy bubble bath. Show a child a bath piled high with bubbles and you'll convert a bath-hater into a happy bather. Make your own with this easy recipe.

No-tears bubble formula

Using a no-tears shampoo will cut the risk of irritating children's eyes. Add a mere capful or two to running water – more if you want more bubbles.

120ml no-tears shampoo
   (clear or light in colour)
180ml water
¼ teaspoon salt
Food colouring (optional)

1 Gently mix shampoo and water in a bowl or a measuring cup with a spout.

2 Add salt and stir until the mixture is slightly thickened. (This will take a minute or so.)

3 If you want to colour the solution, add a drop of food colouring and stir. Continue adding drops and stirring until you have the desired colour.

4 Pour the mixture into a clean bottle.

To make bath time pain free, wear a pair of knee pads!

✱ Cotton gloves and slippery babies

A wriggling infant in a soapy bath can feel as slippery as a wet banana skin, but you can get a grip by wearing a pair of cotton gloves.

✱ Padded knees

Anyone who has bathed a grandchild knows how tough kneeling on the cold hard floor can be. Athletic knee pads are a great remedy.

✱ Soap in a sock

This is an excellent use for the many mismatched socks that your washing machine hasn't swallowed. Fill a sock with soap fragments or a small bar and tightly tie the sock closed. Children like to wash with sock-soap because it doesn't fly out of their hands.

✱ Reusing novelty bottles

Tear-free shampoos and liquid bubble bath in colourful moulded plastic bottles can be expensive everyday products. If your child enjoys shampoo or bubble bath from a bottle shaped like a duck or a frog, save the bottle and refill it with less expensive bath products. Your child will have his bath toy, you'll save money and you'll help the environment by reusing plastic.

✱ Bath-time help from the kitchen

Set a kitchen timer to go off when it's time for a bath – and also time for a bath to end. For youngsters who are inclined to delay, setting the timer to buzz 5 minutes before bath time is an early warning system. If your child likes to stay in the bath until he gets wrinkled, the buzzer will remind him to get a move on. Using a timer can help children acquire a better sense of the time required for a specific task. Timers may also be useful when older siblings are competing for time in the bathroom.

✱ Stop itching with bicarbonate of soda

Adding half of a box of bicarbonate of soda to your child's bath will help to relieve the itching caused by insect bites, heat rashes, sunburn and even chicken pox. Allow the child to have a good soak and then gently pat him or her dry with a clean, soft towel.

Super splashy bath toys

✳ Personalised floaty toys

If you are teaching your child to recognise letters or to spell her name, get personal by picking up some inexpensive floating craft foam at your local craft shop. Available in bright colours, they can be cut to resemble every letter of the alphabet, making them perfect for bath-time learning.

✳ Playthings from the kitchen cupboard

Many of the best bath-time toys are likely to be found in the kitchen. Plastic food containers like margarine/butter tubs, measuring spoons, large cooking spoons, funnels, colanders, cups, milk cartons – if it floats, pours, stirs or drips, it will inspire your child's imagination. Plastic lids become floating platforms. Funnels create waterfalls. Plastic mesh fruit baskets will create masses of bubbles in soapy water. (It's best to avoid wooden and metal items; wood will splinter and get mildewed and metal rusts.) Simple, sturdy plastic items are safe and easy to clean; just wipe down plastic bath toys routinely with a water and bicarbonate of soda solution or run them through the dishwasher.

✳ Go fishing with a kitchen strainer

A small plastic vegetable strainer lets toddlers scoop up sponges or shapes cut from craft foam and promotes hand-eye coordination, too. An aquarium net will also work. (Thoroughly wash and disinfect a used net first.) Help your toddler to drop her 'catch' into a plastic container and count the items together when she gets tired of fishing in the tub.

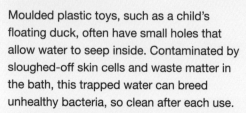

idea

A HYGIENIC RUBBER DUCK

Moulded plastic toys, such as a child's floating duck, often have small holes that allow water to seep inside. Contaminated by sloughed-off skin cells and waste matter in the bath, this trapped water can breed unhealthy bacteria, so clean after each use.

Here's how: squeeze the toy to remove as much bath water as possible. Then submerge it in a mild bleach solution (1 part household bleach to 15 parts water) and squeeze it to suck in the bleach solution. Shake the toy and then let it sit for 10 minutes before squeezing out the cleaning solution. In a separate container filled with clean water, rinse the toy using the same procedure and dry the now-safe toy for the next bath.

✳ Commander of the fleet!

Save wax-coated milk and cream containers, snip the spout off, close the top with a bit of gaffer tape and paint a fleet for your little seafarer in his or her colour of choice, using water-insoluble paint. Give each boat a name, add numbers to the sides and a lollipop stick mast and you'll have a no-cost bath-time armada ready to command.

✳ Throw in the sponge

Raid kitchen drawers and storage cabinets for plain kitchen and household sponges of all sizes and colours and cut them into lots of different shapes. Your child will be able to play stacking games with floating circles, triangles, stars, crescent moons, leaves, keyholes, doughnuts and whatever else your (and his) inventive mind can come up with.

Caution: Before turning the playthings over to your child for the first time, disinfect used sponges by either 1) soaking them in a mild chlorine bleach solution and rinsing well or 2) wetting them and then microwaving on high for 1–2 minutes. After the bath, start a good habit by getting your toddler to help to wipe the tub with a designated 'clean-up' sponge.

✳ Produce-bag storage

Turn a large-size, plastic mesh produce bag from the supermarket into a storage bag for bath toys. (Avoid string bags made of natural materials such as cotton, which can become mouldy and harbour germs.) If a plastic mesh bag has a paper label, it can be soaked off in warm water. If the bag's drawstring isn't strong enough, replace it; a length of plastic-coated washing line, knotted tightly, works well. Be sure to remove any metal staples or plastic tags that may come with the bag. After your child's bath, put the bath toys into the bag and rinse them under running water. Then hang the bag from a tap handle or shower head so that the toys can drip-dry.

Mesh produce bags are perfect for wet toys.

Kitchen solutions for children

✱ Homemade bubbles

The ingredients for a homemade substitute for bubble-blowing liquid are right at the kitchen sink – washing-up liquid and water. Pour 30ml washing-up liquid into a clean plastic measuring jug and fill with tap water (1 part washing-up liquid to 15 parts water), then mix gently. This bubble solution performs best when left to sit overnight before use. Hard water will yield poor results, so test your tap water by making a small batch of solution. If you can't get bubbles to appear, switch to distilled water.

✱ Making salt sculptures

Why buy colourful sculpting dough when you and your child can make your own from inexpensive cupboard staples? Here's how: mix 180g salt together with 150g flour. Using your fist, make a deep indent in the mixture and pour in 180ml water. To add colour, simply use some non-toxic watercolour paint or food colouring. Knead well and shape into a ball. Roll out and hand your child some blunt-edged biscuit

cutters to cut out shapes, mould into sculptures or make into ornaments. Store in an airtight container, and you'll be able to use it again.

✱ Make your own super slime

The slimy green favourite of children everywhere is only a kitchen cupboard or health food shop away. To make it, combine 1 teaspoon of ground psyllium husks (available at pharmacies and health food shops and online) with 280ml of water in a lidded jar and shake vigorously for 3 minutes. Pour into a microwaveable container and add a few drops of green food colouring. Microwave on high for 3 minutes; stop the process if the slime starts to ooze out the top of the container. Let rest for 3 minutes and microwave for another 5 minutes. Remove carefully and let cool for an hour. Store in an airtight container.

✱ A kitchen cupboard toy box

Most babies know that the kitchen is where the real action is – it's full of shiny things, interesting sounds, yummy smells and – food. It's always important to childproof your kitchen, to install safety latches and plugs, and to make sure that anything even remotely dangerous is out of reach. Once you've done this, you can designate one floor cupboard to be a baby's kitchen toy box and stock it with a few specific items that your child can play with: smaller pans and lids, a few plastic containers, a wooden spoon, a sturdy set of measuring spoons and nesting metal measuring cups that he can bang to his heart's content.

✳ Shake, rattle and roll

Some metal and plastic food cans, like containers for stacked potato crisps, come with plastic lids. Turn them into fun noisemakers by cleaning and drying an empty can, making absolutely sure that all sharp edges have been removed or filed down and putting in a small amount of dry pasta, cereal, hard sweets, dried beans or rice. Secure the plastic lid with gaffer tape, testing the noisemaker to be certain the top won't come off. A quieter alternative is to put crunchy cereal into a cardboard biscuit box and secure the top with tape. When rolled on the floor, this homemade rattler makes a great swooshing sound.

✳ From milk bottle to toy caddy

If there are too many small toys under your feet, you can bring some order to the toy invasion by making a simple toy carrier from an empty 4 litre milk bottle or household bleach container with a handle. With scissors or a utility knife, carefully cut a large opening out of the top third of the bottle, leaving the handle area and the plastic cap intact. Cover the cut edge with gaffer or masking tape (although the cut edge could be filed or sanded smooth, taping gives extra protection). Let your child decorate the carrier with permanent markers and then fill it with small toys. Arguing siblings can keep their treasures in separate carriers and perhaps avoid the usual arguments.

✳ Invisible lemon juice 'ink'

If your child has a taste for the mysterious, teach him the secret of invisible writing. All that's required is a small bowl of lemon juice, a cotton bud and a piece of paper. Dip the bud in the juice and write on the paper. When the paper is dry, there will be no sign of the lemon juice 'ink'. Now hold the paper near to, but not touching, a hot lightbulb, moving the paper

make your own...

BATH BOMBS

Nothing makes children happier at bath time than splashing around. Bath bombs, are a literal blast to toss into the tub, but are expensive. Here's how to make your own from scratch:

Natural bicarb bath bombs

2 teaspoons bicarbonate of soda
1 teaspoon cornflour
1 teaspoon citric acid
20 drops glycerine
Food colouring or liquid watercolour paints (optional)
Fragrance (optional)

1 Mix bicarbonate of soda, cornflour and citric acid in a medium bowl.

2 Add the glycerine, 3–4 drops of food colouring and a few drops of fragrance (if desired).

3 Combine well until the mixture becomes crumbly.

4 Form and pack the mixture into golf ball-sized balls (or smaller) and set aside to dry and harden overnight.

5 Place the child and bicarbonate of soda bath bomb in the tub and watch the fun.

Playtime and craft recipes

You've probably come across some or all of the following recipes at one time or another, but they're not always easy to track down when you need them. All are key elements for children's play and crafts – and luckily, all are easy to make.

Finger paint

Keep containers of finger paint safely away from eager little hands. Finger painting is one of the child activities that you should supervise.

> 75g cornflour
> 480ml cold water
> Food colouring

1. Combine cornflour and water in a saucepan and place over a high heat.
2. Bring the mixture to a boil and cook until thickened, stirring constantly.
3. Remove from heat and cool to room temperature.
4. Divide the mixture among containers and stir several drops of food colouring into each.

Storage Pour the finger paint into small plastic containers with snap-on lids and store it at room temperature.

Craft paste

This white paste can be used for craft projects and for making papier-mâché.

> 1 litre water
> 45g salt
> 225g plain flour

1. Bring water to boil in a medium saucepan.
2. Remove from heat and stir in salt.
3. Add flour a little at a time, stirring constantly. Continue to add flour and stir until the mixture is the consistency of thick gravy.
4. Cool the paste to room temperature before using.

Storage Store the paste in an airtight container in the fridge. It may keep for as long as five days, but throw it away immediately if it becomes mouldy or develops a bad smell.

Play clay

Two kitchen staples – bicarbonate of soda and cornflour – are the basis of this easy-to-make clay.

> 360g bicarbonate of soda
> 180g cornflour
> 280g cold water
> Food colouring (optional)

1. In a medium-size saucepan, mix together bicarbonate of soda and cornflour.
2. Add water and stir. Add food colouring to the water, if desired.
3. Set over a medium heat and stir continuously for 10 to 15 minutes. Do not overcook. The mixture should have the consistency of mashed potatoes.
4. Transfer the cooked mixture to a plate and cover with a damp cloth to cool to room temperature.

Storage Between uses, store play clay in a self-sealing plastic bag or an airtight container.
It keeps in the fridge for up to a week.

Hardening Harden clay objects by air-drying overnight on a wire rack. Or place them on a baking sheet in a preheated 180°C/gas 4 oven; then turn off heat and keep objects in the oven until it's cold. To microwave, place objects on a paper towel and microwave at medium power for 30 seconds. Turn objects over and heat for another 30 seconds, repeating as necessary until objects are hard and dry.

slowly over the heat source. Magically, the writing will turn brown and legible – it's a trick worthy of Harry Potter and his friends.

✳ An egg carton game

Here is a fun activity that can help pre school children to master counting and sorting skills. With a marker, write the numbers 1 to 12 (or 15) in the sections of a large egg carton. Then provide edible items such as shaped cereal, raisins or nuts and get the child to put the right amount in each numbered section. You can play a similar sorting game by having him separate different shapes and colours of cereal, dry pasta or dried beans.

Alternatively, give the child a bowl of raw fruit and vegetable pieces – sliced carrots and apples, peas, grapes, mandarin orange segments, cherry tomatoes, broccoli, small button mushrooms – whatever you have on hand and get him to sort the food into the egg sections by type.

✳ Food colouring to brighten snowy-day play

After they have pelted one another with snowballs, children can get fidgety for more fun on a snowy day, so try this: fill several plastic squirt bottles – ketchup bottles are ideal – with water and add a few drops of food colouring to each. Children can 'draw' designs on the snow with the coloured water.

✳ A carrier for precious papers

School children sometimes have important papers to take to school – like the world map your daughter has been working on for weeks for her geography class or a book review that your son has typed up himself. Tubes from rolls of paper towels or standard-size cling film, foil or waxed paper are just the right size for A4 sheets of paper. For larger projects, save longer tubes from wrapping paper or oversized

aluminium foil. Be careful not to cram too much into a cardboard tube or the papers will be difficult to extract.

household superstar

10 THINGS TO DO WITH A CYLINDRICAL CONTAINER

1 Store pencils, crayons and rulers.

2 Make sand-castle towers at the beach.

3 Fill with tennis balls, ping pong balls or shuttlecocks.

4 Fill with dried beans, seal with lid, turn on music and use as a shaker.

5 Seal with lid, turn on music, and use as a drum.

6 Store a secret jewellery hoard.

7 Have mum cut a slice in the middle of the lid, seal and use as a not-quite piggy bank.

8 Store favourite hand-me-down CDs and DVDs.

9 Fill with hairslides, scrunchies, and other hair accessories.

10 Make a time capsule: get your child to write a short essay or draw a picture, add personal items, seal with lid, bury in yard, unearth next year.

Bubbles, bubbles, everywhere

Children love bubbles. Big bubbles. Little bubbles. Clouds of bubbles. And your house is full of items that can make bubbles of all shapes and sizes. Many bubble-ologists swear by a simple blower made of two sheets of plain typing paper. Here's how to make a blower that will be prized for its truly enormous bubbles:

1

Stack the sheets of paper and roll into a cone lengthways, with the tip at the corner of the pages; the diameter at the large end of the cone should be around 3cm.

2

Tape the cone with masking tape starting about 5cm inches above the large end (it's vital that the tape and bubble solution don't touch). Trim the small end of the cone to about 1cm in diameter.

3

To make the flat, smooth-rimmed opening essential for bubble blowing, trim the large end at a point where all layers of paper are overlapping. Cut off any rough spots on the bottom rim, testing for smoothness by running your finger over it; then test it for evenness by making sure that the cone will stand upright on a smooth surface.

4

Dip the large end in bubble solution and blow slowly to make bubbles. Experts advise leaving the cone in the mix for 30 seconds the first time it is used; after that, a 2 or 3-second dip will do.

Try a straw!

We used a metal coat hanger to make a huge blower!

Plastic fruit baskets work as well!

Cupboard crafts

✳ Glitter from salt

Bring some glitz to children's projects, for less. Mix 1 tablespoon liquid watercolour with 45g table salt or rock salt, then shake the salt and colouring in a plastic bag to distribute the colour evenly. Spread the mixture on paper towels on a flat microwaveable plate and microwave on high for 2 minutes. Cool and break up clumps with your fingers. Store in a dry, airtight container.

✳ Play-dough hair with a garlic press

To make hair for play-dough figures, roll up a small ball of play dough, put it in a garlic press and slowly press out the strands. Use a small paintbrush to dab a little water on the spot where a strand will be attached; then press the piece in place with a toothpick or the pointed end of a small knitting needle.

✳ Pasta art

Even little children can make beautiful abstract designs with this project that's old as the hills: look in your cupboard for stray, half-empty boxes of dried pasta. Make different shapes and sizes by breaking up long strands of spaghetti and lasagna, add small macaroni pieces and colour as desired with non-toxic food colouring. When dry, the possibilities are endless:

- Make a personal treasure chest by covering the top and sides of a shoe or cigar box with the pasta, using craft glue.
- Draw designs on folded construction paper or card stock and glue on pasta for a personal holiday or birthday card.
- String coloured macaroni or any tubular pasta to make necklaces and bracelets.
- Glue pasta shapes to hairslides, hairpins and even belt buckles.

A KITCHEN CHRISTMAS TREE

If you want to do something different and have a kitchen-themed tree, use a star-shaped biscuit cutter as a tree topper. Decorating a tree with kitchen items can be a wonderful family project, especially when everyone enjoys cooking together. Almost anything but the kitchen sink can be used as ornaments – here are ideas enough to fill Santa's toy bag:

- Your children's baby cups and spoons
- Biscuit cutters attached with red ribbons
- Old salt and pepper shakers filled with silver and gold glitter
- Stainless-steel spoons, attached with shiny ribbon to add sparkle
- Vintage tea strainers
- Vintage napkin rings
- Colourful pot holders
- Salt clay ornaments (see page 212)

To add pizzazz, string cranberries and popcorn or tiny marshmallows around the tree and tuck colourful cloth or paper napkins into the branches. Finally and most important, have fun creating a delightful memory for everyone.

Kitchen-towel tube creations

Paper-towel tubes make super toy and craft materials and are usually stronger than toilet tissue rolls, so don't throw them out. Here are six child-pleasing ideas that require little more than a few tubes, a bit of tape, glue and scissors:

1

Make a fort by taping cardboard rolls together vertically to form a square and leaving an opening on one side to serve as a door. The size of the fort will depend on the number of tubes you have.

2

Create a log cabin by taping tubes together horizontally and taping ends together to form a square. Cut a door, then add a roof made of flat cardboard. Leave the roof unattached so that children can remove it and set their toy figures inside the cabin.

3

Make Easter egg holders by cutting cardboard tubes crossways into 3-5cm wide sections. Children can decorate the sections with poster paints or washable markers and then set their Easter eggs on the pretty rings. Use the same basic technique to let the children create their own decorative napkin rings.

4

For sandbox play, supply toddlers and pre-school children with a selection of tubes cut in different lengths. They can stick the tubes in the sand and build whatever they imagine.

5

Create a safe magic wand for a toddler by taping or gluing a paper star to one end of a cardboard tube.

6

Make music with a simple flute. Use a pencil to punch four holes in a cardboard tube. Secure wax paper to one end with a rubber band. A child can make music by humming into the open end of the flute.

Inspiration all around

✳ New use for an old aquarium

An unused aquarium or fishbowl can be transformed into a fascinating 3D decoration for a child's room – and your child can pick the theme and do much of the work. Start by cleaning and disinfecting the tank or bowl. Then paint the inside of the glass with a diluted mixture of water and water-soluble craft paint to create the look of ocean water, blue sky, billowy clouds, rainbows, green fields or even abstract designs. The paint should be thin enough to see through, so test it for transparency and thin with more water as needed. On the bottom of the tank, spread a fairly thick layer (5cm or more) of sand or fish bowl pebbles. Now let your child choose what goes inside.

✳ Quick clean-ups

By their very nature, children and dirt go hand-in-hand. Here are some easy ideas to keep your home clean using basic household supplies:

- **Plastic or painted wooden toys** Clean these with a paste made of 2 parts bicarbonate of soda to 1 part washing-up liquid. Apply with a soft cloth. Use a toothbrush to work the paste into small spaces. If the dirt is really stubborn, leave the paste on for a while. Remove it with a damp cloth or sponge.

- **Outdoor toys and children's vehicles** Rub with full-strength white vinegar, applied with a cloth. Remove the residue with a damp cloth or sponge or hose it off and dry with a clean cloth or towel.

- **Stuffed toys** Clean these unwashables by putting them in a plastic or paper bag, adding half or more of a 250g box of bicarbonate of soda and shaking the bag for 30 seconds or so. When the toy looks and smells clean, remove bicarbonate of soda residue by either vacuuming the toy with your machine's curtain attachment or shaking the toy in the open air, brushing off any residue with your fingers.

- **Crayon marks on washable wallpaper** Try warming the marks with a hair dryer. Give it a minute, then wipe the marks away with a damp cloth. Another idea is to apply a coat of latex glue to the marks, let it dry thoroughly and then gently roll off the rubbery glue.

tip BELLS ON THEIR TOES

To keep track of your child as she zips around the house, tightly attach a few **tiny bells** to each of her shoes; not only will you know whether they are in the laundry room or racing around the hall, they'll make music as they do it. Note: Bells should only be used on children over the age of three.

household superstar

6 CHILD FRIENDLY USES FOR TAPE

Tape is indispensable in households with children. The variety of tapes make it easy to find the right tape for every need. Here are a few quick tape solutions for parents and children.

1 Use masking tape to secure disposable nappies when the sticky tabs fail.

2 Wrap the middle part of new crayons and chalk pieces with transparent tape to help keep them from breaking.

3 Wrap clear tape tightly around the ends of string and ribbons to make stringing objects easier.

4 Attach address labels to children's pencils, pens, crayon boxes and other school supplies with transparent tape or clear parcel tape.

5 'Laminate' library cards, bus passes, lunch tickets and other paper take-alongs with clear parcel tape. Apply to both sides; then trim the tape at the edge of card. Scanners are able to read bar codes through clear tape.

6 If you can't find a plaster, substitute a piece of gauze or tissue secured with clear tape.

● **Vomit or urine on a rug** First, wipe up what you can. Pour bicarbonate of soda onto the affected area, pat it in with a paper towel and let it dry completely before vacuuming up the residue. Bicarbonate of soda will clean, sanitise and deodorise the spot. Use the same method to clean a wet mattress.

✱ Dry a baby's cap on a balloon

Machine drying a baby's bonnet or cap, even on the delicate cycle, often leaves it looking wrinkled, limp and less than pretty. To solve the problem, inflate a balloon to the approximate size of the child's head, tie it securely and attach it to a smooth surface with tape (away from baby's reach). Slip the washed and still-damp cap or bonnet over the balloon. With your hands, lightly smooth out creases and gently shape the cap and brim. 'Press' ribbons and ties by running them through your fingers and laying them out straight.

When the cap is dry, pop the balloon and discard it. A few touchups with a warm iron will have the cap looking as good as new.

✱ Secure sewing with dental floss

If you are tired of lost or dangling buttons on your children's coats and jackets, substitute dental floss for sewing thread to get a strong, longer-lasting hold. Also use dental floss when replacing buttons, eyes and ears and stitching ripped seams in stuffed toys.

✱ Tape your troubles away

When toy boxes, paperback book spines and colouring books are falling apart, use clear parcel tape to reinforce corners, spines and edges of books, game boards and game and toy boxes.

Health, safety and hygiene hints

✱ Cover corners with shoulder pads

A great way to protect children who have just started walking is with a pair of old shoulder pads. Cut open the long straight side and slip the pad over a corner so the inner padding encases the edges. Adjust as needed and then tape the pad securely in place. Hiding the pads under an attractive cloth will look better and stop curious youngsters from disturbing them.

✱ Colourful bandages

When a little one has fallen down and scraped his elbow or knee and you're trying to console him, to no avail, distract him from his pain by having him colour his own plaster while you gently clean the wound with a dab of soapy water and antiseptic cream. While you are busy, make him busy: give him a few plain plasters and a rainbow of non-toxic, water-based markers and let his imagination run wild. He'll wear his plaster as a work of art.

✱ Freeze stuffed toys for allergic children

Forestall sniffles in allergy prone children by giving their stuffed toys the deep freeze for 3 to 5 hours, once a week. Slip the toy into a freezer bag, place it among the frozen peas and ice cubes and any dust mites will be killed.

✱ Two tip-to-toe uses for fabric softener sheets

If trainers smell like something has died inside them, stuff each shoe with a fabric softener sheet every night to lessen the odour. And solve a flyaway hair problem by rubbing your child's hair with a softener sheet to control static.

idea

PAINLESS PLASTER REMOVAL

In the old days, parents were advised to rip plasters quickly off a child, causing many a boy or girl to do almost anything to postpone the inevitable. But a quick rip didn't reduce the pain but merely got everything over with more quickly.

A kinder, gentler and generally pain-free approach is to carefully but thoroughly rub baby oil or washing-up liquid along the edges and over the top of the plaster. Use enough to penetrate and lubricate the adhesive (but not the gauze), then slowly lift the plaster off, rubbing on a bit more oil or washing-up liquid if you hit a sticking point. Your children will thank you, if only with an expression of relief.

The great outdoors

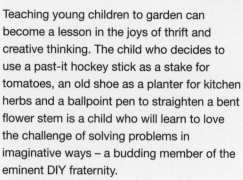

✳ Painting stones

Decorating medium-sized rocks with smooth surfaces is a longtime favourite children's craft. Let their imaginations run wild when they find stones in different shapes. Wash them to remove dirt, grease and any mossy patches and then let the stones dry completely in the sun. Using poster or craft paints, youngsters can paint the tops and sides of the rocks however they like. When the paint is dry, seal the surface with several coats of spray-on, non-toxic, clear varnish, drying between coats. (Avoid brush-on varnishes because brushing is likely to smear the paint.) A sufficiently large stone would make a doorstop, while small stones could be used to decorate a kitchen windowsill or serve as paperweights on a desk.

✳ Cleaning outdoor equipment with vinegar

A simple, inexpensive solution of 1 part white vinegar to 1 part water makes a reliable cleaner for outdoor play equipment, children's cars and bikes. For tough dirt, wipe with the vinegar solution; then rub the spot with bicarbonate of soda on a damp rag or sponge and rinse. It's a good idea to wash swing seats and chains or ropes frequently. You can also use the vinegar solution to clean children's car seats.

✳ Autumn leaf paintings for a Junior Picasso

Nature offers us one of the most versatile and child-friendly paintbrushes in a fallen leaf. For a lovely way to spend an autumn afternoon with a child, take him on a walk in a park and ask him to collect leaves of various shapes and sizes. Bring them home and using an old toothbrush, gently remove any dust or dirt from their surfaces. Mix up a small batch of non-toxic

idea

GARDEN LESSONS

Teaching young children to garden can become a lesson in the joys of thrift and creative thinking. The child who decides to use a past-it hockey stick as a stake for tomatoes, an old shoe as a planter for kitchen herbs and a ballpoint pen to straighten a bent flower stem is a child who will learn to love the challenge of solving problems in imaginative ways – a budding member of the eminent DIY fraternity.

Equip your child with a small spade and bucket to begin and let him get his hands in the dirt. Help him to plant a mix of flowers and vegetable seeds that will produce easy-to-tend compact plants and let him learn by trial and error. Serve as an example by using as many ordinary household items in the garden as you can and he'll soon follow your lead. Also be sure to let him help you compost kitchen waste and autumn leaves for the garden so that he'll learn to think 'outside the plot'.

At the end of the growing season, leave plantings in place so that your child can observe what happens in his garden in the fall and winter. Over the years, your child's plot can grow in size and he can do more of the work on his own – hopefully as a full-fledged apprentice in the art of self-sufficiency.

finger paints (page 214) spread the table with a few pieces of newspaper and top them with sheets of favourite, light-coloured stiff paper. Roll up your child's sleeves and using his index finger as a paint brush, have him paint one surface of

*Make a delicious homemade bird feeder
with pine cones and peanut butter!*

each leaf; immediately press them down onto the paper, paint side down. Count to 20 (another good lesson) and remove the leaf by its stem for instant (and free) art.

✳ Pine cone bird feeders

You can make many kinds of bird feeders from available materials and this one is especially easy and fun to assemble. All you'll need are pine cones, sugarless peanut butter (the amount varies depending on the number and size of cones used) and birdseed. Tightly tie a length of string or yarn around the top or bottom of the cone. Then, using a plastic knife, spread the peanut butter over the cone, pushing it into the nooks and crevices. Now spread a layer of birdseed onto a baking sheet or a pie tin. Roll the cone in the birdseed, making sure it's covered and gently shake off any excess. Hang the cone from a tree branch, fence, gatepost, balcony railing or a secure plant hanger. How could any bird resist such a tempting feeder?

✳ Organising sports equipment

Parents of young athletes are all too familiar with a house overflowing with a jumble of footballs, cricket bats, hockey sticks, tennis rackets, golf clubs, sweatshirts, running shoes and some things you can't even identify. Even one sporty youngster can create a major mess. Here are three suggestions for keeping it under control.

- Put a tall plastic or metal rubbish bin in the garage or utility room to hold long items like bats, sticks, extra golf clubs and cricket stumps. Weight the bottom of the can with bricks or heavy stones so that it won't tip over.
- Install a pegboard and hooks (you may already have one in a work area) for hanging rackets, hats, gloves, protective padding, swimming goggles and caps, wet clothes and shoes.
- Designate one large laundry basket for sports clothing – and do yourself a favour and lay down rules about who is to wash what and when.

Instead of your slippers, puppies can teethe on frozen bagels!

9 Favourite pet subjects

Do you ever feel like your cat or dog is the only one who really understands you? Do you ever find yourself talking to your fish or confiding in your parrot or budgie? If so, don't worry, you're definitely not alone!

Today, you can pay a fortune for specialist pet diets for just about every possible stage of life or health condition – and buy expensive treats and special drinks. Or you can follow the recipe for Arlo and Scamp's favourite biscuits in this chapter, using just a few simple and inexpensive ingredients to make your own delicious doggy delicacies. In the same way, you can buy your cat a toy that costs as much as dinner for two at a restaurant or for a fraction of the cost you can recycle a belt to make a cat-sized collar, fashion a new pet bed by covering a pillow with fabric to match your home decoration and turn an empty pill bottle into a rattling toy.

Read on animal-lovers, for great ideas on how to keep your pets well fed, clean, healthy and happy and your wallet full.

Dogs' dinners

✳ Go bananas!

Add about a third of a soft banana to 1½ cups dry food. Slice it, mash it and stir it into the pellets. Not only does it add variety and a bit of healthy sweetness (which most dogs seem to love), but a bit of banana also will settle your dog's stomach.

✳ Healthy snacks

If you are on a diet, you know all about carrying around little peeled carrots to quell your appetite during snack breaks. The good news is that dogs generally love them, too. They're crunchy, sweet and healthy enough to make them a regular part of his diet in place of a biscuit.

✳ Yoghurt containers as doggie travel carriers

Save plastic yoghurt containers with fitted lids; when you're taking your dog along on a journey, they are the perfect size for his favourite small treats. Though most dogs don't like to eat during travel, you can reward him for his good behaviour once you have reached your destination.

✳ Put the jerk back in the food

Is your faithful friend a little finicky? Try this safe trick: put a stick of beef jerky into a new bag of dry dog food and reseal it for 24 hours. The scent will make the dry food more tempting to your canine.

✳ Get your dog to take a pill

There's no reason to wrestle your dog to the ground to try to get him to take a pill; this is what cheese is for. All you need is some strongly flavoured Cheddar cheese. Grate a small amount (or buy ready grated. Warm a little bit in your hands and roll it into a cheese 'pill'. Then insert the medicine and it should go down in a matter of seconds.

idea

FOODS YOU SHOULD NEVER EVER GIVE A DOG

Chocolate, which contains theobromine, a substance that is poisonous to dogs.

Onions, garlic and other onion family members (leeks, shallots), whose ingredient thiosulphate can destroy your pet's red blood cells.

Add sweetness and flavour to dry dog food with a banana!

make your own...

GOURMET DOG BISCUITS

Here's a delicious, all-purpose, low-salt seasoning that will enhance fish, meat and poultry dishes. Make it in large batches to always have it on hand.

Arlo and Scamp's favourite biscuits

Citric acid, arrowroot and powdered orange peel in this recipe may sound unusual, but they can usually be found in supermarkets.

200g whole-wheat flour
1 tablespoon baking powder
250g natural peanut butter
240ml skimmed milk

1 Preheat oven to 190°C/gas 5.

2 Combine flour and baking powder in one bowl. In another bowl, whisk together peanut butter and milk.

3 Combine wet and dry ingredients and mix until a dough forms. Place the dough on a lightly floured surface and knead until the dough is pliant (about 5 minutes).

4 Roll dough to 0.5cm thickness, then use a dog bone–shaped biscuit cutter to cut out shapes.

5 Place cutouts on a greased baking sheet and bake for 20 minutes or until lightly browned. Cool the biscuits on a wire rack and store in an airtight container.

Gorgeous grooming

* File claws with sandpaper

Most dogs don't like having their claws filed, but doing so will keep their claws in good condition and keep them from splitting in cold weather. To ease your dog's stress about the nail-filing devices used by groomers, cut a small round of medium-grit sandpaper, wrap it around your index finger and *gently* work at it, stopping frequently to praise your dog and reinforcing his good behaviour with a treat.

* Use tube socks for post-shampoo itchiness

Many dogs have skin that is sensitive to shampoos, leaving them scratching and irritated after their bath (which they probably didn't want in the first place). Keep a larger dog from scratching his neck and face by putting his back feet in cotton tube socks and pulling them up as far as you can; if you have a smaller dog (with shorter legs), try a pair of cotton baby socks.

* Use olive oil on matted hair

Loosen your dog's matted hair by rubbing a little olive oil into the knot. Then gently comb through the matted area with a wire brush until the brush teeth glide smoothly through the coat.

* Oil away tar

Remove tar from your dog's foot pads by gently rubbing them with baby oil or petroleum jelly. Then wash away the residue with a mild solution of soapy water. To keep tar pickup to a minimum on your walks, carefully trim the hair that grows between your pet's toes.

* Dab off tear residue with baby oil

Some dogs' tear ducts create a residue that collects in the hair below the corner of the eye. This may stain the hair of light-coloured dogs and despite products sold to 'whiten' it, vets say there is little you can do – so it's best not to fret. Still, you should remove the gunk. Pour a little baby oil onto a cotton ball and gently work it into the area to loosen the residue and make it easier to dab off. You could also use a very mild face-freshening astringent, in which case take great care to keep it out of your dog's eyes.

* Vinegar ear cleaner

All flop-eared dogs – especially water dogs like labradors and retrievers – should have their ears gently cleaned at least once a week to prevent waxy buildup and infections (which result in both pain and odour). Mix 1 part white vinegar to 1 part water; dip a cotton wool ball into the mixture and carefully wipe out your dog's ears, but *without* inserting the cotton wool ball into the ear canal. Use a separate cotton wool ball for each ear to avoid cross contamination in case of infection.

* Prevent dog hair blockages with a pan scrubber

At bath time, you can keep your dog's hair from clogging the drain in your bath by placing a nylon pan scrubber or a snipped-off section of kitchen sponge over the drain. This porous barrier will collect hair, which you can then easily remove and discard.

Playtime for your pet

Buying toys for your dog is a nice gesture, but he'll be just as happy with homemade games, like these:

Blue jean baby

Tiny puppy teeth should chew – but not on your furniture, the cat, slippers or your favourite high heels or boots. How can you stop it? Make sure that your pup has plenty of toys to call her own. Make inexpensive, sturdy toys out of old denim jeans. Cut a double layer of denim into a square, stitch together on three sides, stuff with a few old tennis balls (not tights, which she can choke on if she tears the toy apart) and stitch up the fourth.

Softballs for small dogs

If your furry friend is tiny, he will have a blast chasing around an inanimate object larger than he is; an old tennis ball is just the ticket to occupy his attention for hours.

Chase the flashlight

What could be more fun for a frisky dog than chasing a torch beam in a large, darkened room? Make sure not to shine the light in his eyes and move the furniture to avoid the crashing that generally follows the chase.

Plastic bottle toss

Punch two holes in the cap of an empty plastic soft drink bottle. Fill it with colourful mini pom pons. Then thread a thick string through the cap and knot it, then screw the cap back on tightly. Now throw the bottle towards your puppy and draw it back. He'll enjoy chasing the elusive toy for hours, if you're willing to play along.

Walking the dog

✻ Keep your dog on a tight(s) lead

Your dog will appreciate the elasticity of a lead that's made from an old pair of tights. The idea is to knot it along every 10–12cm and create a handle at the end by looping the tights and knotting it.

✻ Cool him with a wet T-shirt

If you're feeling the heat, your dog may be too. If you're walking him on a very hot day, dampen a large (or small, depending on the dog's size) children's cotton T-shirt with cool water, wring it dry and fit it over his head, pushing his two front paws through the sleeves. Tie a knot on the side to take up the slack, making sure that the shirt fits comfortably – neither too tight nor too loose. (Check it periodically to make sure it stays that way.) If the shirt dries out after a while, spritz it with water.

✻ Glow-in-the-dark collar

Even a few regularly spaced strips of reflective tape placed along your dog's (or cat's) collar will help drivers to see them if they happen to be out at night or at dusk.

✻ Plastic bag pooper-scooper

Never throw away plastic shopping bags. Among many other uses they make prefect pooper-scoopers and they're *free*. Just stick your hand into the bag, pick up the mess with your gloved hand and turn the bag inside out before tying it off and disposing of it.

✻ Cardboard cleaning tool

Cut a section from an empty cereal box to use as a disposable pooper-scooper whenever you walk your dog. Slide it under the pile of dog mess and put both the pile and your scooper directly into a plastic shopping bag. Tie the whole thing up and throw it in the bin.

✻ Soothe paws with petroleum jelly

Extreme temperatures can damage a dog's paws during a walk. Hot pavements, freezing paths and road salts may irritate his foot pads and lead to cracking. To soothe his feet and help initiate healing, rub a little petroleum jelly onto his paws. Before he comes back in the house wipe any excess jelly off his paws so that he won't track it onto the carpet or upholstery.

tip OLD BELT = TEMPORARY LEASH

When you've mislaid your dog's lead **an old belt** will serve as a substitute until you can get to a pet shop to buy a new one. Buckle the belt onto your dog's collar and use gaffer tape to create a handle at the other end. (Twist the tape into a 'rope', loop it and attach it to the end of the belt with several more layers of tape).

Cats and their litter trays

✳ Foil litter tray smells

Once odour penetrates the bottom of a litter tray, it is almost impossible to remove completely – a good reason to whip up this easy-to-make aluminium foil odour barrier. Cut a piece of cardboard box to size, cover it with heavy-duty aluminium foil and secure the foil to the cardboard with masking tape. When changing the cat litter, don't throw away your homemade liner; instead, swab the foil with a wet sponge soaked in a solution of 2 parts vinegar to 1 part bicarbonate of soda. If you treat the liner gently, you should be able to get at least three or four uses out of it.

✳ Slice a lemon to neutralise odour

There's nothing pleasant about the smell of a litter tray – but here's a way to control odour in the area where the box sits. Place half a lemon, cut side up, on a saucer and set it on the floor a few inches from the box. (A scientist could explain to you why the smell of lemon in the air neutralises unpleasant odours, but suffice to say that lemon gives bicarbonate of soda a run for its money when it comes to odour control.) For tough odours, place several lemon halves on a paper plate or try a combination of orange, lemon and lime halves.

✳ Three ways to sweeten a litter tray

If you're buying the kind of litter that neutralises litter tray odours, you're probably spending a lot every week on this cat essential. Here are three suggestions that will help you to achieve the same result at less expense:

- Add 60g bicarbonate of soda to ordinary litter and mix well
- Sprinkle 60g baby powder onto the litter to keep it fresh
- Stir a handful of dried parsley or other aromatic dried herb into the litter.

✳ No-cost litter tray cleaners

Instead of using branded or supermarket own brand cleaning products, choose one of these kitchen cupboard or under-the-sink items to keep a litter tray as fresh as a daisy. After removing the litter and liner (if you use one), clean the box weekly with:

- Vinegar
- Household ammonia
- Lemon oil
- A solution of 1 part household bleach to 10 parts water

Finish the job by rinsing the litter box with plain water. Then wipe it completely dry with a clean cloth before refilling it.

✳ A doormat for cats

To keep your cat from tracking dusty paw prints onto the floor when she leaves her litter tray, place a carpet remnant or an old place mat on the side of the box where she makes her exit.

Cats at play

Cats take as much pleasure in everyday objects as they do in expensive toys. Take aluminium foil. Just scrunch up a piece, throw it and watch your furry friend chase around the house after it. Other 'free' toys are plastic cap guards from bottled water bottles; empty wooden spools; golf balls; plastic bottle tops; corrugated cardboard boxes; shoeboxes; clean plastic buckets and heavy-gauge wire, with one end held in place by closing it in a door or drawer and the other end looped, with a feather or thread attached to it.

Rattlin' good fun

Use plastic medicine bottles or old film canisters to make toys for cats. Fill the vessel with coins, paper clips or buttons – any small items that will rattle when shaken. Roll the toy out on the floor and watch as your cat delights in batting it around.

Sock it to 'em

Clean an old sock, stuff the toe-end with some catnip and tie it off tightly. Dangle the tempting toy from a string and you've got a game going with your cat. Alternatively, tie the filled sock to a doorknob and let your cat bat it about on his own. A sock isn't the only thing to use: You could also stuff a baby bootie with catnip or cut off the sleeve of a worn-out blouse or shirt and turn it into a catnip holder.

'You're pulling my leg!

That's the name of the game you can play with your cat when you stuff a leg of old tights and a feline-human tug of war ensues. Cut off one stocking leg and fill the toe with catnip. Knot the stocking above the filled area and make several more knots along the length of the leg. A catnip-free version of the toy uses old rags or wadded-up tights as stuffing; in this case, engage your cat in a game of 'chase the snake' as you wiggle the toy around on the floor.

Watching your own wild kingdom

If you have a frequently visited bird feeder and a video camera, you have the makings for hours of unbridled entertainment for a little indoor hunter. Video the birds in action, pop in the DVD or tape where your kitten can see the television, turn it on and watch the fun unfold.

Food and drink

✳ Healthy stir-ins

When cooking, save the rich liquid from steamed, vegetables and the drippings from meat and stir a spoonful or two into your cat's food bowl, adding a little warm water to thin the juices if necessary. If your cooking session doesn't coincide with pet-feeding time, put the juices in a jar and store in the fridge for later use. Heat the stir-ins in the microwave to warm, not hot, before sharing them with your cat.

✳ Clean up Kitty's brush with tights

To clean up a cat brush with ease, slip a small piece of a pair of tights over the head of the brush *before* grooming. Make sure the bristles poke through. Once grooming is finished, remove the tights, which should now be laden with cat fur and discard.

✳ A mouse pad for a cat bowl

When you replace your computer mouse pad, use the old one as a place mat for your pet's food bowl. It will be perfect for keeping it from skidding and for catching spills.

✳ Ant-proof your pet's food

When you feed dogs or cats outdoors, keep ants out of the food bowl with this trick: set your pet's bowl in the centre of a baking tray filled with water.

✳ Petroleum jelly = fewer hairballs

Just add 1 teaspoon petroleum jelly to your cat's daily feedings to help to ease hairballs through the digestive tract. (Note: Vegetable oils and other oils won't work because your cat will absorb and digest them.) To control hairballs, give your cat a good brushing every day.

make your own...

CAT TREATS

Rolled oats are the basis of these biscuits just for cats. They have no preservatives or artificial ingredients – if you make your own stock.

Miss Kitty's oatmeal biscuits

Note that your biscuits can be chicken, beef or tuna flavoured. If you choose tuna, you could substitute the liquid in a can of water-packed tuna instead of oil; if the liquid doesn't amount to 120ml, just thin it with tap water.

150g rolled oats
60ml vegetable oil
50ml plain flour
120ml chicken broth, beef broth or oil
or water from canned tuna

1 Preheat oven to 180°C/gas 4.

2 Mix all ingredients into a dough.

3 Dust your hands with flour and shape dough into 1cm thick round biscuits. Set the cookies on a greased baking sheet.

4 Bake for 30 minutes or until the biscuits are lightly browned, then cool for 30 minutes on a cooling rack. Once cool, break them into bite-sized pieces for your cat.

Keeping pets bright-eyed and bushy-tailed

✻ A bicarb bed freshener

In between washings of your pet's bedding, sprinkle it with bicarbonate of soda and let it sit for about an hour. Shake off the bicarbonate of soda outdoors, then vacuum off the rest.

✻ Shrink an old sweater to fit your dog!

To keep your dog warm during cold-weather walks, provide her with a sweater by shrinking one of your old round-necked or v-neck, pullover woollen ones to dog-size. (Use a child's sweater if your dog is small.) First, measure the sweater against your dog; if it's at least three times too big, it should work. Put it into the washing machine with 60ml mild detergent and set the water temperature to hot; set the machine for a large wash, even though the load consists of a single sweater. After removing the sweater, press it between two towels to squeeze out as much water as possible. While the sweater is damp, it's time for a fitting. Reshape the sweater so that the neck is wide enough to fit easily over your dog's head. (If it won't, cut a slit and bind the edges with seam binding to prevent fraying). The arms of the sweater

what's the story?

OLD WIVES' TAIL

You may have heard that adding tomato juice, apple cider vinegar or bicarbonate of soda to a dog's diet will neutralise the acidity in dog urine? The urine that kills your grass? Well, that turns out to be a spurious piece of folklore. Adding any of these ingredients to your dog's diet won't prevent dog pee from killing grass – and anyway, it's not the acidity that does the damage but rather the high concentration of nitrogen in dog urine.

What's worse, following this discredited advice may be quite harmful and it seems that feeding pH-altering supplements such as tomato juice, vinegar or bicarbonate of soda to dogs could result in urinary tract diseases, bladder infections, crystals and bladder stones.

should fit over the dog's two front legs and the body of the sweater should reach about halfway down her back. Lay the sweater on a drying rack and let it dry in a well-ventilated room. Now let your dog strut her stuff in her new winter outfit – which didn't cost a penny.

Store pet supplies in shoe bag pockets!

✳ Recycle a belt as a collar

Save a few pounds by making a pet collar from a small leather belt. (A grosgrain belt is suitable for smaller, lightweight pets, but only if it has a binding along its length.) Cut the belt to the desired length for your little dog or cat. Place the new collar on a block of wood and poke holes in it with an awl, then buckle it around your pet's neck to make sure it fits comfortably. For a cat, split the collar and add in a piece of elastic so that it can slip off if she gets it caught.

✳ Shoe bag pet-stuff organiser

A hanging shoe bag placed inside a kitchen cupboard door or in your laundry room can help you to control all your pet clutter. Use the pockets for storing toys, treats, cloths – even your pet's vital health statistics, including the vet's name and number. With everything in one place, you should find it easier to locate what you need whenever you need it.

✳ Polish makes your pet easy to find

Glow-in-the-dark pet-safe nail polish dabbed onto your cat or dog's collar – and on claws – will make your pet easier to spot when he's out after dark. Available at pet stores or online.

✳ Keep basic info handy

Place all important papers that relate to your pet in a small lidded box (a cigar box is ideal) so that you can easily find it if you have to run to the vet's surgery in an emergency. In the same way, a pet sitter will be able to easily find everything in one place if he needs to.

✳ Don't throw away an old comb

Use it as a belly scratcher for your dog or cat. Your fingernails will do the job, too, but pets seem to love the feel of a fine-toothed comb digging into their fur.

Skin and coat care

✳ Eggs make coats shine

A weekly scrambled egg added to your cat or dog's food will keep her coat shiny and it's a healthy treat your pet will love. Raw eggs are off limits, because they may be contaminated with salmonella.

✳ Unsticking something sticky

That sticky something in your pet's fur could be pine sap, mud or something unmentionable. Before you get out the scissors and cut away the gummy patch, leaving your dog or cat with a bald spot, try mixing 1 teaspoon mild shampoo or washing-up liquid with 60 to 120ml warm water and whisk it well. Wearing rubber gloves, apply some of the solution to your pet's sticky spot, rubbing it in with your fingers. Then comb the spot with a wire-toothed brush. Once you've removed the sticky stuff, wash away any soapy residue with fresh warm water.

✳ Mouthwash for skin problems

You may think that mouthwashes are for oral hygiene only. But they're also a good all-around disinfectant for your dog or cat (and for *you*, for that matter). Use one of the stronger mouthwash brands as an astringent on your pet's skin to disinfect wounds, clean cuts and scrapes and cool down boils and other hot spots. Just moisten a cotton wool ball with mouthwash and dab it on the affected area to help a wounded dog or cat heal more quickly.

 *tip* REVITALISE DRY HAIR WITH TEA

If your pet's coat is looking a little less than lustrous, shampoo Fluffy or Fido as you usually do, then complete the wash by rinsing the coat with a litre of **warm unsweetened tea.**

Chasing away fleas

✷ Mix your own repellants

Homemade flea repellents are easy to mix and bottle, so why not give them a try?

Use them to spray your dog or cat almost all over, especially under the 'armpits', behind the ears and around the head, taking care to shield the eyes. When you spray at the base of the tail, avoid spraying the pet's genitals. Here are two quick and easy recipes:

- **Lemon spray** Cut 2 lemons into small pieces, put the pieces into a saucepan holding 1 litre water and boil the pieces for 1 hour. Remove the pan from the heat and let the mixture stand overnight. Strain the lemony liquid into a spray bottle and spray your pet as directed above.
- **Vinegar flea repellent** Repel fleas with a solution made from 10 parts water to 1 part white vinegar. Pour it into a spray bottle and spray onto your pet as directed above.

✷ Pine scent in the doghouse

A pile of fresh pine needles placed underneath your dog's bed will discourage fleas to settle.

✷ Draw a line in the salt

Pour table salt around all the crevices of the kennel to keep fleas well away from your dog's cosy abode.

✷ Cedar deterrents

Add cedar chips or cedar sawdust to the stuffing for your pet's pillow or bedding. If your dog has a kennel, hang or nail a cedar block inside. The odour of cedar repels fleas as well as other nuisance insects, including moths.

✷ Scent flea collars with essential oils

Shop-bought flea collars often carry an unpleasant odour and you may hesitate to put a chemical-laden collar so close to your pet's skin. Fit your pet with a natural, pleasant-smelling flea collar instead. Rub a few drops of essential oil of tea tree, citronella, lavender, eucalyptus or scented geranium into an ordinary webbed or rope collar or a dog bandana and then refresh the oil weekly.

✷ Kill eggs with salt, too

This flea killer takes a little time to work its magic. Sprinkle salt on your carpets to kill flea eggs; let it sit for a day, then vacuum. Repeat the process a few days later to make sure you haven't missed any flea eggs. Each time you vacuum the salt, tie up and discard the vacuum cleaner bag that you've used.

idea

YEAST FLEA REPELLENT

It's not true that fleas can be repelled only with topical treatments. Brewer's yeast works as a systemic flea repellent when ingested. If you use the powdered form, sprinkle 1 teaspoon into your cat or small dog's food daily (a 20kg dog will need a tablespoon).

You can also use brewer's yeast topically as well; just rub it directly into your pet's fur. Caution: Some animals develop a skin allergy after eating or being rubbed with yeast. If your pet is one, discontinue at once.

Keeping a clean, fresh animal house

✱ Prevent chewing with oil of cloves

Puppies do chew – even on the legs of tables and chairs. Discourage chewing by dabbing the most attractive spots (your shoes, a cardboard box and anything wooden your puppy can get his teeth around) with oil of cloves. The bitter odour and taste are a deterrent to nibbling.

✱ Frozen teething bagels

This is a great method for soothing painful gums in young teething puppies: freeze a few mini bagels until they are rock solid and ice cold. Let the puppy chew on them to ease his painful choppers. When the bagel becomes soft, take it away before he eats it and replace with a dog toy.

✱ Odour-eating vinegar

Accidents do happen, especially with new pets. Eliminate unpleasant urine smells from carpets with a 50:50 solution of white vinegar and warm water. Pour it onto the affected area so that it soaks through to the carpet padding, then allow it to sit for half an hour. Wash the affected area with cool water until the vinegar is rinsed out, then pat the carpet dry with towels. Cover with a 1cm thick layer of dry, clean white rags, towels or paper towels, weight them down with heavy objects (bricks, paperweights, door stops and the like) and let the absorbent material sit for several hours to soak up the moisture.

✱ Clear the air with coffee beans

Some pet owners have found that they can remove pet odours from a room simply by heating a cupful of freshly ground coffee beans

idea

CATS GOTTA SCRATCH

So the cat has ripped one side of a new chair to shreds? While it's being reupholstered, make him a scratching post by stapling or gluing a carpet remnant to a log or a section of board. Attach the post vertically to a 1cm thick section of plywood by hammering nails though the bottom of the plywood and into the log or board.

If you have leftover pieces of carpet, your new scratching post should cost nothing. If you don't have any carpet remnants, you can pick up a small piece for a few pounds at a carpet supplier.

in a cast-iron grillpan over low heat. As soon as the scent is released, remove the pan to the smelly room and set it on a trivet. By the time the ground beans are cool, much of the pet odour should have dissipated.

✱ Do away with pet hair!

It's embarrassing when guests don't want to sit on your sofa because they don't enjoy 'wearing' your pet's coat on their clothing. Here are some ways to remove dog and cat hair from your furniture and clothing – and preventing pet hair from getting there in the first place.

● Lightly mist your hair-covered garment with water, then put it in the tumble dryer with a

Keep Fido off the furniture with a shower curtain!

damp towel and a fabric softener sheet. Dry on the air cycle for a few minutes.

- Gently rub upholstered furniture and your clothing with a slightly damp kitchen sponge to remove pet hair.
- Wrap your hand with masking tape or gaffer tape, sticky side out. Run both your palm and the back of your hand over furniture or clothes to collect hair.
- Put on a rubber glove and rub your fingers back and forth over furniture until the pet hair forms a ball and you can lift it off.

✱ Kill carpet odour with bicarb

If a musty smell has infiltrated the carpet, as often happens with recently cleaned pet urine spots, use bicarbonate of soda to neutralise the odour. Once the carpet has thoroughly dried, sweeten the area by working 20–45ml bicarbonate of soda into the carpet pile. Wait for 15 minutes before vacuuming it up.

- Cover a sponge, a blackboard eraser or your hand with a fabric softener sheet and rub away pet hair.

- Try vacuuming your pet, using the brush attachment on your vacuum. If she doesn't mind the noise, make this a weekly task that will collect loose hairs before they start flying around the house. If your pet doesn't like being vacuumed, try holding the vacuum brush about 5cm away from her fur.

✱ Foil as a noisy deterrent

Noise deters pets from jumping on furniture. To train cats to stay off upholstered couches and chairs, top the cushions with aluminium foil.

If cats jump onto the furniture, the crunching sound of foil under their paws will send them scurrying in a hurry.

✱ Recycle a plastic shower curtain

Covering your furniture with an old plastic shower curtain is likely to keep pets at arm's length. It isn't comfortable to lie on and the crunchy plastic makes an unpleasant noise when your pet climbs onto it.

Equine affairs

✳ Make a tube sock snood
Rather than buying a special tail bag or snood, make one from a tube sock – a cost-effective way to protect your horse's tail on your way to a show. Here's how:
1. On each side of the sock cuff, cut a strip that will remain attached to the sock – each one about 8cm in length and 2cm wide.
2. Braid your horse's tail and slip the tube sock over it.
3. Interlace one of the loose sock strips with the top of the braid, then tie the second sock strip to the first one, knotting it tightly.

✳ Bleach it away
Rain scald or rain rot is a common skin infection affecting horses, particularly in winter when their skin stays wet for long periods of time. Mix 1 part household bleach to 10 parts water and pour the solution into a spray bottle.

Use it to clear up the affected area. Caution: be very careful not to spray it anywhere near the horse's eyes.

✳ Shine her up
After hosing off your horse, sponge on a solution of white vinegar and water (1 part vinegar to 10 parts water). This simple mixture will remove soap residue, repel flies and shine up the coat.

✳ Alternatives to purchased hoof dressing
Keeping your horse's hoofs in good condition is essential to his well-being. While many products are found on the market, here are three dressings you already have at home:
● Margarine
● Aerosol cooking spray
● WD-40

In winter, it's important to apply dressing to the hoofs to prevent snow freezing in a hoof. This makes it hard for a galloping horse to place its feet flat on the ground, often leading to sprains. Just remember that any of these dressings may make the hoof and shoe slippery, so be sure not to apply too much in winter or apply too frequently.

✳ Beat the freeze
Smear petroleum jelly inside your horse's water bucket in winter before filling it with water. When it ices over, you will find it much easier to slide out the ice as it coasts along a coat of slippery gel.

✳ Fight the flies

Keep flies away from your horse's eyes by dabbing a little petroleum jelly around each eye. During summer, smear zinc oxide ointment in and around her ears to repel flies.

✳ Shine up your saddle

Clean and polish your horse's chrome bits, buckles and straps with toothpaste. This handy and inexpensive polish works wonders on the shiny parts of a saddle.

✳ Flies and gnats

These pesky creatures are notoriously annoying to horses. Help your equine companion keep her cool by shading her eyes and giving her a spritz of bath oil spray.

✳ Saddle smarts

When you take apart your saddle for cleaning, it's easy to forget which stirrup strap is left and which is right. Take two empty toilet paper tubes and mark one *Left*, one *Right*. As you remove each strap, lace the strap through the correct paper tube and buckle it.

✳ Hair gel keeps manes tidy

Forget fancy grooming techniques and tools; if hair gel works for you, it will work for your horse, too. Use a dollop to make braiding easy and to keep stray hairs from popping out of place on show day.

✳ Spray stalls with vinegar to keep nibbles at bay

To keep stalls from being chewed on by nickering nags, mix a spray that's half white vinegar, half water; horses hate the taste of anything tart, so they will leave the wood alone.

make your own...

HOOF DRESSING

A horse's hoofs can easily become dry and cracked. This simple homemade hoof dressing, made from equal parts lard and pine tar, will work as well as any purchased product to keep your horse's hoofs in good shape. Pine tar is available at farm supply stores and online.

Pine tar hoof soother

This concoction has a thick consistency in warm weather and hardens to a paste in winter, when you may have to microwave it to make it easy to apply.

500g lard
500g pine tar
¼ teaspoon cayenne pepper

1 Put lard in a large microwave-safe container and microwave on low power until the lard melts.

2 Add pine tar and stir with a large wooden spoon until the dressing is well mixed.

3 Apply the dressing to your horse's hoofs with a soft 6cm-wide paintbrush.

Rabbits, hamsters and other small furries

✱ Give rabbits plenty of paper

A pet bunny with something to burrow into will be a happy one. Offer your rabbit shredded newspaper, crumpled-up phone book pages or other similar paper, placing it in the bottom of his cage so that he can dig away.

✱ A cardboard hidey-hole for a bunny

Rabbits enjoy the comfort of a 'cave'. Remove the lid from a cardboard box and cut out a door shape. Turn the box upside down in the rabbit cage and your pet will use it as a cosy hideaway.

✱ A roll to gnaw on

Almost all pet animals – dogs, cats, rabbits, chinchillas, mice, gerbils, guinea pigs, hamsters, ferrets – enjoy gnawing on an empty cardboard roll. So do some birds, like cockatiels. Put some rolls aside for your pets. They also like to gnaw on cardboard tissue boxes. Remove the plastic liner attached to tissue boxes' dispensing slots.

✱ Let hamsters branch out

Hamsters like fresh branches to climb on and gnaw. Choose small branches of willow or fruit wood for his cage or hutch and make sure that they are pesticide-free.

✱ Coconut gerbil house

Gerbils and other rodents are active creatures and like to stay occupied. A coconut shell suspended from the top of the cage makes a great climb-in, climb-out toy. First, clean the shell well, removing all coconut meat. Then use a jigsaw to cut an opening in the shell, filing down the rough edges. Boil the shell in water for 10 minutes and let it air dry. Insert an eye hook into the shell so that when you suspend it from the cage ceiling, the opening will be on the side (not pointing downward). Hang the shell low enough for your pet to reach.

✱ Nibble, nibble, nibble

Your pet rodents probably enjoy their expensive chew toys. But you can provide just as much munching pleasure for free. As well as all those empty cardboard rolls and small cardboard boxes, give your nibblers small blocks of wood left over from carpentry projects. Caution: Never give them any treated wood to chew on.

tip A LITTLE BIT OF FUN FOR A FERRET

Ping-pong balls and tennis balls make great toys for ferrets, and guinea pigs will find them amusing as well. Ferrets and guinea pigs understand that not every toy has to be a chew toy.

Tortoises, snakes, lizards and other reptiles

✳ Save your tortoise's gravel

Don't throw away the gravel or aggregate in your tortoise's bowl every time you clean it. Dump the gravel, aggregate and any other bowl materials into a colander. Place the colander over a bucket and pour water over the contents until the gravel is clean. Next, pour household bleach over everything. Finally, run water over the contents of the colander until the smell of bleach dissipates.

✳ A lost snake

It sometimes happens, but don't panic. Here are two good ways to find your missing pet:

- Place foil or crinkly plastic packing material around the room in potential hiding places, so you can hear the snake moving around.
- Sprinkle some flour on the floor in areas where you suspect your pet might be hiding.

✳ Bring the outdoors in for a pet lizard

Your pet lizard will enjoy having fresh small tree branches in his cage. Lizards like to climb and hang out on the branches that you can collect from the garden.

✳ Lazin' lizards!

Caged lizards like to relax, so make your pet a little hammock. String a section of old pillowcase or a bandana between two corners of the cage and you will soon see your lizard resting comfortably in her new piece of furniture.

✳ A reptile cage catch-all

Keep the area around a reptile's cage neat by placing an old plastic shower curtain or plastic tablecloth beneath the cage. When it's time to tidy up, bundle up the plastic liner, brush sand or crumbs or any other bits of rubbish into the bin and then wipe the liner with a sponge before returning it to its original spot.

curiosity corner

IS YOUR TORTOISE A BOY OR A GIRL

If you want to give your pet tortoise a gender-appropriate name, finding the answer to the question of female versus male is easier than you might think. Just turn the tortose over and examine its undershell – which is known as the plastron.

If the plastron is convex (curved outward), the tortoise is female; if it's concave (curved inward), the tortoise is male. Because the curves are slight, you may have to hold the tortoise horizontally before your eyes to determine which way the undershell curves.

Creatures of the (not so) deep

✱ Tape fish food dispensers

Some fish food containers have large open tops; others have far too many large holes – and both can lead to overfeeding your aquarium or goldfish-bowl fish. Cover half of the container mouth with masking tape to better control the dispersal of fish flakes.

✱ Tights as tank cleaners

Save an old pair of tights for yet another household use! Once you've removed the fish, the water and any ornaments from an aquarium tank, you can turn your tights into a cleaning tool in two ways: 1) Fit a leg over your arm so you have the foot over your fingers, like a mitten. 2) Ball the tights up and use it as you would a sponge. No matter which method you choose, make a simple vinegar and water solution (1 part white vinegar to 1 part water) and use panty hose to wipe down the sides and bottom of the tank.

✱ Put aquarium water to good use

When you change the water in your tank, don't pour it down the drain. It's excellent for hatching brine shrimp (the favourite food of sea horses, if you keep a sea horse or two in your aquarium) and it makes an excellent fertiliser for houseplants and outdoor ornamentals alike. The nutrients in the water make flowering plants and vegetables thrive like few other fertilisers. And don't be put off by the smell – it will dissipate about an hour after you water your plants.

✱ Pep up a goldfish with salt

Treat your goldfish to a swim in the ocean. Well, a *simulated* ocean. Stir 1 teaspoon marine salt into 1 litre room-temperature water and pour it into a wide-mouthed container. Let your fish swim for about 15 minutes in this slightly salty mix and then return her to her tank. The saltwater will put a little pep in her step. (Caution: It is essential to use marine salt. Never use table salt as the pH is too high. If the fish shows the slightest sign of distress, immediately return it to the tank.)

✱ Tasty treats for hermit crabs

Enhance a hermit crab's diet by adding bits of any of the following to its food dish: mango, papaya, coconut, apples, apple sauce, bananas, grapes, pineapple, strawberries, melons, carrots, spinach, leafy green lettuces (not iceberg), broccoli, grass, leaves, strips of bark from deciduous trees (no conifers), unsalted nuts, raisins, unsalted crackers, unsweetened cereals and plain rice cakes. A wide-ranging crustacean menu indeed.

Our fantastic feathered friends

* Lights-out curtains

An attractive small tablecloth or a pillowcase or scarf can become a nighttime cover for your bird's cage. Covering the cage will help your bird to relax.

* Natural decor for your bird

Clip a small tree branch for your bird's cage. He'll be able to climb and reclimb and also will peck it to sharpen his beak.

* Clean house with vinegar

A 50:50 mixture of white vinegar turns a birdcage into a sparkling clean home and does a good job of cleaning plastic bird toys. After wiping on the mixture, rinse with fresh tap water and then dry the cage with a clean cloth.

* Paper bag fun

Open a brown paper bag and set it on a table or other surface when your bird is out of the cage. He will enjoy peeking in and out.

* Let your bird play peck-the-spools

Make a hanging toy for your bird's cage by stringing wooden spools on a leather cord and tying it diagonally near the top of the cage. Your bird will enjoy pecking at it and making the spools sway back and forth.

* Use your imagination

It's easy to keep a bird occupied. While pet stores sell plenty of toys for caged birds, you can easily entertain your pet with items you have around the house. Milk jugs, mop heads

idea

GLITTERING PLAYTHINGS

Make use of old jewellery to occupy your pet bird. Suspend an old bracelet, necklace or ring from the top of the cage – your budgie doesn't give a hoot what's in fashion as long as she has something shiny to play with. Just be sure not to use anything with gems or parts that your bird could prise off and swallow. For safety's sake, place the item on the outside of the cage so that your bird can peck at it but can't pull it into the cage.

and whisk brooms are good toys for birds that like to pluck feathers. Try some of these:

- Plastic bottle caps
- Plastic milk jugs, with the top cut off and the edges frayed with scissors
- Wads of newspaper
- Shredded computer paper
- A natural-bristle flat broom
- Clothes pegs (without wires or springs)
- Small wooden balls

* A fun (or frustrating?) toy

Add a new dimension to a clear plastic drinks bottle by putting beads, plastic clothespegs or other brightly coloured objects inside and recapping the bottle. Your bird will spend hours on end trying to figure out how he can get to the objects inside.

For safety, cover your suitcase zips with gaffer tape!

10 Top tips for travellers

Holidays have always been our chance to relax, to unwind, to learn and to have fun. But at a time when flights can be cancelled at the drop of a hat and motorway traffic often slows to a snail's pace, you may find yourself worrying more about controlling your rising blood pressure than the relaxation that used to be synonymous with the word 'holiday'.

That said, there are plenty of things you can do to make your trip go more smoothly. Ordinary clear tape and plastic bags take up no space in your suitcase but go a long way toward solving and preventing problems. Then there are pairs of tights, which help to keep your clothes crease free and your bags organised. Whether you are setting off on a camping holiday or a glamorous big-city break, put on your travelling gear and browse the information-packed pages that follow.

Practical packing

✳ Take tape along for the ride

Put a roll of tape into your suitcase and see how useful it is when you are travelling. Use clear tape to:

- Reseal the caps of any liquids that you open, such as shampoo and hair gel
- Make emergency repairs to dropped hems
- Fix a torn map
- Tape postcards and other mementoes into your travel journal
- Tape together earrings, cufflinks or any other tiny items that might go astray
- Remove lint from dark clothes
- Tape driving directions to the dashboard for quick reference
- Tape stray buttons to their respective garments for repair when you return to your hotel room

✳ Save magazine wrappers

The plastic bags that subscription magazines and catalagues come in provide protection in your suitcase as well – and they're just the right shape for shoes and hairbrushes. To keep dirt or hair from getting on to your other belongings, slip shoes and brushes in, one to a bag.

✳ Pack jewellery in the toes of tights

It can be hard to handle jewellery when you're on the move; small items can easily get lost in your suitcase and necklaces and other dangly jewellery tend to become tangled up and snag clothing. Old pairs of tights provide an easy solution. Just cut out the feet, place a single piece of jewellery in each one and tie off the little bags with twist ties. Your jewels and bangles will be easily at hand and in good condition when you need them.

✳ Make a suitcase divider

Take a tip from smugglers: the old false-bottom suitcase trick. You'll keep packed items separated and be spared the annoyance of digging through layers of clothing to get to your toothbrush. Just take some sturdy cardboard and cut out a piece that matches the width and length of your suitcase interior – and you have a portable divider. Put items that you won't need until later on the bottom of the suitcase, lay the cardboard on top and place toiletries, a change of clothing and the other items you will need right away on the cardboard. Or place shoes and other heavy items on the bottom, then put lighter clothing on top to make it less likely to crease.

tip CHUCK IN SOME CLOTHESPEGS

Clothespegs – the lightweight, plastic clip-on type – don't take up much room in a bag and they really earn their place. Use clothespegs to hang up socks and underwear that you wash out in the bathroom sink, clip together maps and other documents and draw curtains for privacy and to keep out light.

Organise your luggage with bits of sturdy cardboard!

✱ Take some tubes

Before setting out, save a few toilet-paper tubes and then put them to work when you pack for a journey. Here are three ways that empty rolls will come in handy:

- Stuff one or two tubes with socks and use them as shoe trees to keep leather shoes from becoming crumpled and creased.
- Wrap necklaces and chains around a tube to prevent tangling.
- Tape small pieces of delicate jewellery inside a tube for protection.

✱ A bit of bicarb

You already know that bicarbonate of soda keeps your fridge smelling fresh – and it can do the same for the contents of your suitcase. There's no need to take a whole box. Just fill a pill bottle or film canister with bicarbonate of soda and poke a few small holes in the top. A little might spill out in the course of your travels, but bicarbonate of soda is unlikely to harm anything in your bag. (To keep any spill contained, tuck the container into one of the open sleeves found in the interior of most suitcases.) Bicarbonate of soda does more than just help to control odour. While travelling, you can dip into your supply to do anything from soaking tired feet to cleaning a Thermos. Caution: bicarbonate of soda may arouse suspicion when travelling by plane, so make sure that you remove it prior to checking in for your flight.

✱ Smooth out creases

When it comes to packing clothing, rolling beats folding. Rolled clothes are far less likely to crease – and take up less room in the suitcase as well. Roll them in:

- **Plastic dry-cleaning bags** Dry cleaners return clothing in sheer plastic bags because plastic prevents fabric from rubbing against fabric and creating tiny creases. Minimise creases by wrapping garments in the bags and rolling up.
- **Stocking legs** Simply cut off the legs of a pair of tights and slip a rolled garment into each one. If you leave the stocking foot

household superstar

12 INVENTIVE USES FOR PLASTIC BAGS

You can hardly have enough self-sealing plastic bags with you when you are on a car journey or camping. Bags of various sizes allow you to:

1 Carry guidebooks and other sightseeing gear in the rain.

2 Make an instant rain hat.

3 Wear as a rain poncho (you'll need a large bin bag for this).

4 Wrap up your feet to keep them dry.

5 Store dirty laundry.

6 Store cottonwool balls and other toiletry items.

7 Organise clothing in a suitcase.

8 Store liquids that might spill.

9 Collect rubbish.

10 Save leftovers.

11 Carry MP3 players and other electronic portables.

12 Carry crayons, pencils and other children's items.

sections on, use these pouches as secure compartments for cameras, MP3 players and other valuables; with a piece of clothing stuffed into a stocking leg, there is no way that these items will fall out and get lost in your bag.

✳ Roll up your tie

A creased tie spoils a smooth business look – but here's a way to ensure ties are crease free every time you take one out of the suitcase. First, lay the tie out full length. Beginning with the narrow end, roll it into a coil. Take a sock and gently stuff the rolled-up tie inside. If you're forgetful, pin a note to the sock so that when you are rummaging through your suitcase for your tie you won't think you have left it behind.

✳ Pack a lunch box

Not with sandwiches but with toiletries and other items that might spill or leak when jostled. Carrying cosmetics and toiletry items in such a compact, sturdy and separate case will also make it easier to get your hands on them. Of course, the lunch box will come in handy when it is time to pack some snacks and drinks to take along on a picnic or day of sightseeing.

Quick fix carriers

✳ A plastic-bag filing system

Various sizes of self-sealing plastic bags provide an easy way to stay organised when you're on the move – small sandwich bags for receipts and large freezer bags for pamphlets, brochures, maps and other memorabilia you collect along the way. The more bags you bring, the more organised you will be. For instance, you might want to use separate bags for each place visited; for each type of receipt (restaurants, hotels, shops); or for each day of your trip.

✳ Pack big bags

It really does make sense: you can fill up bin bags with dirty laundry when you travel. Heavy-duty bags are especially handy because you can just put them over your shoulder and head out to a laundrette. On a picnic or car trip, the bin bag will come in handy for rubbish. And if you don't fancy yourself as a fashionista, you can even cut a couple of slits for your arms and one for your head and wear a bin bag as an improvised raincoat. (Just hope you don't run into anyone you actually know when you are wearing this.)

Note: If you forget to pack bin bags, the plastic laundry bags that you will find in many hotels will serve the same purposes (except for the raincoat).

✳ A handy coin holder

Don't discard torn tights, which can come in handy as a coin holder when you're on the move. To keep all the coins you get as change from cluttering the bottom of a purse or weighing down your pockets, tuck them into the foot of a pair of old tights, tie the top in a loose knot and store this money bag in your suitcase. You won't have to lug around a lot of extra coinage and since the loose change will all be in one place, you can easily dip into your coin reserves as needed.

✳ Little moneybags

Foreign currency can flummox even the worldliest traveller, and it can take a while before you start feeling comfortable with unfamiliar coins and notes. For easier sorting, put notes and coins of various denominations into self-sealing plastic bags – a different bag for each denomination. When it is time to pay for something, you shouldn't have to sort through a pile of confusing currency.

✳ The case for taking a pillowcase

Nothing adds a comforting feel to unfamiliar surroundings like laying your weary head on one of your own pillowcases. This nice touch of home takes up little room in your suitcase and it can do also double duty as:

- **A protector** To keep knitted garments such as sweaters from snagging on other items in you suitcase, slip them into a pillowcase.
- **A laundry bag** When the pillowcase becomes dirty, put your dirty clothes in it. Clothing will be less prone to mould and mildew when kept in a pillowcase than it will in a plastic bag and you can just empty the case and throw it into the wash when you find a laundrette.

A picnic in a bag

One of the best and most delicious ways to be frugal whether you're in Boston or Barcelona is to pack a picnic in a bag. Put a few self-sealing plastic bags into your handbag or backpack and visit a bakery, a cheese shop or a delicatessan; then go to a park or square and enjoy your feast in the outdoors. Fill a bag or two with any combination of the following:

Hard cheese:

Cheddar, Parmesan, Emmental, Gruyère and Gouda are all cheeses that travel well. If you're abroad, ask for advice from the person in the cheese shop. Stay away from very soft cheeses that may not survive hot weather or a long walk to a picnic area or park.

Bread:

Baguettes, rolls or thick slices of fresh bread are ideal for outdoor picnicking and local bakers will often lend their advice on great places to enjoy your meal.

Meats:

Cured meats – smoked turkey and smoked ham, for example – will withstand not being refrigerated for up to 2 hours and are delicious accompaniments to hard cheeses.

Remember to carry a bottle opener, a small picnic knife, a napkin and something to sit on (other than the ground), and enjoy your outdoor feast more than an expensive restaurant meal. When you're finished, put your rubbish into another plastic bag before you go.

The handiest helpers

* Three ways that gaffer tape eases the traveller's life

Do you like to read in bed but need some light on your book? Tape a small torch to the wall above your pillow (but not on the wallpaper). If you want to be able to come and go without the door locking behind you every time you step out? Place a small strip of tape across the bolt. Do you prefer to sleep past dawn? Tape ill-fitting curtains shut to keep out the light.

* Put toilet-paper tubes to good use

You'll find plenty of uses for toilet-paper tubes in a hotel room – so save a few empty tubes at home to take on your trip. Or, in the hotel, you could hoard some empty tubes before the chambermaid has a chance to discard them. Read on for some ways to use them.

- If your laptop computer power cord is unruly or takes up too much space on your desk, loop the cord in a loose coil and stuff it inside the tube to keep it under control.
- Pamphlets, small prints and other fragile paper mementoes almost never make it back home without a crease or two – so roll them carefully and insert them into the tube for safekeeping. For larger papers, you might need to tape two tubes together or bring along a tube from a roll of paper towel.
- Mosquitoes are annoying roommates. If they appear unexpectedly and you're unprepared with spray or other repellants,

household superstar

10 BITS OF GAFFER TAPE GENIUS

When you run up against a problem while driving, hiking or camping, a roll of gaffer tape can bail you out in a flash. Here are 11 ways to make use of the shiny silvery stuff.

1 Tape your trousers tightly around the ankles to keep ticks and other insects away from your legs.

2 Tape your trousers tightly around the ankles to keep the fabric from getting caught up in bike pedals.

3 Twist tape into a 'rope' to use as a clothes line or to tie things together.

4 Twist it into an emergency shoe lace.

5 Repair a rip in a tent.

6 Tape a torch to a wall or tree.

7 Reseal bags of potato crisps and other food.

8 Trap flies by cutting the tape into strips and laying them out, sticky side up.

9 Tape up purchases wrapped in newspaper or bubble wrap.

10 Patch a hole in a canoe, inner tube or an air mattress.

A bag of beans will steady your camera as well as a tripod.

make your own 'flypaper'. Just wrap some adhesive tape around the tube, sticky side out and set it upright on a flat surface.

✳ Buffer sore backsides

Long car rides can take their toll on your rear end and lower back. So why not turn a bit of bubble wrap into a comfy cushion? Just place a long double layer of bubble wrap, bubble side out, against the back and bottom of your car seat. Your body will conform comfortably to this comforable padding. And if you go shopping along the way and come across a fragile item that you just can't resist buying, you'll have some packing material right at hand!

✳ Aromatherapy at 35,000ft

We all know how stressful air travel can be, so take along some relaxants that you can sniff. Before you leave home, drip some lavender oil or clary sage oil onto cotton wool balls. (Herbalists have long prescribed both as for calming.) Pack the cotton wool balls into a small, self-sealing plastic bag or pill bottle and take them out for a good whiff when you want to unwind or doze off. You might also want to dab a dose of these oils onto your skin as you would perfume so you arrive at your destination smelling fresh.

✳ Cap your camera

When shooting a picture in the rain, slip a disposable shower cap over the body of your camera so that the lens pokes out of the cap opening. You'll be able to press any buttons you need to, thanks to the thinness of the plastic.

✳ A beanbag camera steadier

If you want to shoot pictures from a speeding car, a train or a boat, you'll find it almost impossible to keep your camera steady. The answer is a makeshift beanbag. Just pop into a supermarket and buy some dried beans or rice, pour them into the foot of a stocking leg, tie it closed and rest your camera on the beanbag to keep it from vibrating as you snap your picture.

Quick fixes on the road

✳ A hole in your sole

Make a temporary fix with gaffer tape; the backing is waterproof, so your repair might hold up through a couple of downpours. If a broken shoelace is slowing you down, cut off a strip of tape that's about as long as your lace, roll it tightly (lengthways) with the sticky side in and thread your new 'lace' through the holes.

✳ Tape a broken car hose

You can use gaffer tape to fix petrol-powered locomotion, too: tear off a strip to make a quick repair to your car's broken water hose – but don't rely on your handiwork to get you any farther than the nearest garage.

✳ Damp umbrella holders

Hate carrying around a wet umbrella? Make sure that you always have a plastic grocery bag with you; simply stuff the closed umbrella into the bag, roll it tightly like a sausage and stow it in your bag or pocket.

✳ Plastic bag 'galoshes'

Rain can really dampen your enthusiasm for walking or hiking – but you needn't let bad weather get in the way of your fun. Before pulling on your boots, wrap each foot in a sturdy plastic bag. Your feet will stay warm and dry and you can put your wet footwear into one of the bags when it's time to pack and move on.

✳ Wick water from wet shoes

To speed air-drying, stuff water-soaked shoes and boots with crumpled newspaper to wick out the moisture. Speed the drying by placing shoes or boots on their sides, turning over from time to time and replacing damp newspaper.

idea

GAFFER TAPE FIXES AT THE HOTEL OF HORRORS

It's midnight. Severe weather has forced you into an overnight stay and the only hotel you can find looks like it may fall down. A bit of gaffer tape can come to the rescue.

Broken window? Tape a broken pane of glass to keep out the breeze or a ripped screen to keep out mosquitoes if you're travelling in a malaria zone.

Cracked toilet seat? Wrap the break in a little tape for the sake of comfort and safety.

Torn shower curtain? Tape up a ripped shower curtain with gaffer tape. Or use the tape to repair a torn eyelet. Fold a piece of tape and slip it over the eyelet, cut a hole through the tape and place the ring through it.

✳ Freshen car air

When the air in your car is getting a bit stale and the little cardboard pine trees that hang from the rear-view mirror aren't what you have in mind as a solution, plan ahead and bring a plastic bag filled with cotton wool balls soaked in pure vanilla extract, tea tree oil or eucalyptus oil. Take out a couple, put them in the car's ashtray or cup holder and enjoy a natural scent that's far subtler than most over-perfumed commercial products.

Safety measures for travellers

✱ An improvised money belt

If you're feeling very tight with your cash, make your own money belt out of a pair of old tights. Put your money, passport and other valuables into the foot of the tights and tie the top around your waist. Your makeshift (and free) accessory will be concealed by your clothing.

✱ Point your shoes toward the emergency exit

When you check into a hotel, take a few minutes to study the fire-exit diagrams posted on the inside of your door. Then place your shoes by the door before you retire for the night, pointing them in the direction of the emergency exit in your corridor. This way, if an alarm goes off in your hotel room and you wake up and smell smoke, you won't panic trying to remember which way to turn to escape.

✱ Seal luggage latches

When you check your bags onto a flight these days, you'll probably be told to leave them unlocked in case security decides to inspect them. You will probably imagine your luggage being chucked about and the latches popping open – and your belongings suddenly vulnerable to thieves. Allay your concerns by covering the latches of your suitcase with just enough gaffer tape to fit over the fastenings. Security will then be able to inspect the bag by peeling back the tape and they are more than likely to retape the fasteners once they have finished. Use tape that matches the colour of your suitcase or travel bag so that your quick fix won't be obvious to potential thieves.

✱ Thwart pickpockets

A simple safety pin can make your wallet a lot more secure. Put your wallet into a pocket of your trousers or your jacket and close the opening with a safety pin in such a way that you can still squeeze the wallet out – but just barely. The pin is sure to thwart an unsuspecting thief who tries to pickpocket you, since you will undoubtedly notice the tug.

✱ A fine-toothed wallet protector

If you're a man, a wallet and a comb are two items that you are likely to carry at all times. But did you know that you could use them together to prevent pickpockets from taking your wallet? Place your comb in the fold of your wallet so that the teeth extend beyond the open edge; then double-loop a rubber band around the wallet through the teeth of the comb. When you put the wallet in your trousers pocket or the breast pocket of your jacket, the teeth will catch on the fabric when they are moved. So when a thief tries to slip the wallet from your pocket, the comb will act as both a barrier and an alarm.

Hidey holes to outwit thieves

Burglars break into buildings, but thieves look for loot anywhere they can find it – like your suitcase, whether it's en route to the cargo hold of a plane or perched on the luggage rack of a train. One way to protect your valuables from theft is to conceal them in unexpected places. Three safe carriers for expensive items are:

1
An empty film canister
The size and shape of these containers make them especially convenient for rings and earrings.

2
A tampon box
Leave some of these products in the top part of the box and put valuables at the bottom.

3
A tennis ball
Make a slit along one of the seams and put jewellery and other small valuables inside the ball.

Travelling with children

✳ Keep baby essentials organised

Pack a separate self-sealing bag with the essentials your children will need each day – a set of clothing, a change of clothing and some disposable nappies. If you have more than one child in tow, prepare a separate bag for each of the children. The result? You won't have to search through suitcases to put outfits together when dressing the troops every morning.

✳ Save empty washing-up liquid bottles

If you've travelled with children before, you know the mess they can create. Prepare yourself for the inevitable by saving an empty (but unrinsed) bottle of washing-up liquid. Fill the bottle with water before you set out and tuck it away in a leakproof, self-sealing plastic bag, along with some paper towels or facecloths. Use this cleaning kit to wipe faces after snacks, wash hands after bathroom stops and clean up spills and smudges in the car and hotel room.

✳ A mini plastic carrier

Young travellers will enjoy keeping their small personal items – such as coins or tiny toys – in a carrier they've made themselves. All you need is an empty film canister or pill bottle and a key ring with a plastic spring-lock clip that attaches to belts or backpacks (the clips are sold in hardware stores and locksmith shops). Help the child to cut two holes near the top of the canister to accommodate the metal ring, then let her choose beads and ribbons and glue them on for extra pizzazz.

✳ Map fun for little navigators

One way to keep children busy on a road trip – and teach them about geography as well – is to help them to follow your route on a map. While planning the trip, cut out and colour photocopy the portion of a map that corresponds to your route for each day of travel. Attach the segments to a clipboard, give the children some washable markers and get them to chart your course and check off towns and landmarks as you go. If you need directions, you might be able to get some help from the back seat.

✳ A backseat snack tray

Little appetites always seem to get bigger on car trips. This fun way to dish up snacks may be exactly what you need to keep the children satisfied. Thoroughly wash an empty plastic or polystyrene egg carton with warm soapy water (or for short journeys and dried foods use a *clean* cardboard one). After it dries, fill each compartment with a different treat – cheese cubes in one, breakfast cereal in another, sweets in another. When the back seat crew are hungry pass the carton around.

✳ Double duty for fruit and veggie bags

Onions, peppers, citrus fruits and other fruit and vegetables often come in mesh bags. Once the chilren have eaten their way through these healthy staples, keep the bag for a day of outdoor fun. Mesh bags are ideal for taking toys to the beach or anywhere else that gear is likely to become sandy and dirty. At the end of the day, just stick the playthings into the empty bag and rinse the whole lot out under a hose. If you can't find a mesh bag, take a plastic bag and punch holes in it – but only enough holes to allow the water to run out.

✳ Bag it

Family car trips can be a wonderful experience – and even more so when you're equipped with a good supply of self-sealing plastic bags in various sizes. Use them to:

- Store crayons, pencils and other items that can easily go astray.
- Put away rubbish that collects en route (tape a bag to the back of one of the front seats so that it is handy and children get accustomed to using it).
- Save leftovers when children won't eat.
- Serve snacks you can pull out when they claim to be starving.
- Put away soiled garments until you have a chance to launder them.

✳ Delicious pre-trip prep

A great way to prepare your young travellers for the sights, smells and tastes that they will experience on a family excursion is to have a living room picnic with foods that are indigenous to your destination. While your intrepid children are eating, take the opportunity to tell them about the history of the location, its geography and other interesting facts that they'll retain once they get where they're going.

idea
CRAFTY DIVERSIONS

Young travellers do get bored and restless, but less so if you keep their hands busy with a travel activity kit that they have helped to make. Before leaving home, get your children to decorate a paper bag or shoebox, then pack it with materials for activities they can do on the move. Use your imagination, but consider bringing along:

- Colouring books and crayons
- A blank book for writing
- Stickers
- Coloured pipe cleaners
- Plastic safety scissors
- Coloured paper
- Clear tape
- Roll-on glue or glue sticks

✳ Spray-bottle play

On a hot day, a simple spray bottle can be a godsend for young travellers. Recycle a couple of spray bottles from the cleaning cupboard, clean them well, fill them with water and keep them on hand. Use them to:

- Spritz the kids for a cool-down while sitting on a beach, hiking or walking in the city
- Dress children in their swimsuits and set them loose in a park or other public outdoor spot with a couple of spray bottles. Drenching one another with parental approval might be the highlight of your children's trip.

Survival in the outdoors

* Scrounge around for old film canisters

If you still use a film camera, hoard empty film canisters for use when hiking or camping out. These convenient, waterproof containers with their snap-on, leakproof lids are great for storing matches, small batteries or other small items that could leave you high and dry or in danger if they become wet and unusable. If you've made the switch to a digital camera and don't have easy access to film canisters, use old pill bottles instead.

* Zap sap with butter

Sticky tree sap is one of the more harmless hazards you'll encounter when camping out, but it's still annoying to find sap on your skin. To get rid of it, just go to your cooler bag, take out some butter or margarine, rub a little into the sap wherever it happens to be and wash the area with soap and water. This gentle treatment will not only be easy on your skin but has another application for campers: it will help to waterproof tent canvas and other outdoor equipment fabrics.

idea

A COMPASS ON YOUR WRIST

A compass is the standard tool for guiding your way in the wild, but you don't always have access to one. Luckily, your wristwatch and the sun can come to your rescue, so hope that it's not cloudy and then use them to get your bearings. Here's how:

1 Point your watch so that the hour hand faces the direction of the sun.

2 Find the midpoint of the smallest section on the watch face between the hour hand and 12 o'clock – and you've found due south.

An example: If it's 4 o'clock, due south is midway between the 4 and the 12, at the 2; if it's 10 o'clock, due south is midway between the 10 and the 12, at the 11.

When daylight savings are in effect, add an hour. So, if it's 4 o'clock, point the 5 at the sun and you'll see that the midpoint between the 2 and the 3 points due south.

* A tin-can fire starter

Instead of using lighter fluid, try building a fire with this homespun, fluidless charcoal starter.

Cut both ends off an old catering-size tin can. Punch several holes near the bottom of the can, then punch two holes near the top and insert a length of coat hanger wire through them to form a handle. When it comes time to start a fire, set the can into the fire pit, place a piece of crumpled newspaper in the bottom and lay

Store small items in a pastille tin!

briquettes on top of the newspaper. Light the paper through the holes punched at the bottom. When the briquettes are glowing, lift the can away with the wire handle – it will be extremely hot, so be sure to wear gloves or use tongs when grabbing it.

✳ Tin-can candleholder

Don't curse the darkness. Instead, make a reflective candleholder. When opening a large can of cat food or other can with a pull ring, keep the lid partially attached. Once your cat has finished the contents, wash out the can and bend back the lid so it faces straight upward. Put a candle inside and then place the can so the lid blocks the wind. The candle will burn steadily – and seem brighter as the lid will reflect the light.

✳ Great (cotton wool) balls o' fire

Nothing is more frustrating than trying to start a fire when the wood is damp and won't ignite, so here's a trick to warm an outdoor enthusiast's heart. Pack a dozen or so cotton balls heavily saturated with petroleum jelly in a plastic bag. When a fire just won't get going, place several of the balls among the paper scraps and kindling and light them. Then get your food ready to cook, since the petroleum jelly usually burns long enough to get even the most reluctant campfire blazing.

✳ Repurpose throat pastille tins

Once you've finished a tin of throat pastilles, save the tin. A tin with a tight lid is great weatherproof carryall for:
- Fishing hooks and artificial flies
- Matches
- Aspirin
- Packets of sugar and artificial sweeteners
- Safety pins

- Loose change and keys that you don't want to carry in pockets while fishing, hiking or doing other outdoor activities.

✱ Floss it while camping
Dental floss, with its superstrong waxed string is useful for many other purposes when you are camping. These include:
- **Hanging stuff** Floss is so strong you can use it to hang a small lantern, shaving mirror and other gear from a branch.
- **Repairing canvas gear** Floss is slender enough to thread through

the eye of a needle, yet sturdy enough to hold canvas in place, making it ideal for mending tents, backpacks and tarpaulins.
- **Cutting and slicing food** Hold a piece of floss taut and slice your way through cheese, cake and other soft foods.

✱ Shampoo to the rescue
Though shampoo may seem like a luxury item when you are camping, it's well worth putting some into a small plastic container you can easily fit into a backpack or bag. Not only will you keep your hair squeaky clean, but you can also use shampoo to:
- Lubricate a tent zip
- Remove sap and other sticky stuff from your hands
- Stand in for shaving cream when you decide to get rid of stubble.

✱ Vinegar at your campsite
Vinegar will add a bit of zest to campsite meals, but it also:
- **Repels gnats and mosquitoes** Just dab some white vinegar onto exposed skin.
- **Traps flies and mosquitoes** Pour some apple cider vinegar into a container and place it on a picnic table or anywhere else these pests tend to congregate.
- **Helps to kill bacteria in water** Add a few drops of cider vinegar to a water bottle.

✱ Wave goodbye to sand on the beach
You probably come home from a day at the beach with plenty of sand in the car, in your shoes, on your clothes and even the house. Leave the sand where it belongs by taking a plastic bag partially filled with baby powder. When you're ready to go, dip your feet and hands into the powder and dust some more powder over the rest of your body. When you brush off the baby powder, the sand will go too.

what's the story?

MR NELSON'S BACKPACK

In the spring of 1920, a man named Lloyd Nelson set off to explore the Alaskan wilderness for oil. When an Indian lent him a sealskin pouch stretched across willow sticks strapped to the back, Nelson decided that his fortune might lie instead in designing a pack that could be carried over the shoulders for support and comfort. Soon he was back at home sewing together canvas packs and mounting them on wooden boards – to make the precursor of the modern backpack.

Before long, forest rangers and Boy Scouts were carrying what was then known as Trapper Nelson's Indian Pack Boards. They were used by mountaineers to carry their gear while freeing the hands and from the 1960s onwards they became an instant and enduring hit with students setting off to explore the world.

The very many virtues of a walking stick

The humble piece of gear known as the walking stick is easy to come by and needn't cost anything at all. Find a piece of wood that's not too heavy, easy to hold on to and no taller than you are – a broomstick, a fallen branch, a dowel or a piece of thick molding. If you want to get more elaborate, carve convenient hand grips in the stick and sand the wood down and varnish it. Or visit your local antique shop and walk away in style.

Among the stick's many merits are:

A stick helps you keep your balance when you're out walking, especially when you cross streams and rocky terrain.

It reduces stress on your knees, legs, hips and back as you climb uphill.

It's a handy poking-stick for checking crevices, ledges, tall grass and gorse for potential holes and hollows that you want to avoid falling into.

The stick needn't sit idle when you aren't walking. You can lean against it when you want to stop and enjoy the scenery; as a pole to hold up a tent or a tarpaulin; and also as a prop to keep a heavy backpack from falling over when you put it down.

Creature comforts outdoors

✱ Take a dust sheet along

Perhaps you've been spending your spare time painting the house and doing other messy home repairs and you're finally getting a chance to go camping? Leave the work behind but do bring some of the painter's dust sheets you've used to protect floors and furniture. Choose one that more or less matches the dimensions of your tent floor and pitch the tent on top of it. The dust sheet will prevent dampness from seeping in and keep the tent cleaner in the bargain.

You might want to bring another dust sheet (a new plastic one – which are cheap) to use as a tablecloth; campsite tables are often covered with pitch, sap, bird droppings and other unappetising debris.

✱ Pill-bottle salt and pepper shakers

There's no need to eat bland food just because you're roughing it. Pour salt, pepper and any other spices you enjoy into separate small screw-cap pill bottles and label them with an indelible marker – preferably on a piece of masking tape so you'll be able to reuse them. Because these containers are airtight, moisture won't cause the contents to dampen and congeal. For a taste of the comfort of home, take two lids from another set of pill bottles and punch small holes in them with a sharp tool. When you set the table at your camp, put one of the holey lids on the salt and the other on the pepper and then shake away to suit your taste. Be sure to replace the solid caps at the end of the meal to keep moisture at bay.

idea

STAYING CLEAN OUTSIDE

The great outdoors smells great, but you may not smell so good after a few days of roughing it. Here are some ways to clean up in comfort:

Wash up with sun-warmed water Fill a large plastic bottle with water and leave it in the sun; after a few hours you'll have warm water for a soothing sponge bath.

Bathe in a paddling pool For a bit of luxury, pack a small inflatable paddling pool. Find a sunny spot, inflate the pool, fill it with water, wait a while for the sun to do its job, then step into your warm bath.

Shower with a holey bucket Poke sieve-like holes into the bottom of a plastic bucket, then stack it inside a larger (and solid) plastic bucket. When it's time for a shower, hang the bucket with the holes from a branch and fill the bucket without holes with warm water. Stand beneath the hanging bucket, pour warm water into it and enjoy the brief sensation of warm water rushing over you.

✱ Save plastic bottles

Before you throw plastic bottles into the recycling bin, consider the ways you can put them to good use on camping trips and picnics. When you're in the great outdoors, you can use a plastic bottle to:

Keep your sleeping bag smelling
fresh with a bar of soap!

- **Make a bowl** Cut off the bottom portion to make a bowl of any depth you want; you might want to sandpaper the edges to make them less rough.
- **Dispose of liquids** Pour in cooking oils and other liquid rubbish.
- **Create an ice pack** Fill a bottle with water, freeze it and use it to keep a cooler cold. Or put it in a backpack to keep food cool on a long hike.
- **Serve as a makeshift latrine** Keep it just outside the tent so you don't have to wander out into the dark. (This works at least for male campers.)

✱ Plastic tubs are great too

Use your supply of plastic butter or yoghurt containers the next time you go hiking or camping – they have many practical outdoor uses. Plastic containers make it easy to:

- **Snare stinging insects** To keep wasps and other insects from invading your outdoor meals, fill a container with water, add a little sugar, poke a hole in the lid and place this sweet trap off to one side of your dining area. The wasps will fly in but won't be able to fly out.
- **Feed Fido** Fill a container with biscuits so the dog's dinner is ready when he's hungry; use a second container for water.
- **Block ants** Fill four plastic containers with water and put one under each leg of a table. Ants won't be able to get through your makeshift moat and crawl up the table legs to get at your picnic.

✱ Freshen sleeping bags with soap

Sleeping bags can become a bit musty after a couple of uses, but you can freshen a bag by putting a bar of soap or a fabric softener sheet inside. Do it after you get out of the sleeping bag each morning, then zip the bag shut. The next time you slip in, remove the bag freshener and put it aside to use again, then drift off into sweeter-smelling dreams.

✳ Bubble-wrap mattress

Pack a 2m length of bubble wrap and lay it under your sleeping bag before you get in. The air pockets are not only soft, they'll also protect your sleeping bag from damp.

✳ Hula-hoop privacy protector

If you have a hoop, some rope or string, an old shower curtain or table cloth and a few large metal binder clips, bring them along – to build a portable cubicle that you can use for changing, washing up, even showering under a bucket (see 'Staying clean outside', on page 264). Suspend the hoop from a branch with the rope or twine. Drape the shower curtain or tablecloth over the hoop, fastening the material onto the hoop with binder clips or any other fasteners you might have. While your creation probably won't be a thing of beauty, you will welcome the chance to disappear inside it for a bit of privacy.

✳ Shoo off insects with fabric softener

Fabric softener sheets aren't your usual item of technologically advanced outdoor gear, but you'll be glad to have some when mosquitoes start swarming around your tent. Just pin or tie one to your clothing to keep them away.

✳ Foil dampness and grime

For a little extra campsite comfort, take some aluminium foil from the kitchen when packing. Here are three ways to use it:

● Wrap your matches in aluminium foil to protect them from moisture.
● Lay a large piece of foil under your sleeping bag to prevent dampness from seeping in.
● Wad some foil into a ball to use as a scouring pad. Foil is great for scraping grime off a barbecue and blackened residue from the bottom of pans you have used over an open fire.

what's the story?

THE AMAZING SWISS ARMY KNIFE

It's hard to imagine a piece of travel equipment that's handier than a Swiss Army Knife. Depending on the style, this pocket-sized gadget might contain, in addition to a couple of blades, a ballpoint pen, bottle opener, file, magnifying glass, nail file, pliers, saw, scissors, toothpick, tweezers and often lots more. Some recent models are even equipped with USB flash drives, digital clocks and laser pointers.

The first Swiss Army Knife was introduced to the Swiss Army in 1891 and was a relatively simple implement: a pocket knife with a wooden handle that contained a blade, a screwdriver, a can opener and a punch; an improved version with an extra blade, a corkscrew and a special spring mechanism appeared in 1896. In Switzerland, the device was known as Offiziersmesser (officer's knife) – too much for many soldiers to pronounce when they became familiar with the knife during the Second World War and called it 'the Swiss Army Knife'.

There are actually two Swiss Army Knives: the Genuine Swiss Army Knife and the Original Swiss Army Knife. That's because the Swiss government once allowed two companies – Wenger and Victorinox – to produce them. In 2005, Victorinox acquired Wenger and a year later produced a knife with 85 devices and 110 functions: known as The Giant, it's a collector's item nearly 20cm wide that costs around £600.

A traveller's miscellany

✳ Balloon therapy

Balloons lift your spirits and they can be good for the body, too. Pack a durable, uninflated balloon with your travelling medicine kit and use it to make a cold or hot pack to soothe a sprain or muscle soreness. Just fill the balloon with very cold water or hot water from the tap. Tie it off and and lay it over the affected area. If you have a freezer and want to go the whole hog, make an ice pack by freezing a partially water-filled balloon.

✳ Chest rub for painful feet

If a day of sightseeing leaves you with pleasant memories but sore feet, rub a little medicated chest rub on your feet before going to bed (put on a pair of socks to keep the rub from marking the sheets). Your feet will feel like new in the morning.

✳ Pre-soaked insect repellents

You never know when insect repellant spray might come in handy, but cans and bottles can take up a lot of room in a portable medicine kit. Leave bulky containers behind – before leaving home, soak cotton wool balls in insect repellant and store them in a self-sealing plastic bag. When insects make an appearance, just pull out a cotton wool ball and dab some of the protective liquid onto your skin.

✳ A pill-bottle toothbrush protector

Have you ever opened your travel kit to find a toothbrush soaked in shaving cream? An easy and tidy way to keep up with dental hygiene on the road is to make a toothbrush holder kit out of an old plastic pill bottle. Cut a slit in the lid and slide the lid over the handle of your

idea

DON'T LEAVE HOME WITHOUT IT

You might not devote much time to thinking about the marvels of bicarbonate of soda, but put a plastic container into your suitcase and you'll be surprised at how often you reach for it. Use bicarbonate of soda to:

Treat burns Add 1 tablespoon bicarbonate of soda to 1 cup cold water, dip a cloth in the solution and lay the wet cloth on the burned area until it no longer feels hot.

Take the sting out of a bee sting Apply a paste made from 1 teaspoon bicarbonate of soda and 1 teaspoon of water and let it dry.

Brush your teeth and gargle Dip a wet toothbrush in a small amount and brush as you normally would. Finish your dental hygiene routine by mixing 1 teaspoon of bicarbonate of soda with ½ cup water and then gargling the solution.

Soothe sore feet Fill a receptacle – say, a tub, wastepaper basket or large ice bucket – with about a quart of warm water, add 1 tablespoon bicarbonate of soda and soak your tired feet until the water cools.

toothbrush; then replace the lid so the bristles of the toothbrush are inside the container, where they will remain clean.

Start
your garden
by growing
seeds in
paper cups!

11 Handy hints for gardeners

The typical family throws away a surprisingly large amount of food – although we're all trying to reduce the amount of food we waste. But what you don't eat may very well be the perfect food for your plants. Many kitchen staples can either be composted into plant food or can be fed to plants as they are.

And that's just the beginning. Your home is *full* of natural, non-toxic gardening aids, from bananas and soap to peanut butter and pine needles. Not only will using them save you time and money, but you will officially join the ranks of 'green' gardeners who are moving away from factory-made, often-toxic fertilisers, pesticides and weedkillers.

Gardening creatively with what you already own is a rewarding endeavour – a money-saving, eco-friendly approach to one of our favourite hobbies. So whatever the colour of your thumbs, get out in the garden and start growing.

Starting seeds and rooting cuttings

✱ Make seed holes with chopsticks

Instead of buying a dibber – the wooden garden tool used to poke seed holes in the soil – use a chopstick or pencil instead. You'll get the same holes for no cash outlay. Another choice is a full-size pair of folding nail clippers, the blunt arm of which you can poke into the soil and twist. When the time comes to transplant seedlings, use the same arm of the clippers to work a seedling and its rootball from the soil.

✱ No dibbing (or watering) required

An alternative to dibbing holes into the soil of a seed tray is to wet the soil, lay the seeds on the surface and then cover the seeds with another thin layer of soil. Shrink-wrap the tray with cling film and your job is done. Condensation on the wrap will drip down to keep the seeds moist until germination.

✱ Spice jars as seed sowers

Before sowing seeds directly into a seedbed, put them in an empty dried herb or spice jar – the kind with a perforated plastic top. Then shake the seeds out over the seedbed or along a row.

✱ Sowing tiny seeds

Seeds of impatiens, lobelia, carrots, lettuce and a few other flowers and vegetables are so miniscule that they are difficult to sow evenly. To remedy the problem and make seedlings easier to thin out once they sprout, combine the seeds with grainy foodstuffs such as semolina, couscous, oats or dried herbs, all of which will put some space between diminutive seeds.

---

idea

KEEP IT CLEAN

Dirty gardening equipment can carry mould, plant diseases and insects. So don't underestimate the need to thoroughly clean clippers and pots when rooting or otherwise propagating plants. Guard against plant disease with this two-step washing:

1. Scrub any pre-used propagation equipment with a brush dipped in mild washing-up liquid.

2. Fill a large galvanised tub or your bath with a solution of 1 part household bleach to 9 parts water. Then submerge containers or tools for about 5 minutes.

   Once they are completely dry, your germ-free, spore-free implements will be ready to resume their respective jobs.

✱ Make your own plant markers

To label your seeds tray by tray so you won't risk confusing your specially chosen tomato varieties, turn empty yoghurt pots, cottage cheese tubs or other white plastic containers into plant markers. Cut strips from the plastic, trim the ends to a point and use an indelible felt-tip marker to write the plant name (variety included) on each. Stick the strips into the edge of the trays as soon as you plant seeds so you'll know which plant is which from the start.

Transport cuttings to a friend's house in a sliced potato!

✶ Paper cup seed starters

Small paper drinking cups make excellent seed starters. They're the right size, you can easily poke a drainage hole in the bottom and they're easily cut apart when it comes time to plant your seedlings. Note that we specify *paper* cups: polystyrene cups may sit in landfill until your great-great-grandchildren have come and gone.

✶ Dry-cleaning bag humidifier

To provide the humidity needed to root a tray of cuttings, lay a dry-cleaning bag over the cuttings, making sure that it doesn't touch the plants. (Ice cream sticks or pencils can serve as 'tent poles'.) Clip the bag to the rim of the seed tray with clothespegs or small metal clamps.

✶ Root rose cuttings under glass

An easy way to root a cutting from your favourite rosebush is to snip off a 10–15cm piece of stem and plant it in good soil, whether in the garden or a pot. Then cover it with a large fruit jar to create a mini-greenhouse.

✶ Willow tea rooting preparation

Soaking six or eight willow twigs in water gives you a solution of indolebutyric acid (IBA), a natural plant-rooting hormone tea. Cut the twigs from a willow (any species), then split them. Cut twigs into 7cm pieces and steep them in a pail filled with 9–12cm water for 24 hours. Use the tea either to water just-planted cuttings or as an overnight soaker for cuttings.

✶ A rolling seed tray

Turn a child's toy cart into a seed tray on wheels. Poke holes in the cart bottom with a screw-hole punch and hammer, then fill the cart with peat pots or expandable peat pellets, labelling them as you go.

✶ Potatoes as transporters

If you need to take cuttings to another place, use a potato as a carrier. Slice a large potato in half crossways, poke three 2cm deep holes in each cut side with a chopstick or pencil and insert the cuttings, which will stay moist for 3 to 4 hours.

Caring for trees and shrubs

* Newsprint protection for young trees

If you have planted out tree seedlings that look a bit spindly, wrap the trunks in newspaper pages to protect them from the elements. Secure this newsprint sleeve with double-knotted dental floss or garden twine.

* Lichens: love them or hate them?

Lichens are the ruffled, fungus-like organisms that grow on stones, brick walls and tree trunks. Many gardeners love the natural look that lichens lend to trees and paths – but if you're not among them, this is a simple way to make lichens disappear: scrub them with a stiff brush dipped in a solution of 2 tablespoons household bleach and 1 litre water. Be very careful that none of the runoff comes into contact with other garden plants.

* Warm sleeve for standard rose grafts

Standard roses are ordinary rosebushes grafted onto long rootstock trunks. To protect the graft over winter, cut the sleeve off an old sweater or sweatshirt. Prune back the bush's top growth in late autumn so that you'll be able to slip the sleeve over the branches and around the graft scar. Stuff the sleeve with dried leaves, peat moss or straw for insulation, then tie a plastic bag over it for protection against snow and ice. When you remove the sleeve come spring, your rose will grow more vigorously.

* Speed rose-blooming with foil

In late May or early June, place sheets of aluminium foil on the ground beneath your rosebushes and anchor the foil with stones. Sunlight reflecting off the foil will speed up blooming, whether your roses are hybrid teas, floribundas or climbers.

* Feed bananas to roses

Most gardeners know that banana skins make a good fertiliser for tomatoes, peppers and their solanaceous cousins, but roses love them too. Chop banana skins (up to three) into small pieces and dig them into the soil beneath a

tip SOAP YOUR SAW

When trimming tree branches or shrubbery with a garden saw, run the blade through a bar of **anti-bacterial soap**. The soap will not only give the blade more glide but will help to reduce the branch's wound-threatening bacteria population as well.

rosebush. The banana skins provide 3.25 per cent phosphorus and more than ten times that amount of potassium, spurring the growth of sturdier stems and prettier blooms.

✳ A grassy boost for azaleas

After mowing the lawn, lay some of the grass clippings out to dry. Then spread a thin layer of clippings around the base of azalea plants. As the grass decays it leaches nitrogen into the soil, supplementing regular feeds. Many gardeners find this 'something extra' speeds the growth of azaleas and darkens the leaves. Be careful, though: piling the grass clippings too thickly may make them slimy and, in turn, expose the plant's stems to disease.

✳ Cola and tea for gardenias

Occasionally watering a gardenia bush with your favourite cola will increase the acidity of the soil, while the sugar will feed microorganisms and help organic matter to break down. And tea? Place tea bags around the base of a gardenia and cover them with mulch. Whenever you water the plant, the ascorbic acid, manganese and potassium present in the tea leaves will trickle down to the shrub's hungry roots.

✳ Cleaning sap off pruning tools

Taking a saw or shears to tree branches usually leaves sticky sap on the tool. Use a clean cloth to rub any of the following substances onto the blade(s), and say 'so long' to sap:

- Nail varnish remover
- Baby oil
- Aerosol cooking spray
- Suntan oil
- Peanut butter
- Margarine

✳ Lubricate pruning shears

Rubbing petroleum jelly or spraying WD-40 onto the pivot joint of a pair of shears will have you snipping away at shrubs so smoothly that you will feel like a professional pruner.

Growing annuals, perennials and bulbs

✱ Film protection for seeds

If you've just sown flower seeds in a seedbed and are pleased with the spacing and soil coverage, did you know that one simple extra step will warm the soil and speed germination, keep the earth moist and thwart birds foraging for seeds? It will – and all it takes is spreading a layer of clear cling film over the seeded area. Anchor the plastic with rocks and remove it as soon as the seeds have sprouted.

✱ A salt that flowers crave

Epsom salts consist of magnesium sulphate – which, as a supplement to your plants' regular feedings, will deepen the colour of blooms and help to fight disease. Every three or four weeks, scratch 1 teaspoon Epsom salts into the soil around an annual or perennial's stem and water well. Alternatively, dissolve 1 tablespoon Epsom salts in 1 gallon water. Every two weeks or so, pour some of the solution into a spray bottle and spritz the leaves of your flowers.

✱ Prop up tall perennials

Peonies, delphiniums and gladiolus are among a number of tall perennials that generally need support. A wooden stake is the usual answer, but a less obtrusive option is a tall old lampshade frame. Place the metal frame, narrow side down, amid seedlings when they're about 15cm tall, working the frame into the soil to a depth of about a centimetre. As the seedlings grow, tie them loosely to the top of the frame with twist ties. The leaves will obscure the frame as the blooms above stand tall.

✱ Bromeliads like fruit

To encourage a potted bromeliad's rosette of leaves to sprout its pretty flower, place the plant in a plastic dry-cleaning bag with a ripening banana or three or four ripe apples. The ethylene wafting from the fruit will stimulate flower production.

✱ Splints for bent stems

If any of your flower stems are bent, pick one of these common items to use as a splint: for thin stems, a toothpick or cotton bud; for thicker stems, a drinking straw, pencil, ballpoint pen or ice lolly stick. Fix the splints to stems with clear tape, but not too tightly.

✱ Ties for stakes

'Ropes' made from old tights have long been used to tie snapdragons, hollyhocks, tomatoes and other tall flowers and climbing vegetables to stakes (they're soft and pliable), but tights are hardly the only household item that will serve the purpose. Try these ties:

- Gift-wrapping ribbon left over from birthday parties
- Broken cassette tapes
- Plastic bin bag ties
- Dental floss (the thicker kind)
- Velcro strips
- Fabric strips cut from old sheets
- Wool from your knitting basket

✱ Make a flowerdome

Get creative and use an old umbrella – stripped of both its handle and fabric – as a frame for a

Make dried flowers with cat litter

All you need to dry the roses, poppies or peonies that you are so proud of is cat litter, a microwave oven and a deep microwave-safe bowl.

Drying flowerheads

Pick the flowers when they're dry (with no dew or raindrops) and snip off the flowerheads. Pour 4–5 cups litter into the bowl and scoop out space for one or two flowers at most. Nestle the flowers into the litter and gently spoon on more until they are covered. Microwave on high for 2 minutes and then let the litter cool completely – not so much because it's hot to the touch but because the drying continues at this point. Once you remove the dried flowerhead(s), blow off any dust or brush it away with a small paintbrush.

Drying long-stemmed flowers

To dry snapdragons or other long-stemmed flowers for dried arrangements, pour cat litter into an airtight container large enough to accommodate the stems. Arrange the flowers on top so that there's a little space between them, then cap the container. After seven to ten days, your flowers should be dried and ready to display.

flowering climber or vine. In the spot of your choice, drive a 1.5m metal pipe wide enough to accommodate the handle into the ground about 30cm deep, then slide the umbrella stem inside. Plant seedlings of morning glory or any other thin-stemmed flowering vine next to the pipe. Over the next few weeks a unique garden focal point will take shape.

✳ Make hand cleaning easier
If your garden gloves have gone missing but you need to work in the soil of your flowerbeds immediately, just scrape your fingernails over a bar of soap beforehand. The dirt will come out from under your nails more easily when you scrub your hands.

✳ Bag bulbs to prevent rot
Brown paper bags filled with sawdust or peat moss are the easy answer to the winter storage of tender crocus, tulip, daffodil, iris and other bulbs and rhizomes. Put a 5cm layer of sawdust or peat in the bottom of the bag and then arrange bulbs of the same type on top, making sure that they don't touch. Continue layering the bulbs and organic material until the bag is about three-quarters full. Clip the bag closed with clothespegs or metal clamps and use a marker to label each bag with the name of the bulbs contained inside.

✳ Plastic bulb protectors
To keep rodents from nibbling on newly transplanted bulbs, seal the bulbs off in wide-topped plastic containers. Before planting, punch drainage holes into the bottom and sides of a large plastic bottle or carton, bury it in the soil up to the open top and fill it with soil and humus. Plant two or three small bulbs in the container or one or two larger bulbs.

Old plastic storage boxes are more space efficient – and you may find other kinds of potential bulb protectors if you go rummaging through your garage or shed.

✳ Flavour food with scented geraniums
Scented geraniums (*Pelargonium* cultivars, below) have edible leaves that release a fragrance when rubbed. Among the varieties to grow in pots (or in warmer climes, flowerbeds) are those with the aroma of rose, lemon, apple, apricot, mint, cinnamon, ginger or nutmeg. Foods that benefit from the addition of finely chopped scented geranium leaves include fruit compotes, biscuits, cakes and poached pears.

Flowers that you can eat

Many garden flowers are edible and make an attractive and colourful addition to salads, summer dishes and puddings. Pick them fresh for instant use. A warning: never use flowers that have been sprayed with pesticide of any sort. Avoid toxic plants such as as azaleas, crocuses, daffodils, chrysanthemums, hydrangeas, lilies-of-the-valley, oleanders, rhododendrons and sweet peas.

Bee balm These red flowers, said to taste like oregano with a hint of mint, are most often used in fruit dishes and leafy green salads.

Calendulas The golden-orange calendula, a marigold cousin, resembles saffron in taste. Sprinkle the petals on pasta and rice dishes.

Dandelions Dandelion flowers should be eaten only when very young and just-picked; try the honeylike petals as a garnish for rice dishes. The leaves are a great addition to salads, but be aware that dandelions grown in a flowerbed are tastier than those that pop up on the lawn.

Wild pansies The mild wintergreen flavour of these viola flowers is a refreshing complement to salads and soft cheeses.

Nasturtiums Nasturtium blossoms have a sweet-and-spicy taste reminiscent of watercress and the leaves add a peppery tang to salads.

Sage blossoms Sage flowers have a subtler taste than the sage-leaf kitchen herb and add a nice touch to bean, corn and mushroom dishes.

Roses Use larger petals to sprinkle on desserts or salads, smaller petals as a garnish. Rose petals are also used to make syrups and jellies.

Squash blossoms Fried squash blossoms are an Italian speciality but now eaten the world over. A typical recipe calls for dipping the blossoms in beaten egg white, then in bread crumbs and grated Parmesan cheese before frying.

Hints for houseplants

✱ Free houseplants

Every time you eat an avocado, save the stone and grow a houseplant. Just scrub the stone pit clean and insert three sturdy toothpicks into it just above the base. Fill a drinking glass with water and set the stone on its rim. Change the water often and top it off as necessary.

After several weeks, the stone will sprout a shoot and roots, at which point you can pot your fledgling houseplant. Keep the pot in a sunny window and pinch off appropriate new shoots to make the plant bushier. Pinching off the shoot of the central stem after the stem grows to about 15cm tall will result in an even fuller plant.

✱ Coffee filter soil guard

When potting plants in flowerpots, put a small coffee filter in the bottom of the pot first, then add drainage material and soil. This way, excess water will leak out of the drainage hole while the soil stays put.

✱ Cleaning hairy or corrugated leaves

Smooth-leaved houseplants can be cleaned by wiping with a damp paper towel, but hairy or corrugated leaves require special care.

- **Brush dust away** An effective way to clean African violets and other hairy-leaved houseplants is with a soft-bristled toothbrush, a paintbrush or a pipe cleaner. Brush gently from the base of each leaf toward the tip.
- **Breeze dust away** Dust plants with corrugated leaves with a hair dryer. Set the appliance on cool or low and blow air onto every leaf.

✱ The cloth glove trick

Wearing an old cloth glove lets you clean houseplant leaves in half the time. Just run each leaf through your gloved fingers from bottom to top and you've dusted both sides at once.

✱ Go one size larger

To prevent houseplants from becoming rootbound (and dying out too quickly), replant them in a container larger than the one they originally came in. Add extra soil and your plants will grow faster and live twice as long.

✱ A when-to-water pencil gauge

Houseplant manuals tell you to water whenever the soil dries out, but determining dryness is easier said than done. That's not so with a pencil. Push a pencil deeply into the soil and then pull it out. If bits of dirt cling to the bare wood point, the soil is still moist. If the pencil comes up clean, it's time to water your houseplant.

✱ Water with ice cubes

Place ice cubes on top of the soil of potted plants, making sure that they don't touch the stem. The ice will melt slowly, releasing water gradually and evenly into the soil.

✱ Pot within pot

Use a casserole dish, Dutch oven or large saucepan to water cacti and succulents. Just pour a few inches of water into the pot, put in the houseplant and leave it there until no more air bubbles come to the water's surface. Drain the plant well before putting it onto a saucer. Other houseplants that benefit from the pot-in-a-pot method include anthuriums and grassy-leaved sweet flag *(Acorus gramineus)*.

Going away for a while?

When you leave home for a few days, you don't have to ask a neighbour to water your houseplants. Try one of these methods.

1

Plastic bottle/paper towel waterer

Slice the bottom off a 2 litre plastic soft drink bottle and stuff three paper towels into it up to the neck. Turn the bottle upside down and stick the neck into the soil of a houseplant you've just watered. For support, insert a chopstick alongside the bottle and fit two rubber bands around the items. Right before you leave home, fill the bottle with water, which will trickle through the towels and into the soil for about a week.

2

Plastic bag greenhouse

A large plastic bag can become a greenhouse for small houseplants like African violets. Water the plant well and let it drain. Spread a layer of peat moss on the bottom of the bag, then place the plant on top (the peat will absorb excess moisture). Tie the bag loosely with a twist tie, leaving a small gap for ventilation. When the bagged plant is placed in indirect light, the soil will stay moist for two weeks.

3

Bath towel soaker

Dampen a thick bath towel and spread it out in a sink or bath near a sunny window. Turn on the cold water tap just enough that water drips slowly onto the towel. Arrange houseplants (without saucers) on the towel, making sure that the drain holes and towel are in contact. Leave the tap on while you're away and the moisture in the towel will be drawn up by the plants' roots.

Smart tricks for vital vegetables

✱ Sun boxes for veggie seedlings

When you're starting vegetables indoors near a normally sunny south-facing window but the early spring sun won't cooperate, maximise the rays with aluminium foil-lined sun boxes. Cut out one side of a cardboard box and line the three inner 'walls' with foil. When you face the boxes toward the outside, sunlight will reflect back on to your vegetable seedlings. Plants will not only catch more sun, but their stems will grow straight rather than bending toward the light.

✱ Foiling cutworms

Before setting out a tomato seedling, wrap each stem with a 10cm² collar of aluminium foil, leaving it loose enough to allow the stem to grow as it expands. Plant the seedlings with 5cm foil above the soil and 5cm below so that the cutworms won't be able to penetrate the shiny armour.

✱ Nighttime warmers

If the weatherman predicts an unseasonably cold night, get outdoors as early as you can and flank your vegetable plants with something that will absorb the heat of the sun all day and radiate it at night. That 'something' could be large, flat stones or terracotta tiles left over from your new floor. Another solution is to bend wire coat hangers into hoops, secure them over the plants and drape them with black plastic bin bags for the night.

✱ Secure trellis-grown melons with tights

If you grow your melons on a trellis in your greenhouse, a sling made from old tights will keep growing melons from falling to the ground. Cut off a hose leg, slip it over a melon and tie the hose to the trellis.

✳ Keep root vegetables straight with a pipe

To prevent horseradish and special varieties of carrots and parsnips from forming forks or getting bent out of shape, grow them in sections of PVC pipe placed vertically in the ground and filled with rich soil and humus. When you harvest the roots in the autumn, you'll be surprised at how straight and thick they've grown.

✳ Hang a bag of mothballs

Mothball haters include rodents and insects, so consider putting some of the smelly balls into your vegetable garden. Don't let them touch the soil or the toxic chemicals in the mothballs (usually naphthalene or dichlorobenzene) could contaminate it. (If you think you can simply place mothballs on lids, tiles or other flat surfaces to keep them off the ground, think again. In no time at all, wind and garden invaders will knock them off.) For safety's sake, put a few mothballs in small mesh bags and hang them from a trellis.

✳ Grow onions through newspaper

Here's a bit of headline news: one of the easiest ways to grow healthy onions is through newspaper mulch. Why? Because onion stalks cast a very slim shadow at best, letting in the sunlight that will sprout weed seeds. A lights-out mat of newspapers will stop weeds short.

In early spring, wet the soil of the onion patch. Then spread three or four sections of newspapers over the area, hosing down each one. With one or two fingers, punch holes about 12–15cm apart through the wet mat and place an onion set within each. Firm moist soil around the sets and cover the mat with shredded leaves and grass clippings. Weeds won't stand a chance as your onions grow and thrive.

household superstar

10 GARDEN USES FOR A PAIR OF TIGHTS

Among the many places that tights have been used around the house are the flower and vegetable garden – as in the following selection.

1 Slip 'caps' of tights over unpicked produce to thwart birds, squirrels and insects.

2 Tie plant stems and vines to stakes with tights, using a figure of eight loop.

3 Tie climbing roses to a trellis with tights. – white tights for a white trellis, neutral coloured tights for natural wood.

4 Use tights as bags to hold human hair clippings or soap slivers, which when tied to stakes around the garden plot may repel deer.

5 Keep coiled garden hose from coming loose by tying it with tights.

6 Cover a watering can spout with tights when watering delicate flowers.

7 Store bulbs in tights in winter – different varieties in different legs, and labelled.

8 Prevent soil loss in patio plants by laying a piece of stocking over the drainage holes of pots.

9 Use as a tea bag for manure tea.

10 Use tights to strain liquid fertiliser (including manure tea), pesticide or fungicide into a sprayer.

Keep your seedlings warm with aluminium foil.

✳ A tyre tower for potatoes

Increase your potato yield by growing potatoes in a stack of tyres. Fill a tyre with soil and plant two whole or halved seed potatoes about 5cm deep. Once the potatoes have sprouted around 15–25cm of foliage, place a second tyre atop the first and fill with more soil, leaving 8–10cm of foliage exposed.

Repeat the process again and your three-tyre tower will triple your potato crop. Potatoes sprout on the underground stems – and the taller the stems, the greater the number of tasty tubers you will produce.

✳ Two sprays for pumpkins

Ward off fungal diseases in a pumpkin patch by spraying each pumpkin with a homemade mixture of 1 teaspoon bicarbonate of soda and ½ teaspoon corn oil stirred into 1 litre water.

Fungal diseases aside, some gardeners claim that they can enrich a pumpkin's colour with a different spray: aerosol whipped cream, applied around the base of each plant every three weeks.

✳ Grow your own loofahs

The loofah gourd *(Luffa cylindrica)* is a purely practical choice for gardeners: it's grown primarily for its dried pulp, which we know as the exfoliating beauty sponge of the same name. Just plant and cultivate loofahs as directed on the seed packet – though in most places in the UK you'll need to start seeds indoors.

When a gourd lightens in weight and its skin begins to brown, peel it. Wet it thoroughly and squeeze out the seeds with both hands, then set the gourd on a rack to dry for two to four weeks or until hard. (Placing the gourds near to a heating source will speed the process.) Use a sharp knife to slice the dried loofah crossways into rounds to make homegrown skin scrubbers that the whole family can use.

Tending your tomatoes

✳ Fertilise with banana skins

Grow stronger tomato plants by placing three or four banana skins in the bottom of each planting hole. (Note: there is no need to eat all the bananas at once. Freeze the skins in freezer bags until you have enough to work with.) When you plant a tomato seedling, pop the skins in the hole with a mixture of dry leaves, manure and soil. Banana skins act as a kind of time-release fertiliser, leaching potassium and trace minerals into the soil.

✳ Tin foil root-cooler

On really hot days, lay sheets of aluminium foil around the base of tomato plants, shiny side up and anchor them with a few stones. The foil will reflect the sun's rays upward, reduce soil temperature by about 10 per cent and help to keep the tomatoes' root zones from drying out.

✳ An ornamental yet practical support

If you grow tidy tomato plants, that grow to a certain height and then stop, consider painting a stepladder in bright colours and using it as an ornamental A-frame trellis. Plant one seedling 7–10cm from each leg, then tie the stems loosely to the ladder as they grow. As the plants mature, they will be supported by the ladder's sides and treads and no ripening tomatoes will have to rest on the soil and risk rotting.

what's the story?

THE TOMATO: FRUIT OR VEGETABLE?

You're probably aware that the tomato is technically a fruit, which botanists define as the reproductive body of a seed plant, usually having edible sweet pulp. (Actually, it's a berry, but we're not about to bore you with a botany lecture.) Yet for all intents and purposes, the tomato is a vegetable because of the way it's used: as a savoury side dish, in green salads and as a base for the red sauces bequeathed to the world by the Italians.

In 1893 the United States Supreme Court declared the tomato a vegetable. US tomato growers claimed they were being adversely affected by a flood of tomatoes imported from Mexico and Cuba. At that time fruits were not subject to tariffs. Vegetables were taxed and the court ruled that because the tomato is eaten with the main part of a meal rather than with dessert, it should legally be classified as a vegetable. With imported tomatoes now taxed, the tomato industry flourished as growers planted thousands of acres more of everyone's favourite fruit, or do we mean berry ... oh yes, *vegetable.*

✱ Sugar for sweeter tomatoes

When tomato fruits start to show colour, add a spoonful of sugar to the watering can – especially when you have found a variety that you like but that seems a bit too acidic. (That tomato taste we all long for results from an optimum balance of acidity and sweetness.) Your tomatoes will not only be sweeter but juicier.

✱ Prevent blossom end rot with Epsom salts

The bane of many a tomato grower, fruit-spoiling blossom end rot is often caused by a calcium deficiency. Stop the disease before it starts with this simple addition to your tomato bed: pour 90g of Epsom salts into the bottom of each planting hole. Cover the salt with a thin layer of soil before putting in your seedlings.

Epsom salts are comprised of magnesium sulphate, which aids the transport of calcium to the tops of tomato plants and the fruit. As a bonus, Epsom salts help the plants to absorb phosphorus and sulphur.

✱ Grow rooftop tomatoes in hay

If you live in a flat without a garden and don't have anywhere that is suitable for growing tomatoes, haul a bale of hay up to the roof (if building regulations and your roof permit) and you will have a nitrogen-rich medium that heats up like a compost pile. Starting in very early spring, hose the bale daily to activate the heating process.

Once the bale decays into fertile compost (usually after seven to eight weeks), it's cool enough for planting. Stand two stakes in the bale and nestle a tomato seedling into the hay next to each one. Watering daily will keep the plants growing well for the rest of the season.

tip PAINT YOUR SMALL TOOLS

To make small tools easier to spot when you're working in a vegetable patch, **paint their handles** in bright colours – say, fluorescent orange or green. Hopefully you won't have to waste time searching for the trowel you left under a sprawling plant two rows away.

Secrets of fine fruit

✱ Rake-it-up pine tree mulch

Money doesn't grow on trees. But if you grow blueberries, free mulch does – if you have any pine trees in your garden. Naturally acidic pine needles will not only leach the acid blueberries crave into the soil but also will help to protect the plants' shallow roots. Just rake up the pine needles and spread them beneath the blueberry plants to a height of about 5cm.

✱ Aluminium peck-peck prevention

If you grow productive fruit trees and enjoy making fruit pies for friends and neighbours, don't throw away the aluminium pie dishes that come with ready meals or shop-bought pies. Use them to scare away blackbirds, starlings and other fruit-loving birds. Poke a hole in the rim of each plate, thread a 60cm piece of dental floss or string through the hole and triple-knot it tightly. Hang a couple of plates onto the branches of each fruit tree and that's it. Shiny reflective objects that swing in the wind are far more effective bird repellents than the stationary plastic or metal owls, cats and scarecrows you can buy.

✱ Make your own invisible net

You don't always have to buy netting at a garden centre in order to protect ripening cherries and other tree fruit from birds. Just buy two or three spools of black thread. Stand beside the tree, grab the loose end of the thread and toss the spool over the tree to a helper – a child will probably think it's a great game. Continue tossing the spool back and forth until it is empty. The invisible thread won't seal birds off from the tree, but once they run into it a few times they should look for their ripe fruit lunch somewhere else.

idea
THE IMPORTANCE OF NETTING

Dirty gardening equipment can carry mould. If you are serious about growing fruit, you will almost certainly need some netting if you are to keep fruit and berries safe from birds, squirrels and other hungry marauders. Available at garden centres and DIY stores, netting is usually made of nylon or polypropylene and comes in various dimensions and assorted mesh sizes, from a very fine gauge to a much wider net size.

Can we offer an around-the-house alternative to shop-bought netting? Sadly, not really, unless you really want to spend time sewing lots and lots of fishnet T-shirts or supermarket onion bags together.

✱ Ant stick-ups

Ants won't be able to climb your fruit trees and munch on ripe fruit if you wrap the trunks with one of these sticky materials:

- Contact paper, folded in half with sticky-side out
- Two-sided clear tape, wrapped around the trunk in a 7cm deep band
- Sheets of newspaper secured with masking tape and sprayed with an adhesive insect spray
- A cardboard sleeve taped shut and smeared with petroleum jelly

Success with cacti and succulents

Cacti and succulents are some of the most popular houseplants because they come in such a wide variety of shapes and are mostly very easy to care for.

Dust with a soft brush

Always be gentle when dusting potted cacti and brush them lightly with a soft, old toothbrush or shaving brush. In summer, spray the plants lightly with water after brushing.

Rub out pests with alcohol

Two common afflictions of potted cacti and succulents are: 1) White woolly spots that mean mealybugs are present and 2) small beige or brown bumps on the plant's stems that are actually scale insects. If you see only a small number of either of these pests, kill them by wiping them up with a cotton bud soaked in surgical spirit. For heavier infestations, spray the plant with a solution of 240ml surgical spirit, 1 teaspoon corn oil and 1 teaspoon washing-up liquid.

A newspaper gripper

Protect your fingers when re-potting a spiny cactus by making a gripper or pincer, from a couple of sheets of newspaper. Fold the sheets from top to bottom into a 7cm paper band. Wrap the band around the middle of the cactus and grip the ends tightly. Then gently tug upward until the plant comes free of the pot.

Take out the sting with tape

Remove tiny cactus prickles from your fingers by firmly pressing adhesive tape onto the affected area and then ripping it off. For larger or more stubborn prickles, use a pair of tweezers.

A pencil as a pusher

You can easily remove a small cactus or succulent from a pot by pushing a pencil into the drainage hole, eraser end first. As long as the soil is fairly dry, the root ball should emerge from the pot in one clump.

Secrets of lustrous lawns

✱ Lawn tonics

Some highly successful lawn growers achieve great results with homemade lawn tonics made from the most ordinary items. Add any of the following ingredients to the reservoir of a 12–16 litre garden sprayer and water your lawn with the mixture every three weeks or so. Adding 240ml washing-up liquid each time will help to spread the solution more evenly and make it stick to blades of grass.

- A 330ml can of non-diet cola or beer. The sugar in both stimulates microbes that help to break up the soil.
- A 240ml dose of syrup or black treacle. See note on sugar, above.
- A 240ml dose household ammonia. Ammonia adds nitrates, the primary ingredient in most fertilisers.
- A 120ml dose of mouthwash. The alcohol in mouthwash kills bacteria and spores and helps to deter some pests.

✱ Recycle your grass

Take a cue from public parks and golf courses and 'grasscycle' when you mow your lawn – which means leaving clippings on your lawn when you finish. Just mow often enough to make sure no more than a third of the length of the grass blades is chopped off each time. The resulting clippings serve as beneficial mulch and keeps garden waste out of landfill sites.

idea

SECRETS OF LUSTROUS LAWNS

Different types of ground cover are the low-maintenance alternative to lawns, but don't think that you can just plant them and forget about them. All plants need watering and fertilising, though not as often as a picture-perfect lawn. Here's where ground covers really come into their own:

- On hard-to-mow slopes or in tight spaces

- When you want a 'natural' garden

- When you don't have time to spend hours mowing to a perfect finish.

There are lots of potential ground covers you can use – for a fragrant lawn try camomile or wild thyme. Or in a space that gets little light, encourage moss instead of fighting it. Prostrate juniper (*Juniperus horizontalis* 'Wiltoni') has branches that form a carpet of brilliant green foliage. Or if you really aspire to a country look, a wildflower meadow is a delightful possibility.

For greener grass, try a tonic made with mouthwash!

✳ Three temporary trunk protectors

If you are growing a number of fragile tree seedlings that would suffer badly if they were accidentally rammed with your mower, wrap them up before you mow. Wrap slender trunks in bubble wrap or several sheets of newspaper secured with masking tape or gaffer tape. An old towel pinned with two or three large safety pins will also work. All three wraps are easy to put up and take down.

✳ Oil your mower blades

Spraying lawnmower blades and the underside of the lawnmower housing with aerosol cooking oil or WD-40 will help to keep cut grass from building up in your mower, so whip out a can and spray away thoroughly before you use your machine.

✳ A pair of tights for a power mower?

Believe it or not, yes. A few layers of old tights (or, alternatively, two fabric softener sheets) will protect the air intake opening on your power mower – specifically, the carburettor intake horn. Just cut the material to size and secure it to the horn with gaffer tape.

✳ Coat hanger topiary for ground covers

If you take the low-maintenance route and choose a decorative ground cover over a grassy lawn, you can ornament the expanse with a mini-topiary or two. Turn wire coat hangers into frames in the shape of your choice: a circle, a heart, animals and birds – and even your child's initials. Anchor the frame into the soil and train strands of the plants to cover it, using clippers to neaten the growth as necessary.

Watering your garden

✳ Test whether it's time to water with a toothpick

Just as you can test a baking cake for readiness by sticking in a wooden toothpick, you can do the same to see whether a flowerbed is in need of watering. Stick the toothpick into the soil as far as it will go, then examine it. If it comes out clean, it's time to water. If any soil clings to the pick, you don't need to water just yet – test the soil again the next day.

✳ A penny splashed ...

You could take a jar containing £20.57 worth of pennies to the bank or you could use the coins as a splashguard in a window box. Watering plants in window boxes often splashes mud onto windowpanes, as does driving rain. To solve the problem, simply spread some pennies over the surface of the soil.

✳ Recycle unsalted cooking water

Boiled foods release nutrients, so why pour their cooking water down the drain? Let the water cool and then use it to give a garden plants a healthy drink. But take note: when you cook any of the following, do *not* add salt to the water – it is harmful to many plants.

- **Eggs** Hard-boiled eggs leave calcium in the cooking water, so use the liquid to water calcium-loving solanaceous plants: tomatoes, potatoes, aubergines and peppers.
- **Spinach** Plants need iron, too – and spinach

Water used to boil eggs is calcium rich – good for kitchen garden plants

idea

A HOMEMADE RAIN GAUGE

A large plastic soft drink bottle, may not be the most attractive and cutting edge rain gauge in the world – but it has other advantages – it doesn't cost a penny and it works. Just cut off the top third of the bottle, turn the top upside down and fit it into the larger piece to act as a funnel. Then use some waterproof tape to tape the pieces together at the rim.

Lay the bottle on its side and using a ruler and indelible marker mark off lines 0.5cm apart. Set the gauge in an open area in the garden when you are expecting rain, then check to see how high the water rises – a clue to how long you should hold off from watering.

water gives them not only iron but also a good dose of potassium.

- **Pasta** Starchy water will spur the release of plant nutrients in the soil, meaning starch may be better for plants than for you.
- **Potatoes** All the benefits of the pasta water above.

* Milk bottle tricklers

Tomatoes aren't the only garden plants that like lots of water. Other thirsty plants include courgettes and rosebushes. How can you keep their thirst quenched? Bury plastic milk bottle reservoirs alongside each plant. Start by perforating a bottle in several places. Dig a planting hole large enough to accommodate both plant and bottle and bury the bottle so that its opening is at soil level. After refilling the hole

and tamping down the soil, fill the bottle with water. Then top it to overflowing at least once a week and your plant's roots will stay moist.

* Water ferns with weak tea

When planting a fern, put a used tea bag into the bottom of the planting hole to act as a reservoir while the fern adapts to its new spot; the roots will draw up a bit more nitrogen. Another drink ferns like is a very weak solution of household ammonia and water (1 tablespoon ammonia to 1 litre water) which will also feed them a little nitrogen.

* Borax for sun-sensitive plants

To keep direct sunlight from burning the leaves of ferns, azaleas, yews, hollies, hostas and herbs such as thyme and chives, add borax to your watering can – 1 tablespoon dissolved in 4.5 litres water. Wet the leaves of the plants and soak the soil with the solution a couple of times in the spring (more than two treatments is overdoing it), and your plants will be better able to stand up to the sun's hot rays in summer.

* Hose punctured?

If water is leaking from a tiny hole in your garden hose, stick a wooden toothpick into the hole and then break it off at surface level. Wrap electrical tape or gaffer tape around the hose to secure the toothpick. The wet wood will swell up and form a tight seal.

Improving soil and making compost

✴ A hairy nitrogen source

Human hair is by far one of the best nitrogen sources that you can add to your compost heap. Three kilograms of hair contain 500g nitrogen – the same amount yielded by 90kg of manure. Check with local hairdressers or barbers to see if they are prepared to give you a bag of hair.

✴ Help from your pet

Sprinkle unused, alfalfa-based feed or bedding onto your compost pile and toss well. Alfalfa is high in nitrogen – an excellent compost activator – which will help to hasten decomposition.

✴ Attract earthworms with coffee grounds

The larger the number of earthworms wriggling about in your soil, the better its tilth. Attract the worms to planting beds or other garden areas by digging coffee grounds into the soil.

✴ Warm up the soil with clear plastic

What free resource will kill weed seeds, most plant diseases and nematodes in your soil? The sun. Till a patch of soil and water it, then lay a sheet of clear plastic over the area (a split-open dry-cleaning bag will work well) and anchor the edges with stones. After four to six weeks, the sun's heat should have rid the soil of most plant menaces.

✴ Composting in a leaf bag

Turn autumn leaves into compost by storing them over the winter in large black plastic leaf bags. When filling the bag with leaves, add a small spadeful of soil and a handful of 10-10-10 fertiliser as an activator. Then direct a stream of water from your garden hose into the bag to saturate the leaves.

Tie the bag closed and bounce it on the ground a few times to mix the contents. Store the bag in a sunny place so that it absorbs the heat of the sun. By spring the leaves will have rotted into rich compost.

tip COFFEE, TEA OR COLA?

When your compost pile seems a bit slow in producing the fertile organic matter you want to dig into the garden, speed decomposition of its contents by pouring on coffee, **tea or non-diet cola** – all three of which will increase the bacterium population that help both the soil and the compost to break down.

Feeding your plants

✳ A matchbook fertiliser

It's true. But only when you want to add sulphur to the soil to lower the pH for acid-loving plants. Tear out the matches from several matchbooks and throw them into the bottom of planting holes for such plants as impatiens, hydrangeas, azaleas and gardenias.

✳ A freebie from the fireplace

Hardwood ashes from a fireplace will supply potassium and phosphorous to the garden. Don't use wood that has been treated with preservatives or anything else. To fertilise plants, spread a 1cm layer of ashes a few centimetres from the stem and dig into the soil.

A couple of cautions: 1) If you store ashes outside, protect them from the rain or their nutrients will be depleted; 2) don't use ashes around potatoes, as ash can promote potato scab.

✳ Limit your plants' coffee consumption

It isn't the caffeine in coffee grounds that garden plants like azaleas, rosebushes and evergreens love but rather the acidity and aeration that the grounds provide – not to mention nitrogen, phosphorous and trace minerals. Just be sure to dig the grounds well into the soil to keep them from becoming mouldy.

Dig about 100g grounds into the soil near the roots, repeating once a month. And don't overdo it. Fertilising even acid-loving plants with coffee grounds too frequently could increase soil acidity to undesirable levels.

✳ A tree-feeding drill

To make sure that fertiliser reaches a tree's feeder roots, put a power drill to work on something besides wood: the soil. Use a bit at

idea

FINDING FREE MANURE

Not surprisingly, a lot of farmers and stable owners are more than happy for you to take manure away from their property for use in your garden (after drying and ageing, of course). If you live near a zoo or animal park, call the administrative office to see if manure is supplied to gardeners. Caution: never use manure from pets as a fertiliser; it may contain roundworms and potentially toxic parasites.

least 30cm long and 20mm in diameter and bore holes in the soil around the drip line – the imaginary circle beneath the outermost tips of the tree canopy. Space the holes about 60cm apart, then bore a second ring of holes about 75cm from the tree trunk. Funnel a slow-release fertiliser into all of the holes. Plug them with soil and water well.

✳ Add sawdust and leaves to ageing manure

Fresh or raw, manure must be aged so that it doesn't burn your plants' roots – and only the most committed home gardeners will be prepared to wait for the six months it takes. If you're one of those gardeners, water a fresh manure pile, cover it with a tarpaulin so that the nutrients won't leach out during rain and turn the pile with a pitchfork every ten days or so. To control the odour (especially in summer), add sawdust, dead leaves or wood chips.

Myriad mulches

✳ Free mulch quest

Mulch is usually there for the taking if you know where to look for it. Besides the dead leaves and grass clippings you can collect from your own garden, check with agricultural businesses and local governments to see if they have any waste material that they would like to be taken away. In particular, ask for items like chippable bark and wheat straw.

✳ Strawberries like sawdust

A sawdust mulch benefits strawberries in two ways: it gives them the acidity they crave and keeps snails and slugs at bay. Raise the foliage of each plant and mound sawdust 5–7cm high around the stem. But be aware of what you're using: sawdust from certain species such as cedar or chemically treated wood contains toxins that do garden plants no favours.

✳ Foil and paper heat-beaters

A single-layer mulch of aluminium foil (right) or brown paper (the latter coated with clear varnish) will help to decrease soil temperature because both materials reflect the sun's rays. On very hot days, keep the roots of a favourite plant cool by laying foil or paper around the base of the plant.

✳ Recycle the tops of root crops

What can you do with the leafy tops of the carrots, beetroots, radishes and other root vegetables that you grow? Once you have harvested the roots, lay the tops between rows of your veggie garden to mulch the crops that remain.

✳ Black plastic for a small space

If you have a tiny garden – say a 1.5m² patch of soil in a paved courtyard – don't bother to buy the black plastic mulch sold at garden centres. (Black plastic is the standard weed-eliminating underlay for bark chip mulches.) Plain black plastic bin bags will do the job equally well. Just spread out the bags side to side – and when it comes time to restyle your small garden months or years later, you can use the bags for their original purpose: to hold rubbish.

Waging war on weeds

✱ Pinpoint weeds with salt

Salt will kill many weeds that can't be pulled up from the roots. Use a garden fork to scrape the soil away from the base of the weed and then cut the stem as close to the ground as possible. Pour salt onto the wound, trying your best not to spill any into the soil.

✱ Drive weeds from cracks with salt and vinegar

If weeds or grass sprout from cracks in your driveway, path, patio or any other outdoor paved surface, squirt them with a salt and vinegar solution. To make it, combine 480ml vinegar, 45g salt and 2 drops washing-up liquid in a jar, screw the cap on tightly and shake well. A simpler alternative is to pour boiling salted water into the cracks. When applying either weed killer, make sure that no runoff reaches your plants.

✱ Newspaper and plastic smotherers

If one part of your garden seems a little too weed-friendly, try one of these mulches to keep undesirable plants from sprouting:

- **Newspapers** Wet several sheets of newspaper so that they cling together and then set the mat over a patch of weeds. Camouflage the mat by topping it with wood chips or other mulch. Remove it once the weeds have died.
- **Bin bags** Split the seams of black plastic bin bags to double their size and use them to blanket the problem spot. Cover the plastic up with wood chips or a similar camouflage and leave it in place for 10–14 days – by which time the weeds should be dead.

make your own...

WEEDKILLER

Chemical-laden weedkillers do their job effectively but so do greener alternatives that are easy to make at home. Whatever your views on conventional versus organic gardening, it's always a good idea to try weedkillers with low toxicity before using harsher poisons.

Vinegar weed beater

The acetic acid in vinegar kills the leaves of a weed, not the root – but if you apply this spray often enough it will deplete the weed's stored energy reserves and eventually kill off the intruder.

480ml water
360ml vinegar (white or cider)
120ml washing-up liquid

1 Using a funnel, pour all of the ingredients into a 1 litre spray bottle.

2 Shake well to mix.

3 Spray the solution directly on to weeds, taking care not to spray any surrounding grass or desirable plants.

Frost fixers

✳ Coat hanger cold frame

To protect seedlings in heavy planters that you are unable to bring indoors when it's cold, straighten out two coat hangers and then bend the wire into arcs. Cross them and insert the ends into the planter just inside the rim, leaving headroom for the seedlings. Cover this wire frame with a plastic dry-cleaning bag, securing the plastic to the planter by wrapping it with loosely tied string. Temporarily remove the plastic whenever the seedlings need watering.

✳ Extra insulation

If you are keeping seedlings or hardening off young plants in a cold frame and a hard frost is forecast, line the inside of the frame with sheets of newspaper. Newsprint is a first-rate insulator.

✳ A newspaper blanket

When the weather forecaster predicts a frosty night, tent thinnish sections of the newspaper over seedlings and weight them down at the edges with stones. They will keep your plants nicely insulated from the cold until the temperature climbs the next day.

✳ Baskets of warmth

In cold climates, old-fashioned woven baskets make excellent plant protectors, keeping cold winds out while letting in some light – look around for old broken baskets you can leave outside in the wet. At night, drape them with black plastic for extra protection.

✳ Improvised cloches

The French came up with the idea for the glass cloche or bell jar, to protect seedlings from frost. Elegant glass and practical plastic cloches line the shelves at garden centres, but a household substitute will do the job equally well. Some ideas for impromptu plant protectors:

- A tall flower vase, placed upside down over the plant
- A large glass fruit jar
- A 2 litre soft drink bottle. Slice the bottom off with a sharp knife and place the bottle over the seedling.
- A 4 litre milk bottle, used in the same way as the soft drink bottle.

✳ A warm cosy glow

If frost threatens to damage a large container plant that sits on your patio or perhaps a tree that's bearing young fruit, string Christmas lights (below) through the branches. Cover the plant with a sheet or dust sheet and switch on the lights. Your plant will stay warm and frost free through the night.

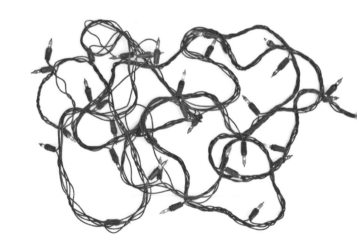

Feathered and furry friends and foes

✳ Help birds to build nests

To attract birds to your garden in spring (they will happily feast on leaf-eating insects when not eyeing up your veggies or fruits in summer), hang some nest-building materials in a tree. Fill a large-mesh onion bag with lint from a tumble drier, hair from your hairbrush, fabric scraps and short pieces of string or wool. Then watch your feathered visitors fashion a new home.

✳ A real flap

If your property is situated in a particularly windy spot – and you are trying to keep birds away from produce – try this trick for keeping birds away from garden plants. Cut plastic rubbish bags into 'flags' or long strips and staple them to tall wooden stakes with a staple gun. When the plastic whips around in the wind, birds will be scared away by both the movement and the noise.

✳ Scarecrow stuffers

If you decide to put a traditional stand-up, hatted scarecrow in your vegetable plot (as much for nostalgia as anything else), be aware that the stuffing materials for his shirt and pants are probably already in your closet or storeroom.

Anything soft and pliable will do as long as you seal it into a plastic bin bag to keep it dry: old pillows, rags, wadded-up newspaper, bubble wrap, polystyrene packing chips, shower curtains or dust cloths. And don't forget old-fashioned hay, straw and dead leaves.

✳ Guard garden plants with garlic

Encircling a flowerbed or vegetable plot with garlic plants will discourage squirrels and other furry pests – including voles, shrews and field mice – from making a meal of your plants. Space the garlic plants about 15cm apart to ward off hungry intruders.

Birds love soft scraps to add to their nests – so make them up a bag!

✳ Make moles run

Run away from their tunnels, that is. Shovelling strong-smelling used cat litter into the tunnel will announce loud and clear that their territory has been invaded and the moles will leave your garden in a hurry.

✳ Oily mole chasers

Soak rags, paper towels or facial tissues in peanut oil or olive oil and stuff them into mole holes. The oils will quickly become rancid and stink the creatures out of their homes. Or take this less smelly route: stick children's windmills around the garden; moles don't like steady clickety-clicking and may escape to a quieter spot.

✳ Rabbit rebuffers

Plenty of repellents will turn rabbits away from your plants. Among those to try:
- Talcum powder, dried red pepper flakes or garlic powder, dusted around your plants
- Hair from humans, dogs or cats
- Bars of strongly fragranced soap placed in vegetable garden rows
- Lemon peel scattered among the plants

✳ Flag down deer

The movement of something white mimics the deer's warning signal that predators or other dangers are imminent: flashing the white underside of its tail. Wind-whipped white 'flags' that could keep deer out of your vegetable garden are white plastic shopping bags, rags or strips torn from some old T-shirts.

Hammer 60 to 90cm tall stakes around your plot at 2m intervals. Tack plastic shopping bags to the stakes so that they will billow in the wind or fix white fabric strips that are long enough to flutter in the breeze. If you're lucky, deer will run the other way when the white flags fly.

Successful strategies for insect pests

✱ Fool codling moths with fake apples

The larvae of these moths attack fruit such as apples and pears, but you can make sure that codling moths never lay eggs by luring them with fake apples – red Christmas tree balls hung in fruit trees. Start by threading a 30cm loop of string through the ball holder, then knot it two or three times. Spray the 'apples' on all sides with an adhesive insect spray and hang three or four on fruit tree branches. The codling moths will home in on the red targets and get stuck.

✱ Bottle up wasps

Wasps follow their noses to sugar, so set them a sweet trap. Slice the top 7cm off the top of a large plastic soft drink bottle and set the piece with the neck aside. Create a hanger by poking holes on either side of the base near the top. Thread 45 to 60cm string through the holes and triple-knot the ends. Place the necked piece into the bottle upside down to form a funnel and tape it tightly.

Pour sugar water into the bottle (use 4 parts water to 1 part sugar, dissolved) and hang your contraption on the branch of a tree that is favoured by wasps. Wasps trying to reach the liquid will either drown or be unable to escape from the bottle.

✱ Repellents in your herb rack

We love herbs and spices, but most garden pests find them unpalatable or even lethal. Sprinkle any of the following around your plants and watch leaf-hungry pests go elsewhere to dine.

- Powdered cinnamon
- Powdered cloves
- Cayenne pepper
- Black pepper
- Chilli powder
- Hot curry powder
- Garlic powder
- Dried lemon thyme
- Dried bay leaves, crumbled.

tip SUCK 'EM UP

Use a battery-operated **handheld vacuum cleaner** to rid your plants of small leaf-eating insects. Run the vacuum over both sides of the leaves of the affected plant to suck up red spider mites, flea beetles, aphids, whiteflies and other tiny pests.

✳ Repel aphids with aspirin

The active ingredient in aspirin, salicylic acid, is produced by plants as a natural protection – and that works to the gardener's advantage. Experiments have shown that plants watered with a weak aspirin and water solution not only repel aphids and other sucking insects but also promote strong plant growth.

To make a systemic solution, fill a bucket with 20 litres water and drop in 3 aspirin tablets. Stir until the tablets dissolve. Water plants as usual with the solution or pour it into a spray bottle to spritz the plants' leaves and stems on all sides. Thereafter, apply the aspirin water every two weeks.

✳ Send insects to a mothball chamber

If whiteflies, mealybugs or other insect pests are attacking houseplants, sentence them to death by mothball. Put an affected plant (pot, saucer and all) into a clear plastic dry-cleaning bag. Water the plant and drop five or six mothballs into the bag.

Now tie the bag closed with a twist tie, then move the bagged plant to a bright, though not directly sunlit, spot. Let it sit for a week before taking the plant from the bag and returning it to its usual place. If necessary, repeat the treatment until all of the pests have given up the ghost.

✳ Attract pests with warm colours

Paint milk cartons red, orange or yellow, coat with an adhesive insect spray and set at 4m intervals in the garden. Flying insects will zoom to them and get stuck fast. To kill aphids in particular, forgo the adhesive and simply fill a yellow container three-quarters full of water. The little green ones will zip straight to the container and end up in a watery grave.

make your own...

INSECTICIDE

Rid garden plants and houseplants of aphids, whiteflies and other insect pests with this garlic-based spray. If you don't have a sprayer, use a well-rinsed cleaning product spray bottle. No matter what equipment you use, be sure to cover both sides of the leaves.

Chase-'em off garlic spray

Use only washing-up liquid in this recipe (not laundry or dishwasher detergent) and store the spray as you would any insecticide: in a capped and labelled bottle kept in a childproof cabinet.

10 garlic cloves, unpeeled
1 tablespoon vegetable oil
750ml hot water
1 teaspoon washing-up liquid

1 Purée the garlic (skins and all) in a blender.

2 Strain the mixture through a fine sieve into a litre jar. Add oil, water and washing-up liquid, screw the jar cap on tightly and shake gently to mix. Pour the mixture into a spray bottle.

3 Apply every three days for a week to control hatching insect eggs. Repeat as needed after rain or when new infestations occur.

✱ Let toads do it

Toads are among the most insect-hungry garden visitors. Attract them by placing a broken flowerpot or two in a shady spot, then sink a dish filled with water and rocks into the soil so that any visiting toads will stick around.

✱ Get a jump on squash vine borers with kerosene

You can prevent squash vine borers from attacking courgettes and pumpkins even before you seed these plants. Soak the seeds in kerosene overnight. The seedlings and mature plants will be able to repel borers – but the kerosene won't infiltrate or affect the fruits.

✱ Eradicate earwig with corn oil

Earwigs are extremely partial to clematis, chrysanthemums, dahlias and gladiolus – so how do you give the hungry little creatures the brush-off? Not with a broom but with oil, an earwig non-botanical favourite. Pour a pool of corn oil onto a saucer, set it on the ground amid your flowers and the earwigs will crawl into the saucer and drown.

✱ Protective fabric softener hankies

Keep mosquitoes from dive-bombing you as you work in the garden by tucking a few fabric softener sheets into your clothing. Pin a sheet to a shirt pocket, loop one through a belt loop and tuck one under the rim of your cap. Once mosquitoes get a whiff of the scented sheets, they will buzz off in a flash.

idea
THREE WAYS TO GET RID OF SLUGS AND SNAILS

The gastropod gourmets we know as slugs and snails have a special taste for dahlias, delphiniums, hostas, lupins, marigolds, zinnias and almost any flower or vegetable seedling. Luckily, there are ways to deprive them of their meals. Use:

Beer Bury shallow containers (a jar lid is the usual choice) so that the rim is level with the soil, then fill it with beer. Slugs and snails love the yeast in beer and overindulge until they drown.

Ashes Sprinkle wood ash along rows of plants. Like salt, the ashes shrivel the skins of slugs and snails.

Fruit peel After enjoying half a grapefruit for breakfast, put the peel upside down in the garden. Slugs and snails will gather under it, making it easier to remove them from vulnerable flower and vegetable areas. Orange and lemon halves work well, too.

Thwarting bugs and plant diseases

✳ Repel caterpillars with onion juice

Spray cabbage and other vegetables that are targeted by caterpillars with onion juice and watch them take a detour. To make a spray, peel 2 medium-size onions, grate them into a large bowl and add 4 litres water. Let the mixture sit overnight, then strain it into a spray bottle. To make the plants smelly enough to repel the pests, you may need to spray the leaves twice.

✳ Soup can stockades

To keep cutworms and other crawling pests from reaching newly planted seedlings, use soup cans as barriers. Cut the top and bottom out of a can, wash it well and place the can over a seedling. Twist it until the bottom is 5cm underground and your tender seedlings will gain protection from all directions.

✳ Fight fungus with bicarbonate of soda

Keep powdery mildew, black spot and other fungal diseases from infecting your fruit trees, vegetables, gardenias, roses and such with a bicarbonate of soda solution. In a large spray bottle, combine 1 teaspoon bicarbonate of soda, 1 teaspoon washing-up liquid and 1 litre warm water. Shake well and spray plant leaves and stems on both sides to discourage fungal diseases from taking hold.

✳ Poison rose black spot with tomatoes

It's long been known that roses grown next to tomatoes are less likely to fall victim to black spot. Make a fungicide by snipping tomato leaves from a plant and whirring them in a blender with a little water; use enough leaves to make 500ml slurry. Combine with 1.5 litres water and 2 tablespoons cornflour and mix well. Store the solution in the fridge, marking it with a warning label. Spray your rosebushes once a week with the fungicide.

The pleasure of the patio

✳ Bleach out pots

When repotting patio plants, sterilise flowerpots and planters to keep your precious newly purchased plants from succumbing to fusarium wilt or leaf curl. First plug the drainage holes with clay or putty. Then scrub off any caked debris with a scrubbing brush or toothbrush. Rinse the pots and fill with a solution of 1 part household bleach to 4 parts water. Let it stand for 2 to 3 hours. Discard the bleach in a utility room sink (not the garden), rinse the pots with fresh water and let them air dry.

✳ A bubble wrap warmer for camellias

Camellias grown in containers are particularly sensitive to the cold because of their shallow roots. When winter comes, wrap the camellia pot with thick plastic bubble wrap or several sheets of newspaper and secure the wrap with gaffer tape. Turn the pot so that the tape is out of the sight line of visitors.

✳ Polystyrene pellets as a drainage aid

Instead of putting rocks or pot shards in the bottom of a patio planter, fill the bottom quarter with the polystyrene pellets used for packing. What do they have over rocks? They make the planters lighter and allow you to use less potting soil.

✳ Plastic raincoats for exposed furniture

When heavy rain is forecast and you don't have enough indoor space to bring your patio or garden tables and chairs inside, cover them with plastic dry-cleaning bags.

make your own...

MOSS

If you want to make a new patio look like it's been around for a while, whip up a special mixture to paint on brick or stone walls or some of your concrete or terracotta patio planters. First, you'll have to search for some moss and collect a few patches to use as a starter.

Do-it-yourself mossifier

A handheld blender works best to purée this mixture, but a long whisking session will do the job in a pinch.

200–300g moss
300ml beer
½ teaspoon sugar

1 Put 200-300g of moss in a bucket.

2 Add beer and sugar and purée the mixture until smooth.

3 Using a paintbrush, spread the mixture about 0.5cm thick on to concrete planters on the areas you want to mossify. The moss should appear in four to seven days.

Help your pots to drain faster with packing pellets!

✱ Bubble away rust with vinegar and bicarb

If you have a concrete patio and metal furniture is leaving rust stains, try pouring full-strength white vinegar on the stains, top the puddle with a little bicarbonate of soda and leave it for about 10 minutes before wiping it off with an absorbent cloth. Older rust stains may need two or three more applications before they disappear.

✱ Wicker basket to hanging plant

Finally, here is a use for the wicker basket you have had stuck in the back of the cupboard for three years. Dig up four or five of the plants in your flowerbed and transfer them to the basket – and you've made a hanging planter for the patio. First use varnish to weatherproof the basket and line the inside with a bin liner poked with a few drainage holes.

✱ Veg out mosquitoes

To stop mosquitoes and other insect larvae from breeding in birdbaths or rainwater barrels, put a few drops of vegetable oil on top of the water. The oil spreads to form a film over the surface, ensuring that mosquito larvae won't be able to breathe through the water surface. Renew the oil every week throughout summer.

✱ Herbal mosquito repellents

Steep a few pennyroyal or fleabane leaves in some hot water and let them sit for 4–6 minutes. Strain the solution into a spray bottle and spray onto patio plants to repel mosquitoes. Or do the same with some garlic. Simmer 8 to 10 peeled garlic cloves in 500ml cooking oil for about an hour. Cool, strain into a spray bottle and spritz away.

Cheers
to a great
windscreen
cleaner –
vodka!

12 Marvellous tricks for motors

Not so very long ago, suburban streets were lined with car owners lovingly washing and polishing their pride and joy – be it a Ford Cortina or a vintage Jaguar E-Type – in a Saturday afternoon ritual. Automatic car washes and time pressures have put a dent in this practice, but that doesn't mean you can't try some old-fashioned car-care tricks, especially if you like saving money.

Forget about expensive car-care contraptions and concoctions and read on for a host of alternatives: Yes you can use peanut butter to clean your car – and a splash of vodka. You will also find ways to keep your wheels in superb running condition, be you a driver or a cyclist and save lots of time (not to mention money) in the process.

What well-known, if somewhat smelly, substance will eliminate the need for a post-wash wax? Which baby care item will clean windscreens in a jiffy? Which fizzy drink has more than one use under the bonnet? The next 21 pages hold the answers to these questions and more.

Superb solutions for a sparkling chassis

✴ Bicarbonate of soda car cleaner

Prepare in advance for your next few car washes by making your own condensed cleaner base. Pour 45g bicarbonate of soda into a 4 litre bottle, then add 60ml washing-up liquid and enough water to fill the bottle almost to the top. Screw on the cap, shake well and store the concentrate for later use. When it is time to wash the car, shake the bottle vigorously and then pour 240ml of the cleaner base into an 8 litre bucket. Fill the bucket with warm water, stir to mix and your homemade cleaning solution is ready to use.

✴ A surprising no-wax washer

Add 240ml kerosene to a 12 litre bucket filled with water and then sponge the solution over the car. You won't have to spray the car before washing or rinse or wax it once you're done. And the next time it rains, rainwater will bead up and roll off the car, decreasing the likelihood of rusting.

✴ Hair conditioner for shine

Wash your car with a hair conditioner that contains lanolin. You'll be amazed when you see the freshly waxed look and see how well the surface repels rain.

✴ You can see clearly now

Add 60ml household ammonia to 1 litre water, pour it into a plastic bottle with a watertight cap and keep it in your car for washing the windscreen and windows. As soon as your windscreen begins to get dirty, take out the solution and apply it with a sponge; then dry the windscreen with a soft cloth or paper towels.

✴ A one-step window cleaner

Clean your windscreen and car windows by rubbing them with baby wipes stored in your glove compartment. What could be easier?

✴ Clean your blades

If your windscreen wiper blades get dirty, they'll streak the glass instead of keeping it clean and clear. Make a solution of 60ml household ammonia to 1 litre cold water. Gently lift the blades and wipe both sides with a soft cloth or paper towel soaked in the solution. Then wipe the blades with a dry cloth before lowering them into place.

✴ Fizz windscreens clean with cola

When it rains after a long dry spell, a dirty windscreen can turn into a filthy disaster area. Get rid of streaks and blotches by pouring cola over the glass. (Stretch a towel along the bottom of the windscreen to protect the paint on the bonnet.) The bubbles in the cola will fizz away the grime. Just be sure to wash the sticky cola off thoroughly or your cleaning efforts will end up attracting more dust and dirt.

✱ Shine your headlights

Keep your headlights polished (and yourself, safe at night) by applying window cleaner and rubbing vigorously with an old pair of tights.

✱ Vodka on the job

When the windscreen-washer reservoir needs filling, raid the drinks cabinet to make your own washing fluid. In a screw-top 4 litre bottle, mix 750ml vodka with 1 litre water and 2 teaspoons washing-up liquid. Screw on the cap and shake well, then pour as much fluid as needed into the reservoir.

make your own...

WINDSCREEN WASHER FLUID

Under the bonnet sits the windscreen-washer fluid reservoir that occasionally needs to be topped up. Don't use a shop-bought cleaning fluid when you can mix up your own. With this recipe, you not only let your car do the work of keeping the windscreen clean, but you may save a few pence.

Keep-it-bright windscreen wash

The alcohol in this solution will speed the drying process when the fluid is sprayed onto the windscreen – and it helps prevent icing in cold winter weather in the bargain.

1 tablespoon liquid washing-up liquid
720ml surgical spirit
2.5 litres water

1 Pour washing-up liquid into a clean 4 litre plastic bottle with a watertight cap.

2 Add the surgical spirit and then the water. Cap the bottle and shake vigorously.

3 Pour as much of the fluid as needed into the car's windscreen washer reservoir. Save the rest for later or use it to wash the windows in your house.

Get gleaming metal trim

✳ Rid chrome of wax

It's easy to get so excited about waxing your car that you go too far: wax can spoil a shiny chrome bumper or radiator with smudges that harden and won't come off. Use a bit of WD-40 to fix the problem. Spray a little of the lubricant over the dried wax, then wipe it off with a clean soft cloth. The wax will dissolve like magic.

✳ De-wax metal trim with ammonia

Car wax mistakenly applied to metal trim can spoil the effect that a keen car cleaner strives for. To rid the trim of wax, wipe it with a rag dampened with household ammonia. The trim will soon sparkle like new.

✳ Oil the trim

When the metal trim on your car is still not shiny enough, squirt a little baby oil onto a paper towel and polish the metal for a shine worthy of a sterling silver trophy.

✳ Get wax off rubber with peanut butter

If you are waxing your car and accidentally get white wax on black rubber trim or mouldings, wipe the area with a bit of peanut butter (below). The rubber will revert to its original blackness.

idea

'LET IT SHINE, LET IT SHINE, LET IT SHINE'

So goes the famous song. If you want to give the metal on your car a shine to end all shines, simply dampen a clean soft cloth with full-strength white vinegar and gently polish the surface to bring out the natural shine of the chrome. Two other shine-it-up methods will have the same effect:

- Dampen a pad of ultrafine steel wool (grade 0000), dip it into a little bicarbonate of soda and squeeze it until it makes a paste. Then use the pad to scrub the chrome a small section at a time, working with small circular movements. When you've finished, rinse the chrome well and dry it with a clean soft cloth.

- Wash chrome with a cloth soaked in apple cider vinegar. After you've dried it, polish the chrome with baby oil.

✳ Make chrome glisten

Brighten chrome trim on your car by wiping it with a small amount of nail varnish remover. (Just be sure to keep it away from the paint.)

Insects, noxious smells and other sticky issues

✳ Counterattack on insect splats

If you're at war with the insects that seem to get splatted on the front of your car, the next time you clean off the insects, try a preventative strategy and spray the front of your car with nonstick cooking spray or vegetable oil or wipe it down with baby oil. Most insects won't stick around and the ones that do can be hosed or wiped off more easily.

✳ Mesh away insect mess

Get rid of the dead insects on your car by squirting a little washing-up liquid over the spot and scrubbing with a mesh bag – the kind that onions are sold in. The mesh is sufficiently rough that it will remove insects, but not so rough that it will scratch the finish or windscreen. Once you have scrubbed away the bugs, wipe the surface with a clean cloth.

✳ A nutty debugger

To get rid of dead insects on your windscreen or bumper, smear the area with peanut butter and let it sit for a while to soften the hardened on substances. Then wash off the mess with a cloth soaked in soapy water.

✳ Keep a radio antenna clean

If grime is clogging your radio antenna and it becomes stuck in an up or down position, extend the antenna to its full height and rub along its length with wax paper. It will be so smooth that it should glide up and down as cleanly as the arm on a trombone.

idea

SUPER EASY BUMPER STICKER REMOVAL

A bumper sticker seems like fun at the time, but wear and tear make it look scruffy and tatty – and the message is lost. But they can be a pain to remove. But once you get round to dealing with it, you may be surprised by how many sticker removers you can find in your cupboards and fridge. Paint a bumper sticker with one of these four substances and let it soak in for 3 or 4 minutes. Then gently scrape off the sticker with the edge of a credit card.

- Brush the sticker with nail varnish remover.
- Apply a thick layer of cold cream.
- Drench the sticker with a citrus cleaner.
- Smear it with mayonnaise.

✳ Rub Christmas tree sap off the car roof

If you've had a fresh Christmas tree strapped to the roof of your car, you'll probably end up with sap stuck to the surface – and soap and water won't do the job. Pour a few drops of surgical spirit over the sap and rub it with your fingertips. Then wipe it off with an alcohol-dampened rag and let the area air-dry.

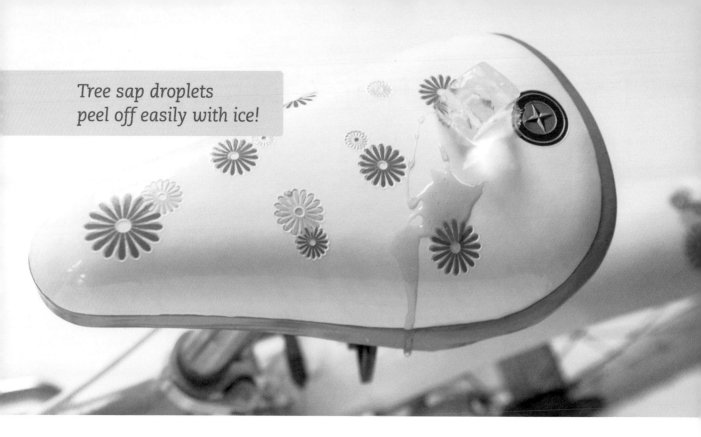

*Tree sap droplets
peel off easily with ice!*

✳ Freeze the sticky stuff

Another way of getting rid of sap is to press an ice cube over it for a minute or so. When the sap hardens, simply peel it off of your car, bicycle or other surface.

✳ Oil away a sticker

To remove a sticker from your windscreen, spray it with vegetable oil or WD-40 and let the spray soak in for a while. Then scrape the sticker off with the edge of a credit card. If bits of it stay stuck, heat the area gently with a blast from a hair dryer and try again.

✳ Removing tar

Tar can be difficult to remove from your car, but you'll win the battle over black goo fast when you try one of these removal methods, rinsing and drying after each one.

- Try spraying the tar with a laundry prewash stain remover. Let it sit for 10–15 minutes and then wipe it off thoroughly.
- Wet a cloth with linseed oil and apply it to the spots of tar. Let the oil soak in for about 10 minutes. Once the tar softens, douse another cloth with linseed oil and wipe the tar away.
- Rub the tar with a bit of peanut butter, leave it on for 10 minutes and then wipe it away with a soft cloth.
- Spray the spots with a squirt of WD-40 and let it soak in for 5 minutes. Then wipe the tar away with a soft cloth.
- Pour a cup of carbonated cola on a clean cloth and rub the tar off the car surface.
- Mix 240ml kerosene with 5 litres water and scrub the tar away with a rag soaked in the potent solution.

Dealing with dents and scratches

✳ Pop goes the dent

If the body of your car has a dent, but the surface is otherwise unblemished, you may be able to pull out the dent with a little suction. Look around your house and find anything that has a large suction cup attached – a sink plunger, for example. Place the cup directly over the dent and push it in straight so that the suction engages the metal. Then pull gently outward and firmly. If you are lucky, you should hear the popping sound that will tell you that the dent is gone.

✳ White out scratches

If you have a white car and it gets scratched, use typewriter correction fluid for a quick touch-up. If your car is another colour, try to find a correction fluid or nail polish colour to match and apply it as a temporary fix.

✳ Brush out scratches

You can often polish out small scratches in a car's finish with dental hygiene staples. Squeeze a dollop of toothpaste onto an old toothbrush and work the paste into the scratch. Buff the area with a clean cloth.

✳ Brighten old paint with scouring powder

If your car is old and painted with oxidised paint that's looking dull, try washing it with low-grit bathroom scouring powder. Apply the cleanser, wet it with a light spray and then rub gently with a car-washing mitt. (Test this first on a small area of the car body that isn't prominent to check that it doesn't remove the paint.) When you have finished, wash the car well and wax it.

Wave goodbye to winter worries and cares

❋ Gain traction with bleach

If your car has become stuck on an icy patch and can't get enough traction, pour a small amount of undiluted chlorine-based bleach over the tyres. The bleach will react chemically to soften both the ice and the rubber, thereby improving traction. Wait for a minute to let the chemical reaction take place and then try driving away. You can also get traction by spreading sand, salt or cat litter over the snow in front of the tyres. (Because bleach accelerates the wear on tyre treads, you should only do this in emergency situations.)

❋ Shovel snow with a hubcap

If your car gets stuck in snow, ice or mud and you don't have a shovel handy, take off a hubcap and use it to dig the car free.

❋ Use oil to prevent stuck doors

Prevent car and boot doors from freezing shut in winter by spraying or wiping the rubber gaskets with a light coating of WD-40 or vegetable oil. The oil will seal out any water that could later freeze, while causing no harm to the gaskets.

❋ Tape a door lock in a car wash

Put a strip of tape over your car's door lock before going through a car wash in cold weather. This will keep out water that could later freeze and make the lock inoperable. Once you're out of the car wash, remove the tape.

❋ Thaw door locks with a straw

If the lock on your car door freezes and you can't insert the key, don't get left out in the cold. Try blowing your warm breath into the keyhole through a straw. The ice should quickly melt, after which you can unlock the door with ease.

❋ Flame frozen locks

If the lock on your car door is frozen, hold the key in your (ideally gloved) hand and heat it with a match or cigarette lighter. Press the key into the lock and turn it gently without forcing.

tip START YOUR CAR WITH A HAIR DRYER

If you get up on a cold morning and your car won't start, connect a **hair dryer** to a long extension lead and direct hot air at the carburettor. Then start up the engine with ease.

idea

SPRAY AWAY SALT

Do you love a heavy snowfall that makes your area look like a Christmas card scene. But don't you hate with a passion the slush that your car's wheels throw up as you drive through the streets? The slush is often full of the salt and grit that the local council has used to clear the roads, but did you know that salt can rust your car's undercarriage?

To get rid of the salt, all you need is an old garden hose and an ice pick to give your car's undercarriage a salt-cleansing shower. Punch holes in a section of the hose equal to the width of the car body. On a day when the temperature rises above freezing, put the hose beneath the car, turn the water on full power and let it spray the underside of the car for 10 minutes or so. Move the hose and repeat the process until the entire undercarriage has had a good shower.

After a few seconds, the hot metal key will melt the ice and you will be able to open the door. Better still, if you have electrical power handy, use a hair dryer to direct hot air into the lock to melt the ice.

✳ Use stockings to tie on a tree

When you buy a Christmas tree, the trick is to get it home without letting it scratch the roof of your car or fall off. Line the roof with an old blanket to protect the roof from sap and scratches, then tie the tree in place with a rope made by twisting an old pair of tights. Tights are strong enough to hold the tree in place, yet soft enough to protect it and the car roof from damage.

✳ Keep ice off wipers

To keep ice from forming on the blades of your car's windscreen wipers and from stopping them working in cold weather, wipe each blade with a soft cloth soaked in full-strength surgical spirit.

✳ Raw onion windscreen rub

To avoid the tedious job of scraping ice off your windscreen on a chilly morning, slice an onion in half and rub the cut sides against your windscreen and car windows the night before a freeze to keep frost from forming.

✳ Shield a windscreen with rubber bath mats

To keep your windscreen from frosting overnight, position inexpensive rubber bath mats over the glass. Hold them in place with the windscreen wipers.

✳ Yoghurt pot scraper and scooper

Scrape ice from windows and windscreen using an empty yoghurt pot. When you scrape with the edge of the rim, the pot will scoop up the ice. As you scrape, empty the ice onto the ground with a quick flick of the wrist.

✳ Bag your side mirrors

On cold nights, slip plastic bags over the car's side mirrors and hold them in place with clothespegs. In the morning, remove the bags and your mirrors will be ice-free.

✳ Don't get steamed up

Winter driving can be dangerous when the inside of a windscreen keeps steaming up. Here are three ways to deal with foggy glass:
● Use a clean blackboard eraser to wipe the inside of the windscreen clean.
● Squirt a little shampoo onto a cloth and wipe the glass with it.
● Use 'outside air' instead of 'recirculated air' and run the de-froster.

Checking under the bonnet

✱ Prevent corrosion

It's not unusual for a car's battery terminals to become so corroded that you can't get a proper connection to jump-start the car. So take a little preventative action. Occasionally coat the terminals with a bit of petroleum jelly to keep them from corroding. Alternatively, tape a copper coin to the top of the battery so that the corrosion is drawn to the coin and not the battery terminals.

✱ A cola loosener-upper

If you need to get at the engine of your car but the nuts and bolts under the bonnet refuse to budge, pour a little carbonated cola over the connections or loosen them with a few squirts of WD-40. Give either substance 2–3 minutes to penetrate, after which you should be able to

loosen the hardware with a wrench. Most jammed metal fixings respond well to the cola trick (below); if you can soak the seized object, so much the better.

✱ Clean corrosion with bicarbonate of soda

If you don't keep your battery terminals clean, you will have to deal with corrosion. To clean the terminals, stir 1 tablespoon bicarbonate of soda into 240ml water, then pour the solution over the terminals. Leave for 4 or 5 minutes, then rinse with clear water.

✱ A sporty shock protector

When you are working on your car and have to disconnect the negative battery cable, don't let the cable come into contact with the car's metal frame or you may suffer a shock. One safe way of handling the cable is to make a slit in a tennis ball and push the ball over the end of the cable.

✱ Foot powder leak-spotter

If oil is leaking from your engine and you can't find the leak's source, clean the engine with an aerosol degreaser such as a silicone spray like WD-40 and then spray its sides and bottom with spray-on foot powder. The leak will reveal itself by turning white.

✱ Dislodge a stubborn oil filter

If you are quite happy to change the oil filter yourself but find that for once it won't budge, a screwdriver and hammer will be your saviours. Hammer the screwdriver right through the filter about 5cm from the engine block. Then take the screwdriver and use it as a lever to turn the filter counterclockwise. Once you get it started, remove the screwdriver and spin the filter off, making sure that there is a tray underneath to catch the leaking oil.

✱ Gum up the works

If the radiator hose in your car springs a leak while you are driving, chew a piece of gum and stick the wad over the leak. Secure it with a bit of strong adhesive tape. It will hold until you can have a proper repair made, but get the car booked in for repair as quickly as possible.

✱ First aid for a fan belt

If the fan belt in your car becomes dry, lubricate it with a little petroleum jelly. With the engine off, dab the inside edges of the belt with the jelly, then start the engine and let it idle for a couple of minutes. Not only will the petroleum jelly lubricate the belt and keep it from cracking but it will eliminate squealing and slippage.

✱ Extend a wrench handle with pipe

Some socket wrenches are so short that it can takes a real muscleman to turn them. If you prefer not to waste a lot of energy when you tighten a bolt under the bonnet, slip a short length of slender metal pipe over the wrench handle and you will get more than enough leverage to use the tool without straining.

✱ Tape a noisy horn

If your car horn gets stuck and won't stop bleating, tap the horn button a few times. If that doesn't stop the din, a piece of tape is the solution. Open the bonnet, disconnect the wire to the horn and tape down the terminal screw. You should enjoy blessed silence until you have the horn repaired.

CLEANING UP GRIMY HANDS

To clean dirty, oily hands, use any of these simple household products.

- Before washing your hands, rub them with salt to get rid of any strong odours, including the smell left by petrol fumes.

- Pour a little olive oil over your hands and rub them together to dislodge the grease. Then wipe them with paper towels and wash as usual.

- Pour a little laundry pre-soak stain remover into your palms and work it into a lather. Rinse off the lather, dry your hands with paper towels and wash them again with soap and water.

- Mix together 210g margarine, 40g cornflour and 40g soap powder. Then grab a small handful of the mixture, wash your hands under the tap and rinse with clear water.

- Wet your hands, sprinkle them with dry bicarbonate of soda and then wash them as usual with soap and water.

- Pour a bit of vegetable oil over your hands (a tablespoon will do) and rub it in. Then wash your hands as usual.

- Add a little sugar to some liquid hand soap, rub in well and rinse away.

- To get greasy dirt from under fingernails, sprinkle bicarbonate of soda over a damp nailbrush and brush nails from every angle. If that doesn't do the job, soak your hands in lemon juice for about 10 minutes and then resume brushing with bicarbonate of soda.

Wheel and tyre care

Wheels do make the world go round. Here's how to keep yours looking good and working well.

Oven cleaner sidewall whitener

To rejuvenate whitewall tyres, spray them with oven cleaner, then thoroughly hose it off. The tyres will be sparkling white once more.

Smarten up hubcaps with oven cleaner

Use oven cleaner to remove brake dust, dirt and grime from a car's aluminium hubcaps. Spray the cleaner onto the hubcap, let it stand for a minute and then rinse it off with a garden hose. Never use oven cleaner on painted hubcaps, as it may take off the paint along with the dirt.

Check for loose wheels

There's an easy way to see whether vibration has caused the nuts and bolts on your car's wheels to loosen. Simply put a dab of paint on each fastener and another dab right next to it. Check the dots from time to time. If they're no longer aligned, the fastener is loose. Tighten them all to keep your wheels safe and sound.

Check your tyres with a penny

To check the tread depth of a tyre, insert a penny into the groove in the tyre, head first. If you can see the top of the queen's head above the tread rubber, it's worn down to less than 2mm and it's time to replace the tyre.

A bubbly hubcap unsticker

If you have trouble removing a hubcap, open a bottle of carbonated cola, hold your thumb over the opening and shake it up. Then spray the cola around the hubcap's rim. After the cola has soaked in for 2–3 minutes, the hubcap should come off with ease.

Your car's interior

✳ An odour-eating pair

Deodorise the interior of your car by sprinkling bicarbonate of soda over everything but the electronic equipment. Take a soft-bristled brush and work the bicarbonate of soda in well. Close the car up for an hour or so and then thoroughly vacuum the interior. To keep the car smelling fresh and clean, place a small open container filled with freshly ground coffee beans where it won't get knocked over. The grounds will absorb any strong odours that you bring into the car.

✳ No butts about bicarbonate of soda

Make good use of the ashtrays in your car by placing about 2cm bicarbonate of soda in the bottom of each one. If you smoke, it will keep cigarettes from smoldering and stinking up the car even after you've put them out. If you're a non-smoker, the bicarbonate of soda will also absorb other stale smells.

✳ Baby-wipe your dash

If your car dashboard gets sticky from spilled drinks or greasy hands, clean it with baby wipes. Once it's clean, you can bring a shine to the dashboard with a little baby oil.

✳ Sweeten bad smells with vinegar

To remove the odour left when someone is carsick, wipe down vinyl upholstery (all of it) with a cloth soaked in a solution of half white vinegar and half water. Then place a bowl of vinegar on the car floor and keep the car closed up tight overnight. In the morning, wipe everything down with a damp cloth.

idea

UPHOLSTERY UPKEEP

You can make your own effective cleaners for car seats using common household products. Here are two recipes, one for vinyl upholstery and the other for leather.

Vinyl shiner. Mix together 60ml liquid soap, 45g bicarbonate of soda and 500ml warm water. Dip a clean cloth in the mixture and wipe the seats and trim, then rinse with clear water. If you encounter any tough spots, rub them with a paste made from bicarbonate of soda and water; let the paste soak in for an hour or more, then wash the entire area with the cleaner and rinse it.

Leather rejuvenator. Mix together 120ml surgical spirit, 120ml white vinegar and 360ml water. Soak a soft cloth in the solution and clean the upholstery with a circular rubbing motion before buffing it dry. To keep the leather from drying out and tearing, occasionally wipe it with a thin layer of baby oil.

✳ Hold taping sessions

Carry a roll of tape in your glove compartment and use it for the following jobs, among others:

- Tape your garage door opener to the underside of the visor on the driver's side of the car. It will be handy, yet out of the way and it won't fall into your lap as you drive.
- Tape a pen to the dashboard just in case you need one; taping it will keep it from rolling around and getting lost.

- Attach permit stickers to the inside of the windscreen instead of using the adhesive on the back so they are easier to remove.
- Whenever you park in a busy supermarket car park, temporarily tape a distinctive paper or cloth flag to the top of your car's antenna. When you come out laden with bags, you should be able to spot the car right away.

what's the story?

DRIVING 100 YEARS AGO

Today, about the only items we carry in our cars are the owner's manual, a road atlas and a spare tyre and tyre-changing equipment – something that would astonish our forebears. In the early 1900s, motorists needed, for starters, a white grease robe, a rubber lap robe, goggles, extra petrol and oil, a towing rope, two sets of tyre chains and a canvas bucket to hold water for both the car and its passengers – not to mention the starter handle they needed to start the engine.

And the roads? A number of pioneer road and civil engineers, including Pierre Trésaguet in the 18th century, Thomas Telford in the early 1800s and John McAdam in the 1820s had refined and improved the road surfaces but it was not until 1845 that the first Tarmac road (a stretch of the London to Nottingham road) appeared.

Gas-lit traffic lights with red for 'stop' and green for 'caution' were installed near Paliament Square in London in 1868, but the three colour system of red, amber and green was not introduced until 1926. Speed limits evolved with the speeds at which cars could travel – a speed limit of 4mph in the country set in 1865 was raised to 12mph in 1896 when the motor car had become established.

✳ Magic carpet cleaner

No matter how meticulous you are, you will probably end up with some greasy stains on the carpet inside the car. But when it does happen, it's not hard to fix. Mix equal parts of salt and bicarbonate of soda and sprinkle the mixture over the grease spot. Use a stiff brush to work the powdery white stuff into the spot and let it sit for 4 or 5 hours. Vacuum it up and the stain with be gone.

✳ Prevent a flat battery with a tennis ball

If for some reason you need to keep a car door open for a while – and the internal light is one of those that you can't switch off – turn to a tennis ball. Just wedge the ball between the door and the switch. The switch will stay off, your battery will stay charged and your jump leads will stay where they belong – in the boot. If you don't have a tennis ball, substitute any soft-surfaced small object, such as a triangular wedge of scrap wood padded with rags.

✳ Bag a steering wheel

If you have to park in the sun on a really hot summer's day, tear a 30cm strip from one side of a large paper bag and slip it over the top of the steering wheel, securing it with a piece of tape if necessary. When you return to the car, the wheel should still be cool enough to touch.

✳ Adjust air temperature with tape

If you have difficulty keeping your car's heating or air conditioning from blowing directly into your face, cover the part of the air vent that's directed at you with gaffer tape. Just be careful not to cover the entire vent.

Along for the ride

✱ Storage basket hold-all

If you tend to collect things in your car and are at risk of drowning in the clutter, here's the simplest way to tidy up: keep a small plastic storage basket on the floor behind the driver's seat and use it to hold the magazines, DVDs, cleaning supplies, catalogues, maps and anything else you accumulate. The clutter will be confined to a single spot and when you give someone a ride, you won't have to fight to make space for your passenger. You also won't have to fib about how you've been 'meaning to clean up all this mess'.

✱ Get a (stocking) leg up on record storage

It's important to keep your car's registration and the records of mileage, maintenance and repair warranties where you can put your hands on them quickly. If they regularly get lost in the mess in your glove compartment, store them in a self-sealing plastic bag.

✱ Pillbox coin holders

Store spare coins in a used pill bottle and keep it in the drinks holder of your car. You will always have the correct change ready for paying for a car park or using in a drink or sweet dispensing machine along the way. You shouldn't have to beg for change for a large note again.

✱ Keep bin bags as a back up

Keep a number of large plastic bin bags in your car for unexpected uses. You never know when you will need a container for things you acquire on the road or when you'll need to wrap up something greasy to keep it from soiling your upholstery. In the same way, if you spill something on the driver or front passenger seat,

idea

NEW USE FOR AN OLD BAG

If you're a woman who likes to hold on to her old handbags, you could keep an old oversized one with lots of pockets and useful zipped compartments in the boot as an emergency kit. Pack it with a container of motor oil, a can of WD-40, a wrench, bottled water and any other odds and ends you might need. You could also tape labels to the compartments to let you see at a glance where everything is.

simply pull a bin bag over the seat if you have to drive off before the offending spill dries. The bags can also protect your upholstery and carpet if children or pets pile into the car wet or muddy.

✱ From briefcase to toolbox

If you have a worn, hard-framed briefcase, don't throw it away; put it to good use. Fill it with the tools that you need to carry in your car and store it in the boot. If you get a flat tyre or engine trouble on the road, the tools will be neatly packaged and readily at hand.

✱ A mini shovel to the rescue

If you're likely to be driving through snowy conditions, keep a shovel handy in case you have to dig out your car. Rather than a classic heavy shovel, in fact your best bet is a child's sturdy toy shovel, which will work better than you may think for digging out your car – and will take up less room in the boot.

✳ A drink tray for auto fluids

Make a convenient carrier for the various fluids that you need to keep on hand for your car, such as bottles of motor oil and windscreen cleaning fluids. Keep a multiple drinks carrier from a local fast-food restaurant and reinforce the bottom with gaffer tape. It will ensure that all of the containers stay in one place and also keep them from sliding around in the boot.

✳ Washing powder as air freshener

Keep your boot smelling fresh even on hot summer days when these enclosed spaces can turn into ovens. Simply place a small open box of washing powder against the spare tyre and the boot will smell fresh in any weather. Keep the box no more than half full to prevent spills.

✳ Put on some weight

If you have a pick-up truck or a car that doesn't have four-wheel drive, you may need to keep something heavy in the boot to prevent slipping and sliding on icy roads. If your boot isn't full of heavy tools or something similar, fill a couple of pairs of thick tights with bricks and store them in the boot over the car's rear wheels. The tights will keep the bricks from sliding around, making a noise and from scattering dust throughout the boot.

Tips for pick-up trucks and other big motors

✳ 'Carpet' a pick-up bed

Line the bed of your pick-up truck with an old carpet remnant to keep your cargo from rattling or being knocked around and damaged. The carpet will make the drive easier on your precious cargo and on your ears.

✳ Shower-curtain rod dividers

A good way to keep things in place in the back of a pick-up truck is to set up a series of movable barriers. Try fitting a series of spring-loaded shower curtain rails at strategic points, wedging them between the sides of the truck bed. You can then move them around to push against any cargo and keep it from rattling or breaking as you drive along.

✳ On board catch-alls for SUVs

Sometimes the amount of stuff that rattles around in a sports utility vehicle that is needed to accommodate a big family knows no bounds. Keep it under control by wedging a plastic milk crate (with a padded rim, if the you have very young children) or laundry basket in a central spot in the vehicle and urging young passengers to keep their playthings and books there when not using them.

✳ Carry-along car wash for motorhomes and caravans

If you travel in a motorhome or tow a caravan and often stay at parks where no water to wash your vehicle is available, make a batch of washing fluid and carry it with you. Pour 80ml fabric softener into a 5 litre bottle and fill it almost to the top with water. Cap the bottle and shake well. When you're ready to wash your vehicle, put the liquid into a spray bottle and spray the vehicle at 1m sections at a time. Let it sit for 10 seconds or so, then dry the area with paper towels or a chamois. You can also rely on this mixture during a water shortage, since it uses far less water than a standard wash.

✳ Keep mice out of your caravan or motorhome with steel wool

The access slots where you hook up your motorhome or caravan to a cable or hose are 'step this way' entries for mice and other small creatures. To take up the welcome mat in one fell swoop, wrap the cable or hose in steel wool before connecting it, making sure that the scratchy material seals the surrounding gap. With their entry barred, mice and other intruders should leave you in peace.

A clean and tidy garage and driveway

✳ Avoid nicks with carpet

If your garage is cramped and you tend to bump your car door on the wall when you get out, attach carpet offcuts to the garage wall where the door hits. The carpet will soften the blow and prevent nicks and dents.

✳ Install a bumper bumper

If you need to pull your car all the way into the garage until it almost hits the back wall, fix an old tyre onto the wall at bumper height. If you do pull in a little too far, your bumper will hit the pliant tyre and save the car and the wall from damage.

✳ A combination work seat and tool caddy

If you're tinkering with something on a low part of your car, you may find it hard to keep squatting or kneeling as you work. But you don't have to. Instead, make an easily constructed combination seat/tool caddy out of a sturdy plastic crate or wooden box. Bolt a 2 x 7cm strip wood onto two parallel sides of the underside of the box or crate. At the ends of each strip, attach screw-cap casters. You can now store your tools inside the crate or box – and you can sit on top of the contraption as you work. Just be sure to put the lid on – or top the box with a sheet of plywood.

✳ Slide right under on vinyl

You don't have to buy a special trolley to work under your car. Simply place a 1.2 x 1.5m scrap of vinyl flooring on your garage floor or driveway pavement – shiny side up – and park the car over it; keep a foot or so of the vinyl protruding from under the car. Lie on your back on the vinyl and you have a slippery mat that lets you easily slide underneath the car.

✳ Out, damned spot

Many garages and driveways are spoiled by unsightly – and sometimes dangerously slippery – grease stains from oil leaks or greasy tools. Prevent stains when you work by covering the area with newspapers or paper bags. If your car is leaking even a little oil, place an unopened brown paper bag or a flattened cardboard box under the leak. Or scatter cat litter in the area; sweep it up whenever it gets saturated and replace it with fresh litter as needed.

✳ Contain dust with newspaper

Before you sweep out a really dusty area of your garage, shred a bunch of old newspaper, dampen it with warm water and scatter it around the area. The soggy paper will keep the dust from rising and resettling as you're sweeping.

✳ Stop water seeping through a garage door with WD-40

If water sometimes seeps in through your garage door during heavy rainfall, spray the seal on the door with WD-40. The seepage should stop even if the rain doesn't.

A galaxy of grease blotters

They're smelly, they're ugly and they're the motoring equivalent of the banana skin: the oil spots on the garage floor or driveway. Luckily there are many methods for making them disappear.

Newspaper

Spread several sheets of newspaper over the oil spots, thoroughly soak the paper with water and weigh it down. When the paper is dry, remove it – and the stain should come up with it.

Cornflour

Mix together equal parts of bicarbonate of soda and cornflour, and sprinkle the mixture over the spot. Let the powder sit and soak up the grease for a couple of hours, then sweep or vacuum the mess away.

Fizzy drinks

Pour fizzy cola over the spot and hose it off with water.

Bicarbonate of soda

For tougher grease spots, sprinkle on bicarbonate of soda and let it stand for about 3 or 4 hours, then scrub it with warm water and a stiff brush.

Laundry stain remover

Spray the area with laundry pre-wash stain remover. Let it sit for about 10 minutes, then sprinkle with powdered detergent and scrub with a broom or stiff brush. Rinse with a hose.

Sawdust, cat litter and sand

Sprinkle the area with sand, sawdust or cat litter and leave it for 4 or 5 hours to absorb the oil. Then sweep it up.

Paint thinners

For really tough spots, pour a little paint thinners over the spot and the surrounding area, sprinkle bicarbonate of soda or cat litter on top and then cover it with newspapers and let everything sit overnight. In the morning, remove the newspaper and sweep up the mess.

Hints for cyclists

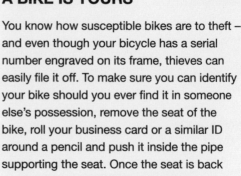

✳ Shine your bike with furniture polish

Once your bike is nice and clean, you may want to shine it up and show it off. Instead of using liquid or paste wax and spending time applying the wax to the bike's various tubes, joints and hard-to-reach spots, all you really need to do is to spray the bike all over with a furniture polish that contains wax – something you probably already have around the house.

✳ Salt-and-lemon juice rust buster

Salt can cause metal to rust – yet it can also be used to remove rust. If any rust spots appear on the handlebars or wheel rims of your bike, try this home remedy. In a small container, mix 60g salt with 2 tablespoons lemon juice to make a paste. Apply the paste to the rusted area with a dry cloth and rub it in. Rinse and dry it thoroughly and then step back and admire your rust-free bike.

✳ Maintain your chain with WD-40

The hardest part of a bicycle to clean is the chain. But you can make the job easier with a little WD-40. Turn the bike upside down and spray some WD-40 onto a soft, clean cloth. Rub the chain with the cloth a few links at a time. Move the pedals forward to work on a new section of chain.

Once the entire chain is clean, carefully dislodge it from the chain ring (the metal toothed wheel that engages it) and use a screwdriver or blunt knife to remove any dirt that is lodged between the chain ring's teeth. Once that is done, use a cloth to polish between the teeth with a back-and-forth flossing motion and then replace the chain.

idea

PROVING THAT A BIKE IS YOURS

You know how susceptible bikes are to theft – and even though your bicycle has a serial number engraved on its frame, thieves can easily file it off. To make sure you can identify your bike should you ever find it in someone else's possession, remove the seat of the bike, roll your business card or a similar ID around a pencil and push it inside the pipe supporting the seat. Once the seat is back in place, no one will think to look there. And the new bike 'owner' will be pretty surprised when you disassemble the bike seat to reveal your ploy.

✳ Spray for a smooth ride

To keep the chain of your bicycle well lubricated, spray it with WD-40 and wipe off any excess with a soft cloth. You can also spray WD-40 into the cables and bearings to drive out moisture and then on the springs in the seat to eliminate squeaking. Finally, spray the frame of the bike to keep dust from sticking to it.

✳ Repair a slash with a folded paper

If a sharp rock or anything else in the road slashes your tyre, you can patch the puncture in the inner tube – but it will bulge out through the slash in the tyre when you try to ride. After patching the inner tube, prevent it from bulging by folding a thickish piece of paper – it could be a paper note – into at least four layers and tucking it between the inner tube and the slash in the tyre. This quick fix should hold for a short ride home.

✻ Let nature help you with a flat tyre

If you get a flat tyre while cycling and don't have a repair kit with you, completely deflate the tyre, turn the bike upside down and pull one side of the damaged tyre out from the rim of the wheel. A good way to work it out is with the wide end of a house key, but any dull metal object will do. Once the tyre is loose around one side, find some leaves and moss along the roadside and stuff them inside the rim. Then squeeze the tyre back into place and ride straight home. The repair will let you ride (carefully) for a while, but not for long – so repair the flat properly as soon as possible.

✻ Baby powder for a smoother ride

If you're a motorcyclist who likes to deck yourself out in leather before taking to the road, sprinkle the bike seat with baby powder before you mount. The fine powder will make it easier for you to slide freely from side to side on the seat, assuring you of a smooth ride.

✻ Keep your visor unfogged

To keep a motorcycle helmet visor from fogging up on the road, put a drop of washing-up or dishwasher liquid on the inside, then rub it over the whole surface with your finger until it's no longer visible. Then say goodbye to a misty visor as you mount your bike and speed off.

✻ Motorbike wash-time protectors

If your motorcycle gets caked with mud and grease from the road, you will probably want to hose it down. Be careful to keep the pressurised water away from the cables and controls. The easiest way to do this is to cover them with plastic. Save the plastic sleeves from subscription magazines and catalogues and slip them over the handlebars at wash time. To keep water out of the ignition lock, put a piece of masking tape over the keyhole.

Keep your visor clear with a drop of dishwasher liquid!

Silence
a squeaky
hinge with a
little shaving
cream!

13 Ingenious DIY repairs

In the last few years, do-it-yourself repairing (or upgrading, for that matter) has taken on a status that has elevated it from drudgery to fun, with money-saving and satisfyingly stylish results. But when push comes to shove, DIYers like to fix and upgrade things for two reasons: keeping costs down and the satisfaction of a good job done.

In the coming pages, we'll take everyday DIY-ing to the next level, and show you how you can save even more money by using common household items to help you to work faster, safer, and more effectively. You don't have to be particularly handy to make use of our advice: these are basic, simple procedures, whether you are re-fixing a hinge, filling a pock-marked wall or doing a little plumbing.

Though the emphasis here is on non-toxic alternatives to commercial chemicals, we recommend that you should always wear gloves and eye protection and take other safety precautions as necessary.

Window wizardry

✱ Rub out a scratch in a window with toothpaste

Squeeze a small amount of toothpaste onto a soft cotton cloth and vigorously polish the scratch for a minute or two. Wipe off the excess with a damp rag and the scratch should be gone. Be sure to use plain, white paste – no gels or striped varieties. You can also use an extra-whitening toothpaste or tooth powder; most have higher amounts of abrasive.

✱ Stop cracks in their tracks with nail polish

You can buy yourself some time before replacing a cracked window by applying a couple of coats of clear nail polish over the crack on both sides of the window. Once dry, the polish will seal any holes in the glass and contain the damage.

✱ Stifle a rattle with a matchbook

A rattling sash window is sure to rattle your nerves, especially when you're trying to sleep. Silence the racket with a small folding book of matches. Slide the thin end of the matchbook in between the sash and the loose corner of the window frame. Wedge it in as far as you can, but leave at least a third of the book exposed for easy removal. Then give the window a few light tugs to make sure it won't shake on blustery nights.

✱ Plug a draughty window leak

A draughty window is guaranteed to suck out precious heat from your home and raise your fuel bills. What can you do if it's winter and you don't have a sealant gun (or the one you have is all dried up)? It's simple. Once you've located the source of the draught (it's often along the top of the lower sash or in a corner between the sash and window frame) take two paper towels, sandwich them together, and fold them up from the bottom 25mm at a time until you have a thick padded strip. Lay the pad over the air leak and secure it on all sides with masking tape.

✱ Straighten that sag

Hinged windows can sag because the corner joints have weakened. A quick fix is to add flat L-shaped steel corner plates, which cost only a few pence with matching countersunk screws. From the outside with the window closed, drive wooden wedges between the window and its frame to close up any loose joints (or to raise a dropped window) and simply screw the plates in place over the corners. Apply metal primer and topcoat to prevent the plate rusting.

✱ Removable secondary glazing

If you have single-glazed windows, you can halve the heat lost through them by fixing plastic sheet double glazing. The plastic sheet can be ordered cut exactly to size and is held in place with a magnetic strip secured to the window and a matching metal strip secured to the frame. The strips need to be cut to length (with sharp scissors or a utility knife) and the backing paper peeled off as they are applied. Unlike film double glazing (see opposite), sheet glazing can be applied just to the window (so it still opens) and it can be removed in summer when it's no longer needed.

Wrap up a window

Ordinary kitchen cling film is the cheapest way to double glaze small window panes. It only lasts a year, but is quick and simple to fix.

1

Thoroughly clean the window frame surface with diluted washing-up liquid to ensure that there is no grease. Wipe dry.

2

Run double sided sticky tape around the window frame. Starting at the top, press the cling film against the tape.

3

Keeping it as taut as you can, unwind the roll by placing a finger in each end. Press it against the tape all the way down then along the bottom. Cut off the excess roll with scissors.

4

Use a hair dryer on a low setting to warm the cling film. This will stretch it taut, removing all the wrinkles.

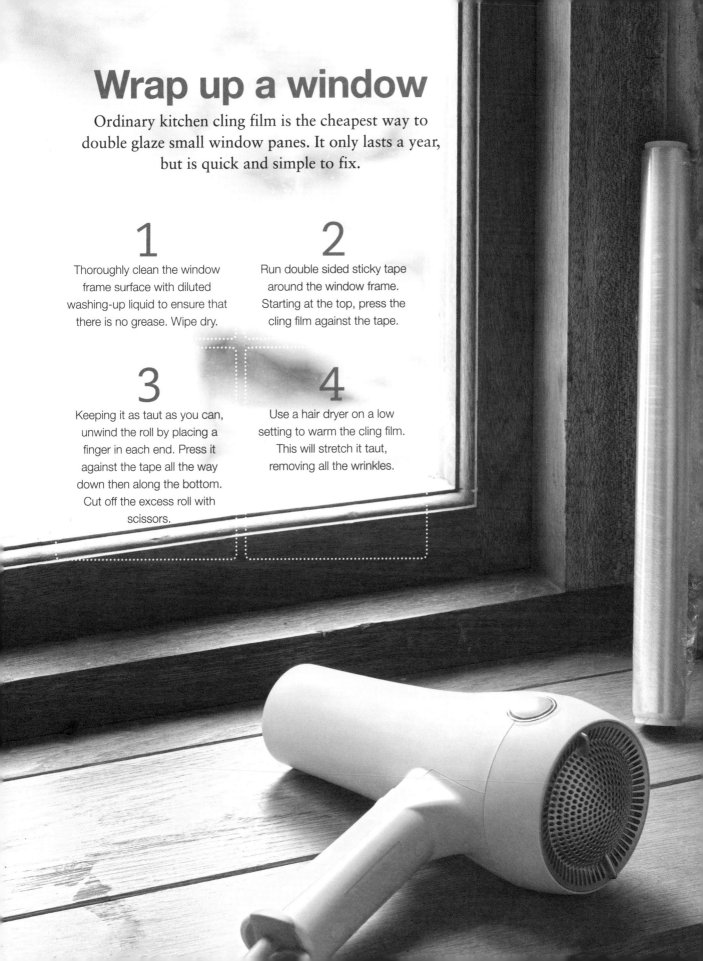

Delightful DIY door fixes

✳ Get the lead in

Forget about oil, which can do more harm than good to a stuck lock. The best lubricant for a lock's inner mechanism is graphite, and a good source of graphite is pencil lead. Rub a sharpened, soft lead pencil (B or HB) repeatedly against the matching key, and insert it several times into the lock. Perform this trick twice a year to keep locks in top working condition.

✳ Remove a broken key

It happens all the time: keys get old and bent and end up breaking off inside the lock. If you can't enter your house or flat through another door, go to a neighbour to borrow a couple of items before calling a locksmith. First, try removing the broken piece with tweezers. If that won't work, apply a tiny drop of superglue to the end of the piece that's still on your key chain. Line it up with the part inside the lock, and carefully insert it. Hold it in place for 40–60 seconds and then slowly pull out the key.

✳ Light up your lock

You know what it's like to come home to a dark porch and have to feel around for the lock on your front door. If you never want to go bump in the night again, dab a few drops of luminous paint around the keyholes of your exterior locks with a cotton bud or small paintbrush. Do the same for any locking bolts on the inside of your house as well, which will make exiting much easier in the event of a power failure, fire or other emergency.

✳ Polish a loose doorknob

A wobbly doorknob is often the result of a loose setscrew (a tiny screw found on the doorknob shank), which keeps the knob firmly in place on the spindle. Everyday usage can cause setscrews to become loosened, but you can keep them in place by brushing a little clear nail polish onto each screw after you have tightened them.

tip SILENCE A PERSISTENT SQUEAK

If freshly oiled door hinges continue to squeak and squawk, the most likely cause is rust, dirt, paint and other debris clogging them up. The best answer is to replace them with **new hinges** of exactly the same size. Prop the door up with magazines and have a helper hold it steady and you will be able to replace each hinge in turn without needing to remove the door completely from the frame.

✱ Pamper a noisy hinge

Is a squeaking door hinge making you feel unhinged? A few drops of baby oil applied around the pin should solve the problem. When you can't find any baby oil and you are out of WD-40, a bit of cooking spray, petroleum jelly or even shaving cream can be used to silence a squeaky hinge.

✱ Re-fix a hinge screw

A loose hinge will cause a door to stick or become difficult to open or close. Tightening the hinge screws usually solves the problem, but if an undamaged screw won't grip, it means the hole has become worn.

To fix it, slide a magazine or two to prop up the opened door, if necessary, and then remove the screws from the loose side of the hinge so that it can be folded back. Loosely fill the screw hole with wooden toothpicks or matchsticks dipped in woodworking adhesive. Keep them flush with the frame by carefully trimming off any protruding ends with a utility knife. When you screw back the hinge, the extra wood should hold the screw firmly in place.

✱ Pop goes the rusted bolt

Loosen a rusted bolt by rubbing it with a few tablespoons of a fizzy drink.

✱ Unstick a stuck door

If a door sticks because it rubs against the floor or threshold, try this simple fix. Gaffer-tape all four edges of a coarse sheet of sandpaper to the floor where the door rubs, then open and close the door back and forth over the sandpaper until it swings smoothly.

A door that is sticking in its frame (because of too much painting or because it has swollen) can be cured by using a bench plane or Surform rasp to remove the high spots from the door where it is binding. Re-paint after removing the offending wood.

curiosity corner

AND YOU THINK YOU HAVE AN OLD DOOR

It may not be the oldest door in the world, but a battered, rarely used storeroom door in Westminster Abbey was recently declared to be the oldest known door in the UK.

According to a dendrochronology test (the scientific analysis of tree-ring growth patterns), the door's five vertical planks came from a single tree that was felled between 1032 and 1064.

That date establishes it as part of the original abbey that was built during the reign of Edward the Confessor and further distinguishes it as the only surviving Anglo-Saxon-era door in England. Some experts additionally believe that the door's 2m high by 1.4m wide size and double-sided form would have made it unique among the Saxon abbey doors and that it might even have secured the entrance to Edward's chapter house.

Professor Warwick Rodwell, Westminster Abbey's consultant archaeologist, credits the late timber expert Cecil Hewett with inspiring the project to discover the door's true vintage. When he first saw the old door in the 1970s, Hewett observed that it could be 'very early'. It turned out to be very early indeed!

Walls and ceilings

✳ White-out wall and ceiling flaws

If you've ever used a typewriter, you know how valuable a small bottle of white correction fluid can be. What you may not know is that it's even more useful around the home for covering up small stains and blemishes on white walls, mouldings, and ceilings. Simply dab it on the defect, and it's gone. When touching up glossy surfaces, coat the dried correction fluid with a little clear nail polish.

✳ Fix small cracks

Don't replaster a ceiling just to cover up a few small cracks. Try this instead: make a paste of equal parts bicarbonate of soda and PVA glue and use it to fill in the gaps. It's easier and it really does the job – but it only works with white ceilings, of course.

✳ Wipe away wallpaper paste

Removing old wallpaper can be a pain, but what's even worse is contending with old wallpaper paste. A window squeegee can make the job a lot easier and neater. Dip the squeegee into a bucket of very hot water; add 240ml vinegar for extra-strength paste. Use the spongy side to apply the solution to the wall; then flip it over and use the blade to remove the glue. Wipe the glue off the blade frequently with a damp rag.

✳ Cover nail holes without filler

If you have run out of filler, look in your medicine cabinet before you go to a DIY store. A little bit of plain white toothpaste should do the job. You can also fill small holes in plasterboard with a paste of equal parts of bicarbonate of soda and woodworking adhesive. Or you could mix 2 tablespoons salt and 2 tablespoons cornflour with just enough water to make a stiff putty.

✳ Stick on a patch

Some people think that the lack of wall studs makes it far more difficult to patch a hole in plasterboard. But they're wrong. In fact, all that's needed is a couple of thin pieces of wood about 25mm wide (the sticks sold for paint mixing are ideal), manoeuvred through the hole and held in place against the back of the plasterboard by a combination of panel adhesive and plasterboard screws. A piece of string tied through a hole in the middle will prevent you losing the wood sticks down the wall! Once the sticks are in place, a matching plasterboard patch can be stuck or screwed in place and damage made good with wall filler.

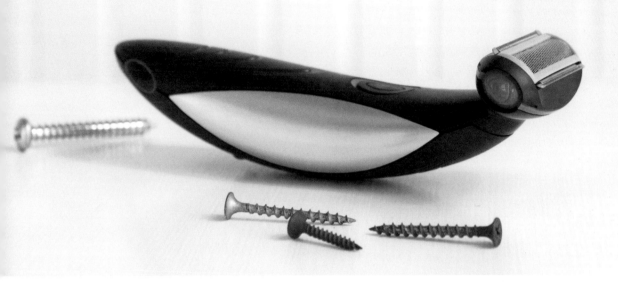

✳ Find a wall stud with a shaver

If you don't have an electronic stud finder, use an electric shaver instead. Switch on the shaver and place it flush against the wall. Move it slowly over the wall, and note the sound of its hum. When the shaver moves over a stud, the pitch of the buzz will rise.

✳ Secure a screw

A screw set into a wall without a rawlplug may work loose over time as the hole surrounding it expands. Take up the slack by cutting one or two twist ties into strips that are equal in length to the screw. Bunch them together in your fingers, stuff the hole and then reset the screw. If the hole has significantly widened, use steel wool, small pieces of cardboard or a cotton wool ball soaked in PVA glue. Let the glue dry for at least 24 hours before attempting to place any weight on the screw.

✳ Banish ceiling stains

Get rid of ugly ceiling stains by putting on a pair of goggles and aiming a long-handled sponge mop moistened with equal parts water and chlorine bleach (toilet cleaner) at the ceiling. Then scrub until the stains are gone.

✳ Match a patch

When repairing damaged textured coating on a section of ceiling, it's worth putting in the extra effort to do the job properly. Once the coating is level, try to match the texture of the surrounding ceiling. You can usually come pretty close by applying some gentle touches with a small scrubbing brush, a pocket comb, or a dry abrasive sponge.

Simple and safe wallpaper removal

You don't have to rent a commercial steamer or use toxic chemicals to strip away old wallpaper. Here are two easy methods that are not only non-toxic but surprisingly inexpensive, too.

1

Fill two-thirds of a spray bottle with hot water and a third with liquid fabric softener. Spray a section of wallpaper until it is saturated. Let the solution soak in for 15–30 minutes, peel or scrape off the covering and repeat. Keep the bottle warm by storing it in a pan of hot water between uses.

2

Use a garden sprayer or a paint roller to apply a solution of equal parts white vinegar and hot water. Saturate an area of wallpaper, wait 10 minutes, then peel it off. For extensive jobs, work with the windows open; vinegar is non-toxic but does have a strong smell.

Fixing your floor

✳ Give scratched floors the boot

Light scratches in wooden floors can often be successfully camouflaged with shoe polish. Just be sure to shop around and find the best colour match for your floor. Apply the polish with a soft cloth, let it dry, then buff with a slightly dampened rag for a quick and easy cover-up.

✳ Iron off a broken tile

To lift a damaged vinyl tile, cover it with a cloth, then give it a rubdown with a clothes iron on a medium setting. Use slow, even strokes. The heat from the iron will eventually loosen the adhesive and the tile, making it easy for you to prise it up with a filling knife. If you don't have an iron at hand, try using a hair dryer.

✳ Tiles on the move

Do you find that your carpet tiles have a tendency to move around and not stay put? Use double-sided adhesive tape to hold them in place. You don't need to stick down all the tiles – just a few key ones and they will hold the others in check. And double-sided tape has loads of other uses.

✳ Repair a rug

If you have a Berber carpet with a number of unsightly pulls, squeeze a bit of latex adhesive into the base of the loose stitch and push it back into place. If the pulled stitch is very long, trim it down with a sharp knife or scissors before gluing. With looped Berbers you may need to thread a toothpick through a loop to keep it free of adhesive.

✳ Renew a burned carpet

To remove slight burns and singes from carpets, use tweezers to lift the threads and then carefully slice off the charred tips with sharp scissors, a razor blade or utility knife. Trim the threads as little as possible to avoid leaving an indentation. The longer and denser the carpet material, the better your results are likely to be.

✳ Stone-cold clean

Tools covered with flooring adhesive can be really hard to clean. Instead of scrubbing, place them in a plastic bag and put them in the freezer overnight. In the morning, the glue will be rock solid and can easily be chipped off with a hammer and chisel. Be sure to wear goggles to protect your eyes from any airborne shards.

tip A GRATER FIX FOR SLASHED VINYL

If a slash has appeared in your vinyl floor, find a small, spare piece of vinyl and grind it down with a **cheese grater.** Remove chunks and mix gratings with clear nail polish. Use the mixture to fill the dent.

Heating up and cooling down

✳ Use grandma's fragrant warming tip

Increase the warmth and moisture level inside your home on bitterly cold days by just simmering a large pan of water on the hob. Don't forget to periodically check the pan and refill the water as needed. Throw a few cloves, some orange peel and one or two cinnamon sticks into the pot and you'll have a delightful air freshener as well.

✳ Get incensed about draughts

To pinpoint the often mysterious source of draughts – and where you'll need to add or renew any draught-proofing – wait for a windy day, then light a stick of incense. Start with the window or door nearest the draught. Hold the incense in a bottom corner of the frame and slowly raise it. The smoke should travel up in a straight line; when it moves sharply in one direction or another, you've located a leak. Repeat the process for all the sealed openings around the house.

✳ Block door draughts

A draughty door can raise your fuel bills as well as being uncomfortable. Until you can replace the draught-proofing, try blocking the draughts under doors with a homemade 'sausage'. Get an old long sock, or cut a sleeve off an old shirt and fill it with sand, rice, or foam padding weighed down with a few small stones. Sew the open ends shut and keep it against the crack at the bottom of the door. For safety's sake, prevent stumbles by spray-painting the draught-blocker a bright colour.

idea

NO MORE COLD ROOMS

Is it nice and snug in the living room, but cold elsewhere in the house? It could be that the room thermostat (which controls the heating) is in the living room and that you've added an extra fuel-effect fire in there with the result that the thermostat is turning the heating off too early. Get an electrician to re-position the thermostat in another room – away from draughts and not in direct sunlight.

✳ Hot bottoms, cold tops

If your radiators are hot at the bottom, but cold at the top, it means that there is air in the system. First check that there is water in the small water cistern in the loft – sometimes, the float valve there can get stuck and be left 'high-and-dry' over an empty cistern where all the water has evaporated. If it is stuck open, free it with WD40 and gentle movement – or replace.

If lack of water isn't your problem (the cistern should be about half full when the water is cold), you'll need to 'bleed' the radiators to get rid of the air. Arm yourself with a cloth and a radiator bleed key and gently unscrew (turn anti-clockwise) the tiny air bleed screw at the top of each radiator, starting with the highest in the house. Don't remove the screw – just loosen it. At first, there will be a hissing as the air rushes out, followed by a spurting of water (caught in your cloth): as soon as no more air is escaping, close the screw before you get water all over the floor.

✳ Hot water too hot?

If you heat your water with an electric immersion heater at any time of the year, the water can be too hot, which is not only dangerous and energy-wasting, but can also cause problems with scale build up in the hot water cylinder. You may not know it, but there is an adjustment within the immersion heater. Turn off the electricity, take a torch and an electrician's screwdriver and remove the cover of the immersion heater (on top of the cylinder). In the middle of the top of the thermostat (a triangular-shaped piece of plastic) is a tiny dial with a central slot. Use the screwdriver to turn the slot so that the arrow points to a lower number – domestic immersion heaters are best set to 65 (60 if you live in a hard water area).

✳ Degrease a dirty fan

Even occasional use can cause an extractor fan to collect dust and grime on its blades and grilles. The built-up of dirt will reduce the fan's air output and worse, places unwanted stress on the motor.

To clean a dirty fan (which you should do at least once a year), unplug at the socket or turn off at the wall switch, and remove the housing. Vacuum off any loose dust using a soft brush attachment, then wipe down the blade and grilles with a rag or sponge dipped in a solution of 60ml ammonia and ¼ teaspoon washing-up liquid in 5 litres warm water. Make sure that all the parts are dry before you reassemble them.

household superstar

11 HOME FIXES WITH NAIL VARNISH

1 Mark off liquid measurement levels (250ml, 500ml, 1 litre) inside a bucket.

2 Mix with ground vinyl dust to repair a gash in vinyl flooring.

3 Fill in light dents in wood floors and wooden furniture.

4 Fill in imprinted numbers on hand tools to make them easier to read.

5 Keep knobs on dressers and cabinets from loosening by dipping screws into clear nail polish before tightening.

6 Coat brass handles and knobs with clear nail polish to prevent tarnish.

7 Paint the buttons of a remote control or the edges of a keyhole with glow-in-the-dark nail polish to make them easier to spot.

8 Stop rust from forming on screws, nails and fasteners by covering them with clear nail polish.

9 Coat scratches on metal appliances to prevent rust.

10 Apply to the bottoms of shaving cream cans and other metal containers to keep them from leaving rust marks.

11 Indicate measurements on the handle of a hammer.

Fixing up furniture

✳ A light through yonder window is damaging

Sunlight can wreak havoc on your furniture, but you can restore it to its former lustre with plain old petroleum jelly. Use a soft cloth to rub a good amount into the wood until the finish perks up. Remove any excess with a clean cloth, and then polish the wood to renew its shine.

✳ Tea time for grime

To remove accumulated grime on wooden furniture, put two tea bags in a litre of boiling water and let it cool. Dip a soft cloth into the solution, wring it out and then test it in an inconspicuous area on the table. If you're pleased with the results, wipe down one section of the piece at a time. Continue dipping, wringing and wiping until all the old polish has been removed. Let it dry, buff with a soft dry cloth, then stand back and watch it glow.

✳ Steam out a dent

You can usually repair a small, shallow dent in wooden furniture with a warm, damp cloth and a steam iron. Fold the cloth and place it over the dent, then press down with the tip of a warm iron for several seconds. If the dent doesn't swell, repeat, but don't overdo it. You need to provide just enough moisture to swell the wood back to its original size.

✳ Repair veneer edging with an iron

If veneer stripping or edging is bulging or popping up from the surface of a piece of furniture, lay a warm, damp cloth over it and press down with the tip of a warm iron for several seconds. Once it's flattened, roll it with a rolling pin.

✳ Unstick a drawer

Wooden drawers can become stuck for all sorts of reasons, but the most common cause is excessive humidity. Although you can't see it, the wood fibres actually swell from the extra moisture in the air. To shrink them back to their original size, use a hair dryer on a warm setting, directing it to the drawer slides and the drawer itself – which should open with ease after a few minutes. For more stubbornly stuck drawers, try rubbing the sides, bottom edges and slides with lip balm, a bar of soap or paraffin wax or beeswax.

✳ Lubricate metal drawer runners

Rust and other deposits can cause metal drawer runners to seize up or to move unevenly. Keep them running smoothly and free of rust by lubricating them occasionally with a smear of petroleum jelly or a squirt of WD-40.

✳ Hassle-free hardware

If you want to keep the shine in decorative brass handles and knobs, give them a coat of clear nail varnish or clear lacquer. This simple task will provide years of protection against the damage wrought by skin oils and tarnishing.

✳ Revive sagging cane seats

The more use it gets, the more a cane seat is likely to sag. To tighten a baggy seat, first soak two or three tea towels in hot water and wring them out lightly. Now turn the chair over and lay the hot towels on the bottom of the seat for about 30 minutes. Remove the towels and let the seat air-dry and then give the cane at least 12 hours to shrink back into place. The revived seat will be tighter and firmer to sit on.

Wiping out water rings

All it takes is one sweating glass or steamy plate and you will be forever reminded of it in the form of an ugly white water ring on a wooden table top. You can often dry up a fresh ring using a hair dryer on a low setting. Most established rings, however, require some form of abrasion. Here are five time-tested methods.

Ashes and mayonnaise

Mix the ash from one cigarette in a tablespoon of mayonnaise. Dip a rough cloth in the mixture and rub it vigorously into the ring. Polish when done.

Salt and lemon oil

Pour a little lemon oil onto a rag and dip it in ½ teaspoon of salt. Gently rub the rag over the spot. If the ring starts to lighten, repeat the process using vinegar instead of lemon oil. (Not recommended for shellac finishes.)

Lemon oil and steel wool

Lightly rub the stain with 0000 extra-fine grade steel wool dipped in lemon oil. Once the ring is gone, polish the table with lemon oil and buff with a clean cloth.

Salt and corn oil

Mix equal parts of corn oil and salt, rub it into the ring and then polish it off with a clean cloth.

Bicarbonate of soda and toothpaste

Mix equal amounts of white toothpaste and bicarbonate of soda and apply it to a rag. Rub in the paste moving parallel to the wood grain, wipe it off and then polish with lemon oil.

✷ Tighten loose joints

A bit of woodworking adhesive is usually all that you need to secure a wobbly chair leg or rail. If the joint is too loose, adhesive alone may not do the job. An easy way to solve the problem is to increase the width of the tenon (the contoured end of the loose piece) by coating it with wood adhesive and wrapping it with cotton thread or by adding a wood shaving. (If you decide on the latter, choose a shaving that's uniformly thick for a consistent fit.) Let the adhesive dry, then glue the tenon back into the mortise.

✷ Reglue it right

Most wobbly furniture can be fixed by simply regluing the parts back together – but since new glue won't stick to old dried glue, the key is to get rid of the old stuff. One of the best tools for getting rid of dried glue is the small wire-bristle brush you can get for cleaning car battery terminals. The external brush (shaped like a tiny fir tree) is ideal for removing glue from mortises and holes, while the internal brush is perfect for scraping dried glue from small tenons and dowel ends.

✷ Paste over a minor burn

Although fewer people smoke in their homes these days, burn marks on wooden furniture are a more common problem than you might think. If the scorch doesn't go below the finish, you can usually rub it out with a paste made of fine ash (wood or cigarette ash) and lemon juice (2 parts ash to 1 part juice). Wipe the area clean, then polish and wax.

ideas
STICKY BUSINESS

The list of items that can end up stuck on a table surface is as long as it is varied. About the only thing that's true in all cases, though, is that you should never simply yank off the offending object, because you may end up damaging the table's finish. To unstick something, follow these instructions:

• A piece of paper placed under a wet or hot object can stick like glue. First, carefully peel off as much of the paper as possible, then dab the remainder with a rag dipped in some olive oil. Let the oil soak in for several minutes and then wipe away the residue with the dry side of the rag.

• If the youngest member of the family has decorated your tabletop with stickers or postage stamps, cover them with a coat of petroleum jelly and let it sit for 2–4 hours. Use an old credit card to gently scrape off the stickers. Repeat if necessary; polish when done.

• If your child parks their half eaten sweet on the table, scrape away as much as you can, then squirt a little baby oil on top of what's left. Give it a few minutes to soak in before sliding off the residue. Buff it to a shine. Baby oil also works well for bubble gum, stuck glassware and candle wax.

• Dried adhesives of all kinds are notoriously difficult to remove, but they can sometimes be softened with an application of cold cream, peanut butter or vegetable oil.

Scratch out scratches

✳ Instant fix for scratched woodwork

You're expecting guests any minute when you happen to notice several fresh, light scratches on your dark wood wall unit. What can you possibly do at such short notice? Go to the kitchen, fetch a small cup or container and mix 1 teaspoon of instant coffee in 1 tablespoon vegetable oil or water. Apply the mixture with a cotton wool ball. (Not recommended for valuable antiques or shellac finishes.)

✳ Cover scratches in leather

You can camouflage unsightly scratches in leather furniture with a permanent marker in a similar shade. Before you start, test the marker on an inconspicuous part of the chair or sofa to make sure that it's a good match. Work slowly and carefully when tracing over the scratch. Medium or fine-point markers work best overall; extra-fine tips may deepen a scratch while thick markers often leave a visible 'edging' around repairs.

✳ Check out the market

These days – especially with the advent of the internet – you can get a whole range of woodcare products, previously available only to professionals. For repairing scratches (and filling small cracks and holes), these include:

- burnishing cream (superficial scratches)
- wax filler sticks (and shellac filler sticks)
- retouch crayons
- touch-up pens

all available in a wide range of wood shades.

✳ Homeopathic scratch care

Most light scratches on wood can be repaired without a trip to a DIY store. That's because

make your own...

LEATHER REJUVENATOR

Heat, sunlight and simple wear and tear can cause leather furniture to dry out and crack. Restore some of the lost pliability and prevent the cracks from spreading by cleaning, oiling and polishing.

Liven-it-up leather lotion

Olive oil rubbed into the leather is left to soak in overnight before you restore leather upholstery to its original shine.

250ml water
250ml white vinegar
1 teaspoon household ammonia
125ml to 250ml olive oil
Furniture cream

1 Combine water, vinegar and ammonia in a large bowl and stir to mix. Pour olive oil into a small bowl.

2 Dip a sponge into the water and vinegar solution, wring it out and use it to wet a section of upholstery.

3 Rub the olive oil into the wet leather with your fingertips, a rag or a cotton wool ball. Let it soak in overnight.

4 The next day, shine leather with furniture cream and buff with a soft cloth.

Say nuts to wood scratches!

masking a scratch is simply a matter of covering it up or adequately lubricating the exposed wood fibres. What's amazing is the number of items that you probably already have around your home that can get the job done. Regardless of which method you use, wax the surface when done.

- Conceal scratches with closely matched shoe polish, a melted crayon or a permanent marker.
- Use the meat of a Brazil nut, walnut or pecan. Rub the nut over the scratch several times, then vigorously massage the oil into the scrape with your thumb.
- Can't find the nutcracker? Rub in a little peanut butter or mayonnaise instead. Wipe it off with a damp rag after 30 minutes or so.
- If that's too messy, try a little baby oil or mix 1 tablespoon olive oil or vegetable oil with 1 tablespoon lemon juice. Apply it with a soft cloth, then buff it off after 30–45 minutes.
- Cover scratches with a generous amount of petroleum jelly. Let it soak for 24 hours, then remove the excess with a soft cloth.

✷ Wax away hairline scratches

High-gloss lacquer finishes are prone to developing hairline scratches when dishes or other items are slid across the surface. You can often get rid of these light scratches with car wax, which contains a light abrasive. Test the wax first on a bottom edge or some other inconspicuous area to make sure it won't discolour or damage the finish. Once you're ready, apply the wax to a soft cloth and polish using a steady circular motion.

Tips for working wood

❋ Make customised wood filler

When working with specific types of wood, save some of the finest sawdust produced by your sanders. Mix a handful of the sawdust with ordinary woodworking adhesive until it becomes a thick paste, then overfill the crack. Let it dry, then lightly sand. Note: Cracks filled with adhesive-based filler will not accept stain in the same way that solid wood does.

❋ Instant wood filler

If you need some wood filler in a hurry for an emergency repair on an inexpensive piece of furniture, mix a couple of tablespoons of ready-mixed all-purpose filler with instant coffee until you achieve the desired shade of brown. Fill in the crack and smooth with a damp rag.

❋ Pluck some filler

An old guitar plectrum makes a great tool for applying small amounts of filler to fill nail holes and small cracks in wood. An easy solution with no strings attached!

❋ Soften wood filler

Acetone-based cellulose wood fillers are designed to dry quickly. If you notice that your acetone filler has started to solidify in the can, you can soften it by adding a little acetone nail polish remover. Stir in just enough to bring the filler to the right consistency or it will become too runny to use. Note: It is not possible to save filler that has already hardened.

❋ Get rid of glue with vinegar

Don't despair when you get a hardened glob of adhesive on your woodwork. Cover it with a rag soaked in warm white vinegar and leave it overnight. The adhesive will slide off with ease in the morning. Vinegar will also soften old glued joints – and even that last bit of woodworking adhesive that's hardening in the bottom of the bottle. Just add a few drops of vinegar to the bottle and let it sit for an hour or two. Shake well, drain the vinegar, and repeat the process as necessary.

idea

HOW TO IDENTIFY DIFFERENT FINISHES

If you're about to strip a piece of furniture but don't know how it's finished, do this test to see which solvent to use. (Note: test solvents first on a hidden section if you don't intend to strip the whole thing.)

1. Start by moistening a rag with some methylated spirit and rubbing vigorously. If the finish stains the rag, it's shellac (French polish).

2. If the finish is unaffected, brush on one or two coats of white spirit. If it loosens the finish, it's wax or oil.

3. Still not budging? Try a coat of cellulose thinner. If that does the job, it's a cellulose varnish finish.

4. If meths, white spirit and cellulose thinner won't work, the piece has a polyurethane finish and requires a chemical stripper.

✳ The last straw for glue spills

Keep some plastic drinking straws nearby when working with wood; they come in handy when working with adhesives and lubricants. If you use too much wood adhesive along a seam, for instance, simply fold a straw in half and use the folded edge to scoop up the excess.

✳ Flip a stripped finish

Stop off in the kitchen before stripping a piece of furniture. The flat, flexible blade on an old plastic spatula is exactly what you need to scrape off used stripper. Hold the spatula by the blade in a reverse position and push it in a straight, steady motion to remove the old finish.

✳ Better ways to stain

Put old pairs of tights to work when staining furniture. Rolled-up tights or stockings make a great alternative to a cotton cloth or a rag. Not only do they drip less, but they also won't leave behind any lint.

A spare paint roller also makes a terrific stain applicator. Cut a 22cm roller into three equal pieces. Whether fixed to an applicator or held in your hand, a roller holds more stain than a brush and applies it more evenly than a rag.

✳ Stop stripper drips

The next time you need to strip a table or a chair, place the legs inside empty (but washed) soup or baked bean cans. The cans will catch the drips, which, besides keeping your work space cleaner, will allow you to re-use the stripper for a second coat.

✳ Baby oil the end grain

If you'd like to save a couple of pounds, don't spend them on a proprietary sealer when finishing your next woodworking project. Instead, seal the end grain with unscented baby oil. It will work just as well as the stuff that you can buy at a DIY store. It keeps the colour uniform by preventing the end from soaking up too much stain.

Rust busters

In the workshop ...

Remove rust from knives, screwdrivers and other tools by rubbing them with a slice of **raw potato** dipped in salt.

Scour rusty tools and machine parts with a steel wool soap pad dipped in **white spirit.**

Dip a rag into a paste made from 4 tablespoons **salt** and 2 tablespoons **lemon juice** to remove rust spots on chrome and other metallic surfaces.

Apply a thin coat of **WD-40** or **petroleum jelly** to spanners, saw blades, screwdrivers, shears or pliers to keep them rust-free during extended periods of non-use.

Rub down tools with **hair conditioner** to help prevent rusting.

Drop in a few recycled **silica gel packs** (the kind found in a new pair of shoes and other leather products) to keep rust out of your toolbox. You can also use a few pieces of **blackboard chalk** or **charcoal briquettes** wherever you store tools in your workshop.

Around the house ...

Rub rust marks on stainless steel with naphtha-based **lighter fluid,** then scrub with a damp sponge sprinkled with scouring powder. Rinse thoroughly.

Plunge a rusty kitchen knife into a large **onion** a few times and it may end up rust-free.

Brush rust stains on porcelain with **toothpaste** (tool of choice: old toothbrush).

Mix **salt** with **white spirit** to remove rust on most surfaces.

Remove rust stains left by metal furniture on patio paving stones by wetting the stain and topping it with the **powder** used to make citrus-flavoured drinks (lemon or orange).

Coat a nick on a metal appliance with clear **nail polish** to keep it from rusting.

Remove rust rings left from metal cans off kitchen and bathroom surfaces with **car polish.**

Put a **coffee filter** in cast-iron cookware to absorb moisture and prevent rust.

Clever kitchen fixes

✱ Rub out scorch marks

If you spot a scorch mark on a laminate worktop, don't use abrasive powder; chances are you'll only remove the finish. If the burn isn't too deep, buff it out with car polish or a mixture of toothpaste and bicarbonate of soda.

✱ A fast fix for dents

If the colour hasn't been altered, you can disguise dents and scratches on practically any kitchen surface – including wood, glass and even some kinds of tiles – with clear nail polish. Brush on the polish in thin coats, letting it dry between applications. When you're finished, smooth the polish with a piece of very fine grit sandpaper, then buff the area with a soft cloth.

✱ Save a rusty dishwasher rack

You can buy pieces of flexible, clear plastic tubing at most DIY stores. For most racks, tubing with an inside diameter of 3mm works best. Cut the tubing into 6mm lengths and slip it over the rack tops.

✱ Check the fridge door gasket

If your fridge or freezer is more than five years old, inspect its door gasket for leaks at least once a year. The easiest method is to place a piece of paper – or a bank note – halfway inside, shut the door, and tug on the paper. Repeat the process in several spots around the seal. The paper should hold firmly; if it's easy to pull out, the gasket needs to be repaired or replaced.

✱ Add ballast to your freezer

Freezers work at maximum efficiency only when they are at least two-thirds full. If you

what's the story?

THE MOTHER OF ALL DISHWASHERS

Homeowners the world over owe a debt of gratitude to Josephine Garis Cochrane of Shelbyville, Illinois, USA. In 1886, Cochrane, a socialite, invented the first automatic dishwasher to prevent her servants from breaking the family china when they hand washed it. Interestingly, Cochrane was not the first inventor in her family; her maternal great-grandfather, John Fitch, received a patent for the steamboat in 1791. (The 'father of steam navigation', Robert Fulton, didn't build his first steamship until nine years after Fitch's death in 1798.)

At a time when women were all but shut out of commerce and trade, Cochrane's hand-operated Garis Cochrane Dishwashing Machine was the hit of the 1893 World's Columbian Exposition in Chicago and subsequently became a staple in many hotels and restaurants.

It wasn't long before Cochrane's invention spawned numerous imitators and competitors, both in the United States and overseas. Yet, her Crescent Washing Machine Company continued producing dishwashers according to her designs well after her death in 1913. In 1926, Crescent was purchased by Hobart Manufacturing Co, which later sold dishwashers under the KitchenAid name, a brand now owned by Whirlpool.

Test the seal on your fridge door with a fiver!

don't have enough food to freeze, add some bulk by filling a few plastic drinks bottles with water and placing them in your freezer. You can easily remove the ice ballast when you get food to replace it.

✳ No-stick kitchen drawers

Most kitchen drawers work on a guide-and-track system. That is, rounded guides on the drawer keep it moving back and forth on tracks mounted inside the cabinet. Accumulations of dust and other impediments can slow down drawers or cause them to stick. Keep them moving freely by spraying the tracks and guides with a little WD-40 once or twice a year.

✳ Stop cabinet doors from banging

If your wooden cabinet doors always close with a bit of a bang, soften the blow by sticking bumpers at each door's top and bottom corners. Inexpensive door bumper pads are one solution, but perhaps a little too obvious for the creative do-it-yourselfer. Instead, try pressing small circular medical sticking plasters into service, testing to see if you need a double layer to silence the bang.

✳ Repair instead of replacing

If you've ever bought a replacement part for a kitchen appliance, you are probably still in recovery from the shock of the high price. The truth is many non-moving parts can be easily repaired for just pence. For instance, a broken handle on a microwave oven or a cracked dishwasher arm can often be easily reattached with some two-part epoxy adhesive. Likewise, a little silicone sealant can be used to patch a small crack in your refrigerator's door gasket, while a few strips of gaffer tape can usually mend broken parts on a fridge door shelf. Remember: you only need to replace that which really can't be fixed.

Plumbing secrets

✳ No plunger, no problem

Use a hollow rubber ball or tennis ball instead. Secure the ball in a vice and cut it in half with a hacksaw or a utility knife. To clear a blocked waste pipe, fit the concave side over the waste outlet and press down with your palms or the base of your thumbs to create pressure.

✳ Clamp down on loose plungers

A plunger with a loose handle makes every job more difficult and can even be dangerous if the handle slips out or breaks off. If your plunger handle is easily separated from the suction cup, tighten it by placing a Jubilee clip around the base of the cup so that it is firmly clamped to the handle.

✳ Saucer as sink shield

Don't let your work go down the drain! Before you take apart a tap in a sink without a plug, take a small plate or saucer out of the kitchen cabinet. Then simply place it upside down over the waste outlet to prevent any small pieces from getting lost.

✳ Loosen a stuck tap

You've tried everything, but a tap handle won't budge. Relax and have a cool soft carbonated drink. After a few sips, pour the rest over the tap. Give the carbonation 5–10 minutes to loosen any rust or corrosion around the tap – followed by a few gentle strikes with a rubber mallet and it'll loosen with ease.

✳ Easy turn-off

It is frustrating when you want to turn the water off at the mains, only to find that the stoptap is jammed tight. It can usually be

make your own...

DRAIN CLEANER

Even if you clean out dirty pots and pans before washing them, grease can still collect inside the waste pipes. It's the same with conditioners and other hair products that you use in the shower. Use this potent non-toxic mixture twice a month in kitchen and bathroom drains to help keep them clog-free.

Super grease buster

This powder gets its powerful punch from the chemical reaction between the alkalinity of the bicarbonate of soda and the acidity of the cream of tartar. Be sure to keep your face pointed away from the drain when adding the water, which triggers the reaction.

180g bicarbonate of soda
180g salt
45g cream of tartar
240ml boiling water

1 Put bicarbonate of soda, salt and cream of tartar in a glass jar, put the lid on tight and shake well to mix.

2 Pour 60ml of the mixture down a dry drain and follow it with 240ml boiling water.

3 Wait for the bubbles to subside, then flush with cold water for 3–4 minutes.

loosened by the judicious application of WD-40 and/or heat – but, to avoid it happening again, try to remember to operate it every month or so and always close it a quarter turn from fully open when you leave it. This way it will work freely when you need it.

✶ Hose off pipe leaks

When you need a quick patch for a leaking water pipe, cut off a section of old garden hose or rubber tubing that's longer than the affected area of pipe. Slice it lengthways, then fit the hose over the leak. Wrap it well with waterproof tape and secure it with three Jubilee clips: one on each end and one in the middle.

✶ Blow-dry a frozen pipe

If a water pipe freezes in the winter cold, close the gate valve by the main cold water cistern and open the nearest tap. Then, starting at the tap, use a hair dryer on a medium setting to thaw out the pipe. Be sure to keep the drier moving all the time so that the pipe doesn't get too hot in one spot; a sudden shift in temperature can cause pipes to crack. After it thaws, cover the pipe in glass fibre or thick foam insulation material to keep it from freezing in the future.

✶ Prevent pipes from freezing in winter

When you know that there's a cold snap on the way, you can keep your waste and drainage pipes from freezing during the winter months by pouring 180g salt followed by 1 litre of boiling water down the waste outlet of your sink, basin and bath once every week or so. And always remember to put the plug in the plughole at night whenever the weather is freezing outside.

Bathroom basics

✱ Fix scratched surfaces

If you have scratches in an acrylic bath, you can fix them with metal polish. Apply it with a soft cloth using a circular motion. The light abrasive in the polish lifts out most fine scratches. To smooth out deeper nicks and scrapes, dampen them with a bit of water and then gently rub with a piece of very fine wet-and-dry abrasive paper before polishing.

Scratches on enamel baths and surfaces can be covered with a few thin coats of enamel touch-up paint (available at most DIY stores) or white correction fluid. Clean the damaged area with some methylated spirit on a cotton wool ball and then sand lightly with wet-and-dry abrasive paper. Let the methylated spirit evaporate thoroughly before applying the paint.

✱ Fill tubs before sealing

Before you seal around a bath, fill the bath with water. The extra weight will widen the gap in the joint between the bath and the wall, which makes for a thicker seal that's less likely to crack or tear later on.

✱ A smarter, simpler way to save water

Some people put bricks inside their toilet cisterns to reduce the amount of water per flush. It's a good way to conserve water, but it can be bad for the toilet because bricks submerged in water often break up and the bits can get into the flushing mechanism. A better option is to use old plastic bottles filled with sand or water. Remove any labels and check that the bottle is tightly sealed before placing it in the cistern.

idea

DETECTING TOILET CISTERN LEAKS

A continuously running toilet is telling you that something is leaking, so don't ignore it. It might be annoying, but it's also wasting water and can be costly if you have a water meter.

To check for leaks, lift off the cistern cover and make sure the water level isn't too high. Gently bend the float arm downward (or use a screwdriver to turn the float valve adjustment screw anticlockwise). If that doesn't stop the water from running, you can easily pinpoint the source of the leak by adding 1–2 teaspoons of food colouring to the cistern water. Don't flush the toilet for an hour or two.

- If the food colouring appears in the water inside the bowl, the leak is coming through the valve – in which case the siphon flap valve needs to be repaired or replaced.

- If the water collects outside the bowl, make sure the flush pipe from the cistern to the pan is properly attached (a loose or misdirected tube can shoot water under the lid). If the pipe isn't the problem, the cistern itself is leaking.

Utility rooms and cellars

✱ Circuit training

Whether your electrical consumer unit (or fuse box) is in the utility room, cellar or garage, it's a good idea to make sure that all the circuit breakers or fuses are properly labelled – so that you know which one to go to when there is a fault or you want to turn a particular circuit off.

Most houses have several circuits. The lighting circuits are the easiest – rated at 5A or 6A, there will normally be two of these (one for upstairs and one for down), but there could be more. Next comes a circuit for an immersion heater (15A) and then various 30 (or 32A) circuits for the socket outlet circuits (and, perhaps, cooker and shower) and finally the 'big' (45A) circuits for a powerful cooker or electric shower. There may be other circuits (burglar alarm, smoke alarms, garden circuits and so on). Make sure you know what they all are and write the names on the labels provided.

If you are working by yourself, an easy way to identify which sockets are on which circuits is to plug a radio into a socket outlet and then see which fuse or miniature circuit breaker makes it go silent. Make sure that it is loud enough for you to hear!

✱ Touch up a scratched washer or drier

Metal buckles, zips and clasps can leave marks and scratches on both washing machines and clothes driers – marks that will undoubtedly rust when exposed to moisture and wet clothing. Don't wait to repair the damage or you will regret it. First, clean the area with a cotton ball dipped in surgical spirit. When the surgical spirit has dried (a few seconds at most), cover the scratch with a thin coat of clear nail varnish or like-coloured car body touchup paint, available from car supply stores.

✱ Catch the ripper

If your clothes come out of the wash with small rips or snags, it's likely that something inside the washer is the guilty party. Rub a wad of recycled tights over the agitator and tub to detect any coarse edges that snag. Then smooth over the rough spots with a piece of very fine grade sandpaper or epoxy.

✱ Cleaner floor

Concrete garage floors can get very dusty, which can make painting jobs a nightmare. It really is worth investing in some garage floor paint, which not only looks smart, but also holds the concrete surface together and makes sweeping the floor very much easier.

✱ A great stand-up routine

Why go through a balancing act every time you need to stand up a mop, duster or broom? Cut off the finger sections from some old latex gloves and slip them over the ends of all those long wooden handles. The rubber provides enough traction to stop a pole from sliding whenever you lean it against a wall.

Soak up musty smells with cat litter!

✱ Mould and mildew treatments

Cellars generally suffer from a lack of ventilation so even the driest basement rooms can have mouldy walls or corners. Wearing rubber gloves and a disposable face mask, brush or scrape the worst of the mould from all surfaces, then scrub the affected areas with a brush dipped in a solution of water, disinfectant and soda crystals. Blot the damp walls with a cloth to minimise moisture, and plug in a fan to keep air circulating and dry the walls thoroughly.

✱ Air out a cellar

You don't have to live with a musty cellar. Once you've taken care of the source of mildew, combat any lingering odours by mixing 2 parts cat litter with 1 part bicarbonate of soda in a large container. Then fill several empty (but clean) large tins to the brim and place them around your basement. Replace with fresh mixture as needed. If the moisture affects the upper corners of the cellar, fill cotton bags or old pillow cases with the mix and hang them close to the damp areas.

✱ Hang up insulation

If you have an attached garage with a flat roof and exposed rafters, warm it up by insulating the roof from below. Buy some rolls of loft insulation (safe to touch these days) plus rolls of garden netting. Push the insulation material up between the exposed rafters and use a staple gun to secure the netting to the underside of the rafters to hold the insulation in place.

Exterior repairs

✱ Get a better handle on glass

If you need to move a large pane of glass and wish there were some way to get a better grip, cut off two short sections from an old garden hose (four sections for a two-person job). Use a sharp knife or scissors to slit each piece down the middle, and then slip them onto the top and bottom edges of the glass. Never attempt to move a large sheet of glass when it is windy.

✱ Bag a lock

Give external padlocks some needed protection in winter by covering them with plastic sandwich bags. The plastic wards off rust and prevents damage when moisture seeps inside the lock and repeatedly freezes and thaws.

Bonus hint: When a lock does ice up, you can usually open it by warming the key for several seconds with a match or lighter before inserting it.

✱ Juice out concrete patio rust stains

When unsightly orange rust stains are defacing your concrete or stone patio you can remove them with the citric acid found in powdered lemonade, lemon-lime or orangeade drink mixes. Wet the surface with water, then pour the powder over the stain. Cover it with a sheet of plastic to keep the moisture from evaporating and put a weight on top to hold it in place. After 30 minutes or so, remove the plastic, scrub with a stiff-bristled brush and rinse. Repeat if necessary.

idea

A WINTER STRATEGY

If you don't attend to the outside of your home in autumn, you can be sure that any problems will be worse in spring – and more expensive to put right!

- Start at the top, examining the roof (use binoculars if necessary), looking for slipped or missing slates and tiles, failed flashing around chimney stacks and leaning chimney pots or stacks.

- Check out the gutters and down pipes to make sure thy are not blocked and are not leaking (have a look when it's raining)

- Look at flat roofs from above and from below (inside a garage or extension) to make sure that there is no damage allowing water through.

- Check exterior woodwork to make sure the paint covering is still sound and that the wood has not started to rot. At the same time, check that there are not gaps between window and door frames that could be letting moisture into the house.

- Clean all patio (and deck surfaces), so that they are not slippery and dangerous in the winter months.

Get as many things sorted as you can – if necessary, with the help of a tradesman.

New life for an old garden hose

Don't throw out a leaky old garden hose. Instead use a thin drill bit to punch a few more holes, crimp the end and you've made a great soaker hose. If you don't need a soaker hose, there are still lots of terrific uses for a retired hose around the house.

Slice open a section of hose and use it as a protective cover for a hand saw's teeth or a circular saw blade between uses.

Cut a piece long enough to cover the tines of a metal rake. (Use a utility knife to slit the hose, but don't cut through to the ends.) Slip it over the rake and use as a squeegee to clear away puddles on decks, patios and paths.

Use it to cover a fraying length of rope to stop it from getting worse.

Staple small, diagonally sliced pieces to the overhead joists in your garage to keep power cords out of your way.

Slit two short pieces down the middle and put them over the shoulders of a spade to cushion your foot and improve grip as you step down on it.

Slip a small section over a metal bucket handle for a more comfortable grip.

✱ Replace slipped slates and tiles

If a roof tile or slate has slipped out of place, it needs to be replaced as soon as possible – or water could get into the roof space and cause untold damage.

Tiles are easiest – you can normally prise up the surrounding tiles and re-hook the tile over its supporting batten. To re-fix a slate, you'll have to make yourself a 'tingle' from a strip of thin lead, around 25mm wide and 230mm long with a small hole drilled in one end. This is nailed in place under the slate (exactly in the gap between the two slates below with the nail through the hole), the slate replaced and the end of the 'tingle' bent up and over to hold the bottom edge of the slate in place.

Caution: don't attempt roof repairs without proper access equipment – a proper extension ladder to reach up to the roof and a roof ladder (hooked over the ridge) to get up on to the roof.

✱ Make a gutter scoop

The next time you need to clean the leaves out of your gutters, don't worry if you haven't got a proper gutter scoop. You can make one out of an empty plastic bottle with a handle (for example a bottle that used to contain toilet cleaner or fabric conditioner). Turn the bottle so that the handle is on top and use a utility knife to cut the end off the bottle so that the handle side is shorter. Leave the cap on the bottle and you have a perfect scoop that should fit virtually every size of gutter.

✱ Foil a leaking gutter

If your steel gutter has sprung a leak, patch the hole by applying a generous coating of silicone sealant to the hole or crack and then covering it with a piece of heavy-duty aluminium foil. Repeat the process and finish off the job with a top coat of sealant.

✱ A quick fix for a loose brick

You don't need to mix up a fresh batch of mortar just to replace a single loose brick in a retaining wall or porch step – but never a brick on the house. Simply get out the two-part epoxy adhesive and apply it to the sides of the brick where the mortar has come loose. Let it cure for 24 hours, then seal any remaining gaps with building silicone sealer.

✱ Instant ageing for new mortar

If you think that new mortar joints are going to stand out like a sore thumb against the old cement, you can 'age' them to match by dabbing the wet mortar with a damp black tea bag. (You may need to experiment a bit to obtain the right shade.)

✱ Pour your own stepping-stones

If you want to put leftover cement to good use, why not make a few concrete stepping-stones? Use a couple of plastic dustbin lids as your moulds. Coat the inside of the lids with a thin, even layer of motor oil so that the cured concrete will slide out. You can even add your own decorative touches by etching shapes in the wet cement using leaves or other objects.

✱ Cover fresh concrete with hay to prevent frost damage while it sets

Any builder who works outdoors has probably had the frustrating experience of working with concrete when the temperature falls. To minimise problems, keep the area covered with hay before the pour, then after the concrete is placed and smoothed, cover it with plastic sheeting followed by hay.

Top tips for tools

✳ Sharpen blades with a matchbox

You can restore the cutting edge to a dull blade on a small craft or utility knife by rubbing it a few times on the striking surface of a box of matches or, if one is handy, an emery board. Be sure to sharpen both sides of the cutting edge.

✳ Be carpet scrap happy

As handy as they are for repairing tears and burns in matching carpeting, carpet remnants may actually be even more useful around the workshop. You can:

- Glue them to the inside of your toolbox to cushion tools in transit.
- Tack them to the tops of workbench surfaces to prevent scratching furniture finishes.
- Staple several remnants inside a narrow cabinet to form cushioned cradles for drills and other power tools.
- Staple remnants (one at a time) to a small block of wood to make a reusable contact-adhesive applicator, where a thin even coating is required.

✳ Hands-on handles

You'll get a firmer (and more comfortable) grip on hammers, spanners, screwdrivers and other tools if you wrap the handles with adhesive tape or flat foam draught proofing strip. Hard tools will become soft to the touch.

✳ Save your fingers

To avoid bruised fingers when hammering home really tiny nails, hold the nails upright in the teeth of a pocket comb rather than between your fingers.

✳ Save the wood

Claw hammers are great for pulling nails out of wood – but you can easily damage the wood's surface as you lever the nail up. Slip a piece of thick cardboard under the hammer head to prevent this from happening.

✳ Shield wood from hammers

Protect wood from accidental hammer blows with a homemade hammer guard. Take the lid from a small plastic container and cut a small hole in the centre large enough to fit over the nail head. Place the lid over each nail before hammering it in. To stop wood from splitting, blunt the tips of your nails with a hammer before using them: simply hold the nail upright on a block of metal and tap its tip lightly.

✳ Pliers as torch holder

Trying to hold a torch and work at the same time is a juggling act that you don't want to perform. But you can still get the illumination you need if you don't have a helper to hold the light. Place the torch between the jaws of a pair of pliers and position it at the required angle. Slip a thick rubber band around the handles of the pliers to keep the torch from slipping.

✳ Fizz away corrosion

Loosen a rusty nut or bolt by covering it with a rag soaked in vinegar or a fizzy drink. Let it sit for an hour to give the liquid time to work into the corrosion. The carbonation in fizzy drinks has another workshop application as well: it will unfreeze a rusted padlock or cabinet lock.

Sealants and adhesives

✳ Cold weather sealing

When you need to do some sealing on a crisp, cool day keep your sealant pliable and running smoothly by wrapping the tubes in a heating pad (the kind sold for pain relief) for 30–45 minutes before using them. Trap the heat by wrapping each tube in cling film before inserting it into the sealant gun.

✳ Clean fingers

Don't use your finger to shape a bead of silicone sealant around a bath or basin unless you don't mind wearing it for a while. A lollipop stick or the back of a old plastic teaspoon is a much better way to go about it; both have smooth, rounded edges and are easy to hold so avoiding getting the silicone on your skin.

✳ Improve your aim

It can be hard to manoeuvre a sealant gun in a tight spot or to properly seal a crevice that's out of reach. But an effective extension tool may be as near as a kitchen drawer: a plastic drinking straw. Push the straw (or any plastic tube of the right size) into the nozzle of the sealant tube. Keep your impromptu extender from slipping off by securing it with gaffer tape.

✳ Mix it up

Old jam jar lids are ideal for mixing two-part epoxy adhesive. The raised edge keeps the adhesive from spreading out as you're mixing it, and the limited interior space prevents you from using too much.

✳ In the bag

If you are looking for an easy way to mix and apply two-part epoxy adhesive there's a solution in the pantry. Take a plastic sandwich bag and squeeze as much adhesive as you need into a corner section. Tie off the rest of the bag and mix the epoxy by rolling it between your fingers (You'll notice the adhesive gets warm as it is mixed.) Use a pin to put one or more small holes in the bag and gently squeeze the epoxy adhesive out.

✳ Unglue the glue

You shouldn't have to fight to get adhesive out of a bottle or tube. Dab a little petroleum jelly on the inside of the lid or on the tip of the tube before replacing the cap. It will prevent the glue from sticking to the cover, and you will have one less frustration to face.

tip TAPE A TUBE

Wrapping sealant tubes in **gaffer tape** can help you to work more neatly and efficiently. The tape helps tubes fit more snugly in the sealant gun and prevents the sticky mess that can follow when tubes swell and collapse as the plunger squeezes out the sealant.

Clamping and sanding

✳ Clamps from the car

If you have an old set of jump leads just lying around collecting dust, cut off the battery clips and take them to your workshop. They make excellent spring clamps and can accommodate objects up to 40mm thick.

You could also use a car hose clamp (Jubilee clip) to secure a cracked wooden leg or spindle while you re-glue it. Just be sure to put a piece of cloth between the clamp and the wood so you won't risk gouging the surface.

✳ Pour on the pressure

It's almost impossible to clamp irregularly shaped items and fragile objects to glue them back together, but you can still provide adequate pressure. Fill a small plastic bag with sand to weigh down repairs on small, fragile items; it will shape itself to the item being glued.

✳ True grit

To extend the life of sanding belts and get the most use out of each sheet of sandpaper, back them with strips of gaffer tape. The tape will prevent the paper from tearing and take some of the stress off the belts. Write down the grit size of the paper and the direction of the belt on the tape using a permanent marker.

✳ Resizing sandpaper

Many sanding jobs require you to cut the paper to odd shapes or sizes. Here are a few household items you can use to get the job done (some require you to tack on the sandpaper):

- A box of playing cards
- Pencils and pencil erasers
- Section of garden hose
- Kitchen sponges
- Traditional round wooden clothespegs
- A wood block secured to a sponge mop holder (for walls and ceilings)

what's the story?

SANDPAPER'S SOUJOURN

The first recorded use of sandpaper took place in 13th-century China, when artisans used natural gum to bond crushed shells, seeds and sand to parchment. Despite this early use, up until the 19th century most woodworkers and cabinet-makers relied on dried sheets of sharkskin to smooth their wooden wares.

In the 1800s the fish skins were replaced by 'glass paper', made by gluing small particles of glass by hand onto sheets of paper. The commercial production of glass paper began in London in 1833 when John Oakey, a former piano manufacturer's apprentice, developed a way to mass produce it. A year later, Isaac Fisher Jr. of Springfield, Vermont, USA, obtained four patents for coating and manufacturing what he called 'sandpaper'.

Sandpaper jumped in popularity in 1921 when 3M introduced Wetordry, the world's first waterproof sandpaper, after purchasing the patent from its unsung inventor. The product, first used for repainting cars, is still sold today – an excellent example of the principle, 'if it ain't broke, don't fix it'.

The lowdown on ladders

✱ Stuck on top

Few things are quite as irritating as dropping a needed screw or tool from the top of a ladder. One way to put an end to such mishaps is to glue a magnetic strip to the top rung of your ladder. It will safely hold on to all your fasteners and small tools until you need them. When it comes to larger tools, secure a canvas tool bag to the ladder to keep them in.

✱ Off on the right foot

A scrap of thick carpet wrapped around the bottom rung of a ladder makes a handy mat for wiping the soles of your shoes before you ascend. It will also let you know that you have reached the bottom when climbing down. Secure the carpet scrap with gaffer tape and replace with a fresh piece when needed.

✱ Don't leave your mark

Cushion the tops of a ladder's rails with an old pair of socks, gloves or a couple of bunched up old T-shirts to prevent it from damaging fascia boards or leaving marks or scratches on interior walls while you are working.

✱ Boot up a ladder

Set the feet of a ladder in a pair of old Wellington boots to give it a skid-free footing on smooth surfaces.

The extraordinary home crisis centre

When a splash of grease burns your hand, the advice in emergency guides (and this book) is to race to the nearest tap and hold the burn under cold running water for 15 minutes. But what about all those other problems that we encounter in daily life? The kind that aren't necessarily emergencies but need a quick fix nonetheless. Ants or mice taking over the kitchen cupboard, a make-up spill on a white silk blouse, nappy rash causing your baby dire distress – you can take care of them all by using the common household items and suggestions that fill the previous chapters in this book. This section, however, will provide you with emergency fixes that will help you to quickly avert virtually any crisis that may come up in your home – and elsewhere.

Culled from a vast well of folk remedies and age-old common sense, it speaks to the imagination of ordinary do-it-yourselfers who possess an extraordinary knack for solving all kinds of problems.

Body repairs

* **You feel a cold coming on** Set your hair dryer to warm, hold it in front of your face and breathe in the warm air. *(Fire up the hair dryer, page 154)*

* **You have a cold or allergy, and your stuffy nose feels as if it may explode** Peel and halve a clove of garlic and hold it on your tongue for as long as you can, taking the fumes into throat and lungs.

Inhale a pinch of ground pepper to precipitate sneezing.

Add 60ml vinegar to the water in a vapouriser, squirt it into the air and inhale the vapour.

* **Your head is pounding like a drum** Soak your feet in hot water laced with mustard powder to calm a thudding headache.
(Head-to-toe headache remedy, page 161)

Tie a scarf, bandana, or necktie tightly around your head at forehead level.
(Wear a headband, page 161)

* **You think you are coming down with flu** Drink a cup of elderberry tea or a glass of water with 20–30 drops of elderberry tincture. *(Swat a flu bug with elderberry, page 156)*

* **You have an excruciating toothache or gum infection** Mix 2–3 teaspoons of table salt in a glass of warm water; and vigorously swish it around in your mouth.
(Saltwater rinse for toothaches, page 163)

Bite down on a cotton wool ball wetted with several drops of clove oil and get to the dentist as fast as you can.
(Clove oil to the rescue! page 163)

Make a pain-relieving mouthwash with 180ml water, ¼ teaspoon salt, and 6–8 drops clove oil. *(Clove oil to the rescue! page 163)*

✻ You have a terrible ear ache Use a clean eyedropper to drop 3 per cent hydrogen peroxide into your ear and let it bubble for 3–5 minutes. *(Bubble away ear trouble, page 162)*

✻ You have a large cold sore that looks (and feels) terrible Dab it with a little bit of yoghurt or vinegar throughout the day.

✻ You have overdone the gardening and now your back muscles are complaining Position a cold, unopened soft drink can between a wall and the painful area and then move from side to side to massage your aching back. *(Tin can massage, page 164)*

✻ You're woken in the night by acute leg cramps that send you hopping out of bed like a frog Stand on a cold stone or ceramic tiled floor. It will help to slow the blood flow and relax tightened, cramped muscles. *(Painful leg cramp relievers, page 164)*

✻ You have burned your tongue badly on a first bite of a hot pizza Sprinkle a pinch or two of sugar on your tongue to ease the pain.

✻ Constipation – an old-fashioned cure Take 1–2 teaspoons castor oil for relief in about 8 hours. *(Old-time constipation cure, page 166)*

✻ Diarrhoea is keeping you on the run Make an infusion from the berries or dried leaves of blackberry, blueberry or bilberry plants. *(Treat diarrhoea with berries, page 166)*

Purée a whole lemon in a blender, add salt and take 1 teaspoon of the mixture two or three times a day.

✻ An upset stomach is spoiling your day Brew an infusion from angelica, anise, caraway seed, camomile, fennel seed, cinnamon, peppermint, ginger, marjoram or oregano. *(Stomach soothers, page 165)*

Drink cold soda water with a dash of Angostura bitters.

---

idea

DON'T SCRATCH AN ITCH!

Whatever the cause – animal, vegetable, or mineral – itchy skin can drive you crazy. But excessive scratching can result in infections and scarring. Control your instinct and try one of these itch-stopping remedies instead.

Mosquito and other insect bites Saturate a clean cloth with white or cider vinegar or surgical spirit and dab the bites. A few drops of ammonia or a generous dab of chest rub applied directly to the bite (but *never* on bleeding or open sores) will also quell itching.

Athlete's foot Soak the affected foot in a salt water footbath. *(Beat athlete's foot, page 170)*. Dust your feet, socks and shoes with baking powder to dry the infection. For stronger relief, make a salve with 1 teaspoon bicarbonate of soda and ½ teaspoon water; rub between the toes and leave for about 15 minutes. Rinsing your feet with undiluted cider vinegar three or four times daily will also calm itching.

Itchy sunburn Make a lotion of 1 part powdered milk, 2 parts water, and a couple pinches of salt, and dab on burned areas. Or treat sunburn with strong green tea. *(Soothe sunburn with green tea, page 172)*

* **Your hiccups aren't responding to the usual cures**
Try this one: eat some peanut butter and leave a little time before swallowing it. (*Peanut butter for hiccups, page 180*)

* **You need a quick treatment for an ordinary skin cut that's bleeding a lot**
Place a peeled, bruised half-clove of garlic over a cleaned cut, secure with a bandage, and leave for up to 10 minutes. (*Treat a cut with garlic, page 171*)
   Use a little mouthwash to disinfect the cut.
   Apply a substantial amount of black pepper directly to the cut. (*Black pepper stops bleeding, page 171*)

* **You've banged your arm or leg so hard you just know it's going to bruise**
Immediately press an onion on the spot for 15 minutes to reduce discoloration. (*Reduce bruising with an onion, page 171*)
   Apply a banana peel, inside down, on to the bruise and secure it with a bandage.
   Apply cotton gauze soaked in cider vinegar for an hour.

* **An inflamed boil needs draining**
Cover the boil with a wet tea bag and secure with a bandage, then leave it on overnight.

* **A wasp or bee sting threatens to ruin a day in the sun**
Apply a paste of 2 parts bicarbonate of soda to 1 part vinegar. (*Double-duty paste for bee stings, page 172*)
   Pour on undiluted vinegar and scrape away stinger with a credit card.
   Place an onion slice over the sting.
   Spray the sting with WD-40 or a window cleaner containing ammonia.

* **Your toddler has a heat rash**
Add 2 teaspoons bicarbonate of soda to every 8 litres of lukewarm bathwater to soothe the rash. (*Soothe heat rash with a bicarbonate of soda bath, page 179*)

* **Your baby has a sudden, painful case of nappy rash**
Apply honey, which will absorb liquid and keep skin dry. (*Nappy rash soothers, page 178*)
   Speed up healing by sealing out moisture with petroleum jelly or toasted cornflour.
   Apply the spice fenugreek. (*A spicy baby powder substitute, page 178*)
   Stir 1 tablespoon salt into 1 litre boiling water and let the solution cool to room temperature. Wipe it onto your baby's bottom then gently dab dry. Apply a zinc oxide lotion to create a barrier to further wetness. (*Prevent nappy rash with salt and zinc, page 178*)

* **Your baby gets a cut or scrape**
Use a baby wipe or hand wipe to clean a dirty cut or scrape when no water is available.
   Squeeze lemon juice, mouthwash, vinegar or a spirit such as gin or vodka directly on the injury, cover with a napkin, and hold in place for a minute or two to stop bleeding.

* **Your child's baby tooth has just fallen out and it's bleeding a lot** Squeeze the excess liquid out of a cool, used tea bag and press the bag onto the empty tooth socket. Hold for 1–2 minutes, then reapply as necessary to stop bleeding.

* **Your beautiful new summer sandals have given you an ugly new blister**
Slice open an aloe leaf and scoop out the gel. Apply gel and bandage blister. (*Aloe for blisters, page 174*)

Household help line

✳ A water pipe is leaking You can make a temporary patch using a garden hose or a piece of rubber tubing that's larger in diameter than the pipe. *(Hose off pipe leaks, page 349)*

✳ You arrive at your country retreat to find the water pipes have frozen Blow warm air from a hair dryer on a pipe until it thaws. *(Blow-dry a frozen pipe, page 349)*

✳ You forgot to cover the outdoor taps and a freeze is predicted Shut off valves and then open the taps and drain remaining water. Wrap spigots and any exposed pipe in several sheets of newspaper to

idea

10 GROOMING AND CLOTHING MISHAPS

Appearance matters, and keeping yourself looking good means knowing what to do in a range of potentially embarrassing fixes.

1. **Too much scent** You went overboard when applying perfume and the scent is overpowering. Dab a little vodka on to the spots where scent was applied.

2. **No lipstick** When you changed handbags, you forgot it. Use a brown eyebrow pencil to add a little colour to your lips. *(Emergency lip colour, page 188)*

3. **No mousse** There's no hair mousse in the bottle and you're hair will droop without it. Mix a little shaving cream with a drop of surgical spirit and rub into the hair where needed. *(A hair mousse alternative, page 189)*

4. **Paint in hair** While you're painting the ceiling, paint drips onto your hair. Rub olive oil on the spots until all traces of paint are gone.

5. **Chlorine-damaged hair** A sip in the swimming pool turns your blonde hair green. Massage ketchup or undiluted tomato juice into your hair. Cover with a shower cap and leave for 10–15 minutes before rinsing.

6. **Blood on clothes** You've cut your hand, and the blood drips onto your trousers. Soak stained portion overnight in a carbonated soft drink, then wash as usual. *(Pop out bloodstains, page 198)*

7. **Chocolate stains** Your three year old smears chocolate on her shirt to wipe her hands. Cover the stain with powdered meat tenderiser, leave for an hour, brush away powder, and wash.

8. **Lipstick marks** Lipstick stains cover your shirt or blouse. Remove the middle from a piece of white bread and knead into a ball. Blot the stain with the bread ball until lipstick is mostly gone. Wash as usual. *(Lipstick smear remover 2: Bread!, page 197)*

9. **Scorch marks** Your favourite white cotton shirt has an obvious scorch mark. Dab the mark with a white cotton cloth moistened with 3 per cent hydrogen peroxide, then wash as usual.

10. **Stuck ring** You tried on your friend's new ring and now can't get it off. Apply mayonnaise liberally to ring and finger to aid the ring's slide. *(Unstick a stuck ring, page 204)*

insulate against cold, and cover with plastic bags secured with gaffer tape.

✳ Your key has broken off in the lock Try to extract the broken part with tweezers or needle-nose pliers.

Use superglue to join the key's two parts. (*Remove a broken key, page 330*)

✳ Someone has left pencil or ink doodles on the wall Rub the marks with rye bread.

For ink marks, dab on white vinegar with clean cloth or sponge, then continue until marks are gone.

✳ A child has decorated the wall with crayons Rub lightly with a clean fabric softener sheet. Rub vigorously with a clean art eraser.

Scrub with shaving cream and a soft toothbrush or nailbrush.

Soften the marks with a hair dryer and remove with baby oil on a cloth. (*Erasing crayon marks from walls, page 72*)

Scrub gently with a damp cloth dipped in bicarbonate of soda or white toothpaste.

For crayon on wallpaper, very lightly skim the surface with a steel wool soap pad, stroking in one direction, until marks disappear.

✳ You've spotted a water mark on a wooden table Mix equal amounts white toothpaste and bicarbonate of soda and rub in, going carefully with the wood grain. (*Get rid of water rings and spots, page 77*)

Lightly rub the ring with fine steel wool dipped in lemon oil.

✳ You're having a dinner party and notice that the table is scratched Apply 2–3 tablespoons instant coffee mixed with just enough water to make a thick paste. (*Instant fix for scratched woodwork, page 341*)

See Homeopathic scratch care (*page 341*) and proceed as directed.

✳ A vinyl or cork tile is about to pop out of the kitchen floor Cover tile with aluminium foil and iron it with a hot iron to heat the glue. Weight with books, bricks, or other heavy flat objects until glue resets.

idea

COMING TO YOUR PET'S RESCUE

Your cat, dog and assorted other pets undoubtedly have their own share of problems – among them, these four situations.

Your dog has itchy ears Mix 1 part white vinegar with 1 part water and wipe your dog's floppy ears using a cotton wool ball taking care not to poke it into the ear itself. (*Vinegar ear cleaner, page 228*)

Fido's kennel is Flea City Wash down the interior walls, plus dog bed and any bedding, with strong salt water. Repeat treatment every few weeks to keep your dog's home flea-free.

Fluffy the cat has rolled in some sticky stuff Mix 1 teaspoon mild shampoo or dishwashing liquid with 60 to 120ml warm water, massage it into the sticky patch and remove the residue with a wire-toothed brush. (*Unsticking something sticky, page 236*)

Your pet snake is not where he's supposed to be Lay sheets of aluminium foil, bubble wrap or crinkly cellophane in potential hiding places so that you can hear him moving. (*Your pet snake is lost? page 243*)

✳ A precious wooden chest has several gouges
Make your own wood putty by adding instant coffee to 2 tablespoons of filler to get the desired colour. *(Instant wood filler, page 343)*

✳ The kitchen sink is blocked and you have no plunger
Use a tennis ball or small rubber ball cut in half as a suction cup. *(No plunger, no problem, page 348)*

Put any of the following into the drain, leave for 10–15 minutes, and then flush with boiling water:

180g bicarbonate of soda and 240ml hot white vinegar.

90g borax, then boiling water added slowly.

2 Alka-Seltzer tablets or 3 denture tablets followed by 240ml vinegar.

180g salt, 180g bicarbonate of soda, and 120ml white vinegar to rid drain of clogs.

✳ Your washing machine is rattling Use a torch to look under the machine when it's in action. If one of the feet isn't resting firmly on the floor, place a sliver of wood, a small carpet scrap or a tile under the unsteady foot.

✳ A drinking glass has crashed to the bathroom floor
First, wear gloves to pick up large pieces. Then choose one of these methods:

Press the area with wet newspaper to take up tiny bits of glass.

Press a slice of bread or a wad of adhesive tape over the tiny slivers and glass dust to remove them from the floor.

✳ Ants are swarming over your worktops
Sugar Make an ant trap by dissolving 2–3 teaspoons sugar in 240ml water, moisten some paper towels or sponges in the sugar water and set out overnight. Next morning, sweep trap and ants into a dustpan. *(Lure ants with sugar, page 90)*
White vinegar Spray windowsills, door thresholds, worktops, cupboards and other surfaces with a mixture of equal parts white vinegar and water. *(Repel ants with vinegar, page 90)*
Cayenne pepper and cinnamon Sprinkle these substances on surfaces where ants gather. *(Spicy ant repellents, page 52)*
Flour or ashes Spread one of these substances over ant trails and the ants will soon find somewhere else to walk. *(Get ants on the run, page 51)*
Lemon juice, etc. Outside the house, pour lemon juice on thresholds, sills, cracks and holes where ants can enter.

Scatter lemon rinds around door entrances. Or use borax, powdered chalk, salt, talcum power, cream of tartar or clove oil in the same way.
Petroleum jelly Apply around the rims of pets' food bowls to keep ants at bay.

✳ There's a cockroach invasion
Mix equal parts bicarbonate of soda and sugar and scatter wherever you have seen the cockroaches.

Making sure there's no danger to children and pets, sprinkle boric acid powder into cracks and crevices and under appliances where cockroaches lurk. Seal off their entrances with equal parts cornflour and plaster of Paris mixed with enough water to make a thick paste.

If you are very quick, you can kill a scurrying roach with a squirt of WD-40.

✳ Your house has been invaded by fleas If the invasion isn't too severe, place bowls of salt in areas where fleas have been seen to attract and trap them.

Wash wood, tile or vinyl floors with the juice and rinds of 4 lemons in 4 litres of water to repel fleas.
Vacuum carpets, rugs and upholstery frequently to remove flea eggs.

On the road

＊ It's a cold morning and the car won't start Get your hair dryer and a long extension lead. Open the bonnet and blow hot air directly at the carburettor to warm the engine for easy ignition. *(Start your car with a hair dryer, page 312)*

＊ The fan belt has broken. Help!
For a temporary fix, twist a pair of tights into a long rope, thread it around the fan pulleys and knot tightly.

＊ Your horn won't stop honking
Stop the incessant blaring by raising the bonnet and taping down the terminal screw. *(Tape a noisy horn page 315)*

＊ You've backed into a post and your back light cover has cracked
If the light itself is okay, make a temporary repair with red or yellow gaffer tape. Stick the tape over the cracks, then turn on the light to be certain it's clearly visible.

＊ It's a dark and stormy night and your headlight has gone out
Covering the dead headlight with reflector tape will help to get you home safely.

＊ Your wheels are spinning on an ice patch
Pour undiluted chlorine bleach over your tyres. *(Gain traction with bleach, page 312)*

Lay a large piece of scrap carpet or a thick pad of newspaper (two or three sheets should be sufficient) where the wheel hits the icy road.

Your car wheels are trapped in snow or mud
Make a shovel dig more efficiently by spraying it with WD-40.

Your car's temperature gauge suddenly goes into the danger zone Check under the bonnet after the engine cools. If you see a cracked or broken water hose, you can probably make a short-term repair – for just long enough to get to a garage – by wrapping the hose with gaffer tape.

Acknowledgments
The writers and editors who produced this book wish to thank the following people and organisations, all of whom graciously shared their knowledge or expertise. American Society of Travel Agents; Arizona Cooperative Extension, Mojave County; Larry Buchwald; Jim Buie; Andrew R. Byers; Trevor Cole; Vicki Coombs; Pat Courtney; Marilyn Dale; Marianne Dervish; Polly DuBose; Carolyn Jackson; Dan Janssen; Pamela Johnson; Marilyn and Gene Kalet; Barbara Kaye; Madelon Konopka; John J. Ligon; Dr Sandra McCurdy; Marty Malone; Men's Garden Club of America; Montana State U. Extension Service, Park County; North Carolina Cooperative Extension, Henderson County; Maurice Ogutu; Oregon State U. Extension Service, Lane County; Penn State Cooperative Extension, Indiana County; Mary Kay Pleyer; Bob Pollock; Angela Ponce; Julia Pryor; Jack Reagor; Linda Renslow; Derek Scasta; Barbara Scott; Aliza Schiff; Hannah Schiff; Mary Skinner; Martha A. Smith; Jim Sorrenti; John Teague; Texas AgriLIFE Extension Service (Texas A & M System), Navarro County; Diane Turner; Sara Beth Warne; Sean Whalen; U. of Illinois Extension, Countryside Extension Center; U. of Nebraska Extension-Lincoln, Lancaster County; U. of Tennessee Extension, Bedford County

Index

Photographs

All copyright Reader's Digest except for: 4 B iStockphoto.com/floortje; 5 iStockphoto.com/Mark Fairey; 22 C iStockphoto.com/Camilla Wisbauer; BR iStockphoto.com/Chris Elwell; 23 ShutterStock, Inc/Norman Chan; 43 CR ShutterStock, Inc/Jason Aron; 57 iStockphoto.com/David Clark; 61 CR iStockphoto.com/Mark Fairey; 80 R; iStockphoto.com/Klaudia Steiner; 142 R iStockphoto.com/Robyn Mackenzie; 162; iStockphoto.com/William Mahar; 165 iStockphoto.com/Bergpuma; 177 R ShutterStock, Inc/Jason Aron; 188 BL ShutterStock, Inc/Jason Aron; 215 R iStockphoto.com/design56; 220 R iStockphoto.com/Ashok Rodrigues; 236 R iStockphoto.com/Matthew Cole; 250 C ShutterStock, Inc/Jason Aron; 253 iStockphoto.com/Paul Tessier; 276 iStockphoto.com/Elena Elisseeva; 295 iStockphoto.com/Winston Davidian; 308 BL iStockphoto.com/Marc Dietrich; 330 iStockphoto.com/Evrim Sen; 337 R iStockphoto.com/Spiderstock

Editor
Lisa Thomas

Art Editor
Conorde Clarke

Designer
Carol Ann Davis

Consultants
David Holloway,
Sheena Meredith

Proofreader
Barry Gage

Indexer
Marie Lorimer

Photographer
Gary Ombler
Ellen Silverman
Kevin Norris

Illustrators
Bill Ledger
Bojana Dimitrovski
Sean Sims

**READER'S DIGEST
GENERAL BOOKS**

Editorial Director
Julian Browne

Art Director
Anne-Marie Bulat

Managing Editor
Nina Hathway

**Head of Book
Development**
Sarah Bloxham

**Picture Resource
Manager**
Christine Hinze

**Pre-press Account
Manager**
Dean Russell

**Product Production
Manager**
Claudette Bramble

**Senior Production
Controller**
Katherine Tibbals

Colour origination
Colour Systems Limited

Printed and bound in China

Note to Readers

The information in this book has been carefully researched, and all efforts have been made to ensure accuracy and safety. Neither the author nor The Reader's Digest Association Limited assumes any responsibility for any injuries suffered or damages or losses incurred as a result of following the instructions in this book. Before taking any action based on information in this book, study the information carefully and make sure that you understand it fully. Test any new or unusual repair method before using it as a remedy or on a highly visible or valuable area or item. The mention of any product or website in this book does not imply an endorsement. All prices, sellers' names, product names and websites mentioned are subject to change and are meant to be considered as general examples rather than specific recommendations.

More Extraordinary Uses For Ordinary Things is published by The Reader's Digest Association Limited, 11 Westferry Circus, Canary Wharf, London E14 4HE.

Also published as a hardback under the title **Bubble wrap, banana peel, baby oil and beyond.**

The text is adapted from **Baking Soda, Banana Peels, Baby Oil and Beyond** published by Reader's Digest Association Inc. in 2008.

We are committed both to the quality of our products and the service we provide to our customers. We value your comments, so please do contact us on 08705 113366 or via our website at www.readersdigest.co.uk

If you have any comments or suggestions about the content of our books, email us at gbeditorial@readersdigest.co.uk

Concept code: US 4972/IC
Book code: 400-448 UP0000-1
ISBN: 978 0 276 44589 7
Oracle code: 250013274S.00.24